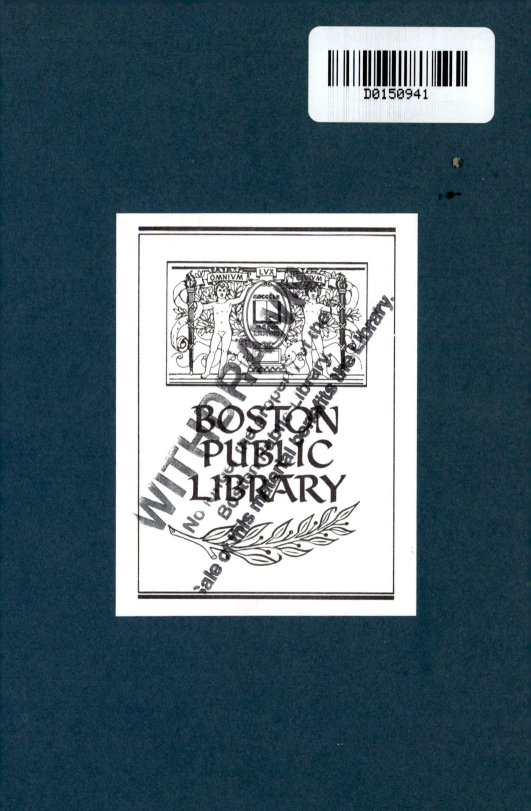

SELECTED LETTERS OF
WALT WHITMAN

Walt

SELECTED LETTERS OF

Whitman

Edited by Edwin Haviland Miller

University of Iowa Press ⚘ Iowa City

University of Iowa Press, Iowa City 52242
Printed in the United States of America
First edition, 1990

Design by Richard Hendel

Printed on acid-free paper

Library of Congress
Cataloging-in-Publication Data

Whitman, Walt, 1819–1892.
[Correspondence. Selections]
Selected letters of Walt Whitman/edited by
Edwin Haviland Miller.—1st ed.
p. cm.
ISBN 0-87745-266-0 (alk. paper),
ISBN 0-87745-267-9 (pbk., alk. paper)
1. Whitman, Walt, 1819–1892—Correspon-
dence. 2. Poets, American—19th century—
Correspondence. I. Miller, Edwin
Haviland. II. Title.
PS3231.A4 1990   89-20478
811'.3—dc20   [B]   CIP

To Pamela and Paul

CONTENTS

ACKNOWLEDGMENTS

Gay Wilson Allen Collection, Duke University
Clifton Waller Barrett Collection, University of Virginia
Henry W. and Albert A. Berg Collection, New York Public Library
Columbia University Library
Dartmouth College Library
Estelle Doheny Collection, Doheny Memorial Library, St. John's Seminary
Ralph Waldo Emerson Memorial Association, Harvard University
Charles E. Feinberg Collection, Library of Congress
Mr. and Mrs. Stephen Greene
T. E. Hanley Collection, University of Texas Library
Florence A. Hoadley
Henry E. Huntington Library
Library of Congress
Oscar Lion Collection, New York Public Library
Melbourne Public Library, Australia
Missouri Historical Society
Pierpont Morgan Library
National Archives, Washington, D.C.
Doris Neale
New Hampshire Historical Society
New-York Historical Society
Ohio Wesleyan Library
University of Pennsylvania Library
Royal Library of Copenhagen
Stanford University Library
Trent Collection, Duke University Library
Walt Whitman House, Camden
Yale University Library

I also want to express my gratitude to Ed Folsom and Arthur Golden
for their encouragement and valuable advice. Finally, there is Rosalind,
who after forty-three years still endures.

PREFACE

I HAVE CHOSEN 250 FROM THE ALMOST 2800 LETTERS IN the six-volume edition of *The Correspondence of Walt Whitman*, which I edited for the New York University Press edition of *The Collected Writings of Walt Whitman*.

The earliest letter was written when Whitman was twenty-one, a schoolteacher fumbling to establish his identity and to find a sense of direction. The last was penned nine days before his death on March 26, 1892, when he was approaching his seventy-third birthday. The final letter, actually a note, consisted of thirteen words. He was barely able to shape the letters of his final "God bless you" to his favorite sister, Hannah.

Whitman had strong convictions that letters were intended to connect people in affectionate bonds, not to provide a vehicle for discussions of literary and intellectual matters. He did not subscribe to the belief that poets are the unacknowledged legislators of the world. He sought fame eagerly, even calculatedly in his self-puffs, but he craved loving relationships more.

The letters constitute an autobiography, but an admittedly limited one, for he also unfolded other self-portraits in his poetry and in his prose writings. From the letters he excluded with notable consistency the struggles, doubts, and ecstasies of the creativity which, almost miraculously in the absence of a preparatory foreground, at age thirty-six, transformed him from a journalist and author of no unusual promise into a revolutionary poet whose "barbaric yawp" sounded "over the roofs of the world," in a new poetry, almost a new language, which outraged many readers because of its frankness, confused others, and inspired, even ravished, a limited audience which longed for a new voice in that century in search of a hero.

We see in these letters the man immersed in the factualities and immediacies of life, not in moments of epiphany. In his poetry he depicts kosmic (he preferred this spelling) immensities and pictures the humble, groping democratic masses as partners of the Homeric heroes in the eternal rhythms and cycles of the universe.

The voice in the prose of the letters is simple, direct, colloquial; only rarely does art intrude with its affectations. Other voices emerge in the prose writings, sometimes oratorical in the nineteenth-century rhetorical tradition, sometimes acerbic, like Mark Twain, in the political and social comments, and sometimes flat in the style of contemporary journalism.

Only when we hear and listen to all the voices will we begin to understand this man whose complexities have confounded and eluded biographers and critics for more than a century.

E X C E P T for the letters written in 1840 and 1841, which surfaced only a few years ago, the texts are those of the New York University Press edition. I have not attempted a so-called diplomatic text, which would be a literal transcription of what Whitman wrote. Fully aware of the objections that can be raised, I have evolved what I hope is a consistent compromise text. I have taken no extreme liberties with Whitman's correspondence, but in my judgment nothing except pedantry would be served by perpetuating in print Whitman's understandable carelessness in personal communications. Therefore, I have made modifications to make the letters more readable, without destroying their informality. I have eliminated confusing double punctuation and have silently inserted commas (and occasionally parentheses) around parenthetical expressions or last-minute interpolations. Spelling errors, on the other hand, I have not corrected, nor have I resorted to the ugly *sic* technique. In the notes I have retained the spelling of Whitman's correspondents, although I have inserted end punctuation out of sympathy for the reader. I have also kept Whitman's ever-present ampersand and *&c.*, as well as his dashes, since they differentiate his letters from his formal prose. I do not attempt, as some editors have done, to approximate the length of the dashes. Initials, abbreviations, and certain words are expanded in square brackets whenever necessary for clarity. As anyone who has read Whitman's letters in manuscript knows, his paragraphing is often bewildering. I have simply used my own judgment; I had no alternative. Finally, I should note that for consistency, I have not hesitated to apply the principles outlined here to the letters which I have had to reproduce from printed sources, the originals not being available.

The headings of the letters have been shortened and standardized both for clarity and convenience. In this selection of Whitman's letters I have deleted repetitious and irrelevant material, with the customary ellipses. Following each letter appears one of three notations: MS, with citation of its location; DRAFT LETTER, which Whitman recopied before mailing; and TEXT, which indicates that the letter is unlocated, probably lost, and that the transcription is based on a copy or a printed source, the accuracy of which cannot be verified.

The letters are arranged chronologically in seven sections: 1840–1841, 1842–1860, 1861–1865, 1866–1873, 1873–1881, 1881–1889, and 1890–1892. There is a commentary preceding each section which clarifies the biographical reasons for these divisions and supplies readers with essential background materials, historical as well as personal.

The notes are compressed versions of those in *The Correspondence of Walt Whitman*.

The following abbreviations appear:

Barrus—Clara Barrus, *Whitman and Burroughs Comrades* (Boston: Houghton Mifflin, 1931).

Corr.—*The Correspondence of Walt Whitman*, ed. Edwin Haviland Miller (New York: New York University Press, 1961–1977), six volumes.

Prose Works 1892—*Walt Whitman: Prose Works 1892*, ed. Floyd Stovall (New York: New York University Press, 1964), two volumes.

Traubel—Horace Traubel, *With Walt Whitman in Camden* (1908–1982), six volumes.

We are having very hot weather here, & it is Dry & dusty — The City is alive with soldiers from both the Army of the Potomac & the Western Armies, brought here by Sherman. There have been some great Reviews here, as you have seen in the papers — & thousands of soldiers are go'g home every day.

You must write to Alfred often, as it cheers up a boy sick & away from home. Write all about Domestic & farm incidents and as cheerful as may be. Direct to him, in Ward C. Armory Square Hospital, Washington, D.C. Should any thing occur, I will write you again, but I feel confident he will continue do'g well. For the present farewell.

Walt Whitman
Washington
D C

INTRODUCTION

IN A CONVERSATION WITH HIS BOSWELL, HORACE TRAU-
bel, in 1888, Walt Whitman observed that the correspondence between Carlyle and Emerson, which had recently been published, "would be impossible
to me, though I see it is all right in itself and for them. It is a matter of
taste—of temperament. I don't believe I ever wrote a purely literary letter—
ever got discussing books or literary men or writers or artists of any sort in
letters: the very idea of it makes me sick. I like letters to be personal—very
personal—and then stop." [1] Literary letters, he insisted, are "too deliberate,
too much prepared, too top-loftical—too infernally top-loftical. God never
made men this way: this is the way men are made when they are made over
by men—creations of strain, creations for effect." [2]

"I never think about literary perfection in letters either," he wrote to a
Civil War soldier. "It is the *man* & the *feeling*." [3] To Hugo Fritsch, a young
New York bohemian of Austrian origin, he said: "You express your thoughts
perfectly—do you not know how much more agreeable to me is the conversation or writing that does not take hard paved tracks, the usual & stereotyped, but has little peculiarities & even kinks of its own, making its genuineness—its vitality?" In another conversation with Traubel, he more or less
summarized his position in regard to letter writing: "My main motive would
be to say things: not to say them prettily—not to stun the reader with surprises—but to say them—to shoot my gun without a flourish and reach the
mark if I can." [4]

Whitman, as one would expect of a man who admitted that his contradic-
tions were mountainous, was not quite consistent. He adopted the epistolary
style appropriate to the occasion and the correspondent, and syntax and diction took on various colorations and intonations. But the finest letters in this
selection—the most feeling and moving and therefore the most Whitman-
esque—are those to the members of his own family, to the soldiers, and to
the various youths who became his comrades. The reason is simple: his heart
was engaged. He never shed with advancing years a childlike excitement and
unquenched enthusiasm for commonplace and seemingly trivial events. "My
darling boy," he wrote to Lewis K. Brown, "when you write to me, you must

write without ceremony, I like to hear every little thing about yourself &
your affairs—you need never care how you write to me, Lewy, if you will
only."[5] If we listen closely to that final clause, we hear the plea of a lonely
man, a solitary singer (to quote the title of Gay Wilson Allen's definitive biography). He offered the same advice to Fritsch after inquiring about oper-
atic performances in New York during the war: "Only dont run away with
that theme, & occupy too much of your letter with it—but tell me mainly
about all my dear friends, & every little personal item, & what you all do, &
say &c." Although he much admired Edward Dowden, the Irish critic,
Whitman was willing to exchange literary chitchat up to a point, but concluded with this suggestion: "My friend, next time you write say more about
yourself, family & Mrs. Dowden, to whom with yourself best love & regards." Despite spurious claims in answer to an insistent inquiry from John
Addington Symonds, he never fathered a family of his own, but the family
was a lifelong preoccupation, an unfulfilled longing.

His letters, then, have little to say about the nineteenth-century intellectual, artistic, and political context, not because he was uninterested in such
matters but because his value system emphasized human bonds. Artistic theory and discussions he left to critics, which may be one of the reasons his
influence on his successors was often limited: his anti-intellectualism provided no clear-cut ideology or guide. "Shoulder your duds, and I will mine,
and let us hasten forth."

A cursory reading of the day-to-day accounts of Traubel during the closing years of the poet's life illustrates how important letters were to him, how
necessary for him was the connection with the world outside. He was always
disappointed, Traubel informs us, if the postman passed without stopping:
"Whitman loves to receive letters—any letters, provided they are in the true
sense human documents."[6] He acknowledged, even somewhat lamented,
the decline of the art of letter writing: "I was never a fulsome correspondent
myself—wrote no superfluous letters: wrote very deliberately: often made a
draft of my notes. . . . It involved a lot of useless work—made a man a slave:
a long letter was half a day's job: God! I used to sweat over it even in cold
weather."[7] As he aged he became a postcard writer, but to close friends,
particularly in the years when his health kept him indoors for extended periods, he dropped a line almost daily, informing them of his health, his visitors, the trivia of existence, to be sure, but it was his way of keeping up inter-
course with the world.

Although Whitman called attention to himself by the garb he self-

consciously assumed—he was always something of a poseur, and knew it—
he never allowed his status as a poet to come between him and the soldiers
in the military hospitals or the people he greeted as he sauntered down the
streets of Brooklyn, New York, Washington, Camden, and Philadelphia. Yet,
beginning with the appearance of *Leaves of Grass* in 1855, he utilized every
available tactic of self-promotion to establish himself as the first great American poet, the bard of a teeming, dynamic democracy. He published anony-
mous reviews of his own poetry on the incontestable principle that no one
else was in a better position to render a critical evaluation, and sent notices
of events in his life to as many as half a dozen newspapers here and in Canada, with a release date. He deliberately kept himself before the American
public. He has been censured for his unauthorized exploitation of Ralph
Waldo Emerson's famous letter written a few weeks after the appearance of
the first edition of *Leaves of Grass*, but he seemingly had no compunctions.
He hungered for acceptance and fame as a poet, but he also hungered for
acceptance as a simple human being named Walt Whitman, the only poet
who has succeeded in establishing a first-name relationship with the public.

One night late in life when Whitman was housebound because of illness,
Traubel read aloud a letter written during the Civil War which described the
reaction of a critically wounded soldier named Caleb Babbitt. "On hearing
your name," the correspondent wrote, "he brightened up and gave me a
warm welcome." "Do you know, Horace," Whitman observed to Traubel,
"such things as that—just little things, insignificant things—are the big
things of life after all? Babbitt didn't say I wrote beautiful poems or did anything that people look at but that he just 'brightened up' on hearing my
name mentioned. Ain't that a thousand times better than writing poems—
just that—to brighten up those who suffer?"[8]

Many years after Whitman's death, John Burroughs, the nineteenth-
century naturalist and friend of the poet, complained of Whitman's "brief
and matter-of-fact letters" and alleged that "he let himself go only in his
poems."[9] Burroughs's judgment of the letters he had received was correct,
but his statement does not apply to Whitman's letters as a whole. For the
best letters are hardly "matter-of-fact"; rather they are lovely prose creations
of an affectionate man who was denied the affection he craved and needed.
In these letters one almost hears Whitman speaking. The letter to the parents of a dead soldier, Erastus Haskell, resonates with the tenderness of a
man who laments the useless loss of youth in war, the loneliness of death, the
grief of the parents, and his own feelings for all the losses he himself has

suffered. In the crescendo which he quietly achieves at the conclusion, he addresses the dead youth, the parents, and himself.

> Poor dear son, though you were not my son, I felt to love you as a son, what short time I saw you sick & dying here—it is as well as it is, perhaps better—for who knows whether he is not better off, that patient & sweet young soul, to go, than we are to stay? So farewell, dear boy—it was my opportunity to be with you in your last rapid days of death—no chance as I have said to do any thing particular, for nothing could be done—only you did not lay here & die among strangers without having one at hand who loved you dearly, & to whom you gave your dying kiss—

Whitman felt early in life what it meant to be a stranger. As he observed to Traubel, "You know how for the most part I have always been isolated from my people—in certain senses have been a stranger in their midst." [10] There were reasons why "my relations with the boys there in Washington had fatherly, motherly, brotherly intimations." [11]

Those "fatherly, motherly, brotherly intimations" appeared early in the life of Walter Whitman, who bore his father's name and was the second child in a family of eight children. One of his earliest prose works is entitled "My Boys and Girls," who, it turns out, bear the names of his own brothers and sisters, as he assumes in fiction the roles which he later partly fulfilled in life.

In "There Was a Child Went Forth," one of his earliest poems, he depicts seemingly an only child's relationship to his parents before he ventures into the larger world beyond. Walter Whitman in fact left home at age eleven, and soon lived in boarding houses as often as at home. He moved, or drifted, from one boarding house to another, from one job to another, as his family moved from one house to another, going back and forth between Long Island and Brooklyn, while his father tried sometimes as farmer, sometimes as builder, to provide for his eight children. The father failed in both and also as a provider. Neither the family nor the young Walter in their restless movements established enduring attachments to neighborhoods or to neighbors. And it perhaps follows that the landscapes the poet was to create were delineated with vague contours and peopled with stereotypes rather than complex, full-blooded humans, and that the "I" of the poetry wanders for the most part alone in vast, vague spaces inhabited by large numbers of people identified by their social function and types, not baptized or dignified with names, nor allowed distinctive voices to engage in dialogue.

Walter Whitman, we would say, was denied his youth, although in his day it had not become an idealized state to be evoked after experiencing at first-hand life's disenchantments and fractures. There is in his poetry a substructure that hints at loss and regret in conflict with the insistent exultations of faith and affirmation of life and American democracy. To Traubel in 1888 he alleged: "Day by day, in these elder years of my life, I see how lucky I was that I was myself thrown out early upon the average earth—to wrestle for myself—among the masses of people—never living in coteries: that I have always lived cheek by jowl with the common people—yes indeed, not only bred that way but born that way." [12] However, according to Grace Gilchrist, Whitman confessed to a "very restless and unhappy" childhood: "I did not know what to do." [13] No doubt both statements unfold the complex truth, the gratifications of personal achievement against formidable odds and lingering anger that in a sense he was pushed out of the house and family in 1830, at age eleven.

Although Whitman never achieved more than a minimal livelihood from his poetry, and then only by resorting to every available tactic such as self-promotion and acting as salesman as well as publisher of his own books, he achieved fame and success despite limited formal education and the handicaps of belonging to a family disadvantaged economically and psychologically. Mary Elizabeth, George Washington, and Thomas Jefferson had relatively normal lives, and the two males were even successful in their careers. Jesse, the firstborn, however, was alcoholic like the father and was so ravaged by syphilis that he had to be institutionalized before his death. Andrew Jackson was also alcoholic and married a streetwalker named Nancy, who bore him a child after his early death. Hannah Louisa was a deeply troubled woman, perhaps a borderline psychotic, who married at her brother Walter's suggestion an itinerant painter, Charles L. Heyde, who in his envy sought to ruin his brother-in-law's reputation and threatened to desert a wife whom, it turned out, he could not live with or without, as often happens in such marriages. Edward, the lastborn of the Whitman children, was feeble-minded and lived out his years as the charge of his mother and later of George and Walt.

Although Walt was her favorite child, the mother could not make anything of his meterless, rhymeless poetry. As Whitman in old age observed seemingly without anger, although discussion of the subject unveils the disappointment and lingering regret that she did not take in his poetry: "my dear, dear mother: she and I—oh! we have been great chums: always next to each other: always: yet my dear mother never took that part of me in." [14]

According to George, "I don't think his father ever had an idea what Walt was up to, what he meant," but George asserted, presumably in answer to suggestions that father and son were not compatible, "His relations with his father were always friendly, always good."[15] That the son almost never referred to his father after his death in 1855 perhaps points to another interpretation.

Though Whitman on the basis of his experience could have assumed the role of Ishmael after the fashion of Herman Melville in his fiction, he was bonded to the family in an ambivalent relationship, spent a lifetime in reconstituting familial structures and familial roles, and at the end arranged for a family reunion not at Huntington, Long Island, his birthplace, but in Harleigh Cemetery in Camden.

1840-1841

This daguerreotype of the 1840s, the earliest known likeness of the future poet, unveils Walter Whitman in his twenties, a fashionable man-about-town, even perhaps a dandy, self-conscious and affected. He was trying on roles—printer, journalist, editor, teacher, builder of houses—as he struggled to establish an identity, to discover, in short, Walt Whitman.

IN 1830, WHEN HE WAS ELEVEN, WALTER WHITMAN LEFT school to work in the offices of two lawyers, James B. Clark and his son Edward. In the following year Whitman was apprenticed to the editor of the *Long Island Patriot* and for the first time boarded away from home. In 1832 he worked in the printing office, it appears, of Erastus Worthington, Jr., and in the fall was employed by Colonel Alden Spooner of the *Long Island Star*. While Walter was with Spooner, the Whitmans moved to Brooklyn, where the son shortly joined them. When the family moved to Norwich, Long Island, in 1834, he remained in Brooklyn and held various jobs there and in New York for short periods, changing boardinghouses almost as often as he changed jobs.

Apparently Walter was briefly reunited with his family when in 1836 he became a schoolteacher in Norwich. He jumped from one teaching job to another: he was at Babylon in the winter of 1836, at Smithtown in the winter of 1837, and at Huntington, his birthplace, in the following spring. He refused to work on his father's farm, and with remarkable aggressiveness, somehow in the unusually difficult climate following the panic of the preceding year, he founded *The Long Islander* in 1837. About that time his brother George, now nine, lived with him and attended his school, as Walter assumed for the first time a kind of paternal role. He sold *The Long Islander* in 1839 and was briefly employed in Jamaica, New York, before he returned to teaching at Woodbury, a village on Long Island.

A few years ago previously unknown letters, the earliest extant ones, were sold to the Library of Congress at auction. All are addressed to Abraham Paul Leech, about whom we know only that he was a bookkeeper and presumably a Democrat, since he was, like Walter, a political activist of sorts. They met perhaps in 1839 when Walter was in Jamaica, where there was seemingly a group of young men of approximately the same age who shunned the somewhat stolid farmers and workers of the area.

The letters to Leech delineate a fop given to affectations in diction, literary analogies more pretentious than substantial, and sophomoric puns mixed in with a condescending, hostile wit. These letters expose with sharp clarity Walter Whitman's awkward and somewhat painful search for identity and a self-image compatible with unstated and perhaps at the time undefined dreams of a future free of middle-class stolidity.

The schoolteacher sneers at the citizens of Woodbury, who are "flatheads," "brutes," "contemptible ninnies," "jackasses," and "puddingbrained bog-trotters." His students are "dirty, ill-favoured young brats" and "coarse brown-faced girls" whose greatest sin is that they waste his time and talent. Repeatedly he attacks the absence of "grace or good breeding" on the part of people who have no interest either in "mental food" or in good dining (only in "pot-cheese"), and whose dialect, which he mocks phonetically, causes him to shudder. He imagines himself a displaced Hamlet as he draws upon the "To be or not to be" speech to dramatize his plight while serving his "period of purgation" buried in Woodbury among people whose lives, he swears in pseudo-Shakespearean grandeur, consist of "the fag ends, the scraps and refuse."

His vituperative language tells us more about Walter Whitman than about the Long Island yahoos, who cart dung and talk at the table of "the colour and consistency of the fluids and solids ejected from the said stomach." There is something almost Swiftian in this excremental vision, or what he calls "the naturality of my metaphor." "Moved by the bowels of compassion," he begins, and then alleges that "conscience spurs me to a full confession; which generally operates on me like a good dose of calomel," which in turn "relieves an overhardened paunch and rumbling intestines."

With his English spellings and his strained diction he sounds like a snotty, disaffected schoolteacher, yet fifteen years later he is to elevate the common people, the "denizens" of Woodbury too, and the "roughs" to heroic and epic heights, casting in his poetic exuberance a Homeric glow over the American landscape.

Beneath the caustic commentary and the posturing and self-pitying emerges a picture of a very lonely young man. In mannered prose he tells us that when he wakens in the morning "the great round face of the sun . . . almost seems to kiss me with a loving kiss.—I am generally dressed and reach to receive him at his first appearance." Then he describes his "sanctum sanctorum, which profane foot invadeth not.—Its hollowed precincts are forbidden ground to every she in the house, except for absolutely necessary entrances, which concern the vital well-being of its lord."

The posturing evokes two extant daguerreotypes of Walter Whitman in the 1840s. In one, attired with a fashionable felt hat, he sits with a gloved hand resting on a dark, beautifully polished cane, and in the other, his right hand behind his head, he looks at us with eyes which keep us at a distance. The daguerreotype of 1854 in which he is a workman with an exposed undershirt introduces us to Walt Whitman.

To Abraham Paul Leech

Woodbury, N.Y., July 30, 1840[1]

My friend

I feel but little in the humour for writing any thing that will have the stamp of cheerfulness.—Perhaps it would be best therefore not to write at all, and I don't think I should, were it not for the hope of getting a reply.—I believe when the Lord created the world, he used up all the good stuff, and was forced to form Woodbury and its denizens, out of the fag ends, the scraps and refuse: for a more unsophisticated race than lives hereabouts you will seldom meet with in your travels.—They get up in the morning, and toil through the day, with no interregnum of joy or leisure, except breakfast and dinner.—They live on salt pork and cucumbers; and for a delicacy they sometimes treat company to rye-cake and buttermilk.—Is not this enough to send them to perdition "uncancelled, unanointed, unannealed?"—If Chesterfield were forced to live here ten hours he would fret himself to death: I have heard the words "thank you," but once since my sojourn in this earthly purgatory.—Now is the season for what they call "huckleberry frolicks."—I had the inestimable ecstasy of being invited to one of these re-fined amusements.—I went.—We each carried a tin pail, or a basket, or a big bowl, or a pudding bag.—It was fun no doubt, but it cost me two mortal pounds of flesh, besides numerous remnants of my apparrel, which still re-main, for what I know, on the briars and bushes.—Was n't it hot!—And then our dinner—our *pic-nic* dinner!—there's the rub!—Guess now what we had.—A broken-bowl half full of cold potatoes; three or four bones thinly garnished with dirty, greasy ham; a huge pie, made out of green apples, molasses, and buckwheat crust; six radishes, and a tin pan of boiled beans!!—And all this had to be washed down with a drink they called "switc*hell*,"[2] a villainous compound, as near as I could discover, of water, vinegar, and brown sugar.—Our conversation, too, was a caution to white folks; it consisted principally, as you may imagine, of ethereal flashes of wit, scraps of Homeric and Italian poetry, disquisitions on science and the arts, quotations from the most learned writers, and suggestions on the speediest way of making butter.—Tim Hewlett, vowed he ought to have a buss from Patty Strong; Patty modestly declined the honour.—A struggle was the re-sult, in which Tim's face received permanent marks of the length of Patty's finger nails; and the comb of that vigorous young damsel lost some of its fair proportions.—It was a drawn battle.—At the conclusion of this performance, we gathered together our forces and the bowls, baskets, and pudding-bags aforesaid, and returned home; for my part feeling "particularly and peculiarly *kewrious*" from the weight of amusement.—

I am much obliged for the paper you sent me.—Write soon.—Send me something funny; for I am getting to be a miserable kind of a dog; I am sick of wearing away by inches, and spending the fairest portion of my little span of life, here in this nest of bears, this forsaken of all Go[d]'s creation; among clowns and country bumpkins, flat-heads, and coarse brown-faced girls, dirty, ill-favoured young brats, with squalling throats and crude manners, and bog-trotters,³ with all the disgusting conceit, of ignorance and vulgarity.—It is enough to make the fountains of good-will dry up in our hearts, to wither all gentle and loving dispositions, when we are forced to descend and be as one among the grossest, the most low-minded of the human race.— Life is a dreary road, at the best; and I am just at this time in one of the most stony, rough, desert, hilly, and heart-sickening parts of the journey.—But Time is the Great Physician who cures, they say, our ills of mind and body.— I pray the fates he may rid me of my spleen ere long.

W. W.

M S: Library of Congress

To Abraham Paul Leech

Devil's den, Woodbury, N.Y., August 11, 1840

My friend,

Why the dickins did n't you come out to the whig meeting at the court house, last Saturday week?—I went there, with the hope of seeing you and one or two others, as much as for any thing else.—I dare say you would have been much gratified; at any rate you would have been astonished, for the *orator* of the day related *facts*, and cut capers, which certainly never before met the eye or ear of civilized man.—Just before sun down the performance concluded, and starting from the C[ourt] H[ouse] I was overtaken by a most impertinent shower, which drenched me to the skin; probably all the whig enthusiasm generated on that occasion was melted down again by this unlucky shower, for we passed loads of forlorn gentlemen, with draggle-tailed coats, crest-fallen hats, and sour-looking phizzes.—The mighty patriotism they felt was *drowned* by a tormenting slipperiness of coat, shirt, and pantaloons.—

Were you ever tried?—I don't mean tried before Squire Searing or Judge

Strong for breach of promise or theft; but tried as they try mutton fat, to make candles of—boiled down—melted into liquid grease?—tried as they try martyrs at the stake?—If you havn't—I have.—The scene was "Huckleberry Plains," the day Friday last—the time, from twelve o'clock, n. until 3½ P.M.—you see I'm not particular.—The awful occasion impressed indelibly upon my memory every agonizing moment of that infernal excursion. It was what the ladies and gentlemen of this truly refined place called a party of *pleasure.*—Yes; it was delightful; fun to the back-bone: but it cost me a sun-burnt face and neck, from which the skin is even now peeling, and four mortal pounds of flesh which ran off in a state of dilution from my body.—The sun poured down whole lumps of red hot fire—not a tree, not a shed to shelter us from the intolerable glare.—I gave you in my last some account of my first "huckleberry frolick," but this beats it all hollow.—I can only wonder why I was such a thundering fool as to try it again.—

How are you all in Jamaica?—What is the news?—Do you have any games at Twenty Questions?—Does "our portrait" yet remain in the condition of the southern banks?—[4] O, how I wish I was among you for a few hours: how tired and sick I am of this wretched, wretched hole!—I wander about like an evil spirit, over hills and dales, and through woods, fields, and swamps. In the manufactory of Nature, the building of these coarse gump-heads that people Woodbury, must have been given to some raw hand, for surely no decent workman ever had the making of them.—And these are the contemptible ninnies, with whom I have to do, and among whom I have to live.—O, damnation, damnation! thy other name is school-teaching and thy residence Woodbury.—Time, put spurs to thy leaden wings, and bring on the period when my allotted time of torment here shall be fulfilled.—Speed, ye airy hours, lift me from this earthly purgatory; nor do I care how soon ye lay these pudding-brained bog-trotters, amid their kindred earth.—I do not believe a refined or generous idea was ever born in this place; the whole concern, with all [i]ts indwellers, ought to be sunk, as Mosher says, "to chaos." Never before have I entertained so low an idea of the beauty and perfection of man's nature, never have I seen humanity in so degraded a shape, as here.—Ignorance, vulgarity, rudeness, conceit, and dulness are the reigning gods of this deuced sink of despair.—The brutes go barefoot, shave once in three weeks, call "brown cow" "*bre*own *ke-ow*;" live on sour milk, rye bread, and strong pork; believe L[ong] I[sland] sound and the south bay to be the ne plus ultra of creation; and the "gals" wear white frocks with red or yellow waist-ribands.—

Think, my friend, think on all this; and pray nightly for my deliverance from this dungeon where grace or good-breeding never were seen, and from whence happiness fled shrieking twenty years ago.—Farewell—and may the blessings of hope and peace, the sunshine of a joyous heart, never be absent from you.—May the bloom of health glow on your features, the tide of joy swell in your heart, and care and grief be strangers to your dwelling

W. Whitman

M S: Library of Congress

To Abraham Paul Leech

Purgatory Fields, Woodbury, N.Y., August 19, 1840

Have you never heard people advance the opinion that earth is man's heaven or hell, according as he acts or is situated, good or evil?—I believe that doctrine; or, at any rate, I believe half of it, as the man said when he was told that his wife had twins.—That this earthly habitation is a place of torment to my miserable self, is made painfully evident every day of existence.— Fate never made a place where dulness perched on every tree, obtuseness located himself on every hill, and despair might be seen "sittin on a rail," every ten yards, as completely as in this cursed Woodbury.—Woodbury! appropriate name!—it *would*-bury me or any being of the least wish for intelligent society, in one year, if compelled to endure its intolerable insipidity, without the hope of relief.—Before many weeks, I expect to be in the condition of those pleasant beings of whom it is said "They are nothing but skin and bone."—You do not know, my friend, nor can you conceive, the horrid dulness of this place.—Making money, plodding on, and on, and on; raising ducks, carting dung, and eating pork, are the only methods of employment that occupy the Woodbury animals.—And as avocations of this nature never met my fancy in any great degree, you may easily imagine what an interesting situation I am in.—

I have eaten my dinner since the last line over leaf was written; but I don't know that I felt any the better as to good-humour.— What do you think I had for dinner?—Guess, now.—Beef?—no.—Mutton?—No.—Pot-pie? No.—Salad and iced champagne?—No, no, no.——I'll tell you in the order that it was put up, or rather put down.—Firstly, two cold potatoes, with the skins on, one of said potatoes, considerably nibbled in a manner which left me in doubt whether it had been done by the teeth of a mouse or the bill of a chicken; secondly three boiled clams, that had evidently seen their best days;—thirdly a chunk of molasses cake made of buckwheat

flour;—fourthly, a handful of old mouldy pot-cheese, with a smell strong
enough to knock down an ox;—fifthly, and lastly, two oblong slats of a mysterious substance, which I concluded, after considerable reflection, must
have been intended for bread;—this last would undoubtedly [have] been
very interesting either to a Grahamite,⁵ or to one fond of analyzing and study-
ing out the nature of the *mineral* kingdom.—Was n't this a feast for an Epi-
cure?—Think, O thou banquetter on good things, think of such an infernal
meal as that I describe, and bless the stars that thy lot is as it is.—Think,
moreover that this diabolical compound was wrapped up in [a] huge piece
of brown paper, and squeezed into a little tin pail, which said pail, being
minus in the matter of a handle or bail, had to be carried by a tow string
instead!—Imagine to yourself, now, that you see me toting along with such
an article as I [have] been describing.—Don't I cut a pretty figure? O, ye
gods, press me not too far—pour not my cup too full—or I know what I
shall do.—Dim and dreadful thoughts have lately been floating through my
brain.—The next you hear of me, I may possibly be arraigned for murder,
or highway robbery, or assault and battery, at the least.—I am getting savage.—There seems to be no relief.—Fate is doing her worst.—The devil is
tempting me in every nook and corner, and unless you send me a letter, and
Brenton remits me an armful of news, there is no telling but what I shall
poison the whole village, or set fire to this old school-house, and run away by
the light of it.—

I suppose all "your folks" are the same as usual, and that Jamaica is "situ-
ate, lying, and being" as in November last.—But do for pity's sake forward
something or other to me soon, in the shape of mental food.—May you
grow fat with peace and good cheer.—May the sun of peace warm you, and
the dews of prosperity fall thick around your path.—May the Fates be busy
with cutting other threads than yours—and may kind fingers shield you in
the hour of death.—Adieu.—Walter Whitman
M S: Library of Congress

To Abraham Paul Leech

Woodbury, N.Y., August 26, 1840
Dearly beloved—⁶ Moved by the bowels of compassion, and pushed onward
by the sharp prickings of conscience, I send you another epistolary gem.—
For compassion whispers in mine ear that you must by this time have become accustomed to the semi-weekly receipt of these invaluable morsels;

and therefore to deprive you of the usual gift, would be somewhat similar to sending a hungry man to bed without his supper.—Besides, conscience spurs me to a full confession; which generally operates on me like a good dose of calomel on one who has been stuffing immoderately, making a clear stomach and comfortable feelings to take the place of overburdened paunch and rumbling intestines.—Excuse the naturality of my metaphor.—

Speaking of "naturality" reminds me of the peculiarities that distinguish the inhabitants, young and old, of this well-bred and highly romantick village.—For instance, I was entertained the other day at dinner, with a very interesting account by the "head of the family," (families of fourteen or fifteen, in these parts, have but one *head* amongst them) of his sufferings from an attack of the gripes; how he had to take ipecachuana, and antimonial wine;[7] the operation of those substances on his stomach; the colour and consistency of the fluids and solids ejected from the said stomach; how long it was before epsom salts could be persuaded to take pity on his bowels; with many and singular concomitant matters, which, you may well imagine, contributed in a high degree to the improvement of my appetite.—I frequently have the felicity of taking my meals surrounded by specimens of the rising generation.—I mean little young ones getting out of bed; and as "to the pure all things are pure," the scene of course is in a high degree edifying to my taste and comfort.—

We have had delightful weather out here for the past few days.—The sun at this moment is shining clear, the cool breeze is blowing, the branches of the trees undulate, and all seems peace and joy but the mind—the *mind*, that strange, unfathomable essence, which is, after all, the main spring of our happiness here.—My period of purgation is almost up in these diggin's.— Thank the pitying fates! in two weeks more I shall wind up my affairs, and with tears in my eyes bid a sorrowful adieu to these hallowed precincts.— Shady walks, venerable old school-house, dismantled farms, innocent young ideas—all—all—will I look upon for the last time.—But I must stop—I cannot carry out the affecting thought any farther.—My heart swells, and my melting soul almost expires with the agonizing idea.—Let me hold out a little longer, O, ye powers!

How are politicks getting along down your way?—Is hard cider in the ascendant; or does democracy erect itself on its tip-toes and swing its old straw hat with a hurrah for "Little Matty?"[8] Down in these parts the people understand about as much of political economy as they do of the Choctaw language;[9] I never met with such complete unqualified, infernal jackasses, in all my life.—Luckily for my self-complacency they are mostly whigs.—If

they were on my side of the wall, I should forswear loco-focoism,[10] and turn
traitor in five minutes.—We had a swinging meeting at the Court house, last
Saturday.—I tell you what, our speakers went as far ahead of "the fat gentleman in striped trousers," as a Baltimore clipper does beyond a North River
dung boat.—There was no 'kimparysun.'

Can't you look round Jamaica and find out whether they dont want a
teacher somewhere, for a quarter?—I shall probably drop down there in the
course of a week or two, and stay a day.—See to it, and oblige me.—I hope
that holy angels will have you in keeping, and that the fragrance of plenty
and the musick of a pleasant heart, will never be foreign to you.—Sweet
blossoms bloom beneath your eyes, and the songs of birds gladden your
hearing!—Farewell.—

Walter Whitman

M S: Library of Congress

To Abraham Paul Leech

Woodbury, N.Y., September 9, 1840

My dear L—I perform the thrice-agreeable office of informing you that
my purgatory here is just finishing.—In a few days more I shall be unbound
and unloosed.—At present I think it improbable that I shall pay any visit to
Jamaica, though I should like to see my friends there.—Write to me on Friday, by the cars, or on Tuesday next, by the baker: after that time I shall not
be here to "receive communications."—O, how my spirit springs and grows
elastick at the idea of leaving this diabolical, and most [p]articularly cursed
locality!—Shades through which I have wandered; orchards that I have
plundered; old school-room, dirty-faced urchins; and moth-eaten desk, I
bid ye all a long farewell.—Pork, cucumbers, and buckwheat bread, we
must part, perhaps forever!—Solemn thought! Rye-sweetcake, sour milk,
and "scented" fish—ye dear companions of the past summer—alas! the
mouth that has known you, will know you no more.—

Dont forget to write on Friday, if you can.—Brenton will send me a pack-
age at that time, and your letter can be slipped in like a knife.—State how
Abel is; and indite the news generally. May the Saints bless you; and may
Peace never get out of humour and cut your acquaintance.

W. Whitman

M S: Library of Congress

To Abraham Paul Leech

Whitestone, Queens, March 25, 1841

By what Overacre would call an "exceedingly natural and extensive con-
catenation of radical causes," I begin thinking, now that I sit down to write
to you, of the time and place that I used to hail from some eight or nine
months ago.—You no doubt remember those precious missives that sprang
almost diurnally from my teeming hand at Purgatory Place.—But that *Place!*
O, it makes my nerves quiver as I think of it.—Yes, anathema! anathema,
curse, curse, upon thee thou fag end of all earthly localities, infernal Woodbury! But I fear I am getting warm.—Let me push the subject no farther.—
The fact is, the most distant mention of that diabolical region, that country
of buckwheat dough-nuts, and pot-cheese, and rye sweet-cake, always makes
me fall a swearing.—Faugh!

Have you never in your travels come across a village where some half
dozen principal characters seemed to give a colour and tone to the whole
place?—Of such a nature is this Whitestone, which your servant now irradi-
ates with the benign light of his countenance.—The principal feature of the
place is the money making spirit, a gold-scraping and a wealth-hunting fiend,
who is a foul incubus to three fourths of this beautiful earth.—Unfortunately,
too, these "leaders" here, set but a poor example to the rest as regards their
strict adherence to the domestick ties and institutions which old Madame
Custom has planted and nourished and made at last so deeply rooted among
us.—Enough of this however.—Do not think I am going to fall into the
splenetic, fault-finding current, on which those Woodbury documents were
set afloat.—

I am quite happy here; and when I say this, may I flatter myself that some
chord within you will throb "I am glad to hear that?"—Yes, as far perhaps
as it falls to mortal lot, I enjoy happiness here.—Of course, I build now and
then my castles in the air.—I plan out my little schemes for the future; and
cogitate fancies; and occasionally there float forth like wreaths of smoke, and
about as substantial, my day dreams.—But, take it all in all, I have reason
to bless the breeze that wafted me to Whitestone.—We are close on the
sound.—It is a beautiful thing to see the vessels, sometimes a hundred or
more, all in sight at once, and moving so gracefully on the water.—Opposite
to us there is a magnificent fortification under weigh.—We hear the busy
clink of the hammers at morn and night, across the water; and sometimes
take a sail over to inspect the works, for you know it belongs to [the] U.S.—[11]

My quarters are quite satisfactory too as regards boarding.—One of the windows of my room commands a pleasant view of the sound.—Another looks to the eas[t] and the great round face of the sun[;] he comes along in the morning, almost seems to kiss me with a loving kiss.[12]—I am generally dressed and ready to receive him at his first appearance.—This said room of mine is something that I much value.—It is my sanctum sanctorum, which profane foot invadeth not.—Its hallowed precincts are forbidden ground to every she in the house, except for absolutely necessary entrances, which concern the vital well-being of its lord.—

I hope this will find you enjoying health and peace.—O that I were a Napoleon that I might load the heads of my friends with golden coronets.— My best wishes I waft to you, wrapped up and sealed with a wafer.—[13] May your shadow never be less.—Adieu

Walter Whitman

M S: Library of Congress

1842-1860

IN THE FALL OF 1840 WHITMAN PUT WOODBURY BEHIND him, probably much to the relief of its citizens and its students. He electioneered for the Democratic party in Jamaica and Queens before he settled briefly in Whitestone as a schoolteacher, but the new setting could neither contain nor sustain Walter Whitman's restless search for a compatible self-image. He moved on, and we hear nothing again of Leech and his Jamaican friends. In 1842 Whitman was in Brooklyn and New York, and for a few months he was the editor of the *Aurora* and then for another few months of the *Tatler*. He changed jobs as well as boardinghouses with amazing frequency. He also submitted articles of no distinction to *The Democratic Review*, a recently founded literary magazine to which Nathaniel Hawthorne contributed.

In 1846, at twenty-seven, he became the editor of the *Brooklyn Eagle*, and this time he lasted for almost two years. The owner of the newspaper fired him early in 1848: Whitman was "without steady principles . . . nor, for that matter, principles of any sort."[1] Perhaps his nonchalant life-style vexed his employers, for he performed his editorial duties early in the day, went to Gray's Swimming Bath in the afternoon, and then took the ferry to Manhattan.

By chance he met the proprietor of the *New Orleans Crescent* about the time he lost his job in Brooklyn. Accompanied by his brother Jeff, he set off to introduce himself to the vast American landscape which he had never seen and to absorb (to use one of his favorite words) life and experiences free of the usual middle-class restrictions and inhibitions. He worked for the *Crescent* for ninety-two days before he was fired. He turned out the usual journalistic pap of the age and perhaps devoted most of his time to self-exploration. Jeff wrote letters to the family, to which Walter added a brief paragraph or so dealing with financial matters. He was preparing himself for a new role in the family.

Shortly after his return to Brooklyn he moved in with the family and, as his father's health deteriorated, assumed paternal responsibilities, supervising the construction of houses which the Whitmans occupied until the completion of another allowed them to sell and to move on. The only constant in the family was the endless, restless motion, not of upward mobility but of failure.

On the other hand, the family provided Walter security and stability and allowed him to assume the role anticipated in "My Boys and Girls" in 1844. He enjoyed the affection of an adoring mother, the respect at least of most of his brothers and all his sisters, but the father's reaction is not known. At thirty Walter was ready to construct houses to insure the family's well-being and to invent a poetic structure and a poetic rhythm which would accommodate what he would call his kosmic vision. Suddenly, or so it appears, he began to find his voice and genius.

The story of his transformation is not recorded in his letters, nor is the battle for recognition which he waged with a largely hostile press. In 1855, with the appearance of the first edition of *Leaves of Grass*, he changed his name and American poetry in one outrageously comic and megalomaniacal line: "Walt Whitman, an American, one of the roughs, a kosmos." In the same month his father died, and the son was now in fact the successor with his boys and girls. In the next few years his hair turned gray prematurely, and soon the flowing Whitman beard appeared.

Poetically he was in a period of dazzling productivity. One great poem followed another, and there seemed no end to his creativity. *Leaves of Grass* was expanded in 1856 and again in 1860, when for the first time Whitman was not his own publisher. He did everything he could with his journalistic skills and contacts to promote his fame and to overcome the opposition of those who found in *Leaves of Grass* everything except fig leaves. Letters were few, because, he explained, "I write to [friends] more to satisfaction, through my poems." He forgot for the moment what he knew full well, that many of his and the family's friends could not understand poetry without conventional rhyme and rhythm.

In the years before the Civil War, he associated with the bohemians, his "darlings and gossips," who gathered at Pfaff's Restaurant on Broadway near Bleeker Street in Greenwich Village. They drank together, discussed everything and anything, and went slumming at Five Corners, where anything went that one desired or had the stomach for. Whitman was the self-styled "old vagabond that so gracefully becomes me," in other words, an elder brother or permissive father figure among younger men.

He characterized his comrades as "all so good, many so educated, traveled, &c., some so handsome & witty, some rich, &c., some among the literary class . . . polished, & brilliant in conversation, &c." Some of those youths, apparently in their twenties, were sons of doctors and wealthy businessmen who lived on or just off fashionable Fifth Avenue. He called it the Fred Gray Association, named after the son of a doctor. Despite the "lambent electricity of real friendship" which he experienced, no lasting relationships developed, and during the war he found a more comfortable, and familiar, home and function among poor, uneducated soldiers in army hospitals.

Jeff and Walter Whitman to their mother

New Orleans, March 27 and 28, 1848

Dear Mother

To day we received the first letter from you, and glad enough we were to get it too. The passage that gave me, and Walter too, the most pleasure was the one that said you were well, and that all the rest were well also. You say the weather is very cold there, here it is just the other way, that is it is pretty warm. I have now begun to wear the summer clothes sister Hannah made me which I find very comfortble.

It would have made you laugh to see me come home from the post office this morning with your letter. Eddy never was so glad when New Year's came, as I was to get your letter.

You must write to us oftener than you have, at least twice a month, which we are going to do.

You need not be alarmed about the yellow fever as that gentleman will (the folks think) not visit this place this summer. The reason they give for that is this. It does not come but once in three or four years, and last season it was very hard and killed a great many persons (I mean it does not come but once in three or four years in such a shape). Besides it is a great humbug, most every one in our office has had (some of them have had it twice) and got well. It is caused mostly (I think all of it) by the habits of the people, they never meet a friend but you have to go drink and such loose habits.[2]

You know that Walter is averse to such habits, so you need not be afraid of our taking it.

Yesterday we were to have a balloon ascension, but just as it was ready to go up the balloon bursted so it did not go up, this is the third time she (it was a lady that was to go up in it) has tried it and each time failed.

We are very nicely situated in our new place;—just "around the corner" is a very fine public park, which we take a walk in every night.

I believe I told you in my last letter that I was also at work at the "Crescent" office at five dollars a week, and I have the exchange papers for which I get twenty five cents per hundred, in a few weeks I expect to get two dollars a week for them.

If you do not get the paper (the "Crescent") regular you must send Andrew or George down to the Eagle office for it, I always see that two copys go every morning. My work is good and light. I have such a part of the mail (and I can do it most over night) and then I have nothing to do for the rest of the day (I generally get through with it about two o'clock) but stay in the office.

We have (I think) got along very well for such a long journey, not a single accident occurred on the way.

Dear Father, I hope you are getting along good with your work &c. Mother says it is cold so you can't work, here it is warm enough. In building houses here they do not do as they do in New York. Here they dig a hole in the ground some two feet deep and about the same width, and in length as far as the wall is to go, (they can not dig cellars here like in the north, you don't dig in the ground more than two feet before it is filled with water.) This trench they cover the bottom with boards (the ground is mostly made of quick-sand) and then build the wall on it. They cannot mak[e] good brick here, so they have to come from a distance. Carpenter's wages are very high here, some forty to fifty dollars a month and found.[3]

I will write a letter to you pretty soon, but in this one I must not forget George and Andrew.

Dear brothers, I should like to see you very much indeed but I suppose I cannot, you must make Mother or Hannah write to us as often as they can. There is nothing, I beleive, there is not any thing here you would like to hear from or of.

Dear Sister [Hannah] I shall never forgive you if you do not write to me. I suppose you would like to hear about the ladies in N.O. They are something like the "critters" in N.Y. except they [wear] one or two more "flonces" and live more in the open air &c&c&c&c&c&c.

To Eddy, you must go to school and learn to read and write and then you must send letters to me, besides you must be a good boy &c.

And now, Dear Mother, I must bid you good bye for a little while but will write to you again shortly.

We are both very well and the warm air agrees with Walter very much.

I have had a little attack of the disentery but I am very very well now, in fact I have not been sick much at all.

Dear Mother, good bye,
                          your son   Jefferson Whitman
My best respects to the rest of the family.

Tuesday morning, 28th March

Dearest Mother;

In one of my late letters, I told Hannah that if you did not receive money, by a letter from me, to pay the interest on the 1st of May, she must go down to the bank and draw $31½, and pay it at the insurance office, and get a receipt for it. However, I may send money in a letter before that time—or part of it. O, mother, how glad I was to hear that you are quite well, again. Do try to keep so; you must not work—and they must all be kind to you. If you only keep well till I get home again, I think I shall be satisfied. I began to feel very uneasy, not hearing from you so long. My prospects in the money line are bright. O how I long for the day when we can have our quiet little farm, and be together again—and have Mary and her children come to pay us long visits. I wrote to Mary yesterday.

W. W.

M S: Berg Collection, New York Public Library

To Moses S. and Alfred E. Beach

Brooklyn, June 17, 1850

To Messrs. Beach, of the Sun: (through Mr. Stuart.)[4]

The accompanying novel, of "*the Sleeptalker*," I consider one of the most interesting, romantic, and full of incident, of any I have ever come across.—It is by the Danish novelist Ingemann, a better writer even than Miss Bremer.—[5]

The work from which I have compiled "*the Sleeptalker*"[6] is an English translation, (I send you the cover and title-page,) whose only fault was, that it was too voluminous, the author going very extensively into the details of old Danish history.—This I have altogether cut out; reducing the work to half its first size.—It has never been republished in this country, and is altogether unknown here.—

The romance is a stirring and lively one, and, it seems to me, fitted to become very popular.—

I take the liberty of leaving it for you to look at, to see if I could dispose of it for serial publication in "the Sun."—I desire but a moderate price.—After running through the Sun, it seems to me it would pay handsomely to print it in a neat 25 cent book form.—

You will see that the title of the original is "The Childhood of Erik Menved"; the latter part of the original story, consisting very much of prolix details of historical events, gives it that name—but that part of the story I have contracted into a few paragraphs—and have taken a singular trait of one of the principal actors in the narrative as the foundation of the name I give it.—

Please, if convenient, make up your minds whether it would suit you, and how much it would be worth to you, so that I can have an answer by the middle or latter part of the week.—

The story would make about 65 leaded short columns of the Sun—so that, at an average of 3 columns a day, it would run through 22 days.—

Walter Whitman

MS: Feinberg Collection, Library of Congress

To John Parker Hale [7]

Brooklyn, August 14, 1852

A word from a stranger, a young man, and a true Democrat I hope.

You must not only not decline the nomination of the Democracy at Pittsburgh, but you must accept it gracefully and cordially. It is well to know when to be firm against others' wishes; but it is better to know when to yield in a manly and amiable spirit.

Out of the Pittsburgh movement and "platform" it may be that a real live Democratic party is destined to come forth, which, from small beginnings, ridicule, and odium, (just like Jeffersonian democracy fifty years ago,) will gradually win the hearts of the people, and crowd those who stand before it into the sea. Then we should see an American Democracy with thews and sinews worthy this sublime age.

It is from the young men of our land—the ardent, and generous hearts—that these things are to come. Do you, then, yield to the decision at Pittsburgh, shape your acceptance to that idea of the future which supposes that we are at [present?] planting a renewed and vital party, fit to triumph over the effete and lethargic organizations now so powerful and so unworthy. Look to the young men—appeal specially to them. Enter into this condition of affairs, with spirit, too. Take two or three occasions within the coming month to make personal addresses directly to the people, giving condensed embodiments of the principal ideas which distinguish our liberal faith from the drag-parties and their platforms. Boldly promulge these, with that temper of rounded and good-natured moderation which is peculiar to you; but abate not one jot of your fullest radicalism. After these two or three speeches, which should be well-considered and not too long, possess your soul in patience, and take as little personal action in the election as may be. Depend upon it, there is no way so good as the face-to-face of candidates and people—in the old heroic Roman fashion. I would suggest that one of these addresses be delivered in New York, and one in Cincinnati—with a third either in Baltimore or Washington.

You are at Washington, and have for years moved among the great men. I have never been at Washington, and know none of the great men. But I know the people. I know well, (for I am practically in New York,) the real heart of this mighty city—the tens of thousands of young men, the mechanics, the writers, &c &c. In all these, under and behind the bosh of the regular politicians, there burns, almost with fierceness, the divine fire which more or less, during all ages, has only waited a chance to leap forth and confound the calculations of tyrants, hunkers,[8] and all their tribe. At this moment, New York is the most radical city in America. It would be the most anti-slavery city, if that cause hadn't been made ridiculous by the freaks of the local leaders here.

O, my dear sir, I only wish you could know the sentiments of respect and personal good will toward yourself, with which, upon seeing a telegraphic item in one of this morning's papers, that you would probably decline, I forthwith sat down, and have written my thoughts and advice. I shall make no apology; for if sentiments and opinions out of the great mass of the common people are of no use to the legislators, then our government is a sad blunder indeed.

How little you at Washington—you Senatorial and Executive dignitaries—know of us, after all. How little you realize that the souls of the people ever leap and swell to any thing like a great liberal thought or principle, uttered by any well-known personage—and how deeply they love the man that promulges such principles with candor and power. It is wonderful in your keen search and rivalry for popular favor, that hardly any one discovers this direct and palpable road there.

Walter Whitman

M S: New Hampshire Historical Society

To Sarah Tyndale[9]

Brooklyn, June 20, 1857

Dear Friend,

Do not suppose, because I have delayed writing to you, that I have forgotten you. No, that will never be. I often recall your visits to me, and your goodness. I think profoundly of my friends—though I cannot write to them by the post office. I write to them more to my satisfaction, through my poems.

Tell Hector I thank him heartily for his invitation and letter—O it is not from any mind to slight him that I have not answered it, or accepted the friendly call. I am so non-polite—so habitually wanting in my responses and ceremonies. That is *me*—much that is bad, harsh, an undutiful person, a thriftless debtor, is me.[10]

I spent an evening with Mr. Arnold and Mrs. Price lately. Mrs. Price and Helen had been out all day with the sewing machine, at Mr. Beecher's— either Henry Ward's, or his father's. They had done a great day's work—as much, one of the Beecher ladies said, as a sempstress could have got through with in six months. Mrs. P. and Helen had engagements for a fortnight ahead, to go out among families and take the sewing machine. What a revolution this little piece of furniture is producing. Isn't it quite an *encouragement*.[11]

I got into quite a talk with Mr. Arnold about Mrs. Hatch. He says the pervading thought of her speeches is that *first* exists the spirituality of any thing, and *that* gives existence to things, the earth, plants, animals, men, women. But that Andrew Jackson Davis[12] puts *matter* as the subject of his homilies, and the primary source of all results—I suppose the soul among the rest. Both are quite determined in their theories. Perhaps when they know much more, both of them will be much less determined.

A minister, Rev. Mr. Porter,[13] was introduced to me this morning, a Dutch Reformed minister, and editor of the "Christian Intelligencer," N. Y. Would you believe it, he had been reading "Leaves of Grass," and wanted *more?* He said he hoped I retained the true Reformed faith which I must have inherited from my mother's Dutch ancestry. I not only assured him of my retaining faith in that sect, but that I had perfect faith in all sects, and was not inclined to reject one single one—but believed each to be about as far advanced as it could be, considering what had preceded it—and moreover that every one was the needed representative of *its* truth—or of something needed as much as truth. I had quite a good hour with Mr. Porter—we grew friends—and I am to go dine with the head man of the head congregation of Dutch Presbyterians in Brooklyn, Eastern District!

I have seen Mrs. Walton once or twice since you left Brooklyn. I dined there. I feel great sympathy with her, on some accounts. Certainly, she is not happy.

Fowler & Wells [14] are bad persons for me. They retard my book very much. It is worse than ever. I wish now to bring out a third edition—I have now a *hundred* poems ready (the last edition had thirty-two)—and shall endeavor to make an arrangement with some publisher here to take the plates from F. & W. and make the additions needed, and so bring out the third edition. F. & W. are very willing to give up the plates—they want the thing off their hands. In the forthcoming Vol. I shall have, as I said, a hundred poems, and no other matter but poems—(no letters to or from Emerson— no notices, or any thing of that sort.) I know well enough, that *that* must be the *true* Leaves of Grass—I think it (the new Vol.) has an aspect of completeness, and makes its case clearer. The old poems are all retained. The difference is in the new character given to the mass, by the additions.

Dear friend, I do not feel like fixing a day on which I will come and make my promised visit. How it is I know not, but I hang back more and more from making visits, even to those I have much happiness in being with.

Mother is well—all are well. Mother often speaks about you. We shall all of us remember you always with more affection than you perhaps suppose. Before I come to Philadelphia, I shall send you or Hector a line.

Wishing Peace & Friendship

Walt Whitman

M S: Henry E. Huntington Library

To an unidentified correspondent [15]

Brooklyn, July 28, 1857

O you should see me, how I look after sea-sailing. I am swarthy and red as a Moor—I go around without any coat or vest—looking so strong, ugly, and nonchalant, with my white beard—People stare, I notice, more wonderingly than ever. . . . I have thought, for some time past, of beginning the use of myself as a public Speaker, teacher, or lecturer. (This, after I get out the next issue of my "Leaves")—Whether it will come to any thing, remains to be seen. . . . My immediate acquaintances, even those attached strongly to me, secretly entertain the idea that I am a great fool not to "*make something*" out of my "talents" and out of the general good will with which I am regarded. Can it be that some such notion is lately infusing itself into me also?

TEXT: *Henkels Catalogue*, June 14–15, 1901

To the editors of *Harper's Magazine*

Brooklyn, January 7, 1860

The theory of "*A Chant of National Feuillage*" [16] is to bring in, (devoting a line, or two or three lines, to each,) a comprehensive collection of touches, locales, incidents, idiomatic scenes, from every section, South, West, North, East, Kanada, Texas, Maine, Virginia, the Mississippi Valley, &c. &c. &c.— all intensely fused to the urgency of compact America, "America always"— all in a vein of graphic, short, clear, hasting along—as having a huge bouquet to collect, and quickly taking and binding in every characteristic subject that offers itself—making a compact, the-whole-surrounding, *National Poem*, after its sort, after my own style.

Is there any other poem of the sort extant—or indeed hitherto attempted?

You may start at the style. Yes, it is a new style, of course, but that is necessitated by new theories, new themes—or say the new treatment of themes, forced upon us for American purposes. Every really new person, (poet or other,) *makes* his style—sometimes a little way removed from the previous models—sometimes very far removed.

Furthermore, I have surely attained headway enough with the American public, especially with the literary classes, to make it worth your while to give them a sight of me with all my neologism.

The price is $40. Cash down on acceptance.

I reserve the use of the piece in any collection of my poems I may publish in future.

Should my name be printed in the programme of contributors at any time it must not be lower down than third in the list.

If the piece is declined, please keep the MS. for me to be called for. Will send, or call, last of next week.

Walt Whitman

MS: Formerly in Richard Gimbel Collection

To James Russell Lowell[17]

Brooklyn, January 20, 1860

Dear Sir,

Mr. House inform'd me that you accepted, and would publish, my "Bardic Symbols." If so, would you, as soon as convenient, have it put in type, and send me the proof?

About the two lines:

(See from my dead lips the ooze exuding at last!
See the prismatic colors glistening and rolling!)

I have in view, from them, an effect in the piece which I clearly feel, but cannot as clearly define. Though I should prefer them in, still, as I told Mr. House, I agree that you may omit them, if you decidedly wish to.

Yours &c

Walt Whitman

MS: Barrett Collection, University of Virginia

To Abby M. Price

Boston, March 29, 1860

As I know you would like to hear from me, my dear friend, I will not yet go to bed—but sit down to write to you, that I have been here in Boston, to-day is a fortnight, and that my book is well under way. About a hundred and twenty pages are set up—it will probably make from six to seven hundred pages, and of a larger size than the last edition. It is to be very finely printed, good paper, and new, rather large-sized type. Thayer & Eldridge, the publishers, are a couple of young Yankees—so far very good specimens, to me, of this Eastern race of yours. They have treated me first rate—have not asked me at all what I was going to put into the book—just took me to the stereotype foundry, and given orders to follow my directions. It will be out in a month—a great relief to me to have the thing off my mind.

I am more pleased with Boston than I anticipated. It is full of life, and criss-cross streets. I am very glad I [have] come, if only to rub out of me the deficient notions I had of New England character. I am getting to like it, every way—even the Yankee twang.

Emerson called upon me immediately, treated me with the greatest courtesy—kept possession of me all day—gave me a bully dinner, &c.[18]

I go on the Common—walk considerable in Washington street—and occupy about three hours a day at work in the printing office. All I have to do, is to read proofs. I wish you lived here—I should visit you regularly every day—probably twice a day. I create an immense sensation in Washington street. Every body here is so like everybody else—and I am Walt Whitman!— Yankee curiosity and cuteness, for once, is thoroughly stumped, confounded, petrified, made desperate.

Let me see—have I any thing else to say to you? Indeed, what does it all amount to—this saying business? Of course I had better tear up this note— only I want to let you see how I cannot have forgotten you—sitting up here after half past 12, to write this precious document. I send my love to Helen and Emmy.

Walt.

MS: Morgan Library

To his brother Jeff

Boston, April 1, 1860

Dear Brother,

I have just finished a letter to my mother, and while my hand is in, I will write you a line. I enclose in my letter to Mother, a note from H[e]yde[19]— nothing at all in it, except that Han is well, and comfortably situated—I have not heard a word from home since I left—write me a few words, Jeff, if mother does not, and let me know how you all are, and whether you have took the house or given it up. I suppose of course if every thing was not going on pretty much as usual, some of you would have written to tell me.

I am having a tolerable fair time here in Boston—not quite enough to occupy me—only two or three hours work a day, reading proof. Still, I am so satisfied at the certainty of having "Leaves of Grass," in a far more complete and favorable form than before, printed and really *published*, that I don't mind small things. The book will be a very handsome specimen of typography, paper, binding, &c.—and will be, it seems to me, like relieving me of a great weight—or removing a great obstacle that has been in my way for the last three years. The young men that are publishing it treat me in a way I could not wish to have better. They are go-ahead fellows, and don't seem to have the least doubt they are bound to make a good spec. out of my book. It is quite curious, all this should spring up so suddenly, aint it.

I am very well, and hold my own about as usual. I am stopping at a lodging house, have a very nice room, gas, water, good American folks keep it—I pay $2—eat at restaurant. I get up in the morning, give myself a good wash all over, and currying[20]—then take a walk, often in the Common—then nothing but a cup of coffee generally for my breakfast—then to the stereotype foundry. About 12 I take a walk, and at 2, a good dinner. Not much else, in the way of eating, except that meal.

If I have any thing to communicate, dear brother, I shall write again.

Walt.

M S: Whitman House, Camden

To his brother Jeff

Boston, May 10, 1860

Dear Brother,

I have nothing particular to write about, yet I know you will be glad to hear from me anyhow. The book is finished in all that makes the reading part, and is all through the press complete—It is electrotyped—that is, by a chemical process, a solution of copper, silver, zinc, &c. is precipitated in a "bath," so as to cover the face of the plates of type all over, and make it very much harder and more enduring. Plates finished by that process wear well for hundreds of thousands of copies, and are probably a neater impression. But perhaps you know about it yourself.

Thayer & Eldridge have put through 1000 copies, for the first pop. They have very accurate ideas of the whole matter. They expect it to be a valuable investment, increasing by months and years—not going off in a rocket way, (like "Uncle Tom's Cabin.") The typographical appearance of the book has been just as I directed it, in every respect. The printers and foremen thought I was crazy, and there were all sorts of supercilious squints (about the typography I ordered, I mean)—but since it has run through the press, they have simmered down. Yesterday the foreman of the press-room (Rand's, an old establishment where all the best work is done,) pronounced it, in plain terms, the freshest and handsomest piece of typography that had ever passed through his mill—I like it, I think, first rate—though I think I could improve much upon it now. It is quite "odd," of course. As to Thayer & Eldridge they think every thing I do is the right thing. We are just now in "suspenders" on account of the engraving. I have about decided, though, to have 1000 copies printed from it, as it is—and then let Schoff,[21] the engraver, finish it afterwards—I do not know for certain whether it is a good portrait or not—The probability is that the book will be bound and ready May 19.

I make Thayer & Eldridge crack on the elegant workmanship of the book, its material, &c. but I won't allow them to puff the poetry—though I had quite a hard struggle—as they had prepared several tremendous puff advertisments—altogether ahead of Ned Buntline and the "Ledger"[22]—I persuaded them to give me the copy to make some little corrections—which I did effectually by going straight to my lodgings, and putting the whole stuff in the fire—Oh, I forgot to tell you, they have printed a very neat little brochure, (pamphlet,) of 64 pages, called "Leaves of Grass Imprints," containing a very readable collection of criticisms on the former issues—This is given away gratis, as an advertisement and circular. Altogether, Jeff, I am very, very much satisfied and relieved that the thing, in the permanent form it now is, looks as well and reads as well (to my own notion) as I anticipated—because a good deal, after all, was an experiment—and now I am satisfied.

And how goes it with you, my dear? I watched the N. Y. papers to see if Spinola's bill passed[23]—but it didn't, of course, or I should of heard of it in many ways. So you must be on the works still—If I get a chance I will take a look at the Boston Works before I leave. The water is almost exactly like the Brooklyn water in taste. I got Mother's letter—tell Mother I may not write next Monday, as I am in hopes to be home, I can't tell exactly what day, but through the week. Oh the awful expense I have been under here, Jeff, living the way I have, hiring a room, and eating at restaurants—7 cents for a cup of coffee, and 19 cts for a beefsteak—*and me so fond of coffee and beefsteak.* Tell mother I think it would have been worth while for her to have moved on here, and boarded me—

I have had a very fair time, though, here in Boston—Very, very many folks I meet I like much—I have never seen finer—they are fine in almost every respect—very friendly, very generous, very good feeling, and of course intelligent people—The great *cramper* of the Bostonian is, though, to be kept on the rack by the old idea of *respectability*, how the rest do, and what they will say. There are plenty of splendid specimens of men come from the other New England states to settle here, especially from Maine, New Hampshire, Vermont, &c, that if they would *let themselves be*, and only make *that* better and finer, would beat the world. For there is no denying that these Yanks are the first-class race. But, without exception, they all somehow allow themselves to be squeezed into the stereotype mould, and wear straight collars and hats, and say "my respects"—like the rest. Of course *I* cannot walk through Washington street, (the Broadway here,) without creating an immense sensation.

I sent a couple of papers to Han this morning. Oh how much I would like to see her once more—and I *must*, this summer—After I recruit a while home, I shall very likely take a tour, partly business and partly for edification, through all the N[ew] E[ngland] states—then I shall see Han—I shall write to her before I leave here—and do you write also, Jeff—don't fail— Should you write to me, in response to this, you must write so that I would get the letter not later than Wednesday morning next—as I feel the fit growing upon me stronger and stronger to move—And the fare is only $3 now from here to New York, cabin passage, in the boat—Besides I could go dead head if I was to apply—Jeff, I feel as if things had taken a turn with me, at last—Give my love to Mat, and all my dear brothers, especially Georgie.

Walt.

M S: Whitman House, Camden

1861-1865

Washington
June 10. 1865.

Mr. & Mrs. Pratt;

As I am visiting your son Alfred occasionally to cheer him up in his sickness in hospital, I thought you might like a few words, though from a stranger, yet a friend to your boy. I was there last night, and sat a while by the bed as usual, & he showed me the letter he had just received from home. He wrote to you yesterday. He has had Diarrhea pretty bad, but is now improved & goes about the hospital — but as the weather is pretty hot & powerful in the midst of the day, I advised him not to go out doors much at present. What he wants most is rest, and a chance to get his strength again. I expect he will

During the horrors of the Civil War Whitman became a self-appointed nurse, or wound dresser, in the military hospitals of Washington, where in awesomely large numbers wounded Union soldiers, often in their teens, came to recover or, all too frequently, to die in soul-wrenching agony. Whitman went through the wards offering comfort, bearing gifts of food and ice cream, holding the hands of the suffering, writing letters for the boys, his "comrades," to their parents.

AFTER WHITMAN'S EXTRAORDINARY BURST OF CREATIV-
ity, the attendant excitement, and the inevitable letdown, he experienced
what he called, in a letter to Emerson, "my New York stagnation." Since
three editions of *Leaves of Grass* produced little income, he supported himself with occasional pieces for Manhattan and Brooklyn newspapers. He
watched as the nation gradually drifted into its greatest tragedy, a fratricidal
strife. Some of the members of the Fred Gray Association departed for military service, usually as officers in specialized roles, not as ordinary enlisted
men who served, it sometimes seemed, as cannon fodder for generals who
learned the art of war at a frightful toll of American youth. Whitman began
to visit military hospitals where wartime casualties arrived in increasing
numbers. At the same time the city prospered, money appeared to flow,
many New Yorkers in their hatred of the blacks sympathized with the South,
and the rich bought their way out of military service.

The Whitman family experienced the war at firsthand when George
volunteered for military service with the Thirteenth New York Regiment
shortly after the firing at Fort Sumter, and he reenlisted for three years of
service the following September. He rose quickly to the rank of lieutenant.
On December 16, 1862, the family learned through the newspapers that
George had been wounded. Walt hastily packed some clothes and set off by
train for Washington. He had his pocket picked in Philadelphia, and with
little or no money in his purse proceeded to Washington, where he searched
futilely for George in the hospitals. He stumbled onto two acquaintances,
William D. O'Connor, a novelist and later the author of various prose tracts,
whom he had met in Boston in 1860, and Charles W. Eldridge, one of the
publishers of the 1860 edition of *Leaves of Grass*. O'Connor loaned him
money, and Eldridge obtained a pass for Fredericksburg, Virginia, where
George's regiment had gone into battle.

Walt did not know that on the day he left New York, George wrote to
their mother from Falmouth, Virginia: "We have had another battle and I
have come out safe and sound, although I had the side of my jaw slightly
scraped with a peice of shell which burst at my feet."[1]

When he found George's regiment, "one of the first things that met my
eyes in camp," Walt wrote to his mother, "was a heap of feet, arms, legs, &c.
under a tree in front a hospital." With the starkness of a canvas by Georgia
O'Keeffe, that pyramid of limbs was to hover over his life and imagination
for the next three years, and it marked the beginning of a rite of passage
which lifted him out of "horrible sloughs," presumably of depression. Those

were "real, terrible, beautiful days!" he remarked in 1888. "I have never left them."[2]

Walt spent a week or so with the members of Captain George Whitman's regiment, and on his return to Washington on December 29, 1862, he told his mother that he had decided to escape "for good" from the drift of his New York life and to settle in Washington. On the same day he informed Ralph Waldo Emerson that "I fetch up here in harsh and superb plight" and asked him to solicit letters of recommendation from various members of Lincoln's cabinet and to send the letters to him for use when he saw fit. Whitman postponed transmitting the letters for several years when it turned out that the articles he wrote for New York newspapers and the copying he did in the Paymaster's Office provided a modest but, for his needs, ample income.

He found himself magnetically drawn to the military hospitals in Washington—to "the beautiful young men in wholesale death & agony." "I get more & more wound round—poor young men," he wrote to his mother in a striking image of birth and death that exposes the symbiotic relationship he was establishing with the dying. To his brother Jeff he confessed, "I never before had my feelings so thoroughly and (so far) permanently absorbed, to the very roots, as by these huge swarms of dear, wounded, sick, dying boys." In still another letter he acknowledged his exhilaration, "how fascinating it is, with all its hospital surroundings of sadness & scenes of repulsion & death." His "presence & magnetism," he declared, saved the lives of soldiers who "would literally sink & give up, if I did not pass a portion of the time with them."

Attired in a floppy wide-brimmed hat, a flowing coat, and military boots, a worn knapsack hanging from his shoulder—he looked like a vagabond— he patiently and slowly walked through the long, endless wards of hospitals. He called the youths by first name. He smiled compassionately and spoke only as the situation demanded, recognizing with characteristic delicacy that some of the young men in their dying days found shelter and perhaps comfort in their own worlds of memories into which he could not enter. He sat at the bedsides of dying soldiers and wrote letters to their families and shared the shattering loneliness of men dying far from their parents and wives, who waited with impatient desperation for news.

For Whitman the hospitals became a kind of home. Although he was neither doctor nor nurse, he took care of needs beyond the reach of medicine, and he fulfilled again, as he had in the Whitman home and in poems such as "Song of Myself," the triple roles of father, mother, elder brother. There were agencies, usually religious, which provided nonmedical services in the hospitals, but characteristically, Whitman preferred to take care of his sons and comrades in his own way. He offered comfort, not moral guidance, tobacco and ice cream, not wafers.

He was humbled by what he saw in the hospitals, "the living soul's, the body's tragedies, bursting the petty bonds of art. To these, what are your dramas and poems, even the oldest and the tearfulest? Not old Greek mighty ones, where man contends with fate, (and always yields)—not Virgil showing Dante on and on among the agonized & damned, approach what here I see and take a part in."

He witnessed day after day an endless procession: some soldiers left to return to their units or their homes, many were silently carried out of the wards on stretchers, and new arrivals at once occupied their beds. In the hospitals where more died than survived and suffered painful amputations, Whitman formed intense friendships and, when his presence eased suffering, experienced deep gratifications. "These letters of yours to the soldiers," Traubel observed, "are the best gospel of comradeship in the language— better than the Leaves itself." Whitman agreed: "Comradeship—yes, that's the thing: getting one and one together to make two—getting the twos together everywhere to make all: that's the only bond we should accept and that's the only freedom we should desire: comradeship, comradeship."[3]

Neither then nor later did Whitman admit the disappointments he sustained in wartime comradeship. He hungered for something more than a symbolic household and a transient relationship. He craved the permanence which had eluded him in life for more than forty years. He became deeply attached to a soldier named Tom Sawyer, one of the patients in Armory Square Hospital, and in his letters dropped his usual caution against self-disclosure. He frankly addresses his "dear, darling comrade," who, he swears, is "the comrade that suits me to a dot." The result of the candor and perhaps the aggressive pursuit was a "pretty" reply written by one of Sawyer's friends. In his next letter Whitman admits his disappointment that Tom had not come up to his room to receive some clothing after he left the hospital: "I should have often thought now Tom may be wearing around his body something from *me*, & that it might contribute to your comfort." "Old wooly-neck loves you," he writes and hopes "God will put it in your heart to bear toward me a little at least of the feeling I have about you." Tom is now "dear brother."

A month later Whitman had not heard from Tom and enclosed a self-addressed envelope. "I do not expect you," he reassures the youth, "to return for me the same degree of love I have for you." Two months later: "I cant understand why you have ceased to correspond with me." In November: "Do you wish to shake me off? That I cannot believe, for I have the same love for you that I exprest in my letters last spring."

About the same time, perhaps on the same day he wrote to Sawyer, Whitman sent a letter to another soldier, Elijah Fox: "I cannot bear the thought of being separated from you—I know I am a great fool about such things." He assures Fox that he is so much "closer" than any of his New York friends "that there is no comparison." The reply of Fox, who after his medical discharge had returned to his home and wife, unveils the sadness of Whitman's quest. "Since coming here I have often thought of what you told me when I said to you I am certain I will come back to Washington. You said to me then that a great many of the boys had said the same thing but none had returned. I am sorry it is so but after I had thought it over I concluded it would be better for me to go into some business that would be a permanent thing."[4]

On reading Whitman's letter to Fox, Traubel said that it "is better than the gospel according to John for love."[5] Whitman agreed but said nothing of the painful recognition, in the words of Robert Frost, of "finalities / Besides the grave."

To his brother George

Brooklyn, July 12, 1861

Dear Brother,

Your letter come to-day. Every thing with us is pretty much the same. Mother is pretty much the same. Some days she [is] better, and some not so well. She has taken a good many sulphur vapor baths. She takes one every other day. She goes down in the cars to the baths, in Willoughby street near the City Hall. Sometimes Mat[6] goes with her, [and once in] a while she goes [alo]ne. They are rather agreeable to take—they make one sweat extremely. Mother goes about the same, around the house. She has better use of her arms and wrists than she did there one time—but an hour or two, now and then, generally in the morning, she has bad pains. Her appetite is pretty good. The weather here lately has been awful—three days the heat was as bad as I ever knew it—so I think that had something to do with mother's feeling weak. To-day it is much cooler.

Jeff and Martha and Cis[7] and Eddy are all well. Jess is the same as usual—

he works every day in the yard. He does not seem to mind the heat. He is employed in the store-house, where they are continually busy preparing stores, provisions, to send off in the different vessels. He assists in that.

We are all very glad the 13th is coming home—mother especially. There have been so many accounts of shameful negligence, or worse, in the commissariat of your reg't. that there must be *something* in it—notwithstanding you speak very lightly of the complaints in your letters. The *Eagle*, of course, makes the worst of it, every day, to stop men from enlisting.

All of us here think the rebellion as good as broke—no matter if the war does continue for months yet.

Walt.

M S: Trent Collection, Duke University

To his mother

Washington, December 29, 1862

Dear, dear Mother,

Friday the 19th inst. I succeeded in reaching the camp of the 51st New York, and found George alive and well—In order to make sure that you would get the good news, I sent back by messenger to Washington (I dare say you did not get it for some time) a telegraphic dispatch, as well as a letter—and the same to Hannah at Burlington. I have staid in camp with George ever since, till yesterday, when I came back to Washington—about the 24th George got Jeff's letter of the 20th. Mother, how much you must have suffered, all that week, till George's letter came—and all the rest must too. As to me, I know I put in about three days of the greatest suffering I ever experienced in my life. I wrote to Jeff how I had my pocket picked in a jam and hurry, changing cars, at Philadelphia, so that I landed here without a dime. The next two days I spent hunting through the hospitals, walking all day and night, unable to ride, trying to get information, trying to get access to big people, &c—I could not get the least clue to anything—Odell[8] would not see me at all—But Thursday afternoon, I lit on a way to get down on the government boat that runs to Aquia creek, and so by railroad to the neighborhood of Falmouth, opposite Fredericksburgh—So by degrees I worked my way to Ferrero's[9] brigade, which I found Friday afternoon without much trouble after I got in camp. When I found dear brother George, and found that he was alive and well, O you may imagine how trifling all my little cares and difficulties seemed—they vanished into nothing. And now that I have lived for eight or nine days amid such scenes as the camps furnish, and had a practical part in it all, and realize the way that hundreds of thousands of good men are now living, and have had to live for a year or more, not only without any of the comforts, but with death and sickness and hard marching and hard fighting, (and no success at that,) for their continual experience— really nothing we call trouble seems worth talking about. One of the first things that met my eyes in camp, was a heap of feet, arms, legs, &c. under a tree in front a hospital, the Lacy house.

George is very well in health, has a good appetite—I think he is at times more wearied out and homesick than he shows, but stands it upon the whole very well. Every one of the soldiers, to a man, wants to get home.

I suppose Jeff got quite a long letter I wrote from camp, about a week ago. I told you that George had been promoted to Captain—his commission arrived while I was there.

Jeff must write oftener, and put in a few lines from mother, even if it is only two lines—then in the next letter a few lines from Mat, and so on. You have no idea how letters from home cheer one up in camp, and dissipate home sickness.

While I was there George still lived in Capt. [Henry W.] Francis's tent— there were five of us altogether, to eat, sleep, write, &c. in a space twelve feet square, but we got along very well—the weather all along was very fine— and would have got along to perfection, but Capt. Francis is not a man I could like much—I had very little to say to him. George is about building a place, half-hut and half-tent, for himself—(he is probably about it this very day)—and then he will be better off, I think. Every Captain has a tent, in which he lives, transacts company business, &c. has a cook, (or man of all work,) and in the same tent mess and sleep his Lieutenants, and perhaps the 1st sergeant. They have a kind of fire-place, and the cook's fire is outside, on the open ground. George had very good times while Francis was away—the cook, a young disabled soldier, Tom, is an excellent fellow, and a first-rate cook, and the 2nd Lieutenant [Samuel M.] Pooley, is a tip-top young Pennsylvanian. Tom thinks all the world of George—when he heard he was wounded, on the day of the battle, he left every thing, got across the river, and went hunting for George through the field, through thick and thin. I wrote to Jeff that George was wounded by a shell, a gash in the cheek— you could stick a splint through into the mouth, but it has healed up without difficulty already. Every thing is uncertain about the army, whether it moves or stays where it is. There are no furloughs granted at present. I will stay here for the present, at any rate long enough to see if I can get any employment at any thing, and shall write what luck I have. Of course I am unsettled at present. Dear mother, my love,

Walt.

If Jeff or any one writes, address me, care of Major Hapgood, paymaster, U. S. Army, corner 15th and F streets, 5th floor, Washington D. C. I send my love to dear sister Mat, and little sis—and to Andrew and all my brothers. O Mat, how lucky it was you did not come—together, we could never have got down to see George.

M S: Feinberg Collection, Library of Congress

To Ralph Waldo Emerson

Washington, December 29, 1862

Dear friend,

Breaking up a few weeks since, and for good, my New York stagnation— wandering since through camp and battle scenes—I fetch up here in harsh and superb plight—wretchedly poor, excellent well, (my only torment, family matters)—realizing at last that it is necessary for me to fall for the time in the wise old way, to push my fortune, to be brazen, and get employment, and have an income—determined to do it, (at any rate until I get out of horrible sloughs) I write you, asking you as follows:

I design to apply personally direct at headquarters, for some place. I would apply on literary grounds, not political.

I wish you would write for me something like the enclosed form of letter, that I can present, opening my interview with the great man. I wish you to write two copies—put the one in an envelope directed to Mr. Seward, Secretary of State—and the other in an envelope directed to Mr. Chase, Secretary of the Treasury—and enclose both envelopes in the one I send herewith so that I can use either one or the other. I wish you also to send me a note of introduction to Charles Sumner.[10]

It is pretty certain that, armed in that way, I shall conquer my object. Answer me by next mail, for I am waiting here like ship waiting for the welcome breath of the wind.

Indeed yours, &c

Walt Whitman

M S: Emerson Memorial Association, Harvard University

To his sister-in-law Martha

Washington, January 2–4, 1863

Dear sister,

You have heard of my fortunes and misfortunes of course, (through my letters to mother and Jeff,) since I left home, that Tuesday afternoon. But I thought I would write a few lines to you, as it is a comfort to write home, even if I have nothing particular to say. Well, dear sister, I hope you are well and hearty, and that little sis keep as well as she always had, when I left home, so far. Dear little plague, how I would like to have her with me, for one day. I can fancy I see her, and hear her talk. Jeff must have got a note from me about a letter I have written to the *Eagle*[11]—you may be sure you will get letters enough from me, for I have little else to do at present. Since I laid my eyes on dear brother George, and saw him alive and well—and since I have spent a week in camp, down there opposite Fredericksburgh, and seen what well men and sick men, and mangled men endure—it seems to me I can be satisfied and happy henceforward if I can get one meal a day, and know that mother and all are in good health, and especially if I can only be with you again, and have some little steady paying occupation in N. Y. or Brooklyn.

I am writing this in the office of Major Hapgood, way up in the top of a big high house, corner of 15th and F. street—there is a splendid view, away down south, of the Potomac river, and across to the Georgetown side, and the grounds and houses of Washington spread out beneath my high point of view. The weather is perfect—I have had that in my favor ever since leaving home—yesterday and to-day it is bright, and plenty warm enough. The poor soldiers are continually coming in from the hospitals, &c. to get their pay—some of them waiting for it, to go home. They climb up here, quite exhausted, and then find it is no good, for there is no money to pay them—there are two or three paymasters desks in this room, and the scenes of disappointment are quite affecting. Here they wait in Washington, perhaps week after [week], wretched and heart sick—this is the greatest place of delays and puttings off, and no finding the clue to any thing—this building is the paymaster general's quarters, and the crowds on the walk and corner, of poor sick, pale, tattered soldiers, are awful—many of them day after day, disappointed and tired out. Well, Mat, I will suspend my letter for the present, and go out through the city—I have a couple of poor fellows in the Hospital to visit also.

Walt.

Saturday evening, Jan 3d.

I write this in the place where I have my lodging room, 394 L street, 4th door above 14th street. A friend of mine, William D. O'Connor, has two apartments, on the 3d floor, very ordinarily furnished, for which he pays the *extra*ordinary price of $25 a month. I have a werry little bedroom on the 2d floor—Mr. & Mrs. O'Connor and their little girl have all gone out "down town" for an hour or two, to make some Saturday evening purchases, and I am left in possession of the premises—so I sit by the fire, and scribble more of my letter. I have not heard any thing from dear brother George since I left the camp last Sunday morning, 28th Dec. I wrote to him on Tuesday last—I wish to get to him the two blue woolen shirts Jeff sent, as they would come very acceptable to him—and will try to do it yet. I think of sending them by mail, if the postage is not more than $1.

Yesterday I went out to the Campbell Hospital to see a couple of Brooklyn boys, of the 51st. They knew I was in Washington, and sent me a note, to come and see them. O my dear sister, how your heart would ache to go through the rows of wounded young men, as I did—and stopt to speak a comforting word to them. There were about 100 in one long room, just a long shed neatly whitewashed inside. One young man was very much prostrated, and groaning with pain. I stopt and tried to comfort him. He was very sick. I found he had not had any medical attention since he was brought there—among so many he had been overlooked. So I sent for the doctor, and he made an examination of him—the doctor behaved very well—seemed to be anxious to do right—said that the young man would recover—he had been brought pretty low with diarrhea and now had bronchitis, but not so serious as to be dangerous. I talked to him some time—he seemed to have entirely give up, and lost heart—he had not a cent of money—not a friend or acquaintance—I wrote a letter from him to his sister—his name is John A. Holmes, Campbello, Plymouth county, Mass. I gave him a little change I had—he said he would like to buy a drink of milk, when the woman came through with milk. Trifling as this was, he was overcome and began to cry. Then there were many, many others. I mention the one, as a specimen. My Brooklyn boys were John Lowery, shot at Fredericksburgh, and lost his left forearm, and Amos H. Vliet—Jeff knows the latter—he has his feet frozen, and is doing well. The 100 are in a ward, (6.)—and there are, I should think, eight or ten or twelve such wards in the Campbell Hospital—indeed a real village. Then there are some 38 more Hospitals here in Washington, some of them much larger.

Sunday forenoon, Jan 4, '63.

Mat, I hope and trust dear mother and all are well, and every thing goes on good home. The envelope I send, Jeff or any of you can keep for direction, or use it when wanted to write to me. As near as I can tell, the army at Falmouth remains the same.

Dear sister, good bye.

Walt.

I send my love to Andrew and Jesse and Eddy and all—What distressing news this is of the loss of the Monitor [12]—

M S: Feinberg Collection, Library of Congress

To his brother Jeff

Washington, January 16, 1863

Dearest brother,

Your letter came last evening containing the $6.[13] Two days since I received one from Probasco, containing $3 (not 5 as you mention.) I send a note, same mail as this, acknowledging the latter. I shall, either by letter giving specific names, hospitals, No. of the particular beds, and dates, or more likely by a letter in print in newspaper, for I am going to print a sort of hospital journal in some paper, send you and Mr. Lane and Probasco, a pretty plain schedule of the manner of my outlays of the sums sent by them to the hospital soldiers through me—as it would interest you all, as you say. Meantime, dear brother, do not crowd the thing in the least—do not ask any one when it becomes unpleasant—let it be understood by our engineer friends &c. that I have mentioned the subscription affair as forwarded, to be left entirely to their sense of what they wish to do, and what they think it would be discreet for them to do. I did not wish you to send $5, for I do not think it right—it is entirely too much—nor mother $1—I think she has enough, present and future, to attend to—but since it has come, I shall use it—I distributed between 2 & $3 yesterday.

What ought to be done by our family, I feel that *I* am doing, and have done myself. I have made $27 while I have been here, and got the money, and I should think I have paid in little items and purchases and money gifts at least $10 of that to the soldiers—I wouldn't take a thousand dollars for the satisfaction it has been to me—but, Jeff, I postpone till we come together again, any attempt to make you realize this whole thing.

Of course you have received, (probably about to-day,) a long letter I have written to Mother. Nothing definite appears to-day about the status or movements of the Army of the Potomac, but my guess, at a venture, is, that they either have moved down the Rappahannock toward Potomac, or are about moving. Whether it is to cross or not and whether for an attack or march, or whether as some think to Fortress Monroe, is quite unknown. You must not be alarmed at hearing of an advance, or engagement—at a distance it is more appalling than it deserves to be thought—Some think a portion goes west to Rosecrans.[14] It is so dangerous and critical for the government to make any more failures like that at Fredericksburgh, that it seems incredible to be any repetition of that most complete piece of mismanagement perhaps ever yet known in the earth's wars. I have not heard from George—it is good that you got a long letter. Jeff, I feel that you and dearest mother are perhaps needlessly unhappy and morbid about our dear brother—to be in the army is a mixture of danger and *security* in this war which few realize— they think exclusively of the danger.[15] [*incomplete*]
M S: Whitman House, Camden

To Ralph Waldo Emerson

Washington, January 17, 1863
Your letters from Buffalo have just come to hand. They find me still hanging around here—my plans, wants, ideas, &c gradually getting into shape.

I go a great deal into the Hospitals. Washington is full of them—both in town and out around the outskirts. Some of the larger ones are towns in themselves. In small and large, all forty to fifty thousand inmates are ministered to, as I hear. Being sent for by a particular soldier, three weeks since, in the Campbell Hospital, I soon fell to going there and elsewhere to like places daily. The first shudder has long passed over, and I must say I find deep things, unreckoned by current print or speech. The Hospital, I do not find it, the repulsive place of sores and fevers, nor the place of querulousness, nor the bad results of morbid years which one avoids like bad s[mells]— at least [not] so is it under the circumstances here—other hospitals may be, but not here.

I desire and intend to write a little book out of this phase of America, her masculine young manhood, its conduct under most trying of and highest of all exigency, which she, as by lifting a corner in a curtain, has vouchsafed me to see America, already brought to Hospital in her fair youth—brought and deposited here in this great, whited sepulchre of Washington itself—(this union Capital without the first bit of cohesion—this collect of proofs how low and swift a good stock can deteriorate—) Capital to which these deputies most strange arrive from every quarter, concentrating here, well-drest, rotten, meagre, nimble and impotent, full of gab, full always of their thrice-accursed *party*—arrive and skip into the seats of mightiest legislation, and take the seats of judges and high executive seats—while by quaint Providence come also sailed and wagoned hither this other freight of helpless worn and wounded youth, genuine of the soil, of darlings and true heirs to me the first unquestioned and convincing western crop, prophetic of the future, proofs undeniable to all men's ken of perfect beauty, tenderness and pluck that never race yet rivalled.

But more, a new world here I find as I would show—a world full of its separate action, play, suggestiveness—surely a medium world, advanced between our well-known practised one of body and of mind, and one there may-be somewhere on beyond, we dream of, of the soul.

Not to fly off to these clouds, however, I must abruptly say to my friends, where interested, that I find the best expression of American character I have ever seen or conceived—practically here in these ranks of sick and dying young men—nearly all I have seen, (five-sixths I think of those I have seen,) farmers' sons from the West, northwest—and from Pennsylvania, New York, and from largely among the rest your Massachusetts, &c—now after great and terrible experiences, here in their barracks they lie—in those boarded Washington hospital barracks, whitewashed outside and in, one story, high enough, airy and clean enough—one of the Wards, for sample, a long stretch, a hundred and sixty feet long, with aisle down the middle, with cots, fifty or more on each side—and Death there up and down the aisle, tapping lightly by night or day here and there some poor young man, with relieving touch—that is one Ward, a cluster of ten or twelve make a current Washington Hospital—wherein this moment lie languishing, burning with fever or down with diarrhea, the imperial blood and rarest marrow of the North—here, at any rate, as I go for a couple of hours daily, and get to be welcome and useful, I find the masses fully justified by closest contact, never vulgar, ever calm, without greediness, no flummery, no frivolity—responding electric and without fail to affection, yet no whining—not the first unmanly whimper have I yet seen or heard.

In the Patent Office Hospital, Dr. Stone,[16] (Horatio Stone the sculptor—in his ward, some 150 men—he has been surgeon here several months—has had successive changes of soldiers in charge—some bad wounds, of course—amputations, sometimes rapidly followed by death, &c.—others from fevers, &c. &c.)—he told me last evening that he had not in memory one single case of a man's meeting the approach of death, whether sudden or slow, with fear or trembling—but always of these young men meeting their death with steady composure, and often with curious readiness—

The Army (I noticed it first in camp, and the same here among the wounded) is *very young*—and far more American than we supposed—ages range mainly from 20 to 30—a slight sprinkling of men older—and a bigger sprinkling of young lads 17 and 18—

As I took temporary memoranda of names, items, &c of one thing and another, commissioned to get or do for the men—what they wished and what their cases required from outside, &c—these memoranda grow bulky, and suggest something to me—so I now make fuller notes, or a sort of journal, (not a mere dry journal though, I hope)—This thing I will record—it belongs to the time, and to all the States—(and perhaps it belongs to me) [17]—

DRAFT LETTER: Barrett Collection, University of Virginia

To his brother Jeff

Washington, February 13, 1863

Dear brother,

Nothing new—still I thought I would write you a line this morning. The $4, namely: $2 from Theo. A. Drake and 2 [from] John D. Martin, enclosed in your letter of the 10th came safe. They too will please accept the grateful thanks of several poor fellows, in hospital here.

The letter of introduction to Mr. [E. D.] Webster, chief clerk, State Department, will be very acceptable. If convenient, I should like Mr Lane to send it on immediately. I do not so much look for an appointment from Mr. Seward as his backing me from the State of New York. I have seen Preston King [18] this morning for the second time—(it is very amusing to hunt for an office—so the thing seems to me just now—even if one don't get it)—I have seen Charles Sumner three times—he says every thing here moves as part of a great machine, and that I must consign myself to the fate of the rest—still [in] an interview I had with him yesterday he talked and acted as though he had life in him, and would exert himself to any reasonable extent for me to get something. Meantime I make about enough to pay my expenses by hacking on the press here, and copying in the paymasters offices, a couple of hours a day—one thing is favorable here, namely, pay for whatever one does

is at a high rate—I have not yet presented my letters to either Seward or
Chase—I thought I would get my forces all in a body, and make one concentrated dash, if possible with the personal introduction and presence of some
big bug—I like fat old Preston King, very much—he is fat as a hogshead,
with great hanging chops—the first thing he said to me the other day in the
parlor chamber of the Senate, when I sent in for him and he came out, was,
"Why, how can I do this thing, or any thing for you—how do I know but
you are a secessionist—you look for all the world, like an old Southern
planter—a regular Carolina or Virginia planter." I treated him with just as
much hauteur as he did me with bluntness—this was the first time—it afterward proved that Charles Sumner had not prepared the way for me, as I
supposed, or rather, not so strongly as I supposed, and Mr. King had even
forgotten it—so I was as an entire stranger. But the same day C. S. talked
further with Mr. King in the Senate, and the second interview I had with the
latter, (this forenoon) he has given me a sort of general letter, endorsing me
from New York—one envelope is addressed to Secretary Chase, and another to Gen. [Montgomery C.] Meigs, head Quartermaster's Dep't. Meantime, I am getting better and better acquainted with office-hunting wisdom,
and Washington peculiarities generally.

I spent several hours in the Capitol the other day—the incredible gor-
geousness of some of the rooms, (interior decorations &c)—rooms used
perhaps but for merely three or four Committee meetings in the course of
the whole year, is beyond one's flightiest dreams. Costly frescoes of the style
of Taylor's Saloon in Broadway, only really the best and choicest of their
sort, done by imported French & Italian artists, are the prevailing sorts
(imagine the work you see on the fine China vases, in Tiffany's—the paint-
ings of Cupids & goddesses &c. spread recklessly over the arched ceiling
and broad panels of a big room—the whole floor underneath paved with
tesselated pavement, which is a sort of cross between marble & china, with
little figures drab, blue, cream color, &c).

These things, with heavy, elaborately wrought balustrades, columns, &
steps—all of the most beautiful marbles I ever saw, some white as milk,
others of all colors, green, spotted, lined, or of our old chocolate color—all
these marbles used as freely as if they were common blue flags—with rich
door-frames and window-casings of bronze and gold—heavy chandeliers
and mantels, and clocks in every room—and indeed by far the richest and
gayest, and most un-American and inappropriate ornamenting and finest interior workmanship I ever conceived possible, spread in profusion through

scores, hundreds, (and almost thousands) of rooms—such are what I find, or rather would find to interest me, if I devoted time to it—But a few of the rooms are enough for me—the style is without grandeur, and without simplicity—These days, the state our country is in, and especially filled as I am from top to toe, of late with scenes and thoughts of *the hospitals,* (America seems to me now, though only in her youth, but brought *already here* feeble, bandaged and bloody *in hospital*)—*these days* I say, Jeff, all the poppy-show goddesses and all the pretty blue & gold in which the interior Capitol is got up, seem to me out of place beyond any thing I could tell—and I get away from it as quick as I can when that kind of thought comes over me. I suppose it is to be described throughout—those interiors—as all of them got up in the French style—well enough for a New York [*incomplete*]

M S: Feinberg Collection, Library of Congress

To his brother Jeff

Washington, March 6, 1863

I go to the Hospitals about the same as ever—the last week or so, I have been most every night to the Capitol, which has been all lit up—I should never get tired of wandering through the Senate wing at night—it is the most costly, splendid and rich-painted place in its interminable mazes (I wander around and lose myself in them) of corridors and halls, that I ever dreamed of, or thought possible to construct—The great Halls of the H[ouse] of R[epresentatives] and the Senate, are wonderful and brilliant at night—they show best then, (in some respects.) They are probably the most beautiful rooms, ornamented and gilded style, in the world.

About what is called the Conscript Bill (an improper name) I hope and pray from the bottom of my heart that, if they (the Government) are indeed going on with the war, they will carry out that bill, and enrol *every man* in the land—I would like to see the people embodied *en-masse*—I am very sure I shall see that my name is in its place on the lists, and my body in the ranks, if they do it that way—for *that* will be something like our nation getting itself up in shape. The Bill however was really meant as a warning to Louis Napoleon, or any other foreign meddler.

With my office-hunting, no special result yet. I cannot give up my Hospitals yet. I never before had my feelings so thoroughly and (so far) permanently absorbed, to the very roots, as by these huge swarms of dear, wounded, sick, dying boys—I get very much attached to some of them, and many of them have come to depend on seeing me, and having me sit by them a few minutes, as if for their lives. . . . [*incomplete*]

M S: Whitman House, Camden

To his brother Jeff

Washington, March 18, 1863

I suppose George must be about leaving you to-day,[19] to return to his regiment—and I can realize how gloomy you will all be for two or three days, especially Mother. Dear mother, you must keep up your spirits, and not get downhearted. I hope you are all well—I think about you all every day—is Mary[20] home?—you must write me all about every thing—I suppose the bundle of George's shirts, drawers, &c came safe by Adams express. I sent it last Saturday, and it ought to have been delivered Monday in Brooklyn. I did not pay the freight. Last Monday 16th I wrote to Mother, and sent her some shinplasters. Saturday previous I sent a note home, enclosing the express receipt.

Jeff, I wrote a letter to the *Eagle*,[21] and sent it yesterday—if it appears, it will probably be to-day or to-morrow (or next day.) I wish you would look out for it, and buy me 20 of the papers, (the afternoon it appears,) and send them, the same as you did the other letter, direct care of Major Hapgood, the same—put the engravings (20 of the large head) in the same package—the postage will be at the rate of ½ cent per oz. You leave one end partially unsealed. Send them as *soon* as convenient, after the letter appears, but no such dreadful hurry.

I suppose you have been in quite a state of pleasure and excitement home, with the visit of dear brother George. I was much pleased to hear by mother's letter that he was so sought for, and treated with so much attention—He deserves it all—you must tell me all the particulars of his visit.

The Hospitals still engross a large part of my time and feelings—only I don't remain so long and make such exhausting-like visits, the last week—as I have had a bad humming feeling and deafness, stupor-like at times, in my head, which unfits me for continued exertion. It comes from a bad cold, gathering I think in my head. If it were not that some of the soldiers really depend on me to come, and the doctors tell me it is really necessary, I should suspend my visits for two or three days, at least. Poor boys, you have no idea how they cling to one, and how strong the tie that forms between us. Things here are just the same with me, neither better nor worse—(I feel so engrossed with my soldiers, I do not devote that attention to my office-hunting, which is needed for success.)

Jeff, you must give my best respects to Mr. and Mrs. Lane, they have enabled me to do a world of good, and I can never forget them. I see you had a great Union meeting in the Academy of Music—it is impossible to tell what the government designs to do the coming season, but I suppose they will push on the war. The south is failing fast in many respects—D'Almeida,[22] the Frenchman I wrote about, told me that he was besieged every where down south to sell (for confederate money) any and every thing he had, his clothes, his boots, his haversack, &c &c. Then their niggers will gradually melt, *certain*. So the fates fight for us, even if our generals do not. Jeff, to see what I see so much of, puts one entirely out of conceit of war—still for all that I am not sure but I go in for fighting on—the choice is hard on either part, but to *cave* in the worst—good bye, dearest brother.

Walt.

M S: Whitman House, Camden

To Nathaniel Bloom and John F. S. Gray[23]

Washington, March 19 and 20, 1863

Dear Nat, and Fred Gray:

Since I left New York, I was down in the Army of the Potomac in front with my brother a good part of the winter, commencing time of the battle of Fredericksburgh—have seen *war-life*, the real article—folded myself in a blanket, lying down in the mud with composure—relished salt pork & hard tack—have been on the battle-field among the wounded, the faint and the bleeding, to give them nourishment—have gone over with a flag of truce the next day to help direct the burial of the dead—have struck up a tremendous friendship with a young Mississippi captain (about 19) that we took prisoner badly wounded at Fredericksburgh—(he has followed me here, is in Emory hospital here, minus a leg—he wears his confederate uniform, proud as the devil—I met him first at Falmouth, in the Lacy house, middle of December last, his leg just cut off, and cheered him up—poor boy, he has suffered a great deal, and still suffers—has eyes bright as a hawk, but face pale—our affection is quite an affair, quite romantic—sometimes when I lean over to say I am going, he puts his arm round my neck, draws my face down, &c. quite a scene for the New Bowery.)

I spent the Christmas holidays on the Rappahannock—during January came up hither, took a lodging room here—did the 37th Congress, especially the night sessions the last three weeks, explored the Capitol then, meandering the gorgeous painted interminable senate corridors, getting lost in them, (a new sensation, rich & strong, that endless painted interior at night)—got very much interested in some particular cases in Hospitals here—go now steadily to more or less of said Hospitals by day or night—find always the sick and dying soldiers forthwith begin to cling to me in a way that makes a fellow feel funny enough. These Hospitals, so different from all others—these thousands, and tens and twenties of thousands of American young men, badly wounded, all sorts of wounds, operated on, pallid with diarrhea, languishing, dying with fever, pneumonia, &c. open a new world somehow to me, giving closer insights, new things, exploring deeper mines than any yet, showing our humanity, (I sometimes put myself in fancy in the cot, with typhoid, or under the knife,) tried by terrible, fearfulest tests, probed deepest, the living soul's, the body's tragedies, bursting the petty bonds of art. To these, what are your dramas and poems, even the oldest and the tearfulest? Not old Greek mighty ones, where man contends with fate, (and always yields)—not Virgil showing Dante on and on among the agonized & damned, approach what here I see and take a part in. For here I see, not at intervals, but quite always, how certain, man, our American man—how he holds himself cool and unquestioned master above all pains and bloody mutilations. It is immense, the best thing of all, nourishes me of all men. This then, what frightened us all so long! Why it is put to flight with ignominy, a mere stuffed scarecrow of the fields. O death where is thy sting? O grave where is thy victory? &c. . . . But let me change the subject—I have given you screed enough about death and Hospitals—and too much, since I got started. Only I have some curious yarns I promise you, my darlings and gossips, by word of mouth, whene'er we meet.

Washington and its points I find bear a second and a third perusal, and doubtless indeed many. My first impressions, architectural, &c. were not favorable; but upon the whole, the city, the spaces, buildings, &c make no unfit emblem of our country, so far, so broadly planned, every thing in plenty, money & materials staggering with plenty, but the fruit of the plans, the knit, the combination yet wanting—Determined to express ourselves greatly in a capital but no fit capital yet here—(time, associations, wanting, I suppose)—many a hiatus yet—many a thing to be taken down and done over again yet—perhaps an entire change of base—may-be a succession of changes. Congress does not seize very hard upon me—I studied it and its members with curiosity, and long—much gab, great fear of public opinion, plenty of low business talent, but no masterful man in Congress, (probably best so.) I think well of the President. He has a face like a hoosier Michael Angelo, so awful ugly it becomes beautiful, with its strange mouth, its deep cut, criss-cross lines, and its doughnut complexion. My notion is, too, that underneath his outside smutched mannerism, and stories from third-class county bar-rooms, (it is his humor,) Mr. Lincoln keeps a fountain of first-class practical telling wisdom. I do not dwell on the supposed failures of his government; he has shown, I sometimes think, an almost supernatural tact in keeping the ship afloat at all, with head steady, not only not going down, and now certain not to, but with proud and resolute spirit, and flag flying in sight of the world, menacing and high as ever. I say never yet captain, never ruler, had such a perplexing, dangerous task as his, the past two years. I more and more rely upon his idiomatic western genius, careless of court dress or court decorums.

I am living here without much definite aim, (except going to the hospitals)—yet I have quite a good time—I make some money by scribbling for the papers, and as copyist. I have had, (and have,) thoughts of trying to get a clerkship or something, but I only try in a listless sort of way, and of course do not succeed. I have strong letters of introduction from Mr. Emerson to Mr. Seward and Mr. Chase, but I have not presented them. I have seen Mr. Sumner several times anent of my office-hunting—he promised fair once— but he does not seem to be finally fascinated. I hire a bright little 3d story front room, with service, &c. for $7 a month, dine in the same house, (394 L st. a private house)—and remain yet much of the old vagabond that so gracefully becomes me. I miss you all, my darlings & gossips, Fred Gray, and Bloom and Russell and every body. I wish you would all come here in a body—that would be divine. (We would drink ale, which is here of the best.) My health, strength, personal beauty, &c. are, I am happy to inform you, without diminution, but on the contrary quite the reverse. I weigh full 220 pounds avoirdupois, yet still retain my usual perfect shape—a regular model. My beard, neck, &c. are woolier, fleecier, whiteyer than ever. I wear army boots, with magnificent black morocco tops, the trousers put in, wherein shod and legged confront I Virginia's deepest mud with supercilious eyes. The scenery around Washington is really fine, the Potomac a lordly river, the hills, woods, &c all attractive. I poke about quite a good deal. Much of the weather here is from heaven—of late, though, a stretch decidedly from the other point. To-night (for it is night, about 10) I sit alone writing this epistle, (which will doubtless devour you all with envy and admiration,) in the room adjoining my own particular. A gentleman and his wife, who occupy the two other apartments on this floor, have gone to see Heron in Medea[24]—have put their little child to bed, and left me in charge. The little one is sleeping soundly there in the back room, and I, (plagued with a cold in the head,) sit here in the front, by a good fire, writing as aforesaid to my gossips & darlings. The evening is lonesome & still. I am entirely alone. "O solitude where are the charms," &c &c.

Now you write to me good long letters, my own boys. You, Bloom, give me your address particular, dear friend. Tell me Charles Russell's address, particular—also write me about Charles Chauncey. Tell me about every body. For, dearest gossips, as the hart panteth, &c. so my soul after any and all sorts of items about you all. My darling, dearest boys, if I could be with you this hour, long enough to take only just three mild hot rums, before the cool weather closes.

Friday Morning, 20th—I finish my letter in the office of Major Hapgood, a paymaster, and a friend of mine. This is a large building, filled with pay-masters' offices, some thirty or forty or more. This room is up on the fifth floor, (a most noble and broad view from my window.) Curious scenes around here—a continual stream of soldiers, officers, cripples, &c &c. some climbing wearily up the stairs. They seek their pay—and every hour, almost every minute, has its incident, its hitch, its romance, farce or tragedy. There are two paymasters in this room. A sentry at the street door, another half way up the stairs, another at the chief clerk's door, all with muskets & bay-onets—sometimes a great swarm, hundreds, around the side walk in front, waiting. (Every body is waiting for something here.) I take a pause, look up a couple of minutes from my pen and paper—see spread, off there, the Poto-mac, very fine, nothing petty about it—the Washington monument,[25] not half finished—the public grounds around it filled with ten thousand beeves, on the hoof—to the left the Smithsonian with its brown turrets—to the right, far across, Arlington Heights, the forts, eight or ten of them—then the long bridge, and down a ways, but quite plain, the shipping of Alexandria—opposite me, and in stone throw, is the Treasury building—and below the bustle and life of Pennsylvania avenue. I shall hasten with my letter, and then go forth and take a stroll down "the avenue" as they call it here.

Now, you boys, don't you think I have done the handsome thing by writ-ing this astounding, magnificent letter—certainly the longest I ever wrote in my life. Fred, I wish you to present my best respects to your father. Bloom and all, one of these days we will meet, and make up for lost time, my dearest boys.

Walt.

Address me, care Major Hapgood, paymaster, U. S. Army, cor 15th & F sts. Washington. How is Mullen? give him my respects—How is Ben Knower? how the twinkling and temperate Towle? remember me to them.

M S: Barrett Collection, University of Virginia

To Thomas P. Sawyer, a soldier[26]

Washington, April 21, 1863

Tom, I thought I would write you a few words, and take chances of its getting to you—though there is great excitement now about the Army of the Potomac, no passes allowed, mails held over, &c. &c.—still I thought I would write, and take chances.

There is nothing very special here about Washington—they seem to be shoving troops off from here now all the time, in small or large bodies—the convalescents are doing guard duty &c in the Hospitals—even the old regiments doing patrol, & provost, are sent off. So I suppose something is up. Tom, I was at Armory last evening, saw Lewy Brown, sat with him a good while, he was very cheerful, told me how he laid out to do, when he got well enough to go from hospital, (which he expects soon), says he intends to go home to Maryland, go to school, and learn to write better, and learn a little bookkeeping, &c.—so that he can be fit for some light employment. Lew is so good, so affectionate—when I came away, he reached up his face, I put my arm around him, and we gave each other a long kiss, half a minute long. We talked about you while I was there. I saw Hiram [Sholes] but did not speak to him. He lay pale and pretty sick, sound asleep. I could not help stopping before I came away, and looking at him—it was pitiful to see him, so pale, sound asleep—Poor Hiram—he is a good boy—he gets no better. Johnny Mahay does not get any better, in Ward E. He is going to have an operation performed on him by Dr. Bliss.[27] Tom, I do not know who you was most intimate with in the Hospital, or I would write you about them.

As to me, there is nothing new with me, or my affairs. I manage to pay my way here in Washington, what I make writing letters for the New York papers, &c. When I stopped here, last January, on my return from Falmouth, I thought I would stop only a few days, before returning to New York, and see if I could not get some berth, clerkship or something—but I have not pushed strong enough—have not got anything—and I don't know as I could be satisfied with the life of a clerk in the departments anyhow. So I have hung along here ever since. I guess I enjoy a kind of vagabond life any how. I go around some, nights, when the spirit moves me, sometimes to the gay places, just to see the sights. Tom, I wish you was here. Somehow I don't find the comrade that suits me to a dot—and I won't have any other, not for good.

Well, Tom, the war news is not lovely, is it? We feel disappointed here about Charleston[28]—I felt as blue about it as anybody. I was so in hopes they would take the conceit out of that gassy city. It seems to me always as if Charleston has done the biggest business of blowing & mischief, on a small capital of industry or manliness, of any city the world ever knew. But for all our bad success at Charleston, and even if we fail for a while elsewhere, I believe this Union will conquer in the end, as sure as there's a God in heaven. This country can't be broken up by Jeff Davis, & all his damned crew. Tom, I sometimes feel as if I didn't want to live—life would have no charm for me, if this country should fail after all, and be reduced to take a third rate position, to be domineered over by England & France & the haughty nations of Europe &c and we unable to help ourselves. But I have no thought that will ever be, this country I hope would spend her last drop of blood, and last dollar, rather than submit to such humiliation.

O I hope Hooker[29] will have good success in his plans, whatever they may be. We have been foiled so often in our plans, it seems as though it was too much. And our noble Army of the Potomac, so brave, so capable, so full of good men, I really believe they are this day the best in the world. God grant Hooker may have success, and his brave boys may at last achieve the victory they deserve. O how much I think about them though. I suppose that does no good. Tom, you tell the boys of your company there is an old pirate up in Washington, with the white wool growing all down his neck—an old comrade who thinks about you & them every day, for all he don't know them, and will probably never see them, but thinks about them as comrades & younger brothers of his, just the same.

These lines may never reach you, as it is talked here that the Army of the Potomac is in for a real fighting march, at last, may be something desperate, it may continue some time when it once begins. Tom, I thought I would write you a few words, hoping they might reach you. Dear comrade, you must not forget me, for I never shall you. My love you have in life or death forever. I don't know how you feel about it, but it is the wish of my heart to have your friendship, and also that if you should come safe out of this war, we should come together again in some place where we could make our living, and be true comrades and never be separated while life lasts—and take Lew Brown too, and never separate from him. Or if things are not so to be—if you get these lines, my dear, darling comrade, and any thing should go wrong, so that we do not meet again, here on earth, it seems to me, (the way I feel now,) that my soul could never be entirely happy, even in the world to come, without you, dear comrade.[30] And if it is God's will, I hope we shall yet meet, as I say, if you feel as I do about it—and if [it] is destined that we shall not, you have my love none the less, whatever should keep you from me, no matter how many years. God bless you, Tom, and preserve you through the perils of the fight.

Good bye, my darling comrade, my dear darling brother, for so I will call you, and wish you to call me the same.

DRAFT LETTER: Berg Collection, New York Public Library

To Thomas P. Sawyer, a soldier[31]

Washington, April 26, 1863

Dear comrade,

I have not heard from you for some time, Lewy Brown has received two letters from you, & Walter in Ward E has received one three weeks ago. I wrote you a letter about a week ago, which I hope you have received. I was sorry you did not come up to my room to get the shirt & other things you promised to accept from me and take when you went away. I got them all ready, a good strong blue shirt, a pair of drawers & socks, and it would have been a satisfaction to me if you had accepted them. I should have often thought now Tom may be wearing around his body something from *me*, & that it might contribute to your comfort, down there in camp on picket, or sleeping in your tent.

Lewy Brown and Hiram [Sholes] are about the same. I saw Lewy & sat with him last evening. I go to see him almost every evening. He sets up a little in the chair, during the middle of the day—his foot is doing pretty well. There is quite a time at Armory about Dr. Bliss—some say he is under arrest for defrauding the government. There is a new surgeon in charge—I have not seen him. In Ward K there is a new surgeon, Dr. Rose. There is quite a change, with men & doctors, going and coming.

Well, Tom, how did you stand the gay old rain storm of Thursday & Friday last? It rained here enough to wet hell itself, and swamp the fires. But yesterday & to-day here have been fine. The talk here previously was all about Hooker's advance—we expected a big fight, on the jump—but of course the storm has laid an injunction on that for some days.

Yet I suppose Hooker must move soon, & that there will be fighting and lots of marches and skirmishes, &c before the summer is through. O my dear comrade & brother, I hope it will prove your good luck to come safe through all the engagements & marches of this war, & that we shall meet again, not to part. I hope this letter will find you in good health & spirits.

Tom, I will not write a long yarn at present. I guess I have not made out much of a letter, anyhow at present, but I will let it go, whatever it is, hoping it may please you, coming from old wooly-neck, who loves you. You must let that make up for all deficiencies now and to come. Not a day passes, nor a night but I think of you. Now, my dearest comrade, I will bid you *so long*, & hope God will put it in your heart to bear toward me a little at least of the feeling I have about you. If it is only a quarter as much I shall be satisfied.

Your faithful friend & brother,

Walt

Tom, it is now about 9 o'clock, a fine moonlight night. I am going to close this up, and then scud out for a walk to the post office. Good by again, & God bless you, dear brother.

DRAFT LETTER: Berg Collection, New York Public Library

To his mother

Washington, May 13, 1863

Dearest Mother,

I am late with my letter this week—my poor, poor boys occupy my time very much—I go every day, & sometimes nights—I believe I mentioned a young man in Ward F, Armory Square, with a bad wound in the leg, very agonizing, had to have it propt up, & an attendant all the while dripping water on night & day—I was in hopes at one time he would get through with it, but a few days ago he took a sudden bad turn, & died about 3 o'clock the same afternoon—it was horrible—he was of good family (handsome, intelligent man, about 26, married) his name was John Elliott of Cumberland

Valley, Bedford Co., Penn., belonged to 2d Pennsylvania Cavalry. I felt very bad about it—I have wrote to his father—have not rec'd any answer yet—no friend nor any of his folks was here & have not been here nor sent, probably didnt know of it at all. The surgeons put off amputating the leg, he was so exhausted, but at last it was imperatively necessary to amputate—mother, I am shocked to tell you, that he never came alive off the amputating table—he died under the operation—it was what I had dreaded & anticipated—poor young man, he suffered much, very *very* much, for many days & bore it so patiently—so it was a release to him—Mother, such things are awful—not a soul here he knew or cared about, except me—yet the surgeons & nurses were good to him—I think all was done for him that could be—there was no help but to take off the leg—he was under chloroform—they tried their best to bring him to—three long hours were spent, a strong smelling bottle held under his nostrils, with other means, three hours. Mother, how contemptible all the usual little worldly prides & vanities & striving after appearances, seems in the midst of such scenes as these—such tragedies of soul & body. To see such things & not be able to help them is awful—I feel almost ashamed of being so well & whole.

Dear mother, I have not heard from George himself—but I got a letter from Fred McReady, a young Brooklyn man in 51st—he is intimate with George, said he was well & hearty—I got the letter about five days ago—I wrote to George four days since, directed to Winchester, Kentucky. I got a letter from a friend in Nashville, Tenn., yesterday, he told me the 9th Army Corps was ordered to move to Murfreesboro, Tenn. I don't know whether this is so or not. I send papers to George almost every day. So far, I think it was fortunate the 51st was moved west, & I hope it will prove to continue so. Mother, it is all a lottery, this war, no one knows what will come up next.

Mother, I rec'd Jeff's letter of May 9th, it was welcome, as all Jeff's letters are, & all others from home. Jeff says you do not hear from me at home but seldom—Mother, I write once a week to *you* regular—but I will write soon to Jeff a good long letter—I have wanted to for some time, but have been much occupied. Dear brother, I wish you to say to Probasco & all the other young men on the Works, I send them my love & best thanks—never any thing came more acceptable than the little fund they forwarded me, the last week, through Mr. Lane—Our wounded, from Hooker's battles, are worse wounded & more of them, than any battle of the war & indeed any I may say of modern times (we have lost from 15,000 to 20,000)—besides, the weather has been very hot here, very bad for new wounds. Yet as Jeff writes so downhearted I must tell him the rebellion has lost worse & more than we have—the more I find out about it, the more I think they, the confederates, have rec'd an irreparable harm & loss in Virginia. I should not be surprised to see them (either voluntarily or by force) leaving Virginia, before many weeks. I don't see how on earth they can stay there—I think Hooker is already reaching after them again—I myself do not give up Hooker yet—

Dear mother, I should like to hear from Han, poor Han—I send my best love to Sister Mat & all. Good bye, dearest mother.

Walt.

M S: Feinberg Collection, Library of Congress

To his mother

Washington, May 19, 1863

Dearest mother,

I received a letter from Heyde this morning, one of the usual sort, about as interesting as a dose of salts. Says Han has not been able to stand erect for the past five months—the doctor told her lately that she might possibly recover in one year if she was careful—then says he thinks, & he don't think, & has taken a little place, & Han has a girl to wait on her, &c. &c. All amounts to nothing more than we knew before, & only serves to make one feel almost heart-sick about Han, & the awful snarl in which we are all fixed about it all, & what to do. I wrote to Han yesterday, (before I received this letter of Heyde's), I wrote a short letter of my own, & sent her George's letter to you, (I cut out what was said about the money, as I did not wish Heyde to see it.)

I also sent George a letter yesterday—have not got any letter myself from Georgy, but have sent him quite a good many & papers—Mother, what a tramp the 51st has had—they only need now to go to California, & they will finish the job complete—

O mother, how welcome the shirts were—I was putting off, & putting off, to get some new ones, I could not find any one to do them as I wear them, & it would have cost such a price—& so my old ones had got to be, when they come back from the wash I had to laugh, they were a lot of rags, held together with starch—I have a very nice old black aunty for a washwoman, but she bears down pretty hard I guess when she irons them, & they showed something like the poor old city of Fredericksburgh does, since Burnside bombarded it—Well, mother, when the bundle came, I was so glad—& the coats too, worn as they are, they come in very handy—& the cake, dear mother, I am almost like the boy that put it under his pillow—& woke up in the night & eat some—I carried a good chunk to a young man wounded, I think a good deal of, & it did him so much good—it is dry, but all the better, as he eat it with tea & it relished—I eat a piece with him & drinked some tea, out of his cup, as I sat by the side of his cot—Mother, I have neglected I think what I ought to have told you two or three weeks ago, that is that I had to discard my old clothes, somewhat because they were too thick & more still because they were worse gone in than any I ever yet wore I think in my life, especially the trowsers—wearing my big boots had caused the inside of the legs just above the knee to wear two beautiful round holes right through cloth & partly through the lining, producing a novel effect, which was not necessary, as I produce a sufficient sensation without—then they were desperately faded—I have a nice plain suit, of a dark wine color, looks very well, & feels good, single breasted sack coat with breast pockets &c. & vest & pants same as what I always wear, (pants pretty full,) so upon the whole all looks unusually good for me, my hat is very good yet, boots ditto, have a new necktie, nice shirts, you can imagine I cut quite a swell—I have not trimmed my beard since I left home, but it is not grown much longer, only perhaps a little bushier—I keep about as stout as ever, & the past five or six days I have felt wonderful well, indeed never did I feel better—about ten or twelve days ago, we had a short spell of very warm weather here, but for about six days now it has been delightful, just warm enough.

I generally go to the hospitals from 12 to 4—& then again from 6 to 9—some days I only go either in the middle of the day, or evening, not both—& then when I feel somewhat opprest, I skip over a day, or make perhaps a light call only, as I have received several cautions from the doctors, who tell me that one must beware of continuing too steady & long in the air & influences of the hospitals—I find the caution a wise one.

Mother, you or Jeff must write me what Andrew does about going to North Carolina[32]—I should think it might have a beneficial effect upon his throat.

I wrote Jeff quite a long letter Sunday—Jeff must write to me whenever he can, I like dearly to have them, & whenever you feel like it you too, dear mother—tell sis her uncle Walt will come back one of these days from the sick soldiers & take her out on Fort Greene again—Mother, I received a letter yesterday from John Elliott's father, in Bedford co[unty,] Pennsylvania, (the young man I told you about, who died under the operation)—it was very sad, it was the first he knew about it—I don't know whether I told you of Dennis Barnett, pneumonia, three weeks since, had got well enough to be sent home—

Dearest mother, I hope you will take things as easy as possible & try to keep a good heart—Matty, my dear sister, I have to inform you that I was treated to a splendid dish of ice cream Sunday night, I wished you was with me to have another—I send you my love, dear sister. Mother, I hope by all means it will be possible to keep the money whole, to get some ranch next spring, if not before, I mean to come home & build it. Good bye for the present, dear mother.

Walt

MS: Feinberg Collection, Library of Congress

To Thomas P. Sawyer, a soldier

Washington, May 27, 1863

Dear brother,

I sit down to rattle off in haste a few lines to you. I do not know what is the reason I have been favored with nary a word from you, to let me know whether you are alive & well—that is, if you are so, which I pray to God you are. My thoughts are with you often enough, & I make reckoning when we shall one day be together again—yet how useless it is to make calculations for the future. Still a fellow will.

Tom, I wrote you one letter April 21st, & then another April 26th. The first one must have gone all right, as a letter was received by me April 28th, (very pretty written)—but I have not heard whether you got my second letter. I enclosed in it an envelope with my address on, in hopes you would write to me.

Well, dear brother, the great battle between Hooker & Lee came off, & what a battle it was—without any decisive results again, though at the cost of so many brave men's lives & limbs—it seems too dreadful, that such bloody contests, without settling any thing, should go on. The hospitals here are filled with the wounded, I think the worst cases & the plentiest of any fighting yet. Was you in the fight? I have made inquiries of two of the 11th Mass. here in hospital, but they could not tell me about you for certain.

Lewy Brown seems to be getting along pretty well. I hope he will be up &

around before long—he is a good boy, & has my love, & when he is discharged, I should feel it a comfort to share with Lewy whatever I might have—& indeed if I ever have the means, he shall never want.

Dr. Bliss was removed from Armory & put for a few days in the Old Capitol prison—there is now some talk however of his going back to Armory.

There is no particular change in my affairs here—I just about manage to pay my way, with newspaper correspondence &c. Tom, I believe I shall have to lay pipe for some office, clerkship, or something—

We had awful hot weather here three or four days ago—O how the grease run off of me—I invested in an umbrella & fan—it must have been gay down there about Falmouth—didn't you want some *ice cream* about last Sunday?

My dearest comrade, I cannot, though I attempt it, put in a letter the feelings of my heart—I suppose my letters sound strange & unusual to you as it is, but as I am only expressing the truth in them, I do not trouble myself on that account. As I intimated before, I do not expect you to return for me the same degree of love I have for you.

DRAFT LETTER: Berg Collection, New York Public Library

To his mother

Washington, June 22, 1863

Dear mother,

Jeff's letter came informing me of the birth of the little girl,[33] & that Matty was feeling pretty well, so far. I hope it will continue—Dear sister, I should much like to come home & see you & the little one, I am sure from Jeff's description it is a noble babe, & as to its being a girl it is all the better. (I am not sure but the Whitman breed gives better women than men.)

Well, mother, we are generally anticipating a lively time here or in the neighborhood, as it is probable Lee is feeling about to strike a blow on Washington, or perhaps right into it—& as Lee is no fool, it is perhaps possible he may give us a good shake—he is not very far off—yesterday was a fight to the southwest of here all day, we heard the cannons nearly all day—the wounded are arriving in small squads every day, mostly cavalry, a great many Ohio men—they send off to-day from the Washington hospitals a great many to New York, Philadelphia, &c. all who are able, to make room, which looks ominous—indeed it is pretty certain that there is to be some

severe fighting, may be a great battle again, the pending week—I am getting
so callous that it hardly arouses me at all—I fancy I should take it very quietly
if I found myself in the midst of a desperate conflict here in Washington.

Mother, I have nothing particular to write about—I see & hear nothing
but new & old cases of my poor suffering boys in Hospitals, & I dare say you
have had enough of such things—I have not missed a day at Hospital I think
for more than three weeks—I get more & more wound round—poor young
men—there are some cases that would literally sink & give up, if I did not
pass a portion of the time with them—I have quite made up my mind about
the lecturing &c project—I have no doubt it will succeed well enough, the
way I shall put it in operation—you know, mother, it is to raise funds to
enable me to continue my Hospital ministrations, on a more free handed
scale—As to the Sanitary Commissions & the like, I am sick of them all, &
would not accept any of their berths—you ought to see the way the men as
they lie helpless in bed turn away their faces from the sight of these Agents,
Chaplains &c. (*hirelings* as Elias Hicks[34] would call them—they seem to me
always a set of foxes & wolves)—they get well paid, & are always incompe-
tent & disagreeable—As I told you before the only good fellows I have met
are the Christian Commissioners—they go everywhere & receive no pay[35]—

Dear, dear mother, I want much to see you & dear Matty too, I send you
both [my] best love, & Jeff too—the pictures came—I have not heard from
George nor Han. I write a day earlier than usual.

                                                                  Walt

We here think Vicksburgh is ours[36]—the probability is that it has capitu-
lated—& there has been no general assault—can't tell yet whether the 51st
went there—we are having very fine weather here to-day—rained last night.
M S: Feinberg Collection, Library of Congress

To his mother

                                              Washington, June 30, 1863
Dearest Mother,

Your letter with Han's I have sent to George, though whether it will find
him or not I cannot tell, as I think the 51st must be away down at Vicksburgh—I have not had a word from George yet—Mother, I have had quite
an attack of sore throat & distress in my head for some days past, up to last
night, but to-day I feel nearly all right again. I have been about the city same

as usual, nearly—to the Hospitals, &c, I mean—I am told that I hover too much over the beds of the hospitals, with fever & putrid wounds, &c. One soldier, brought here about fifteen days ago, very low with typhoid fever, Livingston Brooks, Co B 17th Penn Cavalry, I have particularly stuck to, as I found him in what appeared to be a dying condition, from negligence, & a horrible journey of about forty miles, bad roads & fast driving—& then after he got here, as he is a simple country boy, very shy & silent, & made no complaint, they neglected him—I found him something like I found John Holmes last winter—I called the doctor's attention to him, shook up the nurses, had him bathed in spirits, gave him lumps of ice, & ice to his head, he had a fearful bursting pain in his head, & his body was like fire—he was very quiet, a very sensible boy, old fashioned—he did not want to die, & I had to lie to him without stint, for he thought I knew everything, & I always put in of course that what I told him was exactly the truth, & that if he got really dangerous I would tell him & not conceal it.

The rule is to remove bad fever patients out from the main wards to a tent by themselves, & the doctor told me he would have to be removed. I broke it gently to him, but the poor boy got it immediately in his head that he was marked with death, & was to be removed on that account—it had a great effect upon him, & although I told the truth this time it did not have as good a result as my former fibs—I persuaded the doctor to let him remain—for three days he lay just about an even chance, go or stay, with a little leaning toward the first—But, mother, to make a long story short, he is now out of any immediate danger—he has been perfectly rational throughout—begins to taste a little food, (for a week he eat nothing, I had to compel him to take a quarter of an orange, now & then)—& I will say, whether any one calls it pride or not, that if he *does* get up & around again, it's me that saved his life. Mother, as I have said in former letters, you can have no idea how these sick & dying youngsters cling to a fellow, & how fascinating it is, with all its hospital surroundings of sadness & scenes of repulsion & death.

In this same hospital, Armory Square, where this cavalry boy is, I have about fifteen or twenty particular cases I see much too, some of them as much as him—there are two from East Brooklyn, George Monk, Co A 78th N Y, & Stephen Redgate, (his mother is a widow in E[ast] B[rooklyn], I have written her,) both are pretty badly wounded—both are youngsters under 19—O mother, there seems to me as I go through these rows of cots, as if it was too bad to accept these *children*, to subject them to such premature experiences—I devote myself much to Armory Square Hospital because it contains by far the worst cases, most repulsive wounds, has the most

suffering & most need of consolation—I go every day without fail, & often
at night—sometimes stay very late—no one interferes with me, guards, doctors, nurses, nor any one—I am let to take my own course.

Well, mother, I suppose you folks think we are in a somewhat dubious
position here in Washington, with Lee in strong force almost between us &
you northerners[37]—Well it does look ticklish, if the rebs cut the connection,
then there will be fun—The reb cavalry come quite near us, dash in & steal
wagon trains, &c—It would be funny if they should come some night to the
President's country house, (soldier's home,) where he goes out to sleep every
night—it is in the same direction as their saucy raid last Sunday—Mr.
Lincoln passes here (14th st) every evening on his way out—I noticed him
last evening about ½ past 6, he was in his barouche, two horses, guarded by
about thirty cavalry. The barouche comes first under a slow trot, driven by
one man in the box, no servant or footman beside—the cavalry all follow
closely after with a lieutenant at their head—I had a good view of the President last evening—he looks more careworn even than usual—his face with
deep cut lines, seams, & his *complexion gray*, through very dark skin, a curious looking man, very sad—I said to a lady who was looking with me, "Who
can see that man without losing all wish to be sharp upon him personally?
Who can say he has not a good soul?" The lady assented, although she is
almost vindictive on the course of the administration, (thinks it wants nerve
&c., the usual complaint). The equipage is rather shabby, horses indeed almost what my friends the Broadway drivers would call *old plugs*. The President dresses in plain black clothes, cylinder hat—he was alone yesterday—
As he came up, he first drove over to the house of the Sec[retary] of War, on
K st about 300 feet from here, sat in his carriage while Stanton came out &
had a 15 minutes interview with him (I can see from my window)—& then
wheeled around, & slowly trotted around the corner & up Fourteenth st.,
the cavalry after him—I really think it would be safer for him just now to
stop at the White House, but I expect he is too proud to abandon the former custom—Then about an hour after, we had a large cavalry regiment
pass, with blankets, arms, &c, on the war march over the same track—the
reg't was very full, over a thousand, indeed thirteen or fourteen hundred—it
was an old reg't, veterans, *old fighters*, young as they were—they were preceded by a fine mounted band of sixteen, (about ten bugles, the rest cymbals
& drums)—I tell you, mother, it made every thing ring—made my heart
leap, they played with a will—then *the accompaniment*—the sabres rattled
on a thousand men's sides—they had pistols, their heels spurred—handsome

American young men, (I make no acc't of any other)—rude uniforms, well worn, but good cattle, prancing—all good riders, full of the devil, nobody shaved, all very sunburnt. The regimental officers (splendidly mounted, but just as roughly drest as the men) came immediately after the band, then company after company, with each its officers at its head—the tramping of so many horses (there is a good hard turnpike)—then a long train of men with led horses, mounted negroes, & a long long string of baggage wagons, each with four horses—& then a strong rear guard—I tell you it had the look of *real war*—noble looking fellows—a man looks & feels so proud on a good horse, & armed—They are off toward the region of Lee's (supposed) rendezvous, toward the Susquehannah, for the great anticipated battle— Alas, how many of these healthy handsome rollicking young men will lie cold in death, before the apples ripe in the orchids—

Mother, it is curious & stirring here, in some respects—smaller or larger bodies of troops are moving continually—many just well men are turned out of the hospitals—I am where I see a good deal of them—There are getting to be *many black troops*—there is one very good reg't here black as tar— they go armed, have the regular uniform—they submit to no nonsense— others are constantly forming—it is getting to be a common sight—they press them. [*incomplete*]

M S: Berg Collection, New York Public Library

To his mother

Washington, July 7, 1863

Mother, it seems to be certain that Meade[38] has gained the day, & that the battles there in Pennsylvania have been about as terrible as any in the war— O what a sight must have been presented by the field of action—I think the killed & wounded there on both sides were as many as eighteen or twenty thousand—in one place, four or five acres, there were a thousand dead, at daybreak on Saturday morning—Mother, one's heart grows sick of war, after all, when you see what it really is—every once in a while I feel so hor- rified & disgusted—it seems to me like a great slaughter-house & the men mutually butchering each other—then I feel how impossible it appears, again, to retire from this contest, until we have carried our points—(it is cruel to be so tossed from pillar to post in one's judgment).

Washington is a pleasant place in some respects—it has the finest trees, &

plenty of them every where, on the streets, & grounds. The Capitol grounds, though small, have the finest cultivated trees I ever see—there is a great variety, & not one but is in perfect condition—After I finish this letter I am going out there for an hour's recreation—The great sights of Washington are the public buildings, the wide streets, the public grounds, the trees, the Smithsonian Institute & grounds—I go to the latter occasionally—the Institute is an old fogy concern, but the grounds are fine—Sometimes I go up to Georgetown, about two & a half miles up the Potomac, an old town—just opposite it in the river is an island, where the niggers have their first Washington reg't encamped—they make a good show, are often seen in the streets of Washington in squads—since they have begun to carry arms, the secesh here & in Georgetown (about ⅗ths) are not insulting to them as formerly.

One of the things here always on the go, is long trains of army wagons—sometimes they will stream along all day, it almost seems as if there was nothing else but army wagons & ambulances—they have great camps here in every direction, of army wagons, teamsters, ambulance camps, &c. Some of them are permanent, & have small hospitals—I go to them, (as no one else goes, ladies would not venture)—I sometimes have the luck to give some of the drivers a great deal of comfort & help. Indeed, mother, there are camps here of every thing—I went once or twice to the Contraband Camp,[39] to the Hospital, &c. but I could not bring myself to go again—when I meet black men or boys among my own hospitals, I use them kindly, give them something, &c.—I believe I told you that I do the same to the wounded rebels, too—but as there is a limit to one's sinews & endurance & sympathies, &c. I have got in the way after going lightly as it were all through the wards of a hospital, & trying to give a word of cheer, if nothing else, to every one, then confining my special attentions to the few where the investment seems to tell best, & who want it most—Mother, I have real pride in telling you that I have the consciousness of saving quite a little number of lives by saving them from giving up & being a good deal with them—the men say it is so, & the doctors say it is so—& I will candidly confess I can see it is true, though I say it of myself—I know you will like to hear it, mother, so I tell you—

I am finishing this in Major Hapgood's office, about 1 o'clock—it is pretty warm, but has not cleared off yet—the trees look so well from where I am, & the Potomac—it is a noble river—I see it several miles, & Arlington heights—Mother, I see some of the 47th Brooklyn every day or two—the reg't is on the Heights—back of Arlington House, a fine camp ground—O, Matty, I have just thought of you—dear sister, how are you getting along? Jeff, I will write you truly—Good bye for the present, dearest mother, & all—

Walt

MS: Feinberg Collection, Library of Congress

To his mother

Washington, July 28, 1863

Dear Mother,

I am writing this in the hospital, sitting by the side of a soldier, I do not expect to last many hours. His fate has been a hard one—he seems to be only about 19 or 20—Erastus Haskell, company K, 141st N. Y.—has been out about a year, and sick or half-sick more than half that time—has been down on the peninsula—was detail'd to go in the band as fifer-boy. While sick, the surgeon told him to keep up with the rest—(probably work'd and march'd too long.) He is a shy, and seems to me a very sensible boy—has fine manners—never complains—was sick down on the peninsula in an old storehouse—typhoid fever. The first week this July was brought up here— journey very bad, no accommodations, no nourishment, nothing but hard jolting, and exposure enough to make a well man sick; (these fearful journeys do the job for many)—arrived here July 11th—a silent dark-skinn'd Spanish-looking youth, with large very dark blue eyes, peculiar looking. Doctor F. here made light of his sickness—said he would recover soon, &c.; but I thought very different, and told F. so repeatedly; (I came near quarreling with him about it from the first)—but he laugh'd, and would not listen to me. About four days ago, I told Doctor he would in my opinion lose the boy without doubt—but F. again laugh'd at me. The next day he changed his opinion—I brought the head surgeon of the post—he said the boy would probably die, but they would make a hard fight for him.

The last two days he has been lying panting for breath—a pitiful sight. I have been with him some every day or night since he arrived. He suffers a great deal with the heat—says little or nothing—is flighty the last three days, at times—knows me always, however—calls me "Walter"—(sometimes calls the name over and over and over again, musingly, abstractly, to himself.) His father lives at Breesport, Chemung county, N. Y., is a mechanic with large family—is a steady, religious man; his mother too is living. I have written to them, and shall write again to-day—Erastus has not receiv'd a word from home for months.

As I sit here writing to you, Mother, I wish you could see the whole scene. This young man lies within reach of me, flat on his back, his hands clasp'd across his breast, his thick hair cut close; he is dozing, breathing hard, every breath a spasm—it looks so cruel. He is a noble youngster,—I consider him past all hope. Often there is no one with him for a long while. I am here as much as possible.

TEXT: *Prose Works 1892*, 1:155–56

To Hugo Fritsch [40]

Washington, July 1863

My honest thanks to you, Hugo, for your letter posting me up not only about yourself but about my dear boys, Fred, Nat Bloom—always so welcome to me to hear personally or in any way any & every item about them. Dear friend, the same evening I rec'd your letter, I saw in the New York papers (which get here about 5 every evening) the announcement of Charles Chauncey's death. When I went up to my room that night towards 11 I took a seat by the open window in the splendid soft moonlit night, and, there alone by myself, (as is my custom sometimes under such circumstances), I devoted to the dead boy the silent cheerful tribute of an hour or so of floating thought about him, & whatever rose up from the thought of him, & his looks, his handsome face, his hilarious fresh ways, his sunny smile, his voice, his blonde hair, his talk, his caprices—the way he & I first met—how we spoke together impromptu, no introduction—then our easy falling into intimacy—he with his affectionate heart thought so well of me, & I loved him then, & love him now—I thought over our meetings together, our drinks & groups so friendly, our suppers with Fred & Charley Russell &c. off by ourselves at some table, at Pfaff's off the other end—O how charming those early times, adjusting our friendship, I to the three others, although it needed little adjustment—for I believe we all loved each other more than we supposed—Chauncey was frequently the life & soul of these gatherings—was full of sparkle, & so good, really witty—then for an exception he would have a mood come upon him & right after the outset of our party, he would grow still & cloudy & up & unaccountably depart—but these were seldom—then I got to having occasionally quite a long walk with him, only us

two, & then he would talk well & freely about himself, his experiences, feelings, quite confidential, &c. All these I resumed, sitting by myself.

Hugo, that's the way I sat there Wednesday night till after midnight (the
pleasant Virginia breeze coming up the Potomac) and certainly without
what they call mourning thought of the boy.

Dear Hugo, you speak of your all remembering me and wish to see me, it
would be happiness for me to be with you all, at one of your friendly meetings, especially at Fred's room, so pleasant, with its effect I remember of
pictures, fine color, &c. to have the delight of my dear boys' company &
their gayety & electricity, their precious friendship, the talk & laughter, the
drinks, me surrounded by you all, (so I will for a moment fancy myself,)
tumbled upon by you all, with all sorts of kindness, smothered with you all
in your hasty thoughtless, magnificent way, overwhelmed with questions,
Walt this, Walt that, & Walt every thing. Ah, if one could float off to New
York this afternoon. It is Sunday afternoon now, & perhaps you are at this
moment gathered at Fred's or at your house, & having a good time.

I suppose you were at Charles Chauncey's funeral—tell me about it, & all
particulars about his death. When you write, tell.

DRAFT LETTER: Feinberg Collection, Library of Congress

To Thomas P. Sawyer, a soldier

Washington, July 1863
Dear brother,

You did not write any answer to my last two letters, now quite a while ago,
still I will write again. I still remain here in Washington, finding just about
work enough to pay my expenses. Occasionaly go to Armory Hospital. I see
Lewy Brown always, he has returned from his furlough, he told me a few
days ago he had written to you, & had sent you my best respects—I told him
he must never send my respects to you but always my love. Lewy's leg has
not healed, gives him trouble yet. He goes around with crutches, but not
very far. He is the same good young man as ever, & always will be.

Well, Tom, it looks as though secesh was nearly played out—if they lose
Charleston, as I believe they will soon, seems to be they may as well give it
up—Some think that Lee will make another dash up this way, but I should
think Gettysburgh might last him a while yet.

Dear brother, how I should like to see you—& would like to know how
things have gone with you for three months past. I cant understand why you

have ceased to correspond with me. Any how I hope we shall meet again, & have some good times. So, dearest comrade, good bye for present & God bless you.

DRAFT LETTER: Berg Collection, New York Public Library

To Lewis K. Brown, a soldier[41]

Washington, August 1, 1863

Both your letters have been received, Lewy—the second one came this morning, & was welcome, as any thing from you will always be, & the sight of your face welcomer than all, my darling—I see you write in good spirits, & appear to have first-rate times—Lew, you must not go around too much, nor eat & drink too promiscuous, but be careful & moderate, & not let the kindness of friends carry you away, lest you break down again, dear son—I was at the hospital yesterday four or five hours, was in ward K—Taber has been down sick, so he had to lay abed, but he is better now, & goes around as usual—Curly is the same as usual—most of the others are the same—there have been quite a good many deaths—the young man who lay in bed 2 with a very bad leg is dead—I saw Johnny Mahay in ward E—poor fellow, he is very poorly, he is very thin, & his face is like wax—Lew, I must tell you what a curious thing happened in the chaplain's house night before last—there has been a man in ward I, named Lane, with two fingers amputated, very bad with gangrene, so they removed him to a tent by himself—last Thursday his wife came to see him, she seemed a nice woman but very poor, she stopt at the chaplain's—about 3 o'clock in the morning she got up & went to the sink, & there she gave birth to a child, which fell down the sink into the sewer runs beneath, fortunately the water was not turned on—the chaplain got up, carried Mrs Lane out, & then roused up a lot of men from the hospital, with spades &c. dug a trench outside, & got into the sink, & took out the poor little child, it lay there on its back, in about two inches of water—well, strange as it may seem, the child was alive, (it fell about five feet through the sink)—& is now living & likely to live, is quite bright, has a head of thick black hair—the chaplain took me in yesterday, showed me the child, & Mrs Jackson, his wife, told me the whole story, with a good deal I havn't told you—& then she treated me to a good plate of ice cream—so I staid there nearly an hour & had quite a pleasant visit. Mrs Lane lay in an adjoining room.

Lew, as to me & my affairs there is nothing very new or important—I have not succeeded in getting any employment here yet, except that I write a little (newspaper correspondence &c), barely enough to pay my expenses— but it is my own fault, for I have not tried hard enough for any thing—the last three weeks I have not felt very well—for two or three days I was down sick, for the first time in my life, (as I have never before been sick)—I feel pretty fair to-day—I go around most every day the same as usual. I have some idea of giving myself a furlough of three or four weeks, & going home to Brooklyn, N Y, but I should return again to Washington, probably. Lew, it is pretty hot weather here, & the sun affects me—(I had a sort of sun stroke about five years ago)—You speak of being here in Washington again about the last of August—O Lewy, how glad I should be to see you, to have you with me—I have thought if it could be so that you, & one other person & myself could be where we could work & live together, & have each other's society, we three, I should like it so much—but it is probably a dream—

Well, Lew, they had the great battle of Gettysburgh, but it does not seem to have settled any thing, except to have killed & wounded a great many thousand men—It seems as though the two armies were falling back again to near their old positions on the Rappahannock—it is hard to tell what will be the next move—yet, Lewy, I think we shall conquer yet—I don't believe it is destined that this glorious Union is to be broken up by all the secesh south, or copheads north either—

Well, my darling, I have scribbled you off something to show you where I am & that I have rec'd your welcome letters—but my letter is not of much interest, for I don't feel very bright to-day—Dear son, you must write me whenever you can—take opportunity when you have nothing to do, & write me a good long letter—your letters & your love for me are very precious to me, for I appreciate it all, Lew, & give you the like in return. It is now about 3 o'clock, & I will go out & mail this letter, & then go & get my dinner—So good bye, Lewy—good bye, my dear son & comrade, & I hope it will prove God's will that you get quite well & sound yet, & have many good years yet—

Walt

M S: Library of Congress

To James Redpath (?) [42]

Washington, August 6, 1863

Dear friend,

I am going to write you to ask any friends you may be in communication with for aid for my soldiers. I remain here in Washington still occupied among the hospitals—I have now been engaged in this over seven months. As time passes on it seems as if sad cases of old & lingering wounded accumulate, regularly recruited with new ones every week—I have been most of this day in Armory Square Hospital, Seventh st. I seldom miss a day or evening. Out of the six or seven hundred in this Hosp[ital] I try to give a word or a trifle to every one without exception, making regular rounds among them all. I give all kinds of sustenance, blackberries, peaches, lemons & sugar, wines, all kinds of preserves, pickles, brandy, milk, shirts & all articles of underclothing, tobacco, tea, handkerchiefs, &c &c &c. I always give paper, envelopes, stamps, &c. I want a supply for this purpose. To many I give (when I have it) small sums of money—half of the soldiers in hospital have not a cent. There are many returned prisoners, sick, lost all—& every day squads of men from [the] front, cavalry or infantry—brought in wounded or sick, generally without a cent of money. Then I select the most needy cases & devote my time & services much to them. I find it tells best—some are mere lads, 17, 18, 19 or 20. Some are silent, sick, heavy hearted, (things, attentions, &c. are very rude in the army & hospitals, nothing but the mere hard routine, no time for tenderness or extras)—So I go round—Some of my boys die, some get well—

O what a sweet unwonted love (those good American boys, of good stock, decent, clean, well raised boys, so near to me)—what an attachment grows up between us, started from hospital cots, where pale young faces lie & wounded or sick bodies. My brave young American soldiers—now for so many months I have gone around among them, where they lie. I have long discarded all stiff conventions (they & I are too near to each other, there is no time to lose, & death & anguish dissipate ceremony here between my lads & me)—I pet them, some of them it does so much good, they are so faint & lonesome—at parting at night sometimes I kiss them right & left—The doctors tell me I supply the patients with a medicine which all their drugs & bottles & powders are helpless to yield.

I wish you would ask any body you know who is likely to contribute—It is a good holy cause, surely nothing nobler—I desire you if possible could raise for me, forthwith, for application to these wounded & sick here, (they are from Massachusetts & all the New England states, there is not a day but I am with some Yankee boys, & doing some trifle for them)—a sum—if possible $50—if not, then less—$30—or indeed any am't—

I am at present curiously almost alone here, as visitor & consolator to Hospitals—the work of the different Reliefs & Commissions is nearly all off in the field—& as to private visitors, *there are few or none*—I wish you or some of your friends could just make a round with me, for an hour or so, at some of my hospitals or camps—I go among all our own dear soldiers, hospital camps & army, our teamsters' hospitals, among sick & dying, the rebels, the contrabands, &c &c. What I reach is necessarily but a drop in the bucket but it is done in good faith, & with now some experience & I hope with good heart.

DRAFT LETTER: Feinberg Collection, Library of Congress

To Hugo Fritsch

Washington, August 7, 1863

Dear Hugo,

I rec'd a letter from Bloom yesterday—but, before responding to it (which I will do soon) I must write to you, my friend. Your good letter of June 27th was duly rec'd—I have read it many times—indeed, Hugo, you know not how much comfort you give, by writing me your letters—posting me up.

Well, Hugo, I am still as much as ever, indeed more, in the great military hospitals here. Every day or night I spend four, five, or six hours, among my sick, wounded, prostrate boys. It is fascinating, sad, & with varied fortune of course. Some of my boys get well, some die. After I finish this letter (and then dining at a restaurant), I shall give the latter part of the afternoon & some hours of the night to Armory Square Hospital, a large establishment & one I find most calling on my sympathies & ministrations. I am welcomed by the surgeons as by the soldiers—very grateful to me. You must remember that these government hospitals are not filled as with human débris like the old established city hospitals, New York, &c., but mostly [with] these good-born American young men, appealing to me most profoundly, good stock, often mere boys, full of sweetness & heroism—often they seem very near to me, even as my own children or younger brothers. I make no bones of petting them just as if they were—have long given up formalities & reserves in my treatment of them.

Let me see, Hugo. I will not write any thing about the topics of the horrible riots of last week, nor Gen. Meade, nor Vicksburgh, nor Charleston—I leave them to the newspapers. Nor will I write you this time so much about hospitals as I did last. . . .

I meant to [tell] Nat Bloom that if he expects to provoke me into a dignified not mentioning him, nor writing any thing about him, by his studious course of heart-breaking neglect, (which has already reduced me to a skeleton of but little over 200 lbs & a countenance of raging hectic, indicating an early grave), I was determined not to do any thing of the sort, but shall speak of him every time, & send him my love, just as if he were adorned with faithful troth instead of (as I understand) beautiful whiskers—Does he think that beautiful whiskers can fend off the pangs of remorse? In conclusion I have to say, Nathaniel, you just keep on if you think there's no hell.[43]

Hugo, I suppose you were at Charles Chauncey's funeral—tell me all you hear about the particulars of his death—Tell me of course all about the boys, what you do, say, any thing, every thing—

Hugo, write oftener—you express your thoughts perfectly—do you not know how much more agreeable to me is the conversation or writing that does not take hard paved tracks, the usual & stereotyped, but has little peculiarities & even kinks of its own, making its genuineness—its vitality? Dear friend, your letters are precious to me—none I have received from any one are more so.

Ah, I see in your letter, Hugo, you speak of my being reformed—no, I am not so frightfully reformed either, only the hot weather here does not admit of drinking heavy drinks, & there is no good lager here—then besides I have no society—I expect to prove to you & all yet that I am no backslider—But here I go nowhere for mere amusement, only occasionally a walk.

And Charles Russell—how I should like to see him—how like to have one of our old times again—Ah Fred and you, dear Hugo, & you repentant one with the dark-shining whiskers [Bloom]—must there not be an hour, an evening in the future, when we four returning concentrating New York-ward or elsewhere, shall meet, allowing no interloper, & have our drinks & things, & resume the chain & consolidated & achieve a night better & mellower than ever—we four?

Hugo, I wish you to give my love to all the boys— . . .
DRAFT LETTER: Feinberg Collection, Library of Congress

To the parents of Erastus Haskell, a soldier

Washington, August 10, 1863

Mr and Mrs Haskell,

Dear friends, I thought it would be soothing to you to have a few lines about the last days of your son Erastus Haskell of Company K, 141st New

York Volunteers. I write in haste, & nothing of importance—only I thought any thing about Erastus would be welcome. From the time he came to Armory Square Hospital till he died, there was hardly a day but I was with him a portion of the time—if not during the day, then at night. I had no opportunity to do much, or any thing for him, as nothing was needed, only to wait the progress of his malady. I am only a friend, visiting the wounded & sick soldiers, (not connected with any society—or State.) From the first I felt that Erastus was in danger, or at least was much worse than they in the hospital supposed. As he made no complaint, they perhaps [thought him] not very bad—I told the [doctor of the ward] to look him over again—he was a much [sicker boy?] than he supposed, but he took it lightly, said, I know more about these fever cases than you do—the young man looks very sick, but I shall certainly bring him out of it all right. I have no doubt the doctor meant well & did his best—at any rate, about a week or so before Erastus died he got really alarmed & after that he & all the doctors tried to help him, but without avail—Maybe it would not have made any difference any how—I think Erastus was broken down, poor boy, before he came to the hospital here—I believe he came here about July 11th—Somehow I took to him, he was a quiet young man, behaved always correct & decent, said little—I used to sit on the side of his bed—I said once, You don't talk any, Erastus, you leave me to do all the talking—he only answered quietly, I was never much of a talker. The doctor wished every one to cheer him up very lively—I was always pleasant & cheerful with him, but did not feel to be very lively—Only once I tried to tell him some amusing narratives, but after a few moments I stopt, I saw that the effect was not good, & after that I never tried it again—I used to sit by the side of his bed, pretty silent, as that seemed most agreeable to him, & I felt it so too—he was generally opprest for breath, & with the heat, & I would fan him—occasionally he would want a drink—some days he dozed a good deal—sometimes when I would come in, he woke up, & I would lean down & kiss him, he would reach out his hand & pat my hair & beard a little, very friendly, as I sat on the bed & leaned over him.

Much of the time his breathing was hard, his throat worked—they tried to keep him up by giving him stimulants, milk-punch, wine &c—these perhaps affected him, for often his mind wandered somewhat—I would say, Erastus, don't you remember me, dear son?—can't you call me by name?— once he looked at me quite a while when I asked him, & he mentioned over in[audibly?] a name or two (one sounded like [Mr. Setchell]) & then, as his eyes closed, he said quite slow, as if to himself, I don't remember, I dont remember, I dont remember—it was quite pitiful—one thing was he could not talk very comfortably at any time, his throat & chest seemed stopped—I have no doubt at all he had some complaint besides the typhoid—In my limited talks with him, he told me about his brothers & sisters by name, & his parents, wished me to write to his parents & send them & all his love—I think he told me about his brothers living in different places, one in New York City, if I recollect right—From what he told me, he must have been poorly enough for several months before he came to Armory Sq[uare] Hosp[ital]—the first week in July I think he told me he was at the regimental hospital at a place called Baltimore Corners not many miles from White House, on the peninsula—previous to that, for quite a long time, although he kept around, he was not at all well—couldn't do much—was in the band as a fifer I believe—While he lay sick here he had his fife laying on the little stand by his side—he once told me that if he got well he would play me a tune on it—but, he says, I am not much of a player yet.

I was very anxious he should be saved, & so were they all—he was well used by the attendants—poor boy, I can see him as I write—he was tanned & had a fine head of hair, & looked good in the face when he first came, & was in pretty good flesh too—(had his hair cut close about ten or twelve days before he died)—He never complained—but it looked pitiful to see him lying there, with such a look out of his eyes. He had large clear eyes, they seemed to talk better than words—I assure you I was attracted to him much—Many nights I sat in the hospital by his bedside till far in the night—The lights would be put out—yet I would sit there silently, hours, late, perhaps fanning him—he always liked to have me sit there, but never cared to talk—I shall never forget those nights, it was a curious & solemn scene, the sick & wounded lying around in their cots, just visible in the darkness, & this dear young man close at hand lying on what proved to be his death bed—I do not know his past life, but what I do know, & what I saw of him, he was a noble boy—I felt he was one I should get very much attached to. I think you have reason to be proud of such a son, & all his relatives have cause to treasure his memory.

I write to you this letter, because I would do something at least in his memory—his fate was a hard one, to die so—He is one of the thousands of our unknown American young men in the ranks about whom there is no record or fame, no fuss made about their dying so unknown, but I find in them the real precious & royal ones of this land, giving themselves up, aye even their young & precious lives, in their country's cause—Poor dear son, though you were not my son, I felt to love you as a son, what short time I saw you sick & dying here—it is as well as it is, perhaps better—for who knows whether he is not better off, that patient & sweet young soul, to go, than we are to stay? So farewell, dear boy—it was my opportunity to be with you in your last rapid days of death—no chance as I have said to do any thing particular, for nothing [could be done—only you did not lay] here & die among strangers without having one at hand who loved you dearly, & to whom you gave your dying kiss—

Mr and Mrs Haskell, I have thus written rapidly whatever came up about Erastus,[44] & must now close. Though we are strangers & shall probably never see each other, I send you & all Erastus' brothers & sisters my love—

Walt Whitman

I live when home, in Brooklyn, N Y. (in Portland avenue, 4th door north of Myrtle, my mother's residence.) My address here is care of Major Hapgood, paymaster U S A, cor 15th & F st, Washington D C.

M S: New-York Historical Society

To Lewis K. Brown, a soldier

Washington, August 15, 1863

Lewy, your letter of August 10 came safe, & was glad to hear all about you, & the way you are spending the time—Lew, you must be having first rate times out there—well you need something to make up what you have suffered—You speak of being used well out there—Lewy, I feel as if I could love any one that uses you well, & does you a kindness—but what kind of heart must that man have that would treat otherwise, or say any thing insulting, to a crippled young soldier, hurt in fighting for this union & flag? (Well I should say damned little man or heart in the business)—

Should you meet any such, you must not mind them, dear comrade, & not allow your feelings to be hurt by such loafers—(I agree with you that a rebel in the southern army is much more respectable than a northern copperhead.) Dear son, when I read about your agreeable visit of a week, & how much you enjoyed yourself, I felt as much gratified as though I had enjoyed it myself—& I was truly thankful to hear that your leg is still doing well, & on the gain—you must not mind its being slowly, dear son, if it only goes forward instead of backward, & you must try to be very careful of your eating & drinking &c., not indulge in any excesses, & not eat too much flummery, but generally plain food, for that is always best, & it helps along so much.

Lewy, I believe I wrote you an acc't of the presentation to Dr Bliss—he is now off north for three weeks—Dr Butler (ward D) is in charge—some of the doctors & wardmasters have been drafted—poor Johnny Mahay [45] is not in very good spirits—he was to have an operation performed before Bliss went, but he went off & did not do it—Johnny is pretty low some days— Things in ward K are pretty much the same—they had some improvem'ts in the Hospital, new sinks, much better, & the grounds in front & between the wards nicely laid out in flowers & grass plots &c.—but, Lew, it has been awful hot in the wards the past two weeks, the roofs burnt like fire—

There is no particular war news—they are having batches of conscripts now every day in the Army—Meade is down on the upper Rappahannock & fords, & around Warrenton—Lee stretches down toward Gordonsville, they say his head quarters is there—folks are all looking toward Charleston— if we could only succeed there, I don't know what secesh would do—the ground seems to be slipping more & more from under their feet—Lew, the *Union* & the *American Flag* must conquer, it is destiny—it may be long, or it may be short, but that will be the result—but O what precious lives have been lost by tens of thousands in the struggle already—

Lew, you speak in your letter how you would like to see me—well, my darling, I wonder if there is not somebody who would be gratified to see you, & always will be wherever he is—Dear comrade, I was highly pleased at your telling me in your letter about your folks' place, the house & land & all the items—you say I must excuse you for writing so much foolishness— nothing of the kind—My darling boy, when you write to me, you must write without ceremony, I like to hear every little thing about yourself & your af- fairs—you need never care how you write to me, Lewy, if you will only—I never think about literary perfection in letters either, it is the *man* & the *feeling*—Lewy, I am feeling pretty well, but the sun affects me a little, aching & fulness in the head—a good many have been sun-struck here the last two weeks—I keep shady through the middle of the day lately—Well, my dear boy, I have scribbled away any thing, for I wanted to write you to-day & now I must switch off—good by, my darling comrade, for the present, & I pray God to bless you now & always.

Walt.

Write when you feel like it, Lewy, don't hurry—address still care Major Hapgood, paymaster U S A, cor 15th & F st Washington D C.
M S: Library of Congress

To his mother

Washington, September 15, 1863

Dear Mother

Your letters were very acceptable—one came just as I was putting my last in the post office—I guess they all come right—I have written to Han & George, & sent George papers—Mother, have you heard any thing whether the 51st went on with Burnside, or did they remain as a reserve in Kentucky—Burnside has managed splendidly so far, his taking Knoxville & all together, it is a first class success—I have known Tennessee union men here in hospital, & I understand it therefore—the region where Knoxville is, is mainly union but the southerners could not exist without it, as it is in their midst—so they determined to pound & kill & crush out the unionists—all the savage & monstrous things printed in the papers about their treatment are true, at least that kind of thing is—as bad as the Irish in the mob treated the poor niggers in New York[46]—we north[erners] dont understand some things about southerners, it is very strange—the contrast—if I should pick out the most genuine union men & real patriots I have ever met in all my experience, I should pick out two or three Tennessee & Virginia unionists I have met in the hospitals, wounded or sick—one young man I guess I have mentioned to you in my letters, John Barker, 2d Tennessee Vol. (union)—was a long while a prisoner in secesh prisons in Georgia, & in Richmond—three times the devils hung him up by the heels to make him promise to give up his unionism, once he was cut down for dead—he is a young married man with one child—his little property destroyed, his wife & child turned out—he hunted & tormented, & any moment he could have had any thing if he would join the confederacy—but he was firm as a rock—he would not even take an oath to not fight for either side—they held him about 8 months—then he was very sick, scurvy, & they exchanged him & he came up from Richmond here to hospital, here I got acquainted with him—he is a large, slow, good natured man (somehow made me often think of father), shrewd, very little to say—wouldn't talk to any body but me—his whole thought was to get back & fight, he was not fit to go, but he has gone back to Tennessee—he spent two days with his wife & young one there & then to his regiment—he writes to me frequently, & I to him—he is not fit to soldier, for the rebels have destroyed his health & strength (though he is only 23 or 4), but nothing will keep him from his regiment, & fighting—he is uneducated, but as sensible a young man as I ever met, & understands the whole question—well, mother, Jack Barker is the most genuine Union man I have ever yet met—I asked him once very gravely why he didn't take the southern oath & get his liberty—if he didn't think it was foolish to be so stiff &c—I never saw such a look as he gave me, he thought I was in earnest—the old devil himself couldn't have had put a worst look in his eyes—

Mother, I have no doubt there are quite a good many just such men—he is now down there with his regiment, (one of his brothers was killed)—when he fails in strength, he gets the Colonel to detach him to do teamster's duty for a few days, on a march till he recruits his strength—but he always carries his gun with him—in a battle he is always in the ranks—then he is so sensible, such decent manly ways, nothing shallow or mean, (he must have been a giant in health, but now he is weaker, has a cough too)—Mother, can you wonder at my getting so attached to such men, with such love, especially when they show it to me—some of them on their dying beds, & in the very hour of death or just the same when they recover, or partially recover—I never knew what American young men were till I have been in the hospitals—

Well, mother, I have got writing on—there is nothing new with me, just the same old thing—as I suppose it is with you there—Mother, how is Andrew, I wish to hear all about him—I do hope he is better, & that it will not prove any thing so bad—I will write to him soon myself, but in the mean time you must tell him to not put so much faith in medicine, drugs I mean, as in the true curative things, namely diet & careful habits, breathing good air, &c—you know I wrote in a former letter what is the cause & foundation of the diseases of the throat, & what must be the remedy that goes to the bottom of the thing—sudden attacks &c are to be treated with applications & medicines, but diseases of a seated character are not to be cured by them, only perhaps a little relieved, (& often aggravated, made firmer)—

Dearest mother, I hope you yourself are well, & getting along good— About the letter in the Times, I see ever since I sent it they have been very crowded with news that must be printed—I think they will give it yet. I hear there is a new paper in Brooklyn, or to be one—I wish Jeff would send me some of the first numbers without fail, & a stray Eagle in same parcel to make up the 4 ounces—I was glad to hear Mat was going to write me a good long letter—every letter from home is so good, when one is away—(I often see the men crying in the hospital when they get a letter)—Jeff too I want him to write whenever he can, & not forget the new paper—we are having

pleasant weather here, it is such a relief from that awful heat—(I can't think
of another such seige without feeling sick at the thought)— . . .

Walt

M S: Feinberg Collection, Library of Congress

To William S. Davis [47]

Washington, October 1, 1863

The noble gift of your brother Joseph P Davis of [$20?] for the aid of the
wounded, sick, dying soldiers here came safe to hand—it is being sacredly
distributed to them—part of it has been so already—I may another time
give you special cases—I go every day or night in the hospitals a few hours—

As to physical comforts, I attempt to have something—generally a lot
of—something harmless & not too expensive to go round to each man, even
if it is nothing but a good home-made biscuit to each man, or a couple of
spoonfuls of blackberry preserve, I take a ward or two of an evening & two
more next evening &c—as an addition to his supper—sometimes one thing,
sometimes another, (judgment of course has to be carefully used)—then, after such general round, I fall back upon the main thing, after all, the special
cases, alas, too common—those that need special attention, some little delicacy, some trifle—very often, far above all else, soothing kindness wanted—
personal magnetism—poor boys, their sick hearts & wearied & exhausted
bodies hunger for the sustenance of love or their deprest spirits must be
cheered up—I find often young men, some hardly more than children in age
yet—so good, so sweet, so brave, so decorous, I could not feel them nearer
to me if my own sons or young brothers—Some cases even I could not tell
any one, how near to me, from their yearning ways & their sufferings—it is
comfort & delight to me to minister to them, to sit by them—some so wind
themselves around one's heart, & will be kissed at parting at night just like
children—though veterans of two years of battles & camp life—

I always carry a haversack with some articles most wanted—physical comforts are a sort of basis—I distribute nice large biscuit, sweet-crackers,
sometimes cut up a lot of peaches with sugar, give preserves of all kinds,
jellies, &c. tea, oysters, butter, condensed milk, plugs of tobacco, (I am the
only one that doles out this last, & the men have grown to look to me)—
wine, brandy, sugar, pickles, letter-stamps, envelopes & note-paper, the
morning papers, common handkerchiefs & napkins, undershirts, socks,

dressing gowns, & fifty other things—I have lots of special little requests.
Frequently I give small sums of money—shall do so with your brother's contribution—the wounded are very frequently brought & lay here a long while
without a cent. I have been here & in front 9 months doing this thing, &
have learned much—two-thirds of the soldiers are from 15 to 25 or 6 years of
age—lads of 15 or 16 more frequent than you have any idea—seven-eighths
of the Army are Americans, our own stock—the foreign element in the army
is much overrated, & is of not much account anyhow—As to these hospitals,
(there are dozens of them in [&] around Washington) [there] are no hospitals you must understand like the diseased half-foreign collections under the
name common at all times in cities—in these here, the noblest, cleanest
stock I think of the world, & the most precious.
DRAFT LETTER: Feinberg Collection, Library of Congress

To Hugo Fritsch

                                        Washington, October 8, 1863
Dear Hugo.
   I don't know why I have delayed so long as a month to write to you, for
your affectionate & lively letter of September 5th gave me as much pleasure
as I ever received from correspondence—I read it even yet & have taken the
liberty to show it to one or two persons I knew would be interested. Dear
comrade, you must be assured that my heart is much with you in New York,
& with my other dear friends, your associates—&, my dear, I wish you to
excuse me to Fred Gray, & to Perk, & Ben Knower, for not yet writing to
them, also to Charley Kingsley, should you see him—I am contemplating a
tremendous letter to my dear comrade Frederickus, which will make up for
deficiencies—my own comrade Fred, how I should like to see him & have
a good heart's time with him, & a mild orgie, just for a basis, you know,
for talk & interchange of reminiscences & the play of the quiet lambent electricity of real friendship—O Hugo, as my pen glides along writing these
thoughts, I feel as if I could not delay coming right off to New York & seeing
you all, you & Fred & Bloom, & every body—I want to see you, to be within
hand's reach of you, & hear your voices, even if only for one evening, for
only three hours—I want to hear Perk's fiddle—I want to hear Perk himself,
(& I will humbly submit to drink to the Church of England)—I want to be
with Bloom, (that wretched young man who I hear continually adorns him-

self outwardly, but I hear nothing of the interior &c) & I want to see Charley Russell, & if [when] he is in N. Y. you see him I wish you to say that I sent him my love, particular, & that he & Fred & Charles Chauncey remain a group of itself in the portrait-gallery of my heart & mind yet & forever—for so it happened for our dear times, when we first got acquainted, (we recked not of them as they passed,) were so good, so hearty, those friendship-times, our talk, our knitting together, it may be a whim, but I think nothing could be better or quieter & more happy of the kind—& is there any better kind in life's experiences?

Dear comrade, I still live here as a hospital missionary after my own style, & on my own hook—I go every day or night without fail to some of the great government hospitals—O the sad scenes I witness—scenes of death, anguish, the fevers, amputations, friendlessness, of hungering & thirsting young hearts, for some loving presence—such noble young men as some of these wounded are—such endurance, such native decorum, such candor—I will confess to you, dear Hugo, that in some respects I find myself in my element amid these scenes—shall I not say to you that I find I supply often to some of these dear suffering boys in my presence & magnetism that which nor doctors nor medicines nor skill nor any routine assistance can give?

Dear Hugo, you must write to me often as you can, & not delay it, your letters are very dear to me. Did you see my newspaper letter in N Y Times of Sunday Oct 4?[48] About my dear comrade Bloom, is he still out in Pleasant Valley? Does he meet you often? Do you & the fellows meet at Gray's or any where? O Hugo, I wish I could hear with you the current opera—I saw Devereux[49] in the N Y papers of Monday announced for that night, & I knew in all probability you would be there—tell me how it goes, and about the principal singers—only dont run away with that theme, & occupy too much of your letter with it—but tell me mainly about all my dear friends, & every little personal item, & what you all do, & say &c.

I am excellent well. I have cut my beard short, & hair ditto: (all my acquaintances are in anger & despair & go about wringing their hands). My face is all tanned & red. If the weather is moist or has been lately, or looks as if it thought of going to be, I perambulate this land in big army boots outside & up to my knees. Then around my majestic brow, around my well-brimmed felt hat—a black & gold cord with acorns. Altogether the effect is satisfactory. The guards as I enter or pass places often salute me. All of which I tell, as you will of course take pride in your friend's special & expanding glory.

DRAFT LETTER: Feinberg Collection, Library of Congress

To Abby M. Price

Washington, October 11–15, 1863

Dear friend,

Your letters were both received, & were indeed welcome. Don't mind my not answering them promptly, for you know what a wretch I am about such things. But you must write just as often as you conveniently can. Tell me all about your folks, especially the girls, & about Mr Arnold—of course you won't forget Arthur,⁵⁰ & always when you write to him send him my love. Tell me about Mrs Urner & the dear little rogues. Tell Mrs Black she ought to be here hospital matron—only it is a harder pull than folks anticipate. You wrote about Emma, her thinking she might & ought to come as nurse for the soldiers—dear girl, I know it would be a blessed thing for the men to have her loving spirit & hand, & whoever of the poor fellows had them would indeed feel it so. But, my darling, it is a dreadful thing—you dont know these wounds, sicknesses &c—the sad condition in which many of the men are brought here, & remain for days, sometimes the wounds full of crawling corruption &c—Down in the field hospitals in front they have no proper care & attention, & after a battle go for many days unattended to—

Abby, I think often about you, & the pleasant days, the visits I used to pay you & how good it was always to be made so welcome. O I wish I could come in this afternoon, & have a good tea with you, & have three or four hours of mutual comfort & talk, & be all of us together again. Is Helen home, & well? And what is she doing now? And you, my dear friend, how sorry I am to hear that your health is not rugged—but, dear Abby, you must not dwell on anticipations of the worst. (But I know that is not your nature, or did not use to be.) O I hope this will find you feeling quite well, & in good spirits—I feel so well myself—I will have to come & see you I think—I am so fat, out considerable in the open air, & all red & tanned worse than ever. You see therefore that my life amid these sad & unhealthy hospitals has not yet told upon me, for I am this fall running over with health, so I feel [as] if I ought to go on that account [working] among all the sick & deficient [who are deprived of] it—& O how gladly I would [bestow upon you a] liberal share, dear Abby, if such a thing were possible.

I am continually moving around among the hospitals. One I go to oftenest the last three months is Armory Square, as it is large, generally full of the worst wounds & sicknesses, & is one of the least visited—to this, or some one, I never miss a day or evening. . . . Abby, you would all smile to see me

among them—many of them like children, ceremony is mostly discarded—
they suffer & get exhausted & so weary—lots of them have grown to expect
as I leave at night that we should kiss each other, sometimes quite a number,
I have to go round—poor boys, there is little petting in a soldier's life in the
field, but, Abby, I know what is in their hearts, always waiting, though they
may be unconscious of it themselves—

. . . I give little gifts of money in small sums, which I am enabled to do.
All sorts of things indeed, food, clothing, letter-stamps (I write lots of
letters), now & then a good pair of crutches &c &c. Then I read to the
boys—the whole ward that can walk gathers around me & listens—

All this I tell you, my dear, because I know it will interest you. . . . I like
the mission I am on here, & as it is deeply holding me I shall continue—

October 15

Well, Abby, I guess I will send you letter enough—I ought to have finished
& sent off the letter last Sunday, when it was written—I have been pretty
busy—we are having new arrivals of wounded & sick now all the time—
some very bad cases—Abby, should you come across any one who feels to
help, contribute to the men through me, write me. (I may then send word
some purchases I should find acceptable for the men)—but this only if it
happens to come in that you know or meet any one, perfectly convenient—

Abby, I have found some good friends here, a few, but true as steel—
W D O'Connor & wife, above all. He is a clerk in Treasury—she is a Yankee
girl—then C W Eldridge in paymaster's department. He is a Boston boy
too—their friendship has been unswerving.

In the hospitals among these American young men, I could not describe
to you what mutual attachments & how passing deep & tender these boys—
some have died, but the love for them lives as long as I draw breath—those
soldiers know how to love too when once they have the right person & the
right love offered them. It is wonderful. You see I am running off into the
clouds—but this is my element— . . .

Walt Whitman

M S: Morgan Library

To Lewis K. Brown, a soldier

Brooklyn, November 8 and 9, 1863

Dear son & comrade, & all my dear comrades in the hospital,

I sit down this pleasant Sunday forenoon intending to write you all a good stout letter, to try to amuse you as I am not able at present to visit you, like I did—yet what I shall write about I hardly know until I get started—but, my dear comrades, I wish to help you pass away the time, for a few minutes any how—I am now home at my mother's in Brooklyn, N Y—I am in good health as ever & eat my rations without missing one time—Lew, I wish you was here with me, & I wish my dear comrade Elijah Fox in Ward G was here with me—but perhaps he is on his way to Wisconsin—Lewy, I came through from Washington to New York by day train, 2d Nov., had a very pleasant trip, every thing went lovely, & I got home in the evening between 8 and 9— Next morning I went up to the polls bright & early—I suppose it is not necessary to tell you how I voted—we have gained a great victory in this city—it went union this time, though it went democratic strong only a year ago, & for many years past—& all through the state the election was a very big thing for the union—I tell you the copperheads got flaxed out hand-somely[51]—indeed these late elections are about as great a victory for us as if we had flaxed General Lee himself, & all his men—& as for personal good will I feel as if I could have more for Lee or any of his fighting men, than I have for the northern copperheads—

Lewy, I was very glad to get your letter of the 5th—I want you to tell Oscar Cunningham in your ward that I sent him my love & he must try to keep up good courage while he is confined there with his wound. Lewy, I want you to give my love to Charley Cate & all the boys in Ward K, & to Benton [Wilson] if he is [there still]—I wish you would go in Ward C and see James S Stilwell, & also Thomas Carson in same ward, & Chambers that lays next to him, & tell them I sent them my love. Give Carson this letter to read if he wishes it. Tell James Stilwell I have writ from here to his folks at Comac, L. I., & it may be I shall go down there next week on the L I railroad; & let him have this letter to read if he wishes it—Tell Manvill Wintersteen[52] that lays next to him in Ward C that I send him my love, & I hope his wound is healing good. Lew, I wish you to go in Ward B and tell a young cavalry man, his first name is Edwin [H. Miller?], he is wounded in the right arm, that I sent him my love, & on the opposite side a young man named Charley wounded in left hand, & Jennings, & also a young man I love that lays now up by the door just above Jennings, that I sent them all my

love. So, Lew, you see I am giving you a good round job, with so many messages—but I want you to do them all, dear son, & leave my letter with each
of the boys that wish it, to read for themselves—tell Miss Gregg in Ward A
that I send my love to Pleasant Borley, if he is still there, & if so I hope it will
be God's will that he will live & get strong to go home yet—I send my love
to little Billy [Clements?], the Ohio boy in Ward A, & to Miss Gregg herself—& if Mrs Doolittle is in Ward B, please ask her to tell the boys in the
ward I sent them my love, & to her too, & give her this letter some evening
to read to the boys, & one of these days I will come back & read to them
myself—& the same to Mrs Southwick in Ward H, if she wishes to read it to
the boys for my sake.

Lew, I wish you would go in Ward G & find a very dear friend of mine in
bed 11, Elijah D Fox, if he is still there. Tell him I sent him my best love, &
that I make reckoning of meeting him again, & that he must not forget me,
though that I know he never will—I want to hear how he is, & whether he
has got his papers through yet—Lewy, I wish you would go to him first & let
him have this letter to read if he is there—Lewy, I would like you to give my
love to a young man named Burns in Ward I, & to all the boys in Ward I—&
indeed in every ward, from A to K inclusive, & all through the hospital, as I
find I cannot particularize without being tedious—so I send my love sincerely to each & all, for every sick & wounded soldier is dear to me as a son
or brother, & furthermore every man that wears the union uniform & sticks
to it like a man, is to me a dear comrade, & I will do what I can for him
though it may not be much—& I will add that my mother & all my folks feel
just the same about it, & would show it by their works too when they can—

Well, dear comrades, what shall I tell you to pass away the time? I am
going around quite a great deal, more than I really desire to. Two or three
nights ago I went to the N Y Academy of Music, to the Italian opera.[53] I
suppose you know that is a performance, a play, all in music & singing, in
the Italian language, very sweet & beautiful. There is a large company of
singers & a large band, altogether two or three hundred. It is in a splendid
great house, four or five tiers high, & a broad parquette on the main floor.
The opera here now has some of the greatest singers in the world—the principal lady singer (her name is Medori) has a voice that would make you hold
your breath with wonder & delight, it is like a miracle—no mocking bird
nor the clearest flute can begin with it—besides it is a very rich & strong
voice—& besides she is a tall & handsome lady, & her actions are so grace-
ful as she moves about the stage, playing her part. Boys, I must tell you just
one scene in the opera I saw—things have worked so in the piece that this

lady is compelled, although she tries very hard to avoid it, to give a cup of poisoned wine to her lover—the king her husband forces her to do it—she pleads hard, but her husband threatens to take both their lives (all this is in singing & music, very fine)—so the lover is brought in as a prisoner, & the king pretends to pardon him & make up, & asks the young man to drink a cup of wine, & orders the lady to pour it out. The lover drinks it, then the king gives her & him a look, & smiles & walks off the stage. And now came as good a piece of performance as I ever saw in my life. The lady as soon as she saw that her husband was really gone, she sprang to her lover, clutched him by the arm, & poured out the greatest singing you ever heard—it poured like a raging river more than any thing else I could compare it to— she tells him he is poisoned—he tries to inquire &c and hardly knows what to make of it—she breaks in, trying to pacify him, & explain &c—all this goes on very rapid indeed, & the band accompanying—she quickly draws out from her bosom a little vial, to neutralize the poison, then the young man in his desperation abuses her & tells her perhaps it is to poison him still more as she has already poisoned him once—this puts her in such agony, she begs & pleads with him to take the antidote at once before it is too late—her voice is so wild & high it goes through one like a knife, yet it is delicious—she holds the little vial to his mouth with one hand & with the other springs open a secret door in the wall, for him to escape from the pal- ace—he swallows the antidote, & as she pushes him through the door, the husband returns with some armed guards, but she slams the door to, & stands back up against the door, & her arms spread wide open across it, one fist clenched, & her eyes glaring like a wild cat, so they dare not touch her— & that ends the scene. Comrades, recollect all this is in singing & music, & lots of it too, on a big scale, in the band, every instrument you can think of, & the best players in the world, & sometimes the whole band & the whole men's chorus & women's chorus all putting on the steam together—& all in a vast house, light as day, & with a crowded audience of ladies & men. Such singing & strong rich music always give me the greatest pleasure—& so the opera is the only amusement I have gone to, for my own satisfaction, for last ten years.

But, my dear comrades, I will now tell you something about my own folks—home here there is quite a lot of us—my father is not living—my dear mother is very well indeed for her age, which is 67—she is cheerful & hearty, & still does all her light housework & cooking—She never tires of hearing about the soldiers, & I sometimes think she is the greatest patriot I

ever met, one of the old stock—I believe she would cheerfully give her life
for the Union, if it would avail any thing—and the last mouthful in the
house to any union soldier that needed it—then I have a very excellent
sister-in-law—she has two fine young ones—so I am very happy in the
women & family arrangements. Lewy, the brother [Andrew] I mentioned as
sick, lives near here, he is very poorly indeed, & I fear will never be much
better—he too was a soldier, has for several months had throat disease—he
is married & has a family—I believe I have told you of still another brother
in the army, down in the 9th Army Corps, has been in the service over two
years, he is very rugged & healthy—has been in many battles, but only once
wounded, at first Fredericksburgh.

Monday forenoon November 9.

Dear comrades, as I did not finish my letter yesterday afternoon, as I had
many friends come to see me, I will finish it now—the news this morning is
that Meade is shoving Lee back upon Richmond, & that we have already
given the rebs some hard knocks, there on the old Rappahannock fighting
ground. O I do hope the Army of the Potomac will at last gain a first-class
victory, for they have had to retreat often enough, & yet I believe a better
Army never trod the earth than they are & have been for over a year.

Well, dear comrades, it looks so different here in all this mighty city, every
thing going with a big rush & so gay, as if there was neither war nor hospitals
in the land. New York & Brooklyn appear nothing but prosperity & plenty.
Every where carts & trucks & carriages & vehicles on the go, loaded with
goods, express-wagons, omnibuses, cars, &c—thousands of ships along the
wharves, & the piers piled high, where they are loading or unloading the
cargoes—all the stores crammed with every thing you can think of, & the
markets with all sorts of provisions—tens & hundreds of thousands of
people every where, (the population is 1,500,000), almost every body well-
drest, & appearing to have enough—then the splendid river & harbor here,
full of ships, steamers, sloops, &c—then the great street, Broadway, for four
miles, one continual jam of people, & the great magnificent stores all along
on each side, & the show windows filled with beautiful & costly goods—I
never saw the crowd thicker, nor such goings on & such prosperity—& as I
passed through Baltimore & Philadelphia it seemed to be just the same.

I am quite fond of crossing on the Fulton ferry, or South ferry, between
Brooklyn & New York, on the big handsome boats. They run continually
day & night. I know most of the pilots, & I go up on deck & stay as long as I

choose. The scene is very curious, & full of variety. The shipping along the wharves looks like a forest of bare trees. Then there are all classes of sailing vessels & steamers, some of the grandest & most beautiful steamships in the world, going or coming from Europe, or on the California route, all these on the move. As I sit up there in the pilot house, I can see every thing, & the distant scenery, & away down toward the sea, & Fort Lafayette &c. The ferry boat has to pick its way through the crowd. Often they hit each other, then there is a time—

My loving comrades, I am scribbling all this in my room in my mother's house. It is Monday forenoon—I have now been home about a week in the midst of relations, & many friends, many young men, some I have known from childhood, many I love very much. I am out quite a good deal, as we are glad to be with each other—they have entertainments &c. But truly, my dear comrades, I never sit down, not a single time, to the bountiful dinners & suppers to which I am taken in this land of wealth & plenty without feeling it would be such a comfort to all, if you too, my dear & loving boys, could have each your share of the good things to eat & drink, & of the pleasure & amusement. My friends among the young men make supper parties, after which there is drinking &c., every thing prodigal & first rate, one, Saturday night, & another last night—it is much pleasure, yet often in the midst of the profusion, the palatable dishes to eat, & the laughing & talking, & liquors &c, my thoughts silently turn to Washington, to all who lie there sick & wounded, with bread & molasses for supper—

Lewy, dear son, I think I shall remain here ten or twelve days longer, & then I will try to be with you once again. If you feel like it I would like to have you write me soon, tell me about the boys, especially James Stilwell, Pleasant Borley, Cunningham, & from the cavalry boy Edwin in ward B— tell me whether Elijah Fox in ward G has gone home—Lew, when you write to Tom Sawyer you know what to say from me—he is one I love in my heart, & always shall till death, & afterwards too—I wish you to tell a young man in ward D, 2d bed below the middle door, (his first name is Isaac [Linensparger], he is wounded in left leg, & it has had erysipelas), that I sent him my love, & I wish him to have this letter to read if he desires it, & I will see him again before long.

So, Lew, I have given you a lot of messages but you can take your time to do them, only I wish each of the boys I have mentioned to have my letter that wishes it, & read it at leisure for themselves, & then pass to another. If Miss Hill in ward F or the lady nurse in ward E cares about reading it to the boys in those wards for my sake, you give it them some evening, as I know the boys would like to hear from me, as I do from them.

Well, Lewy, I must bid you good bye for present, dear son, & also to all the rest of my dear comrades, & I pray God to bless you, my darling boys, & I send you all my love, & I hope it will be so ordered to let things go as easy as possible with all my dear boys wounded or sick, & I hope it will be God's will that we shall all meet again, my dear loving comrades, not only here but hereafter.

Walt Whitman

M S: Feinberg Collection, Library of Congress

To Thomas P. Sawyer, a soldier

Brooklyn, November 20(?), 1863

Dear brother,

I am here in Brooklyn, New York, spending a few weeks home at my mother's. I left Washington Nov 2d, & shall return there next week. I wrote to you six or seven weeks ago, the last time.[54] I am well & fat, eat my rations regular, & weigh about 200—so you see I am not very delicate. Here in Brooklyn & New York where I was raised, I have so many friends, I believe, now I am here they will kill me with kindness, I go around too much, & I think it would be policy for me to put back to Washington. I have a brother here, very sick, I do not think he can recover, he has been in the army—I have another brother in the 9th Army Corps, has been out 26 months. But the greatest patriot in the family is my old mother. She always wants to hear about the soldiers, & would give her last dime to any soldier that needed it.

Every thing looks on the rush here in these great cities, more people, more business, more prosperity, & more of every thing to eat & wear, than ever. Tom, I was home in time to vote. The elections went bully. How are you copperheads? I think these last elections will be a settler for all traitors north, & they are the worst.

I shall be back in Washington next Tuesday. My room is 456 Sixth street. But my letters are still addrest care of Major Hapgood, paymaster U S A, Washington D C.

Well, comrade, I must close. I do not know why you do not write to me. Do you wish to shake me off? That I cannot believe, for I have the same love for you that I exprest in my letters last spring, & I am confident you have the same for me. Anyhow I go on my own gait, & wherever I am in this world, while I have a meal, or a dollar, or if I should have some shanty of my own, no living man will ever be more welcome there than Tom Sawyer. So good by, dear comrade, & God bless you, & if fortune should keep you from me here, in this world, it must not hereafter.

DRAFT LETTER: Berg Collection, New York Public Library

To Elijah Douglass Fox, a soldier

Brooklyn, November 21, 1863

Dear son & comrade,

I wrote a few lines about five days ago & sent on to Armory Square, but as I have not heard from it I suppose you have gone on to Michigan. I got your letter of Nov 10th,[55] & it gave me much comfort. . . . Dearest comrade, I only write this, lest the one I wrote five days ago may not reach you from the hospital. I am still here at my mother's, & feel as if [I] have had enough of going around New York—enough of amusements, suppers, drinking, & what is called *pleasure*—Dearest son, it would be more pleasure if we could be together just in quiet, in some plain way of living, with some good employment & reasonable income, where I could have you often with me, than all the dissipations & amusements of this great city—O I hope things may work so that we can yet have each other's society—for I cannot bear the thought of being separated from you—I know I am a great fool about such things, but I tell you the truth, dear son. I do not think one night has passed in New York or Brooklyn when I have been at the theatre or opera or afterward to some supper party or carouse made by the young fellows for me, but what amid the play or the singing, I would perhaps suddenly think of you— & the same at the gayest supper party, of men, where all was fun & noise & laughing & drinking, of a dozen young men, & I among them, I would see your face before me in my thought as I have seen it so often there in Ward G, & my amusement or drink would be all turned to nothing, & I would realize how happy it would be if I could leave all the fun & noise & the crowd & be with you—I don't wish to disparage my dear friends & acquaintances here, there are so many of them & all so good, many so educated, traveled, &c., some so handsome & witty, some rich &c., some among the literary class—many young men—all good—many of them educated & polished, & brilliant in conversation, &c—& I thought I valued their society

& friendship—& I do, for it is worth valuing—But, Douglass, I will tell you the truth, you are so much closer to me than any of them that there is no comparison—there has never passed so much between them & me as we have—besides there is something that takes down all artificial accomplishments, & that is a manly & loving soul—My dearest comrade, I am sitting here writing to you very late at night—I have been reading—it is indeed after 12, & my mother & all the rest have gone to bed two hours ago, & I am here alone writing to you, & I enjoy it too, although it is not much, yet I know it will please you, dear boy—If you get this, you must write & tell me where & how you are. I hope you are quite well, & with your dear wife, for I know you have long wished to be with her, & I wish you to give her my best respects & love too.

Douglass, I havn't written any news, for there is nothing particular I have to write. Well, it is now past midnight, pretty well on to 1 o'clock, & my sheet is most written out—so, my dear darling boy, I must bid you good night, or rather good morning & I hope it may be God's will we shall yet be with each other—but I must indeed bid you good night, my dear loving comrade, & the blessing of God on you by night & day, my darling boy.

DRAFT LETTER: Feinberg Collection, Library of Congress

To his mother

Washington, January 29, 1864

Dear Mother

Your letter of Tuesday night came this forenoon—the one of Sunday night I rec'd yesterday—Mother, you don't say in either of them whether George has re-enlisted or not—or is that not yet decided positively one way or the other?

O Mother, how I should like to be home, (I dont want more than two or three days)—I want to see George, (I have his photograph on the wall, right over my table all the time)—& I want to see California—you must always write in your letters how she is—I shall write to Han this afternoon or to-morrow morning, & tell her probably George will come out & see her, & that if he does you will send her word beforehand—

Jeff, my dear brother, if there should be the change made in the works & things all overturned, you mustn't mind—I dare say you will pitch into something better—I believe a real overturn in the dead old beaten track of a man's life, especially a young man's, is always likely to turn out best, though it worries one at first dreadfully—

Mat, I want to see you most sincerely—they havn't put in anything in the last two or three letters about you, but I suppose you are well, my dear sister—

Mother, the young man that I took care of, Lewis Brown, is pretty well, but very restless—he is doing well now, but there is a long road before him yet—it is torture for him to be tied so to his cot, this weather—he is a very noble young man, & has suffered very much—he is a Maryland boy, & (like the southerners when they *are* union,) I think he is as strong & resolute a union boy as there is in the United States—he went out in Maryland reg't but transferred to a N Y battery—But I find so many noble men in the ranks, I have ceased to wonder at it—I think the soldiers from the New England States & the Western states are splendid, & the country parts of N Y & Pennsylvania too—I think less of the great cities than I used to—I know there are black sheep enough, even in the ranks, but the general rule is the soldiers are noble, very—

Mother, I wonder if George thinks as I do about the best way to enjoy a visit home, after all—When I come home again, I shall not go off gallivanting with my companions half as much, nor a quarter as much as I used to, but shall spend the time quietly home with you, while I do stay—it is a great humbug spreeing around, & a few choice friends for a man, the real right kind, in a quiet way, are enough—

Mother, I hope you take things easy, dont you? Mother, you know I was always advising you to let things go, & sit down & take what comfort you can while you do live— . . .

Mother, I was talking with an (pretty high) officer, here, who is behind the scenes—I was mentioning that I had a great desire to be present at a first class battle—he told me if I would only stay around here three or four weeks longer, my wish would probably be gratified—I asked him what he meant, what he alluded to specifically—but he would not say any thing further—so I remain as much in the dark as before—only there seemed to be some meaning in his remark, & it was made to me only as there was no one else in hearing at the moment—(he is quite an admirer of my poetry)—

The re-enlistment of the veterans is the greatest thing yet, it pleases every body but the rebels—& surprises every body too—

Mother, I am well & fat, (I must weigh about 206)—So Washington must agree with me—I work three or four hours a day copying—Dear mother, I

send you & Hattie my love, as you say she is a dear little girl—Mother, try to
write every week, even if only a few lines—love to George & Jeff & Mat—
Walt

M S: Feinberg Collection, Library of Congress

To John T. Trowbridge[56]

Culpepper, Virginia, February 8, 1864

Dear friend

I ought to have written to you before, acknowledging the good package of
books, duly received by express, & actively used since, changing them
around in places where most needed among the soldiers—(I found a small
hospital of U. S. teamsters, entirely without reading, I go there considerable,
& have given them largely of your reading contribution)—I am down here
pretty well toward the extreme front of the Army, eight or ten miles south of
headquarters, (Brandy Station)—We had some fighting here, below here on
picket lines, day before yesterday—We feared they, the rebs, were advancing upon us in our depleted condition, especially feared their making a flank
movement up on our right. We were all ready to skedaddle from here last
night, & expected it—horses harnessed in all directions, & traps packed up,
(we have held & lost Culpepper three or four times already)—but I was very
sleepy & laid down & went to sleep, never slept fresher or sweeter—but
orders came during the night to stay for the present, there was no danger—
during the night I heard tremendous yells, I got up & went out, & found it
was some of the men returning from the extreme front—As day before yesterday a strong force, three corps, were moved down there—These were
portions of them now returning—it was a curious sight to see the shadowy
columns coming in two or three o'clock at night—I talked with the men—
how good, how cheerful, how full of manliness & good nature our American young men are—I staid last night at the house of a real secesh woman,
Mrs. Ashby—her husband (dead) a near relation of the famous reb Gen
Ashby[57]—she gave me a good supper & bed—There was quite a squad of
our officers there—she & her sister paid me the compliment of talking
friendlily & nearly altogether exclusively with me—she was dressed in very
faded clothes but her manners were fine, seems to be a travelled educated
woman—quite melancholy—said she had remained through fearful troubles
& changes here on acct of her children—she is a handsome middle-aged

woman—poor lady, how I pitied her, compelled to live as one may say on chance & charity, with her high spirit—

Dear friend, I am moving around here among the field hospitals—(O how the poor young men suffer)—& to see more of camp life & war scenes, & the state of the army this winter—Dear friend, I have much to tell you, but must abruptly close—

Walt Whitman

TEXT: Transcription, Stanford University

To his mother

Culpepper, Virginia, February 12, 1864

Dearest Mother,

I am still stopping down in this region. I am a good deal of the time down within half a mile of our picket lines, so that you see I can indeed call myself in the front. I stopped yesterday with an artillery camp, in the 1st Corps, at the invitation of Capt [Henry Lowd] Cranford, who said that he knew me in Brooklyn. It is close to the lines—I asked him if he did not think it danger-ous—he said no, he could have a large force of infantry to help him there, in very short metre, if there was any sudden emergency—The troops here are scattered all around, much more apart than they seemed to me to be op-posite Fredericksburgh last winter—they mostly have good huts & fire-places, &c—I have been to a great many of the camps, & I must say I am astonished how good the houses are almost every where—I have not seen one regiment nor any part of one, in the poor uncomfortable little shelter tents that I saw so common last winter, after Fredericksburgh—but all the men have built huts of logs & mud—a good many of them would be com-fortable enough to live in under any circumstances—

I have been in the Division hospitals around here—there are not many men sick here, & no wounded—they now send them on to Washington—I shall return there in a few days, as I am very clear that the real need of one's services is there after all—there the worst cases concentrate, & probably will, while the war lasts—

I suppose you know that what we call hospital here in the field, is nothing but a collection of tents, on the bare ground for a floor, rather hard accom-modations for a sick man—they heat them here by digging a long trough in the ground under them, covering it over with old railroad iron & earth, &

then building a fire at one end & letting it draw through & go out at the
other, as both ends are open—this heats the ground through the middle of
the hospital quite hot—I find some poor creatures crawling about pretty
weak with diarrhea—there is a great deal of that—they keep them till they
get very bad indeed, & then send them to Washington—the journey aggra-
vates the complaint, & they come into Washington in a terrible condition—
O mother, how often & how many I have seen come into Washington, from
this awful complaint, after such an experience as I have described—with the
look of Death on their poor young faces—they keep them so long in the
field hospitals with poor accommodations, the disease gets too deeply
seated—

To-day I have been out among some of the camps of the 2d division of the
1st Corps—I have been wandering around all day, & have had a very good
time, over woods, hills, & gullys, indeed a real soldier's march—the weather
is good & the traveling quite tolerable—I have been in the camps of some
Massachusetts, Pennsylvania, & New York regiments—I have friends in
them, & went out to see them, & see soldiering generally, as I never cease to
crave more & more knowledge of actual soldiers' life, & to be among them
as much as possible—This evening I have also been in a large wagoners'
camp—they had good fires, & were very cheerful—I went to see a friend
there too, but did not find him in—it is curious how many I find that I know
& that know me—Mother, I have no difficulty at all in making myself at
home among the soldiers, teamsters, or any—I most always find they like to
have me very much, it seems to do them good, no doubt they soon feel that
my heart & sympathies are truly with them, & it is both a novelty & pleases
them & touches their feelings, & so doubtless does them good—& I am sure
it does that to me—

There is more fun around here than you would think for—I told you
about the theatre the 14th Brooklyn has got up, they have songs & bur-
lesques &c, some of the performers real good—As I write this I have heard
in one direction or another two or three good bands playing—& hear one
tooting away some gay tunes now, though it is quite late at night—Mother, I
dont know whether I mentioned in my last letter that I took dinner with Col
Fowler[58] one day early part of the week—his wife is stopping here—I was
down at the 14th as I came along this evening too—one of the officers told
me about a presentation to George of a sword &c, he said he see it in the
papers[59]—the 14th invited me to come & be their guest while I staid here,
but I have not been able to accept—Col Fowler uses me tip top—he is

provost marshal of this region, makes a good officer—Mother, I could get no pen & ink tonight—Well, dear Mother, I send you my love & to George & Jeff & Mat & little girls & all—

Walt

M S: Feinberg Collection, Library of Congress

To his mother

Washington, March 29, 1864

Dearest mother

I have written [to] George again to Knox[ville]—things seem to be quiet down there so far—We think here that our forces are going to be made strongest here in Virginia this spring, & every thing bent to take Richmond—Grant is here, he is now down at headquarters in the field, Brandy Station—we expect fighting before long, there are many indications—I believe I told you they had sent up all the sick from front—about four nights ago we [had a] terrible rainy afternoon [& night]—Well in the middle [of the w]orst of the rain at [night? th]ere arrived a train [of sick?] & wounded, over 600 [soldiers], down at the depot—[It w]as one of the same [old] sights, I could not keep the tears out of my eyes—many of the poor young men had to be moved on stretchers, with blankets over them, which soon soaked as wet as water in the rain—Most were sick cases, but some badly wounded—I came up to the nearest hospital & helped—Mother, it was a dreadful night (last Friday night)—pretty dark, the wind gusty, & the rain fell in torrents—One poor boy (this is a sample of one case out of the 600) he seemed to me quite young, he was quite small, (I looked at his body afterwards)—he groaned some as the stretcher-bearers were carrying him along—& again as they carried him through the hospital gate, they set down the stretcher & examined him, & the poor boy was dead—they took him into the ward, & the doctor came immediately, but it was all of no use—the worst of it is too that he is entirely unknown—there was nothing on his clothes, or any one with him, to identify him—& he is altogether unknown—Mother, it is enough to rack one's heart, such things—very likely his folks will never know in the world what has become of him—poor poor child, for he appeared as though he could be but 18—

I feel lately as though I must have some intermission, I feel well & hearty enough, & was never better, but my feelings are kept in a painful condition a great part of the time—things get worse & worse, as to the amount & sufferings of the sick, & as I have said before, those who have to do with them are getting more & more callous & indifferent—Mother, when I see the common soldiers, what they go through, & how every body seems to try to pick upon them, & what humbug there is over them every how, even the dying soldier's money stolen from his body by some scoundrel attendant, or from some sick ones, even from under his head, which is a common thing—& then the agony I see every day, I get almost frightened at the world— Mother, I will try to write more cheerfully next time—but I see so much— well, good bye for present, dear Mother—

Walt

M S: Feinberg Collection, Library of Congress

To his mother

Washington, April 10 and 12, 1864

Dearest Mother,

I rec'd your letter & sent the one you sent for George immediately—he must have got it the next day—I had got one from him before yours arrived—I mean to go to Annapolis & see him—

Mother, we expect a commencement of the fighting below very soon, there is every indication of it—we have had about as severe rain storms here lately as I ever see—it is middling pleasant now—there are exciting times in Congress—the Copperheads are getting furious, & want to recognize the Southern Confederacy—this is a pretty time to talk of recognizing such villains after what they have done, and after what has transpired the last three years—After first Fredericksburgh I felt discouraged myself, & doubted whether our rulers could carry on the war—but that has past away, the war *must* be carried on—& I would willingly go myself in the ranks if I thought it would profit more than at present, & I don't know sometimes but I shall as it is—

Mother, you dont know what a feeling a man gets after being in the active sights & influences of the camp, the Army, the wounded &c.—he gets to have a deep feeling he never experienced before—the flag, the tune of Yankee Doodle, & similar things, produce an effect on a fellow never such before—I have seen some bring tears on the men's cheeks, & others turn pale, under such circumstances—I have a little flag (it belonged to one of our cavalry reg'ts) presented to me by one of the wounded—it was taken by the secesh in a cavalry fight, & rescued by our men in a bloody little skirmish, it cost three men's lives, just to get one little flag, four by three—our men rescued it, & tore it from the breast of a dead rebel—all that just for the name of getting their little banner back again—this man that got it was very badly wounded, & they let him keep it—I was with him a good deal, he wanted to give me something he said, he didn't expect to live, so he gave me the little banner as a keepsake—I mention this, Mother, to show you a specimen of the feeling—there isn't a reg't, cavalry or infantry, that wouldn't do the same, on occasion—

                                             Tuesday morning April 12th
    Mother, I will finish my letter this morning—it is a beautiful day to-day— I was up in Congress very late last night, the house had a very excited night session about expelling the men that want to recognize the Southern Confederacy—You ought to hear the soldiers talk—they are excited to madness—we shall probably have hot times here not in the Army alone—the soldiers are true as the north star—I send you a couple of envelopes, & one to George—Write how you are, dear Mother, & all the rest—I want to see you all—Jeff, my dear brother, I wish you was here, & Mat too—Write how sis is—I am well as usual, indeed first rate every way—I want to come on in a month, & try to print my "Drum Taps"—I think it may be a success pecuniarily too—Dearest Mother, I hope this will find you entirely well, & dear sister Mat & all.

                                                                        Walt

M S: Feinberg Collection, Library of Congress

To his brother Jeff

                                             Washington, May 23, 1864
Dear brother Jeff
    I received your letter yesterday—I too had got a few lines from George dated on the field, 16th—he said he had also just written to mother—I cannot make out there has been any fighting since in which the 9th Corps has been engaged—I do hope Mother will not get despondent & so unhappy—I suppose it is idle to say I think George's chances are very good for coming out of this campaign safe, yet at present it seems to me so—but it is indeed idle to say so, for no one can tell what a day may bring forth—
    Sometimes I think that should it come, when it *must* be, to fall in battle,

one's anguish over a son or brother killed, would be tempered with much to take the edge off—I can honestly say it has no terrors for me, if I had to be hit in battle, as far as I myself am concerned—it would be a noble & manly death, & in the best cause—then one finds, as I have the past year, that our feelings & imaginations make a thousand times too much of the whole matter—Of the many I have seen die, or known of, the past year, I have not seen or heard of *one* who met death with any terror—Yesterday afternoon I spent a good part of the afternoon with a young man of 17, named Charles Cutter, of Lawrence City, Mass, 1st Mass heavy artillery, battery M—he was brought in to one of the hospitals mortally wounded in abdomen—Well I thought to myself as I sat looking at him, it ought to be a relief to his folks after all, if they could see how little he suffered—he lay very placid, in a half lethargy, with his eyes closed, it was very warm, & I sat a long while fanning him & wiping the sweat, at length he opened his eyes quite wide & clear, & looked inquiringly around. I said, What is it, my dear, do you want any thing?—he said quietly with a good natured smile, O nothing, I was only looking around to see who was with me—his mind was somewhat wandering, yet he lay so peaceful, in his dying condition—he seemed to be a real New England country boy, so good natured, with a pleasant homely way, & quite a fine looking boy—without any doubt he died in course of night—

There dont seem to be any war news of importance very late—We have been fearfully disappointed with Sigel[60] not making his junction from the lower part of the valley, & perhaps harassing Lee's left, or left rear, which (the junction or equivalent to it) was an indispensable part of Grant's plan, we think—this is one great reason why things have lagged so with the Army—some here are furious with Sigel, you will see he has been superseded—his losses in his repulse are not so important, though annoying enough, but it was of the greatest consequence that he should have hastened through the gaps ten or twelve days ago at all hazards & come in from the west, keeping near enough to our right to have assistance if he needed it— Jeff, I suppose you know that there has been quite a large army lying idle, mostly of artillery reg'ts manning the numerous forts around here, they have been the fattest & heartiest reg'ts any where to be seen, & full in numbers, some of them numbering 2000 men—well, they have all, every one, been shoved down to the front—lately we have had the militia reg'ts pouring in here mostly from Ohio, they look first rate, I saw two or three come in yesterday, splendid American young men, from farms mostly—we are to have them for a hundred days & probably they will not refuse to stay another hundred—Jeff, tell mother I shall write Wednesday certain (or if I hear any-thing I will write to-morrow)—I still think we shall get Richmond—

Walt—

M S: Feinberg Collection, Library of Congress

To his mother

Washington, June 3, 1864

Dearest mother

Your letter came yesterday—I have not heard the least thing from the 51st since—no doubt they are down there with the Army near Richmond—I have not written to George lately—I think the news from the Army is very good—Mother, you know of course that it is now very near Richmond in-deed, from five to ten miles—

Mother, if this campaign was not in progress I should not stop here, as it is now beginning to tell a little upon me, so many bad wounds, many pu-trified, & all kinds of dreadful ones, I have been rather too much with—but as it is I shall certainly remain here while the thing remains undecided—it is impossible for me to abstain from going to see & minister to certain cases, & that draws me into others, & so on—I have just left Oscar Cunningham, the Ohio boy—he is in a dying condition—there is no hope for him—it would draw tears from the hardest heart to look at him—he is all wasted away to a skeleton, & looks like some one fifty years old—you remember I told you a year ago, when he was first brought in, I thought him the noblest specimen of a young western man I had seen, a real giant in size, & always with a smile on his face—O what a change, he has long been very irritable, to every one but me, & his frame is all wasted away—the young Massachusetts 1st artil-lery boy, Cutter, I wrote about is dead—he is the one that was brought in a week ago last Sunday, badly wounded in breast—the deaths in the principal hospital I visit, Armory Square, average one an hour—I saw Capt Baldwin[61] of the 14th this morning, he has lost his left arm—is going home soon—

... O I must tell you I gave the boys in Carver hospital a great treat of ice cream a couple of days ago, went round myself through about 15 large wards, (I bought some ten gallons, very nice)—you would have cried & been amused too, many of the men had to be fed, several of them I saw cannot probably live, yet they quite enjoyed it, I gave everybody some—quite a number west-ern country boys had never tasted ice cream before—they relish such things, oranges, lemons, &c—Mother, I feel a little blue this morning, as two young men I knew very well have just died, one died last night, & the other about half an hour before I went to the hospital, I did not anticipate the death of either of them, each was a very, very sad case, so young—well, mother, I see I have written you another gloomy sort of letter—I do not feel as first rate as usual—

Walt—

You don't know how I want to come home & see you all, you, dear Mother, & Jeff & Mat & all—I believe I am homesick, something new for me—then I have seen all the horrors of soldier's life & not been kept up by its excitement—it is awful to see so much, & not be able to relieve it—

M S: Feinberg Collection, Library of Congress

To his mother

Washington, June 7, 1864

Dearest mother,

I cannot write you any thing about the 51st, as I have not heard a word—I felt much disturbed yesterday afternoon, as Major Hapgood came up from the Paymaster General's office, & said that news had arrived that Burnside was killed, & that the 9th Corps had had a terrible slaughter—he said it was believed at the Paymaster general's office—Well I went out to see what reliance there was on it—the rumor soon spread over town, & was believed by many—but as near as I can make it out, it proves to be one of those unaccountable stories that get started these times—Saturday night we heard that Grant was routed completely &c &c—so that's the way the stories fly—I suppose you have the same big lies there in Brooklyn—Well the truth is sad enough, without adding any thing to it—but Grant is not destroyed yet, but I think is going into Richmond yet, but the cost is terrible—

Mother, I have not felt well at all the last week—I had spells of deathly faintness, and bad trouble in my head too, & sore throat, (quite a little budget, ain't they?)—My head was the worst, though I don't know, the faint weak spells were not very pleasant—but I feel so much better this forenoon I believe it has passed over—There is a very horrible collection in Armory Building, (in Armory Square hosp.) about 200 of the worst cases you ever see, & I had been probably too much with them—it is enough to melt the heart of a stone—over one third of them are amputation cases—

Well, mother, poor Oscar Cunningham is gone at last—he is the 82d

Ohio boy, (wounded May 3d '63)—I have written so much of him I suppose you feel as if you almost knew him—I was with him Saturday forenoon & also evening—he was more composed than usual, could not articulate very well—he died about 2 o'clock Sunday morning—very easy they told me, I was not there—It was a blessed relief, his life has been misery for months—the cause of death at last was the system absorbing the pus, the bad matter, instead of discharging it from wound—I believe I told you in last letter I was quite blue from the deaths of several of the poor young men I knew well, especially two I had strong hopes of their getting up—things are going pretty badly with the wounded—They are crowded here in Washington in immense numbers, & all those that come up from the Wilderness, & that region, arrived here so neglected, & in such plight, it was awful—(those that were at Fredericksburgh & also from Belle Plaine)—The papers are full of puffs, &c. but the truth is, the largest proportion of worst cases got little or no attention—we receive them here with their wounds full of worms—some all swelled & inflamed, many of the amputations have to be done over again—one new feature is that many of the poor afflicted young men are crazy, every ward has some in it that are wandering—they have suffered too much, & it is perhaps a privilege that they are out of their senses—Mother, it is most too much for a fellow, & I sometimes wish I was out of it—but I suppose it is because I have not felt first rate myself— . . .

Well, Mother, how do things go on with you all—it seems to me if I could only be home two or three days, & have some good teas with you & Mat, & set in the old basement a while, & have a good time & talk with Jeff, & see the little girls, &c—I should be willing to keep on afterward among these sad scenes for the rest of the summer—but I shall remain here until this Richmond campaign is settled, any how, unless I get sick, & I don't anticipate that—Mother dear, I hope you are well & in fair spirits—you must try to—have you heard from sister Han?

Walt

M S: Feinberg Collection, Library of Congress

To Lewis K. Brown, a soldier

Brooklyn, July 11, 1864

Dear comrade

I have rec'd your letter of the 6th as it has been sent on to me by Major Hapgood. My dear comrade, I have been very sick, and have been brought on home nearly three weeks ago, after being sick some ten days in Washington—The doctors say my sickness is from having too deeply imbibed poison into my system from the hospitals—I had spells of deathly faintness, & the disease also attacked my head & throat pretty seriously—

The doctors forbid me going any more into the hospitals—I did not think much of it, till I got pretty weak, & then they directed me to leave & go north for change of air as soon as I had strength—But I am making too long a story of it—I thought only to write you a line—My dear comrade, I am now over the worst of it & have been getting better the last three days—my brother took me out in a carriage for a short ride yesterday which is the first I have been out of the house since I have been home—the doctor tells me to-day I shall soon be around which will be very acceptable—This is the first sickness I have ever had & I find upon trial such things as faintness, headache & trembling & tossing all night, & all day too, are not proper companions for a good union man like myself—[62]

Lewy, I dont know any news to send you—the acc'ts here to-night are that the railroad & telegraph between Baltimore & Washington are cut, & also between Philadelphia by the rebel invasion—

My dear boy, you say you would like to see me—well I would give anything to see your face again too—I think of you often— . . .

And now good bye, Lewy, & accept my heartfelt & true love, my dearest comrade—& I will try to write again before a great while & tell you how I am getting along, & which way I expect to move, &c. And I hope you will do the same to me—

So good bye again, Lew, & God bless you, dear son, now & through life—

Walt Whitman

M S: Berg Collection, New York Public Library

To William D. O'Connor

Brooklyn, September 11, 1864

Dear friend

I have nothing of consequence to write, but I thought I would send you a few lines anyhow. I have just written Nelly a letter, & send to Little Compton—We are full of politics here, the dispute runs high & hot everywhere—I think the Republicans are going to make a stout fight after all, as there is confusion in the opposition camp—the result of course I do not pretend to foretell—

My health is quite re-established, yet not exactly the same unconscious state of health as formerly—The book is still unprinted—Our family are all well as usual—I go two or three times a week among the soldiers in hospital here—

I go out quite regularly, sometimes out on the bay, or to Coney Island—& occasionally a tour through New York life, as of old—last night I was with some of my friends of Fred Gray association, till late wandering the east side of the City—first in the lager bier saloons & then elsewhere—one crowded, low, most degraded place we went, a poor blear-eyed girl bringing beer. I saw her with a McClellan medal on her breast—I called her & asked her if the other girls there were for McClellan[63] too—she said yes every one of them, & that they wouldn't tolerate a girl in the place who was not, & *the fellows* were too—(there must have been twenty girls, sad sad ruins)—it was one of those places where the air is full of the scent of low thievery, druggies, foul play, & prostitution gangrened—

I don't know what move I shall make, but something soon, as it is not satisfactory any more in New York & Brooklyn—I should think nine tenths, of all classes, are copperheads here, I never heard before such things as I hear now whenever I go out—then it seems tame & indeed unreal here, life as carried on & as I come in contact with it & receive its influences— . . .

                                                                          Walt

MS: Berg Collection, New York Public Library

To William D. O'Connor

                                                        Brooklyn, January 6, 1865
Dear friend

Your welcome letter of December 30 came safe. I have written & sent my application to Mr Otto, & also a few lines to Mr Ashton,[64] with a copy of it. I am most desirous to get the appointment, as enclosing, with the rest of the points, my attentions to the soldiers & to my poems, as you intimate.

It may be Drum-Taps may come out this winter, yet, (in the way I have mentioned in times past.) It is in a state to put right through, a perfect copy being ready for the printers—I feel at last, & for the first time without any demur, that I am satisfied with it—content to have it go to the world verbatim & punctuation. It is in my opinion superior to Leaves of Grass—certainly more perfect as a work of art, being adjusted in all its proportions, & its passion having the indispensable merit that though to the ordinary reader let loose with wildest abandon, the true artist can see it is yet under control. But I am perhaps mainly satisfied with Drum-Taps because it delivers my ambition of the task that has haunted me, namely, to express in a poem (& in the way I like, which is not at all by directly stating it) the pending action of this *Time* & *Land we swim in*, with all their large conflicting fluctuations of despair & hope, the shiftings, masses, & the whirl & deafening din, (yet over all, as by invisible hand, a definite purport & idea)—with the unprecedented anguish of wounded & suffering, the beautiful young men, in wholesale death & agony, everything sometimes as if in blood color, & dripping blood. The book is therefore unprecedently sad, (as these days are, are they not?)—but it also has the blast of the trumpet, & the drum pounds & whirrs in it, & then an undertone of sweetest comradeship & human love, threading its steady thread inside the chaos, & heard at every lull & interstice thereof—truly also it has clear notes of faith & triumph.

Drum Taps has none of the perturbations of Leaves of Grass. I am satisfied with Leaves of Grass (by far the most of it) as expressing what was intended, namely, to express by sharp-cut self assertion, *One's-Self* & also, or may be still more, to map out, to throw together for American use, a gigantic embryo or skeleton of Personality, fit for the West, for native models—but there are a few things I shall carefully eliminate in the next issue, & a few more I shall considerably change.

I see I have said I consider Drum-Taps superior to Leaves of Grass. I probably mean as a piece of wit, & from the more simple & winning nature of the subject, & also because I have in it only succeeded to my satisfaction in removing all superfluity from it, verbal superfluity I mean. I delight to make a poem where I feel clear that not a word but is indispensable part thereof & of my meaning.

Still Leaves of Grass is dear to me, always dearest to me, as my first born, as daughter of my life's first hopes, doubts, & the putting in form of those days' efforts & aspirations—true, I see now, with some things in it I should not put in if I were to write now, but yet I shall certainly let them stand, even if but for proofs of phases passed away—

Mother & all home are well as usual. Not a word for over three months from my brother George[65]—the probabilities are most gloomy. I see the Howells now & then. I am well, but need to leave here—need a change. . . .

Love to dear Nelly & Jeannie & all.

Walt Whitman

M S: Berg Collection, New York Public Library

To his brother Jeff

Washington, January 30, 1865

My dear brother,

Your letter has only just reached me though I see the Brooklyn post office stamp is January 27th—I was gratified with [Lt. William E.] Babcock's and [Aaron] Smith's letters, though I am very sorry they neither of them mentioned the date of Lt [William] Caldwell's letter from Danville. If it should be much later than George's, which was November 27th, it would be a relief to know it—but I presume it was one of the same batch. Jeff, I have this morning written to Capt [Julius W.] Mason, telling him where George is, & asking him, as that would be ten times more likely to get through, if he will have (or direct some proper person) to put up a box of things to eat, & given him George's address to send it through the lines, & said that I or you would pay the bill of course, & be most deeply obliged to him & that I would have enclosed the money in the letter I sent him, but thought it safer to wait & see whether it reached him. I have written to George since I have been here in Washington. Also a few lines to Han. We have had very cold mean weather here ever since I arrived till to-day—it is now moderated & very pleasant overhead.

I am quite comfortable, have a comfortable room enough, with a wood stove, & a pile of wood in the room, a first rate & good big bed, & a very friendly old secesh landlady whose husband & son are off in the Southern army—she is different from any I have found yet here, is very obliging, starts my fire for me at 5 o'clock every afternoon, & lights the gas, even, & then turns it down to be ready for me when I come home. I get my meals where I can—they are poor & expensive—You speak of the Indian office—it is a Bureau in the Department of the interior, which has charge of quite a large mass of business relating to the numerous Indian tribes in West & Northwest, large numbers of whom are under annuities, supplies, &c for the government. All I have hitherto employed myself about has been making copies of reports & Bids, &c for the office to send up to the Congressional Committee on Indian Affairs. It is easy enough—I take things very easy—the rule is to come at 9 and go at 4—but I don't come at 9, and only stay till 4 when I want, as at present to finish a letter for the mail—I am treated with great courtesy, as an evidence of which I have to inform you that since I began this letter, I have been sent for by the cashier to receive my *PAY* for the arduous & invaluable services I have already rendered to the government—I feel quite well, perhaps not as completely so as I used to was, but I think I shall get so this spring—as I did indeed feel yesterday better than I have since I was taken sick last summer.

I spent yesterday afternoon in Armory Square Hospital, & had a real good time, & the boys had too. Jeff, you need not be afraid about my overdoing the matter. I shall go regularly enough, but shall be on my guard against trouble. I am also going to some of the camps about here, there is a great chance among them to do good, & they are interesting places every way, for one who goes among the men. I have thought every day of Mother—dear Mother, I hope she gets along well this bitter weather—(about the hoop iron, I think it was the right thing to do—the least they can do is to take it off)—My dear brother, you must by all means *come* & see me—Martha, my dear sister, I send you & the dear little torments my best, best love—Jeff, give my respects to Mr. Lane & Dr Ruggles[66]—

Walt

M S: Feinberg Collection, Library of Congress

To the mother of a soldier, Mrs. Irwin

Washington, May 1, 1865

Dear madam:

No doubt you and Frank's friends have heard the sad fact of his death in hospital here, through his uncle, or the lady from Baltimore, who took his things. (I have not seen them, only heard of them visiting Frank.) I will write you a few lines—as a casual friend that sat by his death-bed. Your son, Corporal Frank H. Irwin, was wounded near Fort Fisher, Virginia, March 25th, 1865—the wound was in the left knee, pretty bad. He was sent up to Washington, was receiv'd in ward C, Armory-square hospital, March 28th—the wound became worse, and on the 4th of April the leg was amputated a little above the knee—the operation was perform'd by Dr. Bliss, one of the best surgeons in the army—he did the whole operation himself—there was a good deal of bad matter gather'd—the bullet was found in the knee. For a couple of weeks afterwards he was doing pretty well. I visited and sat by him frequently, as he was fond of having me. The last ten or twelve days of April I saw that his case was critical. He previously had some fever, with cold spells. The last week in April he was much of the time flighty—but always mild and gentle. He died first of May. The actual cause of death was pyaemia, (the absorption of the matter in the system instead of its discharge). Frank, as far as I saw, had everything requisite in surgical treatment, nursing, &c.

He had watches much of the time. He was so good and well-behaved and affectionate I myself liked him very much. I was in the habit of coming in afternoons and sitting by him, and soothing him, and he liked to have me—liked to put his arm out and lay his hand on my knee—would keep it so a long while. Toward the last he was more restless and flighty at night—often fancied himself with his regiment—by his talk sometimes seem'd as if his feelings were hurt by being blamed by his officers for something he was entirely innocent of—said, "I never in my life was thought capable of such a thing, and never was." At other times he would fancy himself talking as it seem'd to children or such like, his relatives I suppose, and giving them good advice; would talk to them a long while. All the time he was out of his head not one single bad word or idea escaped him. It was remark'd that many a man's conversation in his senses was not half as good as Frank's delirium. He seem'd quite willing to die—he had become very weak and had suffer'd a good deal, and was perfectly resign'd, poor boy. I do not know his past life, but I feel as if it must have been good. At any rate what I saw of him here, under the most trying circumstances, with a painful wound, and among strangers, I can say that he behaved so brave, so composed, and so sweet and affectionate, it could not be surpass'd. And now like many other noble and good men, after serving his country as a soldier, he has yielded up his young life at the very outset in her service. Such things are gloomy—yet there is a text, "God doeth all things well"—the meaning of which, after due time, appears to the soul.

I thought perhaps a few words, though from a stranger, about your son, from one who was with him at the last, might be worth while—for I loved the young man, though I but saw him immediately to lose him. I am merely a friend visiting the hospitals occasionally to cheer the wounded and sick.

W. W.

TEXT: *The Complete Writings of Walt Whitman* (1902), 4:122–25

To the parents of a soldier, N. M. and John P. Pratt

Washington, June 10, 1865

Mr. & Mrs. Pratt:

As I am visiting your son Alfred occasionally, to cheer him up in his sickness in hospital, I thought you might like a few words, though from a stranger, yet a friend to your boy. I was there last night, and sat a while by the bed, as usual, & he showed me the letter he had just received from home. He wrote to you yesterday. He has had diarrhea pretty bad, but is now improved & goes about the hospital—but as the weather is pretty hot & powerful in the midst of the day, I advised him not to go outdoors much at present. What he wants most is rest, and a chance to get his strength again. I expect he will improve by degrees, & I hope it will not be very long before he will be sent home—though I don't know, as I am only a friend, occasionally visiting the hospitals. Alfred has good accommodations where he is, & a good doctor, & nursing—so you must not worry about him. I shall stop & see him a little every day, as he likes to have me, & I like him too. Poor young men, there are hundreds & thousands of them here, wounded or sick, in the great army hospitals—many of them suffering with amputations & wounds—others with sickness, & so faint & weak, this weather—it is enough to make one's heart bleed—

As to Alfred, he is comparatively well off, there are so many with bad wounds &c.—the deaths are quite frequent. He will soon be restored, according to present appearances.

We are having very hot weather here, & it is dry & dusty—The City is alive with soldiers from both the Army of the Potomac & the Western Armies, brought here by Sherman. There have been some great Reviews here, as you have seen in the papers—& thousands of soldiers are going home every day.

You must write to Alfred often, as it cheers up a boy sick & away from home. Write all about domestic & farm incidents, and as cheerful as may be. Direct to him, in Ward C, Armory Square Hospital, Washington, D. C. Should any thing occur, I will write you again, but I feel confident he will continue doing well. For the present farewell.

Walt Whitman

M S: Feinberg Collection, Library of Congress

To Anson Ryder, Jr., a soldier

Washington, August 15 and 16, 1865

Dear Anson,

As there is a sort of lull and quiet for a short time in my work, I will improve the opportunity to write to you, dear friend. In this office, I am in the part where the Pardons are attended to. There is a perfect stream of Rebels coming in here all the time to get pardoned. All the Southerners that are worth more than $20,000 in property, have to get special pardons, & all who have been officers of the rank of Brig. Gen'l, or upwards, the same. Many old men come in here, and middle-aged and young ones too. I often talk with them. There are some real *characters* among them—(and you know I have a fancy for any thing a little out of the usual style)—Quite a good many women come up to Washington, and come to this office, about their pardons—some old, some young—all are drest in deep black—Then there are bushels of applications arriving every week by mail—when they are recommended by the Provisional Governors, or some well known Union person, they get their papers—Many have got their papers—but nearly all are waiting for the President's signature—I should think 3 or 4000. He is not in any hurry to sign them. . . . Blue coats here are getting quite scarce. Your letter of the 9th came safe, and was welcome. I envy you the pure fresh country air and healthy influences and I doubt not fine scenery and quiet. When you write tell me about the neighborhood—where is Cedar Lake, and what kind of place? Well, Anson, I must close. God bless you, my loving soldier-boy, now and always.

                                                                Walt Whitman

Wednesday morning, 16th Aug.

Anson, as I neglected to send this yesterday, I have brought down a couple of little pictures, & enclose them, after all. But you shall have a larger & better one, dear son. I will have it prepared [*indecipherable*] was to send it to you. They have commenced breaking up Armory Square. The picture in shirt sleeves was taken in 1854 (the year of the first edition of *Leaves of Grass*)—you would not know it was me now, but it was taken from life & was first-rate then. Anson, when you write tell me all particulars of yourself, folks, place & about Wood &c—your true friend.

                                                                        W W

TEXT: *The Flying Quill at Goodspeed's Book Shop* (March 1968)

To Alfred Pratt, a soldier

                                        Washington, August 26 and 29, 1865
Dear Al,

Your letter came all right—& I was glad to hear from you, boy, & to know that you had got home to your own folks at last—& now I hope you will get well & strong again, dear son—& I hope it may be God's will that you will not only get so, but keep so. Armory Square hospital is broken up, & all the sick & wounded have been taken away, or forwarded home. . . . Al, you was quite low, one time there in the Hospital—& the worst of it was you was down-hearted & homesick, & said nothing to any body—only when I came around, & we soon had quite a love toward each other, & no doubt that did you good—only I now regret that I did not do more for you, & come to see you oftener.

I am working now in the Attorney General's office. This is the place where the big southerners now come up to get pardoned—all the rich men & big officers of the reb army have to get special pardons, before they can buy or sell, or do any thing that will stand law—Sometimes there is a steady stream of them coming in here—old & young, men & women—some of the men are odd looking characters—I talk with them often, & find it very interesting to listen to their descriptions of things that have happened down south, & to how things are there now, &c. There are between 4 & 5000 pardons issued from this Office, but only about 200 have been signed by the President—The rest he is letting wait, till he gets good & ready—What I hear & see about Andrew Johnson, I think he is a *good man*—sometimes some of the letters he gets are sent over to this office to be answered—& occasionally that job falls to me—One of them was a letter a few days ago from a widow woman in Westfield, N Y. Her husband was in Texas when the war broke out, joined *our* army—& was killed by the rebels—they also confiscated his property in Texas, leaving his family helpless—this lady wrote to the President for aid, &c—I wrote the President's answer—telling her that she should have her husband's pension, which would be pretty good, as he was a captain—& that the rebs in Texas could not hold any such property, but that she could bring a suit & get it back, &c.—then put in a few words to cheer her up, &c.—

Aug 29.

Dear son, I did not finish my letter because I have not been able to get the little picture of Lincoln & Washington—but I succeeded in getting one this morning—I send it as a little present to my dear boy, & I hope it will please him, for there is something about it that is both pleasing & solemn to me, though but a small picture—We are having a cloudy drizzly day here & heavy mist—There is nothing very new or special—

There was a big match played here yesterday between two base ball clubs, one from Philadelphia & the other a Washington club—& to-day another is to come off between a New York & the Philadelphia club I believe—thousands go to see them play—

I keep well, & every body says I am getting fat & hearty—I live at the same place in M street, 468—only I have moved into the front room—it is pleasanter—I have my meals brought up to me—my landlady gives me very good grub, $32.50 a month—Well I must draw to a close, as the sheet is most full—When you write, to let me know how you are, & if you have rec'd this, direct to me, *Attorney General's office*, Washington D. C.

Now, Ally, I must bid you good by, & I send you my love, my darling boy, & also to your parents, for your sake—you must try to be a good young man & behave right & manly, for that is far more than worldly prosperity—Farewell, dear son,

Walt Whitman

M S: Feinberg Collection, Library of Congress

1866-1873

BY 1866 WHITMAN HAD PUBLISHED *DRUM-TAPS*, CONTAIN-ing the greatest war poems in our literature, drawn from his empathic experiences in the field and in military hospitals. The assassination of Abraham Lincoln was commemorated in "When Lilacs Last in the Dooryard Bloom'd," which has become our national elegy. Whitman was preparing to publish the fourth edition of *Leaves of Grass*, which was to include *Drum-Taps*.

He was an employee of the United States government. The hours and the labor were not burdensome, and the salary, $1200 or more, was ample for his simple life-style. One day in 1865 he lost his post when James Harlan, the recently appointed Secretary of the Interior, peremptorily fired him, pronouncing *Leaves of Grass* an obscene book and its author unworthy of public office. Whitmanites and the poet himself were outraged, but in their desire to exploit the situation, they overlooked that on the day following his dismissal Whitman had a full-time position in the Attorney General's Office. William D. O'Connor and others saw to that.

Harlan's prudery presented the opportunity for O'Connor to come to Whitman's defense with his considerable powers in vituperative rhetoric. Volatile, given to deep depressions and to excited hyperbole, O'Connor delighted the partisans but increased the almost irrational fury of the opponents in *The Good Gray Poet* (1866) and "The Carpenter" (1868), which endowed Whitman with a messianic aura. Whitman has always incited excessive reactions like that of one speaker who declared with deep sincerity and passion, "There are three great men in human history, Jesus, Buddha, and Walt Whitman, and the greatest of these is—Walt Whitman." At the time of the deification O'Connor, with Whitman's assistance, sought to modify the public image of the poet as a decadent or immoralist who narcissistically flaunted himself and refused in the age of Victoria to cover the genitals with the mandatory fig leaves.

William Michael Rossetti, the brother of Dante Gabriel and Christina Rossetti, expressed interest in publishing in England a selection from *Leaves of Grass* without the sexual poems and the objectionable phraseology found in other poems. Whitman consented, although his public stance was always to be that he refused to modify a single word in his poetry to satisfy conventional morality. As soon as he heard of Rossetti's proposed edition, Whitman prepared a preface which O'Connor was to recopy and forward to Rossetti. It insisted upon Whitman's cleanliness, physical and verbal, and sought without saying so to conventionalize the "rough" for the sake of public acceptability. Whitman granted himself heroic dimensions—"a kosmos"—

and never discouraged the extravagances of idolators like O'Connor, but at the same time he wanted to be the democratic bard loved by the people.

One of the readers of Rossetti's selection was Anne Gilchrist (1828–1886), the widow of the biographer of William Blake, Alexander Gilchrist, and the mother of four children. A woman of incredible enthusiasms and idealism in search of a hero in a century of hero worship, she discovered in Whitman a hero with the body of a Titan and the soul of a lover. At last she had found the physical and poetic embodiment of her ideal. So impassioned were her letters about Whitman's verse to Rossetti that he advised her to publish them anonymously as "A Woman's Estimate of Walt Whitman" (1870), which was the first major defense by a woman of the controversial poet. Hers was an amorous critique masquerading as criticism.

In despair because Whitman did not write directly to her—she had a nervous collapse in 1870—she waited and pined. Finally, the "life force" was too much for her. The books which Whitman had sent to Rossetti to transmit to her served as an excuse, and on September 3, 1871, she wrote one of the most extraordinary love letters in the language. This well-bred Victorian lady swept aside conventional amenities to declare her love feverishly and to offer her soul and body to the poet. She rapturously envisaged herself as the poet's spiritual mate and the mother of a noble progeny. Whitman, understandably, waited six weeks before he replied to her letter. His brevity and evasiveness did not dampen her passion, nor did his subsequent warning: "You must not construct such an unauthorized & imaginary ideal Figure, & call it W. W. and so devotedly invest your loving nature in it. The actual W. W. is a very plain personage, & entirely unworthy such devotion."

She, however, was powerless to deny a shattering passion that cried for spiritual and physical satisfaction. He was equally powerless to offer the fulfillment she craved. And so we have a spectacle, the stuff of tragedy for some writers, of comedy to others. The poet who shocked the world because of his anatomical candor and who boldly summoned lovers to embrace him wherever he walked did not know how to handle a woman whose ardor his verses had inflamed. She exposed her feelings without shame and without stint; he was awed by her emotional excesses—and perhaps frightened. He retreated as she pursued. She wanted to come to America to offer herself to him; he preferred to have an ocean between them.

Late in 1865 Whitman met a veteran of the Confederate Army, Peter Doyle, now a streetcar conductor in Washington. Though there were to be stresses or "perturbations" in the relationship of a man approaching fifty

and an ex-soldier in his twenties, life for Whitman was to center about Pete
and his friends, who also worked for the railroads in Washington. O'Connor,
Charles W. Eldridge, and John Burroughs, all of whom remained in Washington after the war, never satisfied Whitman's need for comrades who,
whether he realized it or not, resembled his own brothers in education and,
more important, in their need of an elder brother to guide them.

Pete was born in Ireland about 1845 and came to the United States as
a young man. He lived in Washington with his mother and four brothers,
who were either policemen or laborers. Like most of the young men whom
Whitman befriended, Pete was semiliterate: he believed *Leaves of Grass*
was "without sense or meaning," which was pretty much the judgment of
Whitman's own family. For eight years they saw each other almost daily.
Whitman took long walks with Pete at night, sent a bouquet to him now and
then,[1] had clothes made for him, and coaxed the excitable young man out
of his blues or depressions. It was a passionate involvement which filled
Whitman with happiness and despair. He was not happy when he was absent from Pete, but the poet had to retreat to Brooklyn, where "I think of
you very often, dearest comrade, & with more calmness than when I was
there." He feared that his love was not returned but was surprised to discover, after he left Washington for a visit to Brooklyn in 1870, that "you
made so much of having me with you, [and] that you could feel so downcast
at losing me. I foolishly thought it was all on the other side."

It was the longest sustained relationship of Whitman's life, with many
gratifications but also many uncertainties. Pete was unstable and troubled,
perhaps even troubled about his involvement with Walt Whitman, who in
his poetry had to confess his own homosexual desires but, at the same time,
to render them problematic in the recurrent evasiveness of his "faint clews &
indirections."

In 1872, probably in August, there was a painful rupture in Whitman's
life. For ten years he had been an intimate of O'Connor and his family. He
admired, even perhaps overrated, O'Connor's brilliance and virtuosity, and
he dined with the family frequently. The two men had very different views
on slavery, and Whitman's ambivalent attitude toward black people annoyed
O'Connor. One night there was a violent quarrel. Infuriated and deeply
wounded, O'Connor refused Whitman's gesture of reconciliation, abruptly
moved out of his own home, and for the next ten years saw the members of
his own family infrequently. There must have been other reasons beyond dif-
ferences in racial attitudes. Ellen O'Connor, like Anne Gilchrist, was in love

with Whitman, and O'Connor may have been jealous, yet there is no reason to believe that Whitman was ever in love with a woman. Since those intimately involved with Whitman—O'Connor, Burroughs, Richard Maurice Bucke, Traubel, among others—chose to remain silent about Whitman's private life, for whatever reasons, there will always be large gaps in our knowledge.

Still in Washington, early in 1873 Whitman suffered a stroke. Doyle and Eldridge alternated as nurses, attending him day and night. Ellen O'Connor came frequently with food. About the same time, Jeff's wife, Martha, became ill and died of cancer in February. Whitman's mother now lived in Camden, New Jersey, with George and his wife, Louisa, but not contentedly. Mrs. Whitman had difficulty surrendering her independence and admitting to the toll of the years. Walt wrote to her vaguely about having her live with him in Washington, although how he was to manage in his paralyzed state he never said. Suddenly the mother became ill, and Walt hurried to Camden. She died on May 23, 1873. Her "last lines" were: "farewell my beloved sons farewell i have lived beyond all comfort in this world   dont mourn for me my beloved sons and daughters   farewell my dear beloved Walter."[2]

Whitman returned to Washington, but, recognizing his physical condition—the continuing paralysis in the left arm and leg—as well as the formidable problems of living alone, dependent upon his friends, he decided to live with George and Louisa in Camden.

To John Burroughs[3]

New York, September 10, 1866

My dear friend,

My book[4] has been delayed among the printers—but I shall stay till it is all printed—it is a little over half done, & they promise that it shall be done, or mainly so, this week. If convenient, send me a draft for the $100. If practicable send a draft payable to me, at Atlantic National Bank, of Brooklyn, New York. Write me a note separate, also. Direct to me at 279 East 55th street, New York City.

The book is going to suit me pretty well—it will make a volume of 500 pages, size & style & type, &c fully equal to Drum Taps. I shall feel glad enough when it is completed—I have a constant struggle with the printers—They are good fellows & willing enough—but it seems impossible to prevent them making lots of ridiculous errors—it is my constant dread that the book will be disfigured in that way—though we have got along pretty well thus far— . . .

I have been well & hearty. My mother is pretty well for an old woman of 72—John, I hope this will find you, & the wife too, in good health. I send you both my love. The weather is perfect here, & if it wasn't for the worriment of the book, I should be as happy as a clam at high water, as they say down on old Long Island.

Walt.

MS: Feinberg Collection, Library of Congress

To Alfred Pratt, a soldier

Washington, September 27, 1866

Dear boy, & comrade,

I am not only alive, but as well & hearty as ever I was—& more than that, I often think about you, Alfred, & retain the same friendship that we formed when I used to sit down on your bed when you was so low in the hospital. If I hadn't got your letter of 23d, I should likely have written to you very soon, of my own accord, for I thought about you the last few weeks in particular. I have been home in Brooklyn the last two months, to see my mother, & pay a visit to New York, &c. and I only returned day before yesterday. I am still employed in this Department, shall probably remain here through the winter, (although nothing is certain now-days)—Washington is rather dull—no more soldiers around like there used to be—no more patrols marching around the streets—no more great racks of hospitals—I get along well enough in this city in pleasant weather, when one can go around, but it's rough in bad weather.

Al, I got the picture, dear boy, & I have it yet, & take good care of it, & take a good look at it every now & then—I think it is a good likeness. It is now a year ago since you sent it—you spoke in that letter of your parents—You must give my love to them, & if it should be practicable I should like much to make them a call—but yet it does not seem likely as things are at present. But I wonder whether we shall ever come together again, you & I, my loving soldier boy. O how much comfort it would be to me, if things were so that we could have each other's society—for I think so much of such things.

I am writing this at my table by a big window in the Office, where I can look out & see the Potomac away down to Alexandria, & across all up & down Arlington Heights, & near at hand the grounds south of the President's House—it is a splendid day to-day, bright & clear & just cool enough—& I feel in good health—& all the better on account of your letter arriving. Well I must draw to a close.

I hope, dear comrade, you are trying to be an honorable & upright young man, for that is more than the greatest worldly prosperity, or learning either.

I send you my love, & must now bid you farewell for present, dear soldier boy.

Walt Whitman

M S: Feinberg Collection, Library of Congress

To Anson Ryder, Jr., a soldier

Washington, December 14, 1866

Dear boy & comrade,

I rec'd your letter of the 9th—& am real glad to hear from you, & that you are well & in good spirits, as appears by your letter. You speak how much you would like to see me, & we could be together a while. I too, dear friend, would be so glad if we were near each other where we could have each other's company often.

I am still working here in the same office—We have lately a new Attorney General[5]—One of the first things he did was to *promote me!*—Sensible man, wasn't he?—May the Lord reward him. I have been absent on leave the past summer two months—went to New York—spent most of the time with my mother, in Brooklyn—I have been well since I last wrote to you, mostly—only the last six weeks have had rather a bad time with neuralgia—but am getting over it.

Things with friend Hiram Frazee have gone poorly. He went from Harewood hospital here, to Brooklyn, to the City Hospital there—he had a terrific operation there that nearly cost him his life, & after all did no good—it was a pay hospital, & his stay in it cost him $300—The last I heard of Frazee was about two months ago—he was then home—his address is *Hiram W. Frazee, Camden, Oneida Co. New York*—he wrote me, & said he was as comfortable as one in his condition could be—he spoke about you in his letter, & wanted much to know about you— . . .

Dear Comrade, you don't give me the particulars what you are doing, &c.

you must, when you write again—you speak of not being overburdened with green backs, & profits &c.—Well, boy, one can bear that, if one only keeps hearty & fat & in good spirits, as I guess you are.

Well, I keep about as stout as ever, and my face red & great beard just the same as when I used to see you—I eat my rations every time, too—I am writing this in the office by a big window with a splendid view of the Potomac & Arlington Heights—Well I find I must close—I send my love to you, darling boy, & I want you always to keep me posted wherever you go, dear Comrade.

Walt Whitman

M s: Gay Wilson Allen Collection, Duke University

To his mother

Washington, December 24, 1866

Dearest mother,

I got Jeff's letter sending the money toward the soldiers' dinner—it was more than I asked for, & was very good of them all[6]—I have not had any trouble myself, worth mentioning—the dinner has been got up at my instigation—I have contributed handsomely—but they, (the Hospital steward, &c.) have done the work.

Mother, I sent Han a handsome little volume of "Florence Percy's Poems,"[7] & $5 for a Christmas present. Sent it to-day. Poor Han—I suppose every such thing does her so much good—

Don't you believe that fool Heyde lately wrote a long letter to Mr. Raymond,[8] editor of the N. Y. Times—in it he said "Walt was a good fellow *enough—but*"—& then he went on to run down Leaves of Grass, like the rest of 'em—

The way I know is, Wm. O'Connor was invited by Raymond to come & see him—& he told O'Connor he had received a number of letters about that piece in the *Times* of Dec. 2, which I sent you. He said they all praised the piece, & thanked him (Raymond) for printing it, except one he got from a fellow in Vermont who called himself Walt Whitman's relation—a brother in law, he believed—quite a good deal of stuff. Raymond seemed to think the man was either crazy or a fool, & he treated the letter with contempt.

I dont want you to write any thing about it, to Han, of course—only if she was here, we would tell her. The puppy thought I suppose that he could get his letter printed, & injure me & my book.

We are likely to have a pleasant day for Christmas—when I next write I will tell you about the dinner—I must inform you that I have had a present of a beautiful knife, a real Rogers' steel, to-day from the Attorney General—Mother, $2 is for Nance—you can give it to her in money, or any way you like—

Well, dear mother, this is Christmas eve, & I am writing it in the office by gas light, so as it will be ready to go to-morrow— I have not heard since from Mrs. [Edward B.] Grayson. Good night, mother dear.

Walt.

M S: Barrett Collection, University of Virginia

To his mother

Washington, April 16, 1867

Dearest mother,

I rec'd your letter last week a couple of hours after I sent mine. I have written to Hannah. Well, mother, we have had a spell of warm weather here—& last night & this morning we are having quite a rain—I can see the difference this morning already—the grass & trees are beginning to look green—they have made a large flower garden right in front of my window at the office. . . .

I went to a concert last night—Brignoli & Parepa[9]—nothing very great—

There is nothing new at the office—I went up to the Supreme Court last Friday, & heard the Attorney General Mr. Stanbery make quite a great speech—he is a good speaker—you would have liked it.

I was down at the hospital Sunday—there was one poor young man, a Maryland boy, very bad from delirium tremens—(such cases are getting quite common)—this young man saw such sights & terrible things, he took it into his head that the Almighty was in a rage, & punishing him—& he just got on his knees, & *remained so for over 12 hours*, praying away for mercy—so the wardmaster told me—I sat by him some time—he told me, "*they*" went away while I was with him—he said he could hear "*them*," a good ways off—but they wouldn't come near him while I was there—he got into quite a little nap while I remained—you know if the delirium tremens patients can only get a few hours good sleep the worst is over—they are rational on most things—One of these men, in the hospital, had an idea there was a great cat gnawing at his arm, & eating it—he had this idea for days &

days, & of course suffered awfully—One of the watchmen of the Treasury, (formerly a Captain in the army, in an Ohio reg't,) is there in the hospital, with delirium tremens—So you see what troubles there are in the world, of one kind & another—

We are quite busy at the office—have a good many people coming—so it is quite lively—We had a clerk here, who was a great nuisance to every body, a young sprig of a Virginian—he has cleared out, forced to resign—we are all very glad—it makes a great relief—all the rest of us get along like brothers—I like them all, & they like me.

Walt

M S: Trent Collection, Duke University

To Ellen M. O'Connor

Brooklyn, September 21, 1867

My dear friend,

As you see by the date, &c. I am home, on a visit to my mother & the rest. Mother is about as well as usual—has occasionally some trouble with rheumatism, but is cheerful & keeps up amazingly. We speak of you every day, & I have to give minute particulars of you, William, little Jenny, & all. My brother George is very well, looks hearty & brown as ever—much like he used to, only more serious—Jeff is at St. Louis, on the Water Works. Martha & the little girls are well—they are here in Brooklyn, occupying temporary apartments.

I am well as usual, & go daily around New York & Brooklyn yet with interest, of course—but I find the places & crowds & excitements—Broadway, &c—have not the zest of former times—they have done their work, & now they are to me as a tale that is told—Only the majestic & moving river & rapid sea-water scenery & life about the islands, N. Y. and Brooklyn, tower into larger proportions than ever. I doubt if the world elsewhere has their equal, or could have, to me—The waters about New York & west end of Long-Island are real sea-waters, & are ever-rolling & rushing in or out—never placid, never calm—surely they please this uneasy spirit, Me, that ebbs & flows too all the while, yet gets nowhere, & amounts to nothing—

I am trying to write a piece, to be called *Democracy*, for the leading article in the December or January number of the *Galaxy*—in some sort a counterblast or rejoinder to Carlyle's late piece, *Shooting Niagara*, which you must have read, or at least heard about. Mr. Church strongly wishes it written. Mother & Martha send love, & I also, most truly—I shall probably return to Washington last of the week.

Walt.

M S: Berg Collection, New York Public Library

To Moncure D. Conway

Washington, November 1, 1867

Dear friend,

My feeling and attitude about a volume of selections from my Leaves by Mr. Rosetti,[10] for London publication, are simply passive ones—yet with decided satisfaction that if the job is to be done, it is to be by such hands. Perhaps, too, "good-natured," as you advise—certainly not ill-natured. I wish Mr. Rosetti to know that I appreciate *his* appreciation, realize his delicacy & honor, & warmly thank him for his literary friendliness.

I have no objection to his substituting other words—leaving it all to his own tact, &c.—for "onanist," "father-stuff" &c. Briefly, I hereby empower him, (since that seems to be the pivotal affair, & since he has the kindness to shape his action so much by my wishes—& since, indeed, the sovereignty of the responsibility is not at all mine in the case,)—to make verbal changes of that sort, wherever, for reasons sufficient to him, he decides that they are indispensable. I would add that it is a question with me whether the introductory essay or prose preface to the first edition is worth printing.

"Calamus" is a common word here. It is the very large & aromatic grass, or rush, growing about water-ponds in the valleys—spears about three feet high—often called "sweet flag"—grows all over the Northern and Middle States—(see Webster's Large Dictionary—Calamus—definition 2). The recherché or ethereal sense of the term, as used in my book, arises probably from the actual Calamus presenting the biggest & hardiest kind of spears of grass—and their fresh, aquatic, pungent bouquet.

I write this to catch to-morrow's steamer from New York. It is almost certain I shall think of other things—moving me to write you further in a week or so.

Walt Whitman

M S: Formerly in Robert H. Taylor Collection

To Moncure D. Conway

Washington, about November 10, 1867

My dear Conway: [11]

Mr. Whitman has shown me your letter of October 12, with news of Mr. Hotten's proposed London print of Leaves of Grass or selection therfrom, edited by Mr. Rosetti, with an Introductory Essay or preface, by Mr. R.

Now, in view of the latter, if I may take the liberty, I wish to speak of two or three points, or rather, enforce them—for no doubt they will, to a certain extent, have occurred to Mr. Rosetti. But as I have made Leaves of Grass & their author my study for the last seven years, & have had some fortuitous advantages, perhaps Mr. Rosetti would not consider it intrusive in me, that I send this letter, which I wish you to hand him.

Considering the attitude of the public, and their average calibre, and also considering the general bearing of most of the criticisms on Mr. Whitman's poetry, I would suggest the expediency, in any forthcoming, friendly examination of his genius & writings, of dwelling pretty strongly on the following points, & making them unmistakably appear:

1st—That personally the author of Leaves of Grass is in no sense or sort whatever the "rough," the "eccentric," "vagabond" or queer person, that the commentators, (always bound for the intensest possible sensational statement,) persist in making him. He has moved, & moves still, along the path of his life's happenings & fortunes, as they befall or have befallen him, with entire serenity & decorum, never defiant even to the conventions, always bodily sweet & fresh, dressed plainly & cleanly, a gait & demeanor of antique simplicity, cheerful & smiling, performing carefully all his domestic, social, & municipal obligations, his demonstrative nature toned very low, but eloquent enough of eye, posture, & expression, though using only moderate words; and offering to the world, in himself, an American Personality, & real Democratic Presence, that not only the best old Hindu, Greek, and Roman worthies would at once have responded to, but which the most cultured European, from court or academy, would likewise, on meeting to-day, see & own without demur. All really refined persons, and the women more than the men, take to Walt Whitman. The most delicate & even conventional lady only needs to know him to love him.

2. Critically, a significant, if not the most significant, fact about Leaves of Grass, is, that the genesis & fashioning of them have evidently not been for literary purposes, merely or mainly. Neither in mass nor detail have their

pages been tried by the *sine qua non* of current literary or esthetic standards. Instead of that, the Book is the product of the largest universal law & play of things, & of that sense of kosmical beauty, of which even literature is but a fraction. This is probably the clue to the explanation of the puzzle of the widely-vexatious formal & esthetic argument involved in Leaves of Grass.

3. The idea, however, which is this man's highest contribution, and which, compared even with the vastness of Biblical & Homeric poetry, still looms & towers—as, athwart his fellow-giants of the Himalayas, the dim head of Kunchainjunga rises over the rest—is the idea of Totality, of the All-successful, final certainties of each individual man, as well as of the world he inhabits. Joyousness, out of such sure ultimate happiness & triumph, rings throughout his verse. He holds the solution of each & every problem—the spell, giving full satisfaction; and his talisman is *Ensemble*. This is the word that epitomises the philosophy of Walt Whitman. Add the word *modernness*, & you begin to unlock Leaves of Grass.

These are the points, my dear Conway, that I wish, through you, to submit to Mr. Rosetti. I have mentioned to Mr. Whitman my intention of writing him, & he, W., has made no objection. I would add, for myself, for Mr. Rosetti, that I hope he will not be deterred from giving fullest swing to what I am sure I have discovered in him, namely, an intuitional admiration & appreciation of our Poet, by the ostensibly timid attitude held at present by the critical & reading world toward Leaves of Grass—but hope he will strike at that loftier, honestly enthusiastic range of minds & readers, which, perhaps by the time Mr. Hotten's volume gets well in the hands of the public, will prove the genuine audience Mr. Whitman is certain of.

Again asking pardon of Mr. Rosetti for perhaps intruding these suggestions—yet placing them in any & every respect at his service should they be so fortunate as to strike him favorably—I remain &c &c

DRAFT LETTER: Berg Collection, New York Public Library

To William M. Rossetti

Washington, November 22, 1867

My dear Mr. Rosetti:

I suppose Mr. Conway has received, & you have read, the letter I sent over about three weeks since, assenting to the substitution of other words, &c. as proposed by you, in your reprint of my book, or selections therefrom.

I suppose the reprint intends to avoid any expressed or implied character

of being an expurgated edition. I hope it will simply assume the form &
name of a selection from the various editions of my pieces printed here.
I suggest, in the interest of that view, whether the adjoining might not be a
good form of Title page: [12]

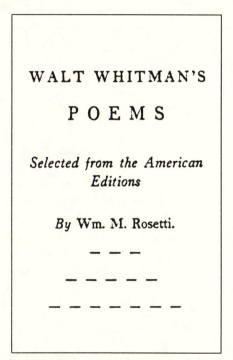

WALT WHITMAN'S

POEMS

*Selected from the American
Editions*

By Wm. M. Rosetti.

I wish particularly not only that the little figures numbering the stanzas,
but also that the larger figures dividing the pieces into separate passages or
sections be carefully followed & preserved, as in copy.

When I have my next edition brought out here, I shall change the title of
the piece "When lilacs last in the dooryard bloom'd," to *President Lincoln's
Funeral Hymn*. You are at liberty to take the latter name, or the old one, at
your option, (that is, if you include the piece.)

It is quite certain that I shall add to my next edition (carrying out my plan
from the first,) a brief cluster of pieces, born of thoughts on the deep themes
of Death & Immortality.

Allow me to send you an article I have written on "Democracy"—a hasty
charcoal-sketch of a piece, but indicative, to any one interested in Leaves of
Grass, as of the audience the book supposes, & in whose interest it is made.
I shall probably send it next mail.

Allow me also to send you (as the ocean-postage law is now so easy,) a copy of Mr. Burroughs's *Notes*,[13] & some papers. They go same mail with this.

And now, my dear sir, you must just make what use—or no use at all—of any thing I suggest or send—as your occasions call for. Very likely some of my suggestions have been anticipated.

I remain, believe me, with friendliest feelings & wishes,

Walt Whitman.

M S: Formerly in Robert H. Taylor Collection

To William M. Rossetti

Washington, December 3, 1867

My dear Mr. Rossetti:

I have just received, & have considered your letter of November 17. In order that there be the frankest understanding with respect to my position, I hasten to write you that the authorization in my letter of November 1st to Mr. Conway, for you, to make verbal alterations, substitute words, &c. was meant to be construed as an answer to the case presented in Mr. Conway's letter of October 12. Mr. Conway stated the case of a volume of selections in which it had been decided that the poems reprinted in London should appear verbatim, & asking my authority to change certain words in the Preface to first edition of poems, &c.[14]

I will be candid with you, & say I had not the slightest idea of applying my authorization to a reprint of the full volume of my poems. As such a volume was not proposed, & as your courteous & honorable course & attitude called & call for no niggardly or hesitating response from me, I penned that authorization, & did not feel to set limits to it. But abstractly & standing alone, & not read in connection with Mr. C's letter of October 12, I see now it is far too loose, & needs distinct guarding.

I cannot & will not consent of my own volition, to countenance an expurgated edition of my pieces. I have steadily refused to do so under seductive offers, here in my own country, & must not do so in another country.

I feel it due to myself to write you explicitly thus, my dear Mr. Rossetti, though it may seem harsh & perhaps ungenerous. Yet I rely on you to absolve me, sooner or later. Could you see Mr. Conway's letter of October 12, you would, I think, more fully comprehend the integrity of my explanation.

I have to add that the points made in that letter in relation to the proposed reprint, as originally designed, exactly correspond with those, on the same subject, in your own late letter—& that the kind & appreciative tone of both letters is in the highest degree gratifying, & is most cordially & affectionately responded to by me—& that the fault of sending so loose an authorization has surely been, to a large degree, my own.

And now, my friend, having set myself right on that matter, I proceed to say, on the other hand, for you, & for Mr. Hotten, that if, before the arrival of this letter, you have practically invested in, & accomplished, or partially accomplished, any plan, even contrary to this letter, I do not expect you to abandon it, at loss of outlay, &c. but shall *bona fide* consider you blameless if you let it go on, & be carried out, as you may have arranged. It is the question of the authorization of an expurgated edition proceeding from me, that deepest engages me. The facts of the different ways, one way or another way, in which the book may appear in England, out of influences not under the shelter of my umbrage, are of much less importance to me. After making the foregoing explanation, I shall, I think, accept kindly whatever happens. For I feel, indeed know, that I am in the hands of a friend, & that my pieces will receive that truest, brightest of light & perception coming from love. In that, all other & lesser requisites become pale.

It would be better, in any Introduction, to make no allusion to me, as authorizing, or not prohibiting, &c.

The whole affair is somewhat mixed—& I write offhand to catch tomorrow's New York steamer. But I guess you will pick out my meaning. Perhaps, indeed, Mr. Hotten has preferred to go on after the original plan—which, if so, saves all trouble.

I have to add that I only wish you could know how deeply the beautiful personal tone & passages of your letter of November 17, have penetrated and touched me. It is such things that go to our hearts, and reward us, & make up for all else, for years. Permit me to offer you my friendship.

I sent you hence Nov. 23d a letter, through Mr. Conway. Also a copy of Mr. Burroughs's *Notes*, Mr. O'Connor's pamphlet [*The Good Gray Poet*], & some papers containing criticisms on *Leaves of Grass*. Also, later, a prose article of mine named *Democracy*, in a magazine.

Let me know how the work goes on, what shape it takes, &c. Finally I charge you to construe all I have written, through my declared & fervid realization of your goodness toward me, nobleness of intention, &, I am fain to hope, personal, as, surely, literary & moral sympathy & attachment. And so, for the present, Farewell.

Walt Whitman.

M S: Formerly in Robert H. Taylor Collection

To Moncure D. Conway

Washington, February 17, 1868

My dear Conway,

Your letter of February 1st has just come to hand. I am willing that Mr. Hotten should sell his English publication of my Poems in the United States, on condition of paying me one shilling on every copy disposed of here—& hereby give consent to that arrangement. Furthermore, to save trouble, I hereby fully empower you to decide & act for me in any matters or propositions relating to the book, in England, should any such arise—& what you agree to is agreed to by me. If convenient I should like Mr. Hotten to send me two copies of the book, by mail, immediately. I should also consider it a special favor if you would forward me from time to time any of the English magazines or journals that might contain *noteworthy* criticisms of my poems. But you must allow me to repay you the favor. . . .

Our American politics, as you notice, are in an unusually effervescent condition—with perhaps (to the mere eye-observation from a distance) divers alarming & deadly portending shows & signals. Yet we old stagers take things very coolly, & count on coming out all right in due time. The Republicans have exploited the negro too intensely, & there comes a reaction. But that is going to be provided for. According to present appearances the good, worthy, non-demonstrative, average-representing Grant will be chosen President next fall. What about him, then? As at present advised, I shall vote for him non-demonstrative as he is—but admit I can tell much better about him some five years hence.

I remain well & hearty—occupy the same quite agreeable & quiet berth in the Attorney General's office—and, at leisure, am writing a prose piece or two, (which I will send you, when printed.) [15] . . .

I wish to send my sincerest thanks & personal regards to Mr. Rossetti. To have had my book, & my cause, fall into his hands, in London, in the way they have, I consider one of the greatest pieces of good fortune. . . .

I have not yet seen the February Fortnightly—nor the book William Blake—but shall procure & read both. I feel prepared in advance to render my cordial & admirant respect to Mr. Swinburne—& would be glad to have him know that I thank him heartily for the mention which, I understand, he has made of me in the Blake.

Indeed, my dear friend, I may here confess to you that to be accepted by those young men of England, & so treated with highest courtesy & even honor, touches one deeply. In my own country, so far, from the organs, the press, & from authoritative sources, I have received but one long tirade of shallow impudence, mockery, & scurrilous jeers. Only since the English recognition have the skies here lighted up a little.

With remembrance & love to you, Rossetti, & all my good friends—I write, for the present, Farewell.

Walt Whitman.

MS: Columbia University

To his mother

Washington, June 6–8, 1868

Dearest Mother,

I rec'd your letter day before yesterday—& am sorry you are troubled with rheumatism—it must be quite bad—Do you have any one to do the rougher house-work? I hope you have. Mother, every thing is pretty much the same with me—I remain very well, go around a good deal in the open air—we have it pretty hot in the middle of the day, & dusty—but the nights are beautiful—

I know the Mr. [Joseph M.] Simonson you saw at the post office—he has been a sort of Deputy post master a good many years—Notwithstanding what he says, the Brooklyn p. o. has a very bad name, & a great many money letters sent there never get to their destination—but I should think by what you have said, that the carrier who brings your letters must be a good safe man—

We had the strangest procession here last Tuesday night, about 3000 darkeys, old & young, men & women—I saw them all—they turned out in honor of *their* victory in electing the Mayor, Mr. [Sayles J.] Bowen—the men were all armed with clubs or pistols—besides the procession in the street, there was a string went along the sidewalk in single file with bludgeons & sticks, yelling & gesticulating like madmen—it was quite comical, yet very disgusting & alarming in some respects—They were very insolent, & altogether it was a strange sight—they looked like so many wild brutes let loose—thousands of slaves from the Southern plantations have crowded up here—many are supported by the Gov't.

Yesterday I went up to the Presidents to see the reception of the Chinese Embassy—there were eight or nine Chinese, headed by our Mr. [Anson]

Burlingame, who is head of them all, (O'Connor knows him quite well)—
you will see the speech made to them by the President, in the papers—I
think it is first rate [16]—

Sunday noon, June 7.

I am sitting awhile in the office—we are having a spell of hot oppressive
weather—It is generally thought we clerks will get our extra compensa-
tion—but I wait to see whether Congress will pass it—if they do I will make
you a present, mother dear—So you like the ticket, Grant & Colfax,[17] do
you, mother? Well, I do, too—Chase is cutting up, trying to get somebody
to nominate him, & doing his best to injure the Republican ticket—He
is just the meanest & biggest kind of a shyster—He tried the same game at
Lincoln's second nomination—Mother, I send the Chicago News, No. 7—
have you rec'd the six others all safe?—I have sent them all—

Monday forenoon, June 8. Nothing special to write about this morning,
mother. We had a thunder-shower last night & very pleasant this morning—
I was up to O'Connors as usual last evening to tea—they are all well. Well,
I believe this is all—only to send you my love, mother dear—same to
George—write all the domestic news, & about George's work, & the house.

Walt

M S: Trent Collection, Duke University

To Pete Doyle [18]

New York, September 25, 1868

Dear Boy,

I rec'd your second letter yesterday—it is a real comfort to me to get such
letters from you, dear friend. Every word does me good. The *Star* came all
right, & was quite interesting. I suppose you got my second letter last
Wednesday. There is nothing new or special to write about to-day—still I
thought I would send you a few lines, for Sunday. I put down off hand, &
write all about myself & my doings, &c. because I suppose that will be really
what my dear comrade wants most to hear, while we are separated.

I am doing a little literary work, according as I feel in the mood—
composing on my books. I am having a small edition of the Leaves of Grass
for 1867, fixed up & printed. This & some other things give me a little occupation. Upon the whole though I don't do much, but go around a great

deal—eat my rations every time, sleep at night like a top, & am having good times so far, in a quiet way, enjoying New York, the society of my mother, & lots of friends. Among other things I spend a portion of the day, with the pilots of the ferry boats, sailing on the river. The river & bay of New York & Brooklyn are always a great attraction to me. It is a lively scene. At either tide, flood or ebb, the water is always rushing along as if in haste, & the river is often crowded with steamers, ships & small craft, moving in different directions, some coming in from sea, others going out. Among the pilots are some of my particular friends—when I see them up in the pilot house on my way to Brooklyn, I go up & sail to & fro several trips. I enjoy an hour or two's sail of this kind very much indeed. My mother & folks are well, & are engaged just these times in the delightful business of moving. I should assist, but have hired a substitute in the shape of a stout young laboring man.

I send you, by mail, a copy of *the Broadway*, with the piece [19] in the same as I had in the car one day. It will not interest you much, only as something coming from me.

I think of you very often, dearest comrade, & with more calmness than when I was there—I find it first rate to think of you, Pete, & to know that you are there, all right, & that I shall return, & we will be together again. I don't know what I should do if I hadn't you to think of & look forward to.

Tell Tom Hasset, on No. 7, that I wish to be remembered to him particular. Pete, I hope this will find you entirely well of your cold. I am glad to hear that your mother is all right of her cold. This is the time of year when they are apt to be pretty troublesome. I should like to have seen that match played between the Nat. & Olympics.[20]

DRAFT LETTER: Feinberg Collection, Library of Congress

To John Swinton, of the *New York Times*

New York, about September 28, 1868

(qu?) To make a *Personal* item or ¶ for "*Minor Topics.*"[21]

qu? To commence for instance

       "With the bright, crispy autumn weather,

WALT WHITMAN again makes his appearance on the sidewalks of Broadway," &c &c

      (three or four lines on *personnel* as lounging along)

item the obstinacy, pertinacity or continuity of Leaves of Grass & of the personality of W. W. in current Literature notwithstanding all attacks & objections

---

The poems have been republished in England, & are being translated by Freíligrath for publication in Germany.[22]

---

allude to the proposed prose work—"Democratic Vistas."

Cant you put in the idea of an obstinate, tenacious, determined *living man*, appearing with a will, in our easy-going imitative literature.

DRAFT LETTER: Feinberg Collection, Library of Congress

To Henry Hurt[23]

New York, October 2, 1868

Dear friend Harry Hurt,

I thought I would just drop you a line for yourself—but no doubt you keep fully posted about me by my letters to Pete, as I am willing you or any of my particular friends who wish to, should read them. (He knows who I would be willing should read them—I leave it to him)—Harry, you would much enjoy going round N. Y. with me, if it were possible, & then how much I should like having you with me. This great city, with all its crowds, & splendor, & Broadway fashion, & women, & amusements, & the river & bay, & shipping, & the many magnificent new buildings, & Central Park & 5th Avenue, & the endless processions of private vehicles & the finest teams I ever saw, for miles long of a fine afternoon—altogether they make up a show that I can richly spend a month in enjoying—for a change from my Washington life. I sometimes think I am the particular man who enjoys the show of all these things in N. Y. more than any other mortal—as if it was all got up just for me to observe & study. Harry, I wish when you see Ben. Thompson, conductor, you would say I sent him my love, & have not forgot him. Let him read this letter. I send him a newspaper, the N. Y. Clipper. I have marked the piece about the Five Points.[24] I went down there myself just for fun, three nights ago, with a friend of mine, a policeman, & that account in the Clipper is a very good description—only not half rank enough. I wish you to tell John Towers, conductor, I sent him my love, & we will see each other again one of these days. I send him a Clipper also with an acc't of the Five Points—Harry, you let one of them lend you the paper, & read the

acc't—it will amuse you—I was there two hours—it was instructive but disgusting—I saw one of the handsomest white girls there I ever saw, only
about 18—blacks & white are all intermingled—
DRAFT LETTER: Feinberg Collection, Library of Congress

To Pete Doyle

New York, October 6, 1868

Dear Pete,

There is nothing special with me to write to you about. The time slips
away mighty quick. It seems but a day or two since I left Wash, yet I am now
on the fourth week of my furlough. Last night was about the greatest political show I ever saw, even in New York—a grand Democratic meeting &
torch-light processions. I was out in the midst of them, to see the sights.
I always enjoy seeing the city let loose, and on the rampage, as it was last
night to the fullest extent. I cannot begin to tell you how the Democrats
showed themselves by thousands & tens of thousands. The whole city was lit
up with torches. Cannons were fired all night in various parts of the city. As I
was on my way home in a 2d av. car between 12 & 1 o'clock we got blocked
in by a great part of the returning procession. Of course we had to just stand
& take it. I enjoyed it hugely from the front platform. They were nearly an
hour passing us, streaming both sides. In the procession were all sorts of
objects, models of ships, forty or fifty feet long, full-manned, cars of liberty
with women, &c &c. The ranks spread across the street, & every body carried a blazing torch. Fireworks were going off in every direction. The sky
was full of big balloons, letting off rockets & Roman candles, 'way up among
the stars. The excitement, the rush, & the endless torches, gave me great
pleasure. Ever & anon, the cannon, some near some distant. I heard them
long after I got to bed. It sounded like a distant engagement. I send you the
Herald with a sort of account of the show, but it doesn't do half justice to it.
The speeches were of no account at all.

. . . We are having pleasant weather just now, seems like Indian summer.
So long, dear Pete. From your loving comrade.
DRAFT LETTER: Feinberg Collection, Library of Congress

To Pete Doyle

New York, October 9, 1868

Dear Pete,

It is splendid here this forenoon—bright and cool. I was out early taking a short walk by the river—only two squares from where I live. I received your letter of last Monday—also the [*Washington*] *Star* same date—& glad enough to hear from you—the oftener the better. Every word is good—I sent you a letter, on the 6th, which I suppose you rec'd next day. Tell Henry Hurt I received his letter of Oct. 5 all right, & that it was welcome. Political meetings here every night. The coming Pennsylvania & Ohio elections cause much talk & excitement. The fall is upon us. Overcoats are in demand. I already begin to think about my return to Washington. A month has nearly passed away. I have received an invitation from a gentleman & his wife, friends of mine, at Providence, R. I.[25] & shall probably go there & spend a few days, latter part of October. . . .

Every day I find I have plenty to do—every hour is occupied with something. Shall I tell you about it, or part of it, just to fill up? I generally spend the forenoon in my room, writing &c., then take a bath, fix up & go out about 12, & loafe somewhere, or call on some one down town, or on business, or perhaps if it is very pleasant & I feel like it, ride a trip with some driver-friend on Broadway from 23d street to Bowling Green, three miles each way. You know it is a never-ending amusement & study & recreation for me to ride a couple of hours, of a pleasant afternoon, on a Broadway stage in this way. You see everything as you pass, a sort of living, endless panorama—shops, & splendid buildings, & great windows, & on the broad sidewalks crowds of women, richly-dressed, continually passing, altogether different, superior in style & looks from any to be seen any where else—in fact a perfect stream of people, men too dressed in high style, & plenty of foreigners—& then in the streets the thick crowd of carriages, stages, carts, hotel & private coaches, & in fact all sorts of vehicles & many first-class teams, mile after mile, & the splendor of such a great street & so many tall, ornamental, noble buildings, many of them of white marble, & the gayety & motion on every side—You will not wonder how much attraction all this is, on a fine day, to a great loafer like me, who enjoys so much seeing the busy world move by him, & exhibiting itself for his amusement, while he takes it easy & just looks on & observes.[26] Then about the Broadway drivers, nearly all of them are my personal friends. Some have been much attached to me, for years, & I to them. But I believe I have already mentioned them in a former letter. Yesterday I rode the trip I describe with a friend, on a 5th Avenue stage, No. 26—a sort [of] namesake of yours, Pete Calhoun. I have known him 9 or 10 years. The day was fine, & I enjoyed the trip muchly. So I try to put in something in my letters to give you an idea of how I pass part of my time, & what I see here in N. Y. Of course I have quite a variety—some four or five hours every day I most always spend in study, writing, &c. The other serves for a good change. I am writing two or three pieces.

I am having finished about 225 copies of Leaves of Grass bound up, to supply orders. Those copies form all that is left of the old editions. Then there will be no more in the market till I have my new & improved edition set up & stereotyped, which it is my present plan to do the ensuing winter at my leisure in Washington.[27]

Mother is well, I take either dinner or supper with her every day. Remember me to David Stevens & John Towers. . . . I send you my love, & *so long* for the present. Yours for life, dear Pete, (& death the same).

DRAFT LETTER: Feinberg Collection, Library of Congress

To Pete Doyle

New York, October 14, 1868

Dear Boy Pete,

There is great excitement here over the returns of yesterday's elections, as I suppose there is the same in Washington also—the Democrats look blue enough, & the Republicans are on their high horses.[28] I suppose Grant's success is now certain. As I write, the bands are out here, parading the streets, & the drums beating. It is now forenoon. To-night we will hear the big guns, & see the blazing bonfires. It is dark & cloudy weather here to-day. I was glad to get your letter of Friday, 9th which is the last— . . . I am about as well as usual. Mother is well, & my brothers the same. I am going to-morrow to Providence, R. I., to spend a few days. Should you write any time within four or five days after receiving this, direct to me *care of Hon. Thomas Davis, Providence, R. I.*[29]

My friend O'Connor is quite unwell, and is absent from Washington away down on the New England coast. I received a letter from him yesterday. I believe I told you I was finishing up about 230 copies of my book, expecting to sell them. I have had them finished up & bound &c. but there is a hitch about the sale, & I shall not be able to sell them at present. There is a pretty strong enmity here toward me, & L. of G., among certain classes—

not only that it is a great mess of crazy talk & hard words, all tangled up, without sense or meaning, (which by the by is, I believe, your judgment about it)—but others sincerely think that it is a bad book, improper, & ought to be denounced & put down, & its author along with it. There are some venemous but laughable squibs occasionally in the papers. One said I had received 25 guineas for a piece in an English magazine, but that it was worth all that for any one to read it. Another, the *World*, said "Walt Whitman was in town yesterday, carrying the blue cotton umbrella of the future." (It had been a drizzly forenoon)—So they go it. When they get off a good squib, however, I laugh at it, just as much as any one.

Dear Pete, I hope this will find you well & in good spirits. Dear boy, I send you my love. I will write you a line from Providence. So long, Pete.

Walt

DRAFT LETTER: Feinberg Collection, Library of Congress

To Pete Doyle

Providence, Rhode Island, October 17, 1868

Dear boy & comrade,

I sent off a letter to you yesterday noon, but towards evening Mr. Davis brought me up from the p. o. yours of the 15th,[30] which I was so glad to get that you shall have an answer right off. After the flurry of snow I told you of yesterday morning, we had a pleasant clear afternoon. I took a long walk, partly through the woods, and enjoyed it much. The weather was pretty cold & sharp, & remains so yet. As I left my overcoat in Washington, I have been compelled to get something here—so I have bought me a great iron-grey shawl, which I find very acceptable. I always had doubts about a shawl, but have already got used to mine, & like it first rate. In the evening, I went by invitation to a party of ladies & gentlemen—mostly ladies. We had a warm, animated talk, among other things about Spiritualism. I talked too, indeed went in like a house afire. It was good exercise—for the fun of the thing. I also made love to the women, & flatter myself that I created at least one impression—wretch & gay deceiver that I am. Then away late—lost my way—wandered over the city, & got home after one o'clock.

The truth is, Peter, that I am here at present times mainly in the midst of female women, some of them young & jolly—& meet them most every evening in company—& the way in which this aged party comes up to the scratch & cuts out the youthful parties & fills their hearts with envy is abso-

lutely a caution. You would be astonished, my son, to see the brass &
coolness, & the capacity of flirtation & carrying on with the girls—I would
never have believed it of myself. Brought here by destiny, surrounded in this
way—& as I in self defence would modestly state—sought for, seized upon
& ravingly devoured by these creatures—& *so* nice & smart some of them
are, & handsome too—there is nothing left for me—is there—but to go in.
Of course, young man, you understand, it is all on the square. My going in
amounts to just talking & joking & having a devil of a jolly time, carrying
on—that's all. They are all as good girls as ever lived. I have already had
three or four such parties here—which, you will certainly admit, considering
my age & heft, to say nothing of my reputation, is doing pretty well.

I go about quite a good deal—this is as handsome a city, as I ever saw.
Some of the streets run up steep hills. Except in a few of the business streets,
where the buildings are compact—in nine-tenths of the city, every house
stands separate, & has a little or quite a deal of ground about it, for flowers,
& for shade or fruit trees, or a garden. I never saw such a prosperous looking
city—but of course no grand public buildings like Washington.

This forenoon I have been out away down along the banks of the river &
cove, & making explorations generally. All is new to me, & I returned quite
tired. I have eat a hearty dinner. Then I thought I would come up & sit a
while in my room. But as I did not feel like reading, I concluded to write this
precious screed. Fortunate young man, to keep getting such instructive
letters—aint you? It is now four o'clock & bright & cool, & I have staid in
long enough. I will sally forth, on a walk, & drop this in the P. O. before
supper. So long, dear Pete—& my love to you as always, always.

W

DRAFT LETTER: Feinberg Collection, Library of Congress

To Ralph Waldo Emerson

Washington, November 30, 1868

Dear Mr. Emerson:

On the eve of sending the enclosed piece[31] abroad, I have taken a notion
to first offer it to the *Atlantic*—and, if not too great a liberty, to solicit your
services for that purpose.

I would be much obliged if you would take it in to Mr. Fields the first time
you go to Boston—show him this letter—If available at all, I propose it for
about the February number of the magazine. The price is $100, & 30 copies

of the number in which it may be printed—and I will ask Mr. Fields to do me the favor to send me an answer within a week from the time he receives the piece—or perhaps he can give his decision at once on receiving it.

With best respect & love,

Walt Whitman.

The piece appears in printed form because I have had it put in type for my own convenience, and to insure greater correctness—I forgot to say, above, that I scrupulously reserve the right to print this piece in future in my book—(which, however, will not be for several months.)

W. W.

M S: Dartmouth College

To Pete Doyle

Brooklyn, August 21, 1869

Dear Pete—

I have been very sick the last three days—I dont know what to call it—it makes me prostrated & deathly weak, & little use of my limbs. I have thought of you, my darling boy, very much of the time. I have not been out of the house since the first day after my arrival. I had a pleasant journey through on the cars Wednesday afternoon & night—felt quite well then. My Mother & folks are all well. We are in our new house—we occupy part & rent out part. I have a nice room, where I now sit writing this. It is the latter part of the afternoon. I feel better the last hour or so. It has been extremely hot here the last two days—I see it has been so in Washington too. I hope I shall get out soon. I hanker to get out doors, & down the bay.

And now, dear Pete, for yourself. How is it with you, dearest boy—and is there any thing different with the face?[32] Dear Pete, you must forgive me for being so cold the last day & evening. I was unspeakably shocked and re-pelled from you by that talk & proposition of yours—you know what—there by the fountain. It seemed indeed to me, (for I will talk out plain to you, dearest comrade,) that the one I loved, and who had always been so manly & sensible, was gone, & a fool & intentional murderer stood in his place. I spoke so sternly & cutting. (Though I see now that my words might have appeared to have a certain other meaning, which I didn't dream of, insulting to you, never for one moment in my thoughts.) But I will say no more of this—for I know such thoughts must have come when you was not yourself, but in a moment of derangement—& have passed away like a bad dream.

Dearest boy, I have not a doubt but you will get well, and entirely well—& we will one day look back on these drawbacks & sufferings as things long past. The extreme cases of that malady, (as I told you before) are persons that have very deeply diseased blood, probably with syphilis in it, inherited from parentage, & confirmed by themselves—so they have no foundation to build on. *You* are of healthy stock, with a sound constitution, & good blood—& I *know* it is impossible for it to continue long. My darling, if you are not well when I come back I will get a good room or two in some quiet place, (or out of Washington, perhaps in Baltimore,) and we will live together, & devote ourselves altogether to the job of curing you, & rooting the cursed thing out entirely, & making you stronger & healthier than ever. I have had this in my mind before, but never broached it to you. I could go on with my work in the Attorney General's office just the same—& we would see that your mother should have a small sum every week to keep the pot a-boiling at home.

Dear comrade, I think of you very often. My love for you is indestructible, & since that night & morning has returned more than before.

Dear Pete, dear son, my darling boy, my young & loving brother, don't let the devil put such thoughts in your mind again—wickedness unspeakable—murder, death & disgrace here, & hell's agonies hereafter—Then what would it be afterward to the mother? What to *me?*—

Pete, I send you some money, by Adam's Express—you use it, dearest son, & when it is gone, you shall have some more, for I have plenty. I will write again before long—give my love to Johnny Lee, my dear darling boy, I love him truly—(let him read these three last lines)—Dear Pete, *remember*—

Walt

M S: Feinberg Collection, Library of Congress

To Pete Doyle

Brooklyn, September 3, 1869

Dear Pete,

. . . Dear Pete, I hope every thing is going on favorably with you. I think about you every day & every night. I do hope you are in good spirits & health. I want to hear about the face. I suppose you are working on the road.

There is nothing new or special in my affairs or doings. The weather is pleasant here—it is pretty cool & dry. My folks all continue well—mother first rate, & brothers ditto. I do not have such good luck. I have felt unwell most every day—some days not so bad. Besides I have those spells again, worse, last longer, sick enough, come sudden, dizzy, & sudden sweat—It is hard to tell exactly what is the matter, or what to do. The doctor says it is all from that hospital malaria, hospital poison absorbed in the system years ago—he thinks it better for me in Washington than here.

About one third of the time I feel pretty well. I have taken three or four of my favorite rides on Broadway. I believe I described them to you in my letters a year ago. I find many of my old friends, & new ones too, & am received with the same warm friendship & love as ever. Broadway is more crowded & gay than ever, & the women look finer, & the shops richer— then there are many new & splendid buildings, of marble or iron—they seem to almost reach the clouds, they are so tall—some of them cost millions of dollars.

Staging in N. Y. has been very poor this summer—9 or $10, even on the big Broadway lines—Railroading has also been slim. New York is all cut up with railroads—Brooklyn also—I have seen Jimmy Foy—he was over to Brooklyn, looking for work on a road. He was well & hearty, & wished to be remembered to you. They pay $2½ on many of the roads here, & 2¼ on the rest. The work is pretty hard, but the hours not so long as in Washington.

There is all kinds of fun & sport here, by day & night—& lots of theatres & amusements in full blast. I have not been to any of them—have not been to see any of my particular women friends—though sent for, (the papers here have noticed my arrival)—have not been down to the sea-shore as I intended—In fact my jaunt this time has been a failure—Better luck next time—

Now Pete, dear, loving boy, I don't want you to worry about me—I shall come along all right. As it is, I have a good square appetite most of the time yet, good nights' sleep—& look about the same as usual, (which is, of course, lovely & fascinating beyond description.) Tell Johnny Lee I send him my love, & hope he is well & hearty. I think of him daily. I sent him a letter some time ago, which I suppose he rec'd about Aug. 26, & showed you[33]—but I have not had a word from him. Lend him this letter to read, as he will wish to hear about me.

God bless you, dear Pete, dear loving comrade, & Farewell till next time, my darling boy.

Walt.

M S: Feinberg Collection, Library of Congress

To Pete Doyle

Brooklyn, September 10, 1869

Dear Pete—dear son,

I have received your letter of the 8th to-day—all your letters have come safe—four altogether. This is the third I have sent you (besides that one by Adams' Express, Aug. 23d.)[34]

Pete, you say my sickness must be worse than I described in my letters—& ask me to write precisely how I am. No, dearest boy, I wrote just as it really was. But, Pete, you will now be truly happy to learn that I am feeling all right, & have been mainly so for the last four days—& have had no bad spells all that time. Yesterday I thought I felt as strong & well as ever in my life—in fact real young & jolly. I loafed around New York most all day—had a first-rate good time. All along Broadway hundreds of rich flags & streamers at half-mast for Gen. Rawlins'[35] funeral—From the tall buildings, they waved out in a stiff west wind all across Broadway—late in the afternoon I rode up from the Battery to look at them, as the sun struck through them—I thought I had never seen any thing so curious & beautiful—On all the shipping, ferry boats, public buildings &c. flags at half mast too. This is the style here. No black drapery, for mourning—only thousands of flags at half mast, on the water as well as land—for any big bug's funeral.

To-day I am all right too. It is now towards 3—Mother & I have just had our dinner, (my mammy's own cooking mostly.) I have been out all the forenoon knocking around—the water is my favorite recreation—I could spend two or three hours every day of my life here, & never get tired—Some of the pilots are dear personal friends of mine—some, when we meet, we kiss each other (I am an exception to all their customs with others)—some of their boys have grown up since I have known them, & they too know me & are very friendly.

Pete, the fourth week of my vacation is most ended. I shall return the middle of next week. . . .

I suppose you got "Kenilworth" I sent.

Well, boy, I shall now take a bath, dress myself & go out, cross the river, put this letter in the p. o. & then ramble & ride around the City, awhile, as I think we are going to have a fine evening & moonlight &c.

Good bye, dear son—We will soon be together again.

Walt.

M S: Feinberg Collection, Library of Congress

To William M. Rossetti

Washington, December 9, 1869

Dear Mr. Rossetti,

Your letter of last summer to William O'Connor with the passages transcribed from a lady's[36] correspondence have been shown me by him, and a copy lately furnished me, which I have just been re-reading. I am deeply touched by these sympathies & convictions coming from a woman, & from England, & am sure that if the lady knew how much comfort it has been to me to get them, she would not only pardon you for transmitting them to Mr. O'Connor, but approve that action. I realize indeed of such an emphatic & smiling *Well done* from the heart & conscience of a true wife & mother, & one too whose sense of the poetic, as I glean from your letter, after flowing through the heart & conscience, also comes through & must satisfy Science, as much as the esthetic, that I had hitherto received no eulogium so magnificent.

I send by same mail with this, same address as this letter, two photographs, taken within a few months. One is intended for the lady (if I may be permitted to send it her)—and will you please accept the other with my respects & love? The picture is by some criticized very severely indeed, but I hope you will not dislike it, for I confess myself to a (perhaps capricious) fondness for it as my own portrait over some scores that have been made or taken at one time or another.

I am still at work in the Attorney General's office. My p. o. address remains the same, here. I am, & have been, quite well & hearty. My new editions, considerably expanded, with what suggestions &c. I have to offer, presented, I hope, in more definite, graphic form, will probably get printed, the coming spring. I shall forward you early copies.

I send my love to Moncure Conway, if you see him. I wish he would write to me, soon & fully. If the pictures don't reach you, or if they get injured on the way, I will try again by express. I wish you to read or loan this letter to the lady—or, if she wishes it, give it to her to keep.

Walt Whitman

MS: University of Pennsylvania

To Charles Warren Stoddard

Washington, April 23, 1870

Dear Charles Stoddard,[37]

I received some days since your affectionate letter, & presently came your beautiful & soothing South Sea Idyll which I read at once.

Now, as I write, I sit by a large open window, looking south & west down the Potomac & across to the Virginia heights. It is a bright, warm spring-like afternoon. I have just re-read the sweet story all over, & find it indeed soothing & nourishing after its kind, like the atmosphere. As to you, I do not of course object to your emotional & adhesive nature, & the outlet thereof, but warmly approve them—but do you know (perhaps you do,) how the hard, pungent, gritty, worldly experiences & qualities in American practical life, also serve? how they prevent extravagant sentimentalism? & how they are not without their own great value & even joy?

It arises in my mind, as I write, to say something of that kind to you—

I am not a little comforted when I learn that the young men dwell in thought upon me & my utterances—as you do—& I frankly send you my love—& I hope we shall one day meet—

—I wish to hear from you always,

Walt Whitman

M S: Feinberg Collection, Library of Congress

To Pete Doyle

Brooklyn, July 30–August 2, 1870

Dear Pete,

Well here I am home again with my mother, writing to you from Brooklyn once more. We parted there, you know, at the corner of 7th st. Tuesday night. Pete, there was something in that hour from 10 to 11 oclock (parting though it was) that has left me pleasure & comfort for good—I never dreamed that you made so much of having me with you, nor that you could feel so downcast at losing me. I foolishly thought it was all on the other side. But all I will say further on the subject is, I now see clearly, that was all wrong.

I started from the depot in the 7:25 train the next morning—it was pretty warm, yet I had a very pleasant journey, & we got in New York by 5 o'clock, afternoon. About half an hour before we arrived, I noticed a very agreeable change in the weather—the heat had moderated—& in fact it has been pleasant enough every day since. I found mother & all as well as usual. It is now Saturday between 4 & 5 in the afternoon—I will write more on the other side—but, Pete, I must now hang up for the present, as there is a young lady down stairs whom I have promised to go with to the ferry, & across to the cars. . . .

Monday, Aug 1

The carrier brought quite a bunch this forenoon for the Whitman family, but no letter from you. I keep real busy with one thing & another, the whole day is occupied—I am feeling well quite all the time, & go out a great deal, knocking around one place & another. The evenings here are delightful and I am always out in them, sometimes on the river, sometimes in New York— There is a cool breeze & the moon shining. I think every time of you, & wish if we could only be together these evenings at any rate.

Tuesday—Aug 2.

Well, Pete, you will have quite a diary at this rate. Your letter came this morning—& I was glad enough to get word from you. I have been over to New York to-day on business—it is a pleasure even to cross the ferry—the river is splendid to-day—a stiff breeze blowing & the smell of the salt sea blowing up, (sweeter than any perfume to *my* nose)—It is now 2 o'clock—I have had my dinner & am sitting here alone writing this—Love to you, dear Pete—& I wont be so long again writing to my darling boy.

Walt.

M S: Feinberg Collection, Library of Congress

To Pete Doyle

Brooklyn, September 2, 1870

Dear Pete,

. . . there is nothing particular to write about this time—pretty much the same story—every day out on the bay awhile, or going down to Coney Island beach—and every day from two to four or five hours in the printing office—I still keep well & hearty, & the weather is fine—warm through the middle of the day, & cool mornings & nights—

I fall in with quite a good many of my acquaintances of years ago—the young fellows, (now not so young)—that I knew intimately here before the war—some are dead—& some have got married—& some have grown rich—one of the latter I was up with yesterday & last night—he has a big house on Fifth avenue[38]—I was there to dinner (dinner at 8 p.m.!)—every thing in the loudest sort of style, with wines, silver, nigger waiters, &c. &c. &c. But my friend is just one of the manliest, jovialest best sort of fellows— no airs—& just the one to suit you & me—no women in the house—he is single—he wants me to make my home there—I shall not do that, but shall go there very frequently—the dinners & good wines are attractive—then there is a fine library.

Well, Pete, I am on the second month of my furlough—to think it is al-most six weeks since we parted there that night—My dear loving boy, how much I want to see you—it seems a long while—I have rec'd a good letter from Mr. O'Connor, & also one from John Rowland who is in the office for me. Nothing new in office—Well, Pete, about half our separation is over— the next six weeks will soon pass away—indeed it may be only four, as John Rowland told me he might wish to go away—

Good bye for the present, my loving son, & give my respects to any of the boys that ask about me.

Walt

MS: Feinberg Collection, Library of Congress

To Pete Doyle

Brooklyn, September 6, 1870

Dear son,

. . . I keep pretty busy, writing, proof-reading, &c. I am at the printing office several hours every day—I feel in capital health & spirits—weigh sev-eral pounds heavier—but, as a small drawback, & something new for me, find myself needing glasses every time I read or write—this has grown upon me very rapidly since & during the hot weather, & especially since I left Washington—so I read & write as little as possible, beyond my printing matters, &c—as that occupies several hours, & tires my eyes sometimes.

We are having splendid fall weather, both days & nights. Last night I was out late—the scene on the river was heavenly—the sky clear, & the moon shining her brightest—I felt almost chilly at last with the cold—& so put for home. One of the prettiest sights now is to see the great German steamers, and other ships, as they lay tied up along shore, all covered with gay flags &

streamers—"dress ship" as they call it—flaunting out in the breeze, under a
brilliant sky & sun—all in honor, of course, of the victory of the German
armies[39]—all the spars & rigging are hid with hundreds & hundreds of
flags—a big red-white-& black flag capping all—

Of course you may know that the way the war turns out suits me to
death—Louis Napoleon fully deserves his fate—I consider him by far the
meanest scoundrel, (with all his smartness) that ever sat on a throne. I make
a distinction however—I admire & love the French, & France as a nation—
of all foreign nations, she has my sympathy first of all.

Pete, I was just reading over your last letter again. Dear son, you must try
to keep up a good heart. You say you do—but I am afraid you are feeling,
(or have felt,) somewhat unhappy. One soon falls into the habit of getting
low spirited or deprest & moody—if a man allows himself, he will always
find plenty to make him so—Every one has his troubles, disappointments,
rebuffs, &c. especially every young & proud-spirited man who has to work
for his living. But I want you to try & put a brave face against every thing
that happens—for it is not so much the little misfortunes of life themselves,
as the way we take them & brood over them, that causes the trouble.

About the "*tiresome*,"[40] all I have to say is—to say nothing—only a good
smacking kiss, & many of them—& taking in return many, many, many,
from my dear son—good loving ones too—which will do more credit to his
lips than growling & complaining at his father.

Walt

M S: Feinberg Collection, Library of Congress

To Pete Doyle

Brooklyn, July 14, 1871

Dear Pete,

It is pretty much the same with me, as when I wrote my former letters—
still home here with my mother, not busy at any thing particular but taking a
good deal of comfort—It has been very hot here, but one stands it better
here than in Washington, on account perhaps of the sea-air—I am still feeling well, & am out around every day.

There was quite a brush in N. Y. on Wednesday[41]—the Irish lower orders
(Catholic) had determined that the Orange parade (protestant) should be
put down—mob fired & threw stones—military fired on mob—bet. 30 and

40 killed, over a hundred wounded—but you have seen all about it in papers—it was all up in a distant part of the city, 3 miles from Wall street— five-sixths of the city went on with its business just the same as any other day—I saw a big squad of prisoners carried along under guard—they reminded me of the squads of rebel prisoners brought in Washington, six years ago—

The N. Y. police looked & behaved splendidly—no fuss, few words, but *action*—great, brown, bearded, able, American looking fellows, (Irish stock, though, many of them)—I had great pleasure in looking on them— something new, to me, it quite set me up to see such chaps, all dusty & worn, looked like veterans—

Pete, dear son, I rec'd your two letters, & was glad to get them—

Mother has been quite sick, & I have been sort of nurse, as she is here alone, none of my sisters being home at present—she is much better this morning, under my doctoring—

Pete, I see by your letters that every thing goes on right with you on the road—give my best regards to my friends among the drivers & conductors—Dear son, I shall now soon be coming back, & we will be together again, as my leave is up on the 22d [42]—I am now going to take a bath & dress myself to go over to New York. Love to you, my dearest boy, & good bye for this time—

Walt.

M S: Feinberg Collection, Library of Congress

To Pete Doyle

Coney Island, July 16 and 21, 1871

Dear Pete,

I will write you a few lines as I sit here, on a clump of sand by the sea shore—having some paper in my haversack, & an hour or two yet, before I start back. Pete, I wish you were with me the few hours past—I have just had a splendid swim & souse in the surf—the waves are slowly rolling in, with a hoarse roar that is music to my ears—the breeze blows pretty brisk from south-west, & the sun is partially clouded—from where I sit I look out on the bay & down the Narrows—vessels sailing in every direction in the distance—a great big black long ocean steamship streaking it up toward New York—& the lines of hills & mountains, far, far away, on the Jersey

Coast, a little veiled with blue vapor—here around me, as I sit, it is nothing but barren sand—but I don't know how long I could sit here, to that soothing, rumbling murmuring of the waves—& then the salt breeze—

Pete, if you are still working, and all is going on smooth, you can send me that $50—you might get Mr. Milburn to send it to me by post-office order—give it to him, with this envelope, & ask him to go to p. o. & send a p. o. order to me—it will save you the trouble—But Pete, dear boy, if any thing has turned up in mean time, you needn't send it, as I can get along otherwise—

I am doing very well, both in health & *business prospects* here—my book is doing first rate—so every thing is lovely & the goose hangs high—Your loving comrade & father

Walt.

Friday July 21.

Dear son, I wrote the preceding nearly a week ago, intending to finish & send it then—Nothing very new or special with me—Mother has been quite unwell, gets better, & then worse again—I have applied for a few days further leave—The weather here remains nearly perfect—we have had but three or four uncomfortably hot days the past five weeks—every day a fine breeze smelling of the sea—

M S: Feinberg Collection, Library of Congress

To Anne Gilchrist

Washington, November 3, 1871

Dear friend,

I have been waiting quite a long while for time & the right mood to answer your letter[43] in a spirit as serious as its own, & in the same unmitigated trust & affection. But more daily work than ever has fallen upon me to do the current season, & though I am well & contented, my best moods seem to shun me. I wished to give to it a day, a sort of Sabbath or holy day apart to itself, under serene & propitious influences—confident that I could then write you a letter which would do you good, & me too. But I must at least show, without further delay, that I am not insensible to your love. I too send you my love. And do you feel no disappointment because I now write but briefly. My book is my best letter, my response, my truest explanation of all. In it I have put my body & spirit. You understand this better & fuller &

clearer than any one else. And I too fully & clearly understand the loving & womanly letter it has evoked. Enough that there surely exists between us so beautiful & delicate a relation, accepted by both of us with joy.

Walt Whitman

M S: University of Pennsylvania

To Edward Dowden

Washington, January 18, 1872

Dear Mr Dowden,

I must no longer delay writing, & to acknowledge your letters of Sept 5 and Oct 15 last. . . . All—letters & Review—have been read & reread. I am sure I appreciate you in them. May I say you do not seem to stand afar off, but very near to me. What John Burroughs [44] brings adds confirmation. I was deeply interested in the acc'ts given in the letters of your friends. I do not hesitate to call them mine too. . . . I wish each to be told my remembrance (or to see this letter if convenient).

I like well the positions & ideas in your Westminster article—and radiating from the central point of assumption of my pieces being, or commencing "the poetry of Democracy." It presents all the considerations which such a critical text & starting point require, in a full, eloquent, & convincing manner. I entirely accept it, all & several, & am not unaware that it probably afforded, if not the only, at least the most likely gate, by which you as an earnest friend of my book, & believing critic of it, would gain entrance to a leading review—Besides, I think the main theme you exploit is really of the first importance—and all the rest can be broached & led to, through it, as well as any other way.

I would say that (as you of course see) the spine or verteber principle of my book is a model or ideal (for the service of the New World, & to be gradually absorbed in it) of a complete healthy, heroic, practical modern *Man*—emotional, moral, spiritual, patriotic—a grander better son, brother, husband, father, friend, citizen than any yet—formed & shaped in consonance with modern science, with American Democracy, & with the requirements of current industrial & professional life—model of a Woman also, equally modern & heroic—a better daughter, wife, mother, citizen also, than any yet. I seek to typify a living Human Personality, immensely animal, with immense passions, immense amativeness, immense adhesiveness—in the woman immense maternity—& then, in both, immenser far a *moral con-*

science, & in always realizing the direct & indirect control of the divine laws through all and over all forever.

In "Democratic Vistas" I seek to make patent the appalling vacuum, in our times & here, of any school of great imaginative Literature & Art, fit for a Republican, Religious, & Healthy people—and to suggest & prophesy such a Literature as the only vital means of sustaining & perpetuating such a people. I would project at least the rough sketch of such a school of Literatures—an entirely new breed of authors, poets, American, comprehensive, Hegelian, Democratic, religious—& with an infinitely larger scope & method than any yet—

There is one point touched by you in the Westminster criticism that if occasion again arises, might be dwelt on more fully—that is the attitude of sneering denial which magazines, editors, publishers, "critics" &c. in the U. S. hold toward "Leaves of Grass." As to "Democratic Vistas" it remains entirely unread, uncalled for here in America. If you write again for publication about my books, or have opportunity to influence any forthcoming article on them, I think it would be a proper & even essential part of such article to include the fact that the books are hardly recognized at all by the orthodox literary & conventional authorities of the U. S.—that the opposition is bitter, & in a large majority, & that the author was actually turned out of a small government employment & deprived of his means of support by a Head of Department at Washington solely on account of having written his poems.

True I take the whole matter coolly. I know my book has been composed in a cheerful & contented spirit—& that the same still substantially remains with me. (And I want my friends, indeed, when writing for publication about my poetry, to present its gay-heartedness as one of its chief qualities.)

I am in excellent health, & again & still work as clerk here in Washington.

I saw John Burroughs very lately. He is well. He showed me a letter he had just rec'd from you.

I wish more & more (and especially now that I realize I know you, & we should be no strangers) to journey over sea, & visit England & your country.

Tennyson has written to me twice—& very cordial & hearty letters. He invites me to become his guest. . . .

Emerson has just been this way (Baltimore & Washington) lecturing. He maintains the same attitude—draws on the same themes—as twenty-five years ago. It all seems to me quite attenuated (the *first* drawing of a good pot of tea, you know, and Emerson's was the heavenly herb itself—but what must one say to a *second*, and even *third* or *fourth* infusion?) I send you a newspaper report of his lecture here a night or two ago. It is a fair sample.[45]

And now, my dear friend, I must close. I have long wished to write you a letter to show, if nothing more, that I heartily realize your kindness & sympathy, & would draw the communion closer between us. I shall probably send you any thing I publish, and any thing about my affairs or self that might interest you. You too must write freely to me—& I hope frequently—
Walt Whitman

TEXT: Dowden's transcription, Berg Collection, New York Public Library

To John Addington Symonds

Washington, January 27, 1872

J. A. Symonds,[46]

Not knowing whether it will reach you, I will however write a line to acknowledge the receipt of your beautiful & elevated "Love & Death," and of the friendly letter from you, of October 7th last. I have read & re-read the poem, & consider it of the loftiest, strongest & tenderest. Your letter was most welcome to me. I should like to know you better, & I wish you to send me word should this reach you—if the address is the right one. I wish to forward you a copy of my book—as I shall presently bring out a new edition.

I am, as usual, in good health, and continue to work here in Washington in a government office, finding it not unpleasant—finding, in it, indeed sufficient and free margin.

Pray dont think hard of me for not writing more promptly. I have thought of you more than once, & am deeply touched with your poem.

DRAFT LETTER: Feinberg Collection, Library of Congress

To William M. Rossetti

Washington, January 30, 1872

My dear Mr. Rossetti,

I send you my newest piece,[47] (in a magazine lately started away off in Kansas, fifteen or eighteen hundred miles inland)—And also improve the occasion to write you a too-long-delayed letter. Your letters of July 9 last, & Oct. 8, were welcomed—since which last nothing from you has reached me.

John Burroughs returned with glowing accounts of England, & heartiest satisfaction from his visits to you, & talks, &c. I saw him day before yesterday. He is well & flourishing.

I still remain here as clerk in a government department—find it not unpleasant—find it allows quite a free margin—working hours from 9 to 3—work at present easy—my pay $1600 a year (paper)—

Washington is a broad, magnificent place in its natural features—avenues, spaces, vistas, environing hills, rivers, &c. all so ample, plenteous—& then, as you go on, fine, hard wide roads, (made by military engineers, in the war) leading far away down dale & over hill, many & many a mile—Often of full-moonlight nights I have a habit of going on long jaunts with some companion six, eight miles away into Virginia or Maryland over these roads. It is wonderfully inspiriting, with such new presentations. We have spells here, night or day, of the finest weather & atmosphere in the world. The nights especially are at times miracles of clearness & purity—the air dry, exhilarating. In fact, night or day, this whole District affords an inexhaustible mine of explorations, walks—soothing, sane, open air hours. To these mostly my habits are adjusted. I have good sturdy health—am fortunate enough to almost always get out of bed in the morning with a light heart & a good appetite—I read or study very little—spend two or three hours every day on the streets, or in frequented public places—come sufficiently in contact with all sorts of people—go not at all in "society" so-called—have however the blessing of some first-rate women friends—My life, upon the whole, toned down, flowing calm enough, democratic, on a cheap scale, popular, suitable, occupied sufficiently, enjoying a good deal—flecked, of course, with some clouds & shadows. I still keep in good flesh & weight. The photos I sent you last fall are faithful physiognomical likenesses. (I still have yours, *carte*, among a little special cluster before me on my desk door.)

My poetry remains yet, in substance, quite unrecognized here in the land for which it was written. The best established magazines & literary authorities (eminencies) quite ignore me & it. It has to this day failed to find an American publisher (as you perhaps know, I have myself printed the successive editions).[48] And though there is a small minority of approval & discipleship, the great majority result continues to bring sneers, contempt & official coolness. My dismissal from moderate employment in 1865 by the Secretary of the Interior, Mr. Harlan, avowedly for the sole reason of my being the author of *Leaves of Grass*, still affords an indication of the high conventional feeling. The journals are often inveterately spiteful. For example, in a letter in the correspondence of a leading New York paper (*Tribune*) from a lady tourist,[49] an authoress of repute, an allusion in the letter to mountain scenery was illustrated by an innocent quotation from, & passing complimentary allusion to me. The letter was all & conspicuously published, except that the editors carefully cut out the lines quoting from & alluding to me, mutilating the text & stultifying the authoress to her great vexation. This to give you a clearer notion—(and I distinctly wish my friends in England writing about my book for print, to describe this state of things here.)

Of general matters here, I will only say that the country seems to have entirely recuperated from the war. Except in a part of the Southern States, every thing is teeming & busy—more so than ever. Productiveness, wealth, population, improvements, material activity, success, results—beyond all measure, all precedent—& then spreading over such an area—three to four millions square miles—Great debits & offsets, of course—but how grand this oceanic plenitude & ceaselessness of domestic comfort—universal supplies of eating & drinking, houses to live in, farms to till, copious traveling, migratory habits, plenty of money, extravagance even—true there is something meteoric about it, and yet from an overarching view it is Kosmic & real enough—It gives glow & enjoyment to me, being & moving amid the whirl & din, intensity, material success here—as I am myself sufficiently sluggish & ballasted to stand it—though the best is with reference to its foundation for & bearing on the future—(as you doubtless see in my book[50] how this thought prevails with me.)

But I will turn to more special, personal topics.

Prof. Dowden's Westminster Review article last fall made us all feel pleased & proud. He and I have since had some correspondence, & I have come to consider him (like yourself) fully as near to me in personal as literary relations. I have just written to him at some length.

I have received word direct from Mrs. Gilchrist. Nothing in my life, nor result of my book, has brought me more comfort & support every way—nothing has more spiritually soothed me—than the warm appreciation & friendship of that true, full-grown woman—(for I still use the old Saxon word, for highest need.) . . .

I received some time since a most frank & kind letter, and brief printed poem, from John Addington Symonds, of Bristol, England. The poem *Love and Death* I read & re-read with admiration. I have just written to Mr. Symonds.

I received Roden Noel's "Study" in *Dark Blue*[51] for Oct. & Nov. last, & appreciate it—& also a letter from himself. I have sent him a copy of my last edition, & intend to write to him.

I proposed by letter to Mr. Ellis, (Ellis & Green) of London to publish my poems complete, verbatim. Mr. Ellis has written me a good friendly letter, but declined the proposition.

I shall be happy to receive a copy of your *Selections from American Poets,*[52] when ready—& always, always, glad, my friend, to hear from you—hope, indeed, you will not punish me for my own delay—but write me fully & freely.

Walt Whitman

MS: Lion Collection, New York Public Library

To Anne Gilchrist

Brooklyn, March 20, 1872

My dear friend,

Your letter is rec'd, having been sent on to me from Washington. My address still remains Solicitor's office, Treasury there. I am moving about a good deal the past year, & shall be for the ensuing year—I am to start for northern New England, & remain awhile—am also arranging for a trip afterward to California—a journey I have had in contemplation for several years, & which has been two or three times fixed, but postponed, during that time.

I have been stopping for two months, (Feb. & March,) home with my Mother, & am writing this home. Mother is towards eighty—has had an active domestic & maternal life—has had eight children—has brought them all up—has been healthy & strong, always worked hard—now shows the infirmities of age (indeed rapidly advancing) but looks finely, & is cheerful hearted—will probably soon give up her housekeeping & go to live with one of my brothers, who is married[53]—My father died seventeen years since.

Dear friend, I am quite sure that *every one* of your letters has safely reached me—sometimes after delays & circuits, (as you will now understand better) on account of my more & more frequent wanderings[54]—The letter with the photographs gave me great pleasure—& was acknowledged by a letter I sent you—Have you not received it?

Walt Whitman

Dear friend, let me warn you somewhat about myself—& yourself also. You must not construct such an unauthorized & imaginary ideal Figure, & call it W. W. and so devotedly invest your loving nature in it. The actual W. W. is a very plain personage, & entirely unworthy such devotion.[55]

M S: University of Pennsylvania

To Alfred Tennyson

Washington, April 27, 1872

My Dear Mr. Tennyson:

This morning's paper has a vague sort of an item about your coming to America, or wanting to come, to view the working of our institutions, etc. Is there anything in it? I hope so, for I want more and more to meet you and be with you. Then I should like to give my explanations and comments of America and her shows, affairs, persons, doings, off-hand, as you witness them, and become puzzled, perhaps, dismayed by them. America is at present a vast seething mass of varied material human and other, of the richest, best, worst, and plentiest kind. Wealthy inventive, no limit to food, land, money, work, opportunity, smart and industrious citizens, but (though real and permanently politically organized by birth and acceptance) without fusion or definite heroic identity in form and purpose or organization, which can only come by native schools of great ideas—religion, poets, literature— and will surely come, even through the measureless crudity of the States in those fields so far, and to-day.

The lesson of [Henry Thomas] Buckle's books[56] on civilization always seemed to me to be that the preceding main basis and continual *sine qua non* of civilization is the eligibility to, and certainty of boundless products for feeding, clothing, and sheltering everybody, infinite comfort, personal and intercommunication and plenty, with mental and ecclesiastical freedom, and that then all the rest, moral and esthetic, will take care of itself. Well, the United States have secured the requisite bases, and must now proceed to build upon them.

I send you by same mail with this, a more neatly printed copy of my "Leaves"; also "Dem. Vistas."

Your letter of last fall reached me at the time. Have you forgotten that you put a promise in it, to send me your picture when "you could lay hands on a good one?"

I have been in Brooklyn and New York most of the past winter and current spring, visiting my aged dear mother, near eighty. Am now back here at work. Am well and hearty. I have received two letters from you, July 12 and September 22, of last year. This is the second letter I have written to you. My address is: Solicitor's Office, Treasury, Washington, D. C., United States. Write soon, my friend. Don't forget the picture.

Walt Whitman.

TEXT: Thomas Donaldson, *Walt Whitman the Man* (New York: Harper, 1896), 224–26

To Charles W. Eldridge

New York, July 19, 1872

Dear friend,

I rec'd your letter yesterday, and was particularly pleased to get it, bringing late intelligence about you all. It was a good letter. What you say about William [O'Connor], fagged with work & I suppose the weather—& Nelly, half-sick, & Jeannie about the same (but she will soon spring up)—aroused my sympathies—Mother & I talked about them all—I send love to all. Nelly, I shall return next week, & then I shall surely come to the house, & see you & all.

Charley, I went leisurely up the Connecticut valley, by way of Springfield, through the best part (agriculturally, & other) of Massachusetts, Connecticut & New Hampshire, June 24th & 25th by day light—26th & 27th at Hanover, N. H.—28th & 29th slowly up the White River valley, a captivating wild region, by Vermont Central R. R. & so to Burlington, & about Lake Champlain where I spent a week, filling myself every day, (especially morning & sunsets) with the grandest ensembles of the Adirondacks always on one side, and the Green Mountains on the other—sailed after that down Champlain by day—stopt at Albany over night, & down the Hudson by boat, 4th of July, through a succession of splendid & magnificent thunderstorms (10 or 12 of them) alternated by spells of clearest sunlight—Then home some five or six days—immediately following I was ill, real ill—I suppose the excessive heat, &c &c—but am now feeling all right.

Upon the whole, I have stood the unprecedented heat pretty well. Mother is not very well—has spells of weakness—has rheumatism—then good days again—will break up from Brooklyn in September, & go with George, at Camden—as they are vehement for it.

My sister Martha at St. Louis is better far than one would expect, after the alarm of two months ago[57]—she has since no trouble with the cancer, (or supposed cancer)—Jeff & the children well—My sister Hannah, (Mrs Heyde,) in Burlington, I found better than I had anticipated—*every thing much better*[58]—

Charley, who do you think I have been spending some three hours with to-day, from 12 to 3—(it is now 4½)—*Joaquin Miller*[59]—He saw me yesterday toward dusk at 5th av. on a stage, & rushed out of the house, & mounting the stage gave me his address, & made an appointment—he lives here 34th st. in furnished rooms—I am much pleased, (upon the whole) with him—*really pleased & satisfied—his presence, conversation, atmosphere*, are infinitely more satisfying than his poetry—he is, however, mopish, ennuyeed, a *California Hamlet*, unhappy every where—but a natural prince, may-be an illiterate one—but tender, sweet, & magnetic—Love to you, dear Charley, & to all—I will soon be with you again—

Walt

MS: Philo Calhoon

To his mother

Washington, January 26, 1873

Dearest mother,

I have been not well for two or three days, but am better to-day. I have had a slight stroke of paralysis, on my left side, and especially the leg—occurred Thursday night last, & I have been laid up since—I am writing this in my room 535 15th st, as I am not able to get out at present—but the doctor gives me good hopes of being out and at my work in a few days—He says it is nothing but what I shall recover from in a few days—Mother, you must not feel uneasy—though I know you will—but I thought I would write & tell you the *exact truth—neither better nor worse—*

I have a first rate physician, Dr. Drinkard—I have some very attentive friends, (& if I have occasion can & will telegraph to you or George—but do not expect to have any need)—

I have had no word from St Louis or any where by letter for some days—The weather here is mostly stormy & cold the last week—I rec'd your last letter with Jeff's—it is ½ past one—Lizzie the servant girl has just brought me up some dinner, oyster stew, toast, tea, &c, very good—I have eaten little for two days, but am to-day eating better—I wrote to Mat early last week—

Later—I have been sitting up eating my dinner—
Love to you, dearest mother, & to George & Lou—

Walt

I will write again middle of the week—
M S: Yale University

To his mother

Washington, January 29, 1873

Dearest mother,

I am writing this lying in bed—the doctor wishes me to keep as much in bed as possible—but I *have* to keep in, as I cannot move yet without great difficulty, & I am liable to dizziness & nausea, at times, on trying to move, or even sitting up—But I am certainly over the worst of it, & *really*—though slowly—*improving*. The doctor says there is no doubt of it—

Yesterday afternoon I eat something like a meal for the first time—boiled chicken, & some soup with bread broken up in it—relished it well—I still have many callers—only a few particular ones are admitted to see me—Mrs. O'Connor comes & a young woman named Mary Cole—Mrs. Ashton[60] has sent for me to be brought to her house, to be taken care of—of course I do not accept her offer—they live in grand style & I should be more bothered than benefitted by their refinements & luxuries, servants, &c—

Mother, I want you to know truly, that I do not want for any thing—as to all the *little extra fixings* & superfluities, I never did care for them in health, & they only annoy me in sickness—I have a good bed—a fire—as much grub as I wish & whatever I wish—& two or three good friends here—So I want you to not feel at all uneasy—as I write, Peter Doyle is sitting by the window reading—he & Charles Eldridge regularly come in & do whatever I want, & are both *very helpful* to me—one comes day time, & one evening—I had a good night's sleep last night—My mind is just as clear as ever—& has been all the time—(I have not been at all down hearted either)—(My January pay is due me, & as soon as I get up, I shall forward you your $20.)[61]

Dear sister Lou,[62]

Your letter came this morning & was very pleasant to get it—I shall be getting well soon—am on a fair way to it now—

latest ½ past 4

I have just set up & had my bed made by Pete—I am already beginning to feel something like myself—will write in 2 days—

M s: Yale University

To his mother

Washington, February 23, 1873

Well, mother dear, here I sit again in the rocking chair by the stove—I have just eat some dinner, a little piece of fowl & some toast & tea—my appetite is good enough—& I have plenty brought to me—I have been sitting up all day—have some bad spells, but am decidedly gaining upon the whole—think I have fully recovered where I was a week ago, and even a little better—went down stairs yesterday and out for five minutes into the street—& shall do so again this afternoon—as I think it did me good yesterday—though I was very tired, on returning—as I have to go down & up 4 flights of stairs—The doctor comes every day—(I must tell you again I have a first-rate doctor—I think he understands my case exactly—I consider myself very lucky in having him)—

Mother, yesterday was a very serious day with me here—I was not so very sick, but I kept thinking all the time it was the day of Matty's funeral—Every few minutes all day it would come up in my mind—I suppose it was the same with you—Mother, your letter came Friday afternoon—it was a very good letter, & after reading it twice, I enclosed it in one to Han—she must have got it Saturday night—

There are great preparations here for 4th of March—inauguration—if you & I had a house here,[63] we would have George & Lou come on & see the show, for I have no doubt it will be the finest ever seen here—(but I am in hopes to be able to get away for all that)—

½ past 4.

Mother, I have just been down & out doors—walked half a block—& have come back—*went all alone*—(got a little assistance at the steps)—this is the most successful raid yet—& I really begin to feel something like myself—

Hope this will find you all right, dearest Mother—

Walt.

M s: Lion Collection, New York Public Library

To his mother

Washington, March 28, 1873

Dearest mother,

The sun shines out bright & cheerful this morning—& in my east window I have a fine healthy rose-bush—I see it has got two roses, in bloom, & one just budding out—(it was a present from Mrs. Channing[64] of Providence—she sent on here, and had it got for me, when I was first sick)—I think I am feeling better to-day, & more like myself—I have been in the habit of soaking my feet in hot water every night for two months now—& I think lately it has done me more harm than good—one thing is, it has probably made me catch a slight cold—so I have stopt it, & I have a notion I feel better from stopping it—I have just had my breakfast, & am sitting here alone by the stove, writing this—Charles Eldridge will be here in a few minutes, & bring the morning papers—he comes & sits a few minutes every morning before going to work—he has been very good indeed—he & Peter Doyle hold out through every thing—most of the rest have got tired & stopt coming—(which is just as well)—Mrs. O'Connor comes whenever she can, & generally brings a dish of roast apples, or something—

I go over to the office about 12 or 1 most every day—but only for a few minutes—have not resumed work there yet, but hope to, Monday—I find there a great deal of paralysis around, and they say I have got along very well—but it is so slow, so aggravating, to be disabled, so feeble, cannot walk nor do any thing, when one's mind & will are just as clear as ever—Still *I feel* I shall get as well as usual yet, dearest mother—& then I shall *surely* get here or buy or build a little place here, rooms enough to live in for you & Ed and me—I realize it more, far more now, than ever—even for my own comfort—this spring is better to buy here than usual—I think we could get along *very well* indeed—you could visit George & Lou as often as you liked (& George & Lou could come & pay us a visit in winter when Congress is in full blast)—

I miss John & Mrs. Burroughs—they are at a place called Waukill, N. Y. state—they have hired out their house furnished, 6 mo's, $50 a month. I have not heard any thing further from Jeff—I hope to come on soon & pay you all a visit, but wait to see how things go in the office—& how I feel—(as I have been absent now nine weeks)—Every thing looks pleasant here to-day—quite spring like—Mother dear, I hope this will find you feeling well, & in good spirits, as that is the main thing. Mother, as I cannot get down to the p. o. I send the money once more enclosed—write me Sunday, if convenient—Chas. Eldridge has been in—it is now later, towards 12—I have washed & put on some clean clothes, & am going over to the office—

Walt.

M S: Ohio Wesleyan

To his mother

Washington, April 19, 1873

It is now about noon, & I have just come over to the office, and have put up the window for a few moments, to stand & get the fresh air, & then put it down again. Right opposite the window—in the President's grounds a man in his shirt-sleeves is raking up the grass that has been already cut on a ¾ acre patch—so you can see spring has advanced here—the trees are quite green—

Mother, I have had the second application of electricity to-day, quite a good application by Dr. Drinkard—he rubs the handles over my leg & thigh, for perhaps twenty minutes—the shock is very perceptible—it is not painful at all, feels something like pressing a sore—I feel as I said before, that it will be beneficial to me, (though there are different opinions about it)—I feel better to-day than yesterday—I think, mother dear, there is no doubt at all that I progress surely though very slowly, (& with an occasional bad spell)—

Did you read in the morning papers to-day about the fight with the Modocs out in California—& Col. Mason—I think (but am not sure) it is Jule Mason[65]—it is quite interesting—I am going to work for a couple of hours now at my work in the office books—I am feeling quite comfortable this afternoon.

TEXT: *In Re Walt Whitman* (1893), 88–89

1873-1881

Harry Stafford, whose family had a farm in New Jersey, met the poet when he was
recovering from the effects of his stroke of 1873 and the death of his mother
in the same year. Theirs was a tempestuous relationship as Whitman shared Harry's
growing pains and troubled search for identity. The ring on Harry's right hand
may be the one Whitman gave him. Late 1870s.
Edward Carpenter Collection, Sheffield Library

WHITMAN'S RECOVERY WAS FRUSTRATINGLY SLOW, AND then only partial. "My left arm never fully recovered from the shock of 1873, though it has always been a useful remnant," he observed years later. "My left leg was never itself again—was not restored—never reawakened."[1] He characterized the first years in Camden as "the worst, darkest, doubtfullest, period of my life, all told."[2]

He was "down in the dumps," he said on another occasion, before he got "a bit more spruce again."[3] "I don't know a soul here," he wrote to Pete Doyle a few months after he settled in Camden, "am entirely alone— sometimes sit alone & think, for two hours on a stretch—have not formed a single acquaintance here, any ways intimate . . . (then, for a fellow of my size, the *friendly presence & magnetism needed*, somehow, is not here—I do not run foul of any)." Soon he managed to limp to the docks nearby and began to board the ferries to Philadelphia, sometimes making three or four crossings during the day, as he had years earlier when he lived in Brooklyn and crossed by ferry to New York. He became acquainted with railroad men in two cities—as always he sought out men of the working class—but he found no successor to Pete Doyle. In his letters "lonesome" resounded as a motif such as one hears in the reveries of Huck Finn or Holden Caulfield. A year later he still had "no near friends, (in the deepest sense) here at hand."

His mourning for his mother was to be long and painful. "It is the great cloud of my life," he informed Pete, "nothing that ever happened before has had such an effect on me." He slept in the room in which she had died and for years lay on her pillow. On the first anniversary of her death he spoke of "a sorrow from which I have never entirely recovered, & likely never shall."

In July 1874 he was dismissed from his government post, even though he had sent a note to President Grant asking him to intervene. Given his physical condition, the absence of friends, and now the loss of income, he had little choice but to settle in Camden. He asked Doyle to send on the rest of his possessions and hoped "that we can yet be with each other, at least from time to time—& meanwhile we must adapt ourselves to circumstances." Such adaptations Whitman had begun to learn when he was eleven. The Doyle relationship was over, amicably, it would appear. The two men met infrequently in subsequent years, but as we shall see, another comrade was to appear, and the same story was to unfold, for the last time.

With the loss of his government salary Whitman's financial situation changed dramatically. As long as he was on the payroll he received $1600 and paid a substitute $600 annually and his sister-in-law $30 monthly for room and board. At the end of 1874, even with the expenditure of $450 for a lot on which he planned to build "a little two or three room house for my-self," he had $1116.80 in the bank. In 1875 he deposited $129.14 and with-drew $645.00, and at the end of the year the balance was $600.94. He now paid George and Louisa only $15 or $16 a month for room and board.[4]

Whitman began to submit poems and prose pieces to magazines and newspapers and to prepare a two-volume edition of his writings, consisting of the sixth edition of *Leaves of Grass* and a miscellany entitled *Two Rivulets*, which was to be issued during the 1876 centenary celebration. Always aware of the uses of publicity, he—anonymously, of course—began to inform the American people of his plight. His "needy circumstances" were referred to in an article in the *New York Sun* in November 1875, and the *New York Herald* on January 2, 1876, commented: "He is poor in purse, but not in actual want." An article in the *West Jersey Press* on January 26, titled "Walt Whitman's Actual American Position," alleged that "the determined denial, disgust and scorn of orthodox American authors, publishers and editors, and in a pecuniary and worldly sense, have certainly wrecked the life of their author. . . . No established house will yet print his books."[5]

As Clifton Joseph Furness demonstrated years ago in *Walt Whitman's Workshop*, Whitman wrote that article and sent it to Rossetti, who printed excerpts in *The Athenaeum* in March, with the inclusion of two sentences from Whitman's letter: "My theory is that *the plain truth* of the situation here is best stated. It is even worse *than* described in the article."[6] Whitman overstated.

Rossetti and others in England launched an ambitious campaign on Whitman's behalf, and there was a similar subscription in the United States. Contributors received copies of Whitman's new volumes, for which they paid $10 and sometimes more. In 1876 Whitman received at least $1081 in book orders from England and at least $457 from Americans. Although Whitman delighted in the pose of the loafer—the fifth line of "Song of My-self" reads, "I lean and loafe at my ease . . . observing a spear of summer grass"—he had learned early to be a practical man of business. To the end of his life, he ran from his home what turned out to be a profitable business, and more important, he retained complete control over the publication of his writings.

The daybooks which Whitman began to keep in 1876 confirm his vigor-ous activity as distributor of his books but also record an active reentry into society. The lists of youths, tradespeople, and railroad employees are longer. He also attached himself to newspaper men in Camden and Philadelphia; few knew better than Whitman how to use the press for his own ends.

In 1876 Anne Gilchrist came to Philadelphia with three of her children. Although Whitman had forbidden the trip, her genuine passion was not to be checked by a male's fears: she trusted that her physical presence would achieve the consummation her body and soul longed for. Her erotic fantasy of the poet, based upon the erotic fantasy of his poetry, shortly gave way to the painful recognition that the man could fulfill neither her fantasy nor his own. Her disappointment she never revealed, not even to her children, and after she returned to England in 1879 she continued to write and occasionally to confess her feelings for the bachelor bard of love. In the months before her death in 1885 she composed a second defense of the American poet, and as she was dying she instructed her son to notify Walt. She was faithful to the last.

The important event in 1876 was not Whitman's resumption of publication, the appearance of Mrs. Gilchrist, or even the slight improvement in his physical condition. He became part of the Stafford family, who lived on a farm in Kirkwood, New Jersey. Nearby was a creek with a swimming hole, where Whitman could bathe and loaf, alone or with members of the family. It was a lovely setting reminiscent of the childhood environment which he evokes in poems like "There Was a Child Went Forth" and "Out of the Cradle Endlessly Rocking." The child left home but in search of another home among people who resembled his parents and his brothers and sisters.

Among the Staffords he found an almost exact duplication of his early life. The father, George, was hard-working but not very prosperous. Family life centered around the mother. Of Susan Stafford, Whitman wrote, "There is not a nobler woman in Jersey." There were seven living children, five boys and two girls, a situation that paralleled closely the six boys and two girls of the Whitman family. Like his own brothers and sisters, the Stafford children did not have time to be educated, and they had to pitch in and help with the chores to keep the family going.

Apparently Whitman met Harry Stafford early in 1876 while the boy was employed in the printing office of the *Camden New Republic*. He was eighteen, uncertain of his goals, emotionally troubled as he was crossing the bridge from childhood into manhood, subject to the blues. Again we perceive a pattern. For Harry was the counterpart of the soldiers Whitman had met in the Washington hospitals, of Peter Doyle, and probably of many others in the early years who have escaped literary detection.

Harry came eagerly for guidance to a fatherly figure, and Whitman attempted to teach him penmanship and to obtain jobs for him. But the poet was not able to play the paternal role consistently: like a brother or a buddy he indulged in roughhousing with the youth. Burroughs in 1877 complained in his diary after Harry and Whitman had visited him, "They cut up like two boys and annoyed me sometimes."[7] On November 24, 1878, after a visit to Camden, Harry wrote about his team of horses, "They wanted to troot all the way home, they felt good I guess . . . so they wanted to show off, you know how it is you'r self when you feel like *licking* me; but I held them down as I do you, when you feel that way."[8]

Whitman generally referred to their relationship guardedly and some-times deceitfully. In accepting an invitation to visit John H. Johnston, a New York jeweler, he informed his host that he was to be accompanied by "my (adopted) son" in one letter and, in another six days later, "My nephew & I when traveling always share the same room together & the same bed." Just before Christmas Whitman sent Johnston a check for $35 for a gold watch, "a Christmas present for a young man." In a letter on February 22, 1878, he mentioned Harry cryptically through concealed initials,[9] much as years ear-lier he alluded to Pete Doyle in a diary jotting through the use of numbers. The indirection that Whitman spoke of as characteristic of the new Ameri-can poetry is paralleled by the secretiveness with which he, of painful ne-cessity apparently, camouflaged troubled emotions. Fearfully he trod un-trodden paths.

Although the bard and the boy could caper like children, relations were not always smooth. On May 1, 1877, Harry wrote, "Can you forgive me and take me back and love me the same. I will try by the grace of God to do better. I cannot give you up." He signed the letter "Your lovin but bad tem-pered Harry."

Continually Harry repented and promised to "do my best to-ward you in the future. You are all the true friend I have, and when I cannot have you I will go away some ware, I don't know where." Whitman forgave and re-created the same erotic ambience. "Dear son, how I wish you could come in now, even if but for an hour & take off your coat, & sit down on my lap." Harry boasted of defeating a friend in a wrestling match and thought of beating up his employer. For, he explained, "when I am not thinking of my business I am thinking of what I am shielding, I want to try and make a man of myself, and do what is right, if I can do it."

On another occasion Harry pleaded, "I wish you would put the ring on my finger again, it seems to me ther is something that is wanting to com-pleete our friendship when I am with you. . . . You know when you put it on there was but one thing to put it from me and that was death."[10]

Slowly the relationship changed. "Times have become settled," Harry wrote, not quite accurately, "and our love sure (although we have had very many rough times to-gather) but we have stuck too each other so far and we will until we die, I know." But life rarely conforms to clichés. Whitman's health was so improved that he began to travel about, to give lectures on Abraham Lincoln in Boston and elsewhere, to undertake extensive trips to the West and later to Canada, where he visited Dr. Richard Maurice Bucke, the Canadian neurologist and mystic.

With renewed vigor he gathered his prose jottings for a miscellany which he called *Specimen Days*, a kind of autobiography. He wrote less frequently and more quietly to Harry, and sent long gossipy letters to Harry's mother, Susan, as well as to other members of the family. In a letter to Harry on February 28, 1881, he said that he owed his life to the Staffords, "*& you, my darling boy, are the central figure of them all.*" The letter, however, was signed "Your loving ever-faithful old friend & comrade." Whitman was now sixty-two. Harry was to marry Eva Westcott on June 25, 1884. There were three children, two girls and a boy who was named after his grandfather, not Walt Whitman.

To Pete Doyle

Camden, June 18–20, 1873

Dear Pete,

It has been a good move of me coming here, as I am pleasantly situated, have two rooms on 2d floor, with north & south windows, so I can have the breeze through—I can have what I wish in the grub line—have plenty of good strawberries—& my brother & sister are very kind—It is very quiet, & I feel like going in for getting well—There is not much change so far— but I feel comparatively comfortable since I have been here—& better satisfied—

My brother is full of work (inspecting pipe, manufactured here at the foundries for Water Works, & Sewers, northern cities)—he is in splendid health—a great stout fellow—weighs more than I do—he is building a handsome new house here, to be done latter part of August—

Thursday, 19th

Nothing very new—I have had some bad feeling in the head yesterday afternoon & this morning—but it will pass over, no doubt—It is warm weather here, days, but pleasant nights so far—Pete, when you get the *Star* save it & send to me—you can send two in a wrapper with a one cent stamp, (I enclose some, for fear you havn't any)—

Friday, 20th

Pretty hot weather here & needs rain badly—I am about the same—feel pretty well for a while, & then have a bad spell—have distress in the head at times, but keep up a good heart—or at any rate try to—Give my respects to all inquiring friends—tell them I expect to return to Washington in about a couple of months—tell me who you meet, & every little thing, & who asks about me, &c. as it will interest me—

I have made a raise of some new summer clothes, real nice—thin black pants & vest, a blue flannel suit, & some white vests—Love to Wash Milburn[11]—let him read this letter if he wishes—Write how you are getting along—good bye, dear son,

Walt

M S: Feinberg Collection, Library of Congress

To John and Ursula Burroughs

Camden, June 29, 1873

My dear friends John and 'Sula Burroughs,

I am here again in Camden, stopping awhile, with the intention, as soon as I can move with comfort, of getting to the sea-side—probably Atlantic City—about an hour & three quarters from here, by rail—I am not much different from when I saw you last—have been a good deal worse, (by spells, several of them)—but have now brought round again to where I was six or eight weeks ago.

Mother died here on the 23d of May—I stood it all better than I would have expected. I returned to Washington about nine days afterwards—but I was very restless & dissatisfied there—staid about a couple of weeks—obtained two months leave of absence, & (after almost making up my mind to go into quarters at a Hospital, as boarder, but was persuaded out of it)—here I am & have been for about two weeks—(I think comparatively better the last two days)—occupying the rooms in which my mother died—waiting for time to restore my health, which I still think it will—but I feel that the blank in life & heart left by the death of my mother is what will never to me be filled—

I am comfortably fixed here, have great kindness—I try to compose my-self to writing at some of my themes, already outlined, but it don't amount to much yet. 'Sula, O how I wish you was near-by keeping house—I should consider it such a privilege to hobble there for an hour or two every day, while I am in this condition—The last nine or ten days in Washington, I left my den on 15th, & visited the Ashton's on K st. & lived there.

John, I don't think I have any news either of Washington, or of literary affairs or persons, to tell you, nor have I heard any thing since from abroad. Love to you & 'Sula. I hope you will write me soon, and spread yourself about gossip, about self & 'Sula, and the place & every thing—a letter writ-ten when you are in the mood, & let your pen run—I depend much on letters, as I am tied up here, & it is pretty lonesome.

Walt

M S: Yale University

To Pete Doyle

Camden, July 24 and 25, 1873

Dear son Pete,

It is still the same old story with me—the best I can say is that I dont seem to get worse, even if I don't get better. Your letter came—and the Star, with the item about Tasistro.[12] It must be very hot there in Washington, but you stand it better than most any one I know. I too never used to think any thing of heat or cold, from 20 to 50—but last summer I felt the heat severely, for the first time.

Pete, as I have told you several times, I still think I shall get over this, & we will be together again & have some good times—but for all that it is best for you to be prepared for something different—my strength cant stand the pull forever, & if continued must sooner or later give out—Now, Pete, don't begin to worry, boy, or cry about me, for you havn't lost me yet, & I really don't think it is likely yet—but I thought it best to give a word of caution, if such a thing should be—

I am quite comfortable here & have every thing I want—I went out at ½ past 5 yesterday afternoon, & rode in the cars here to the ferry, & crossed the Delaware from Camden to Philadelphia four or five times—very pleas-ant. To-day is burning hot, but I am feeling as well as usual.

Friday 25th—4 o'clock—Pretty hot again to-day here, but not so op-

pressive to bear as in Washington—I am feeling about as usual to-day—
shall try to get out a few steps, after I send this—Good bye for this time,
dear loving son.

Walt.

MS: Feinberg Collection, Library of Congress

To Pete Doyle

Camden, August 14 and 15, 1873

Pete, dear son, I am not sinking nor getting worse—I have had some *very*
bad times, & have some pretty bad ones yet, mostly with my head—& my
leg is about as useless as ever—still I am decidedly no worse, & I think now
I am even *getting better*—it is slow & with great alternations—but I have
the feeling of getting more strength, & easier in the head, more like myself—
something like what I was before mother's death—I cannot be reconciled to
that yet—it is the great cloud of my life—nothing that ever happened before
has had such an effect on me—but I shall get well, yet, dear son, probably,
(of course not certainly) and be back in Washington this fall, & we will be
together again. I think I am now about as I was the day you came down to
Baltimore depot with me, 20th May I think—

Friday after dinner

I have thought of you the nights of this week, the heaviest rains here almost ever known—great trouble & loss to railroads—was you in any tight
spot?—that described in your last made me feel a little nervous—That was a
fearful disaster of the Wawasset [13]—sad beyond description—

So Tasistro is around yet—The Chronicle came—Mr. Eldridge has returned to Washington from his month's leave—he stopt here and paid me a
3 or 4 hours visit—John Burroughs has an article in the Sept. number of
Scribner's Magazine, just out, in which I am extracted from [14]—Pete, it is
now towards 3, and I am going to try to get down to the ferry boat, & cross
to Philadelphia—so you see I am not altogether disabled—but it is awful
tough work—when the weather is cooler, (which will be soon) I shall be
better off in Washington, as it is very lonesome to me here, & no one to
convoy me—I shall return there—I want to get a couple of unfurnished
rooms, or top floor, somewhere on or near the car route—Pete, if you see

Charley Towner give him my love, & ask him to give you his address to send me—He works in the Printing Bureau (M'Cartee's) [15] Treasury.

Good bye, my dear loving boy.

Walt.

M S: Feinberg Collection, Library of Congress

To Pete Doyle

Camden, September 26, 1873

Dear son Pete,

Your letter of yesterday came this forenoon—that was a rather serious runaway of cars in the tunnel a week ago—& mighty lucky to get off as you all did—Pete, I got a few lines from Parker Milburn—he told me you had a very bad sore on a finger of right hand—they are plaguey bad things—I am in hopes yours will partly make up in giving you a little resting spell. I sent you "The Children of the Abbey," [16] an old novel that used to be all the rage—did you get it? To-day here is a great turn out & dedication of the *Masonic Temple* in Philadelphia—it is truly a handsome & noble building. A rain last night here, & to-day is really perfect. The Camden free masons marched by here this morning, about 250, the finest collection of men I thought I ever saw, but poor music, all brass, a lot of fat young Dutchmen, blowing as if they would burst, & making a hell of a hullabaloo—

Pete, I am about the same—may-be a little improved in general strength—had bad spells a good deal all the earlier part of the week—some very bad—but feel better yesterday & to-day—I am making some calculations of the cool weather—think it may be favorable to me—did not go out any yester-day—shall try to get out this afternoon a couple of hours—I don't know a soul here—am entirely alone—sometimes sit alone & think, for two hours on a stretch—have not formed a single acquaintance here, any ways inti-mate—My sister-in-law is very kind in all housekeeping things, cooks what I want, has first-rate coffee for me & something nice in the morning, & keeps me a good bed & room—All of which is very acceptable—(then, for a fel-low of my size, the *friendly presence & magnetism needed*, somehow, is not here—I do not run foul of any)—Still I generally keep up very good heart—still think I shall get well—When I have my bad spells, I wait for them to fade out—I have got a letter from Charley Towner—I am finishing this by the open window—still in the rooms where my mother died, with all the old familiar things—but all drawing to a close, as the new house is done, & I shall move on Monday.

Walt.

M S: Feinberg Collection, Library of Congress

To Abby M. and Helen Price

Camden, about January 11, 1874

Dear Abby, & Dear Helen, not forgetting Emmy, & all

As I am sitting here alone in the parlor, the sun near setting pleasantly & brightly, (though cold to-day,) I just think that I ought to write you, even if but a line—that I am neglecting you—that perhaps you will be glad enough to hear from me. Well, I am still here—still alive, after quite a many pretty hard pulls & pressures—maintain pretty good spirits—which *would* be, quite *first-rate & good*—but every day & every night comes the thought of my mother—I am not despondent or blue, nor disposed to be any more *ennuyeed* than ever—but that thought remains to temper the rest of my life.

I am probably improving, though very slowly—go out a little most every day—go over to Philadelphia—get along pretty well in the cars & crossing the ferry. (The car fellows & ferrymen are very kind & helpful—almost all know me, I suppose instinctively)—appetite fair—rest at night tolerable—general strength better than at any time—(it is now just a year since I was paralyzed.)—Can't use my left leg yet with any freedom—bad spells in the head too frequent yet—then, with all those, I am certainly encouraged to believe I am on the gain. (But I am not out of the woods yet.) I write some—(must occupy my mind.) I am writing some pieces in the *Weekly Graphic*—my reminiscences of war times—first number appears in *Weekly Graphic* of Jan. 24 [17]—three or four others to follow—

We are in the new house my brother has built—very nice. I find myself *very lonesome* here, for all social & emotional consolation—(Man cannot live on *bread alone*—can he?)—I want to come & see you—*must* do so before long—want to pay a moderate board, (same as I do here,) if convenient for you to have me—*Shall not come on any other condition*—Well, Abby, I have just *skurried* rapidly over the sheet, & will send it to you just as it is, with love.

Walt Whitman

M S: Morgan Library

To Ulysses S. Grant

Camden, February 27, 1874

Dear Mr. President,

Hoping, (should time & inclination favor,) to give you a moment's diversion from the weight of official & political cares—& thinking, of all men, you can return to those scenes, in the vein I have written about them—I take the liberty of sending, (same mail with this) some reminiscences I have printed about the war, in nos. of the N. Y. *Weekly Graphic.*

I am not sure you will remember me, or my occasional salute to you, in Washington.

I am laid up here with tedious paralysis, but think I shall get well & return to Washington.

Very respectfully

Walt Whitman

DRAFT LETTER: Feinberg Collection, Library of Congress

To Rudolf Schmidt

Camden, March 19, 1874

My dear Rudolf Schmidt, [18]

My lonesomeness & sickness here, (for I am still sick, & here,) have been much rejoiced to-day by my getting your good & copious letter of 28th February, on your return of Kopenhagen. I rec'd with it the *Fatherland* with Mr. Rosenberg's criticism [19]—which (perhaps luckily for me) I cannot now read— but will one of these day have translated & read to me. I keep it very carefully—as I do all you send me—& shall yet read and commune with, & dwell upon & absorb *all* thoroughly & at leisure—(especially your own review in the *Ide.*) I think probably *all*—certainly *most*—papers, sheets, &c. you have sent me to Washington, have reached me here—the post office forwards them here—I rec'd two complete copies *Demokratiske Fremblik,* & one copy in sheets—also three copies picture paper *Folkeblad,* with my portrait, which is most excellent—(and the notice I will have read to me)—I rec'd at the time, a year ago, the translation of Swedish and Norwegian poems, you sent me, acknowledged it, but the letter seems to have missed you, & have read it & had much pleasure, & am to read it more—I also rec'd from [Carl F.] Clausen [20] your picture, which I have with me—& prize.

A friend lately looking at it said, "Why, he looks like a born Yankee—& of the best."

I wrote you March 4th, acknowledging *Demokratiske Fremblik*, & sent you (one in *Harper's Magazine*, & one extracted in the N. Y. *Tribune*) my two latest pieces *Song of the Redwood Tree*, (California,) and *Prayer of Columbus*, which I suppose you have rec'd all—For the last ten weeks I have not felt inclined to write—have suffered in the head—walk hardly any, (from the paralysis,) but maintain good spirits, keep up in body & face, (my brother & sister said at dinner yesterday that portrait in the *Folkeblad* looks greatly like me now, & has caught the true *expression* better than any of them.) In body I have always been, & still remain, *stout*, in the American sense, (i.e. *not* corpulent)— . . .

The same *hardness*, crudeness, worldliness—absence of the spiritual, the purely moral, esthetik, &c—are in Democracy here too—(though there are signs & awakenings here very plain to me)—probably in Great Britain, & in Europe & everywhere—*Here*, it is much counterbalance & made up by an immense & general basis of the eligibility to manly & loving comradeship, very marked in American young men—but generally, I am the more disposed to be satisfied with the case as it is because I see that the only foundations & *sine qua non* of popular improvement & Democracy are *worldly & material success established first*, spreading & intertwining everywhere—*then* only, but then surely for the masses, will come spiritual cultivation & art—they will then firmly assert themselves—

Thank you for the graphic line-sketch you write of Bismark, in your letter. My own opinion is, that we can well afford—I will say, *such as you & I*, can well afford, to let those little & great *chunks of brawn*—Attilas, Napoleons, Bismarks—prepare the way, & cut the roads through, for *us*.

Write me *here*, till further notice—let me hear what is said about *Vistas* or my poems—let me hear always of yourself fully.

Walt Whitman

M S: Royal Library of Copenhagen

To Ellen M. O'Connor

Camden, March 22, 1874

Dearest Nelly,

I will just write you a word (for I feel to.) I am feeling well enough to be hopeful—Whether it is because I *am* hopeful—or whether the precursor of health yet, after all—tedious as it is a-coming—this deponent cannot swear—but we will think it the latter. I have had a bad week since I wrote you—feel more comfortable to-day. Saw the doctor ([Matthew J.] Grier) day before yesterday—he made a careful auscultation of my heart—pronounced it all right there—(I have been suffering considerable pain & oppression on left side)—He still thinks I will recover—says he is not disposed to recommend galvanism, (though the electric business is his specialty)—says he is sure the main trouble is the *cerebral* anæmia—cure, great care, good surroundings, time & hygiene—arrives, in fact, at the same conclusions as Dr. Drinkard—(though an entirely different man from Dr. D., a great talker, & very demonstrative)—

Nelly, you needn't send the photos of my nieces back yet. Keep them a while yet.

Nelly, your last letter is very blue, mainly about political & public degradation—Sumner's death & inferior men &c. being rampant &c—I look on all such states of things exactly as I look on a cloudy & evil state of weather, or a fog, or long sulk meteorological—it is a natural result of things, a growth of something deeper, has its uses, & will hasten to exhaust itself, & yield to something better—

Walt.

M S: Berg Collection, New York Public Library

To Pete Doyle

Camden, March 26 and 27, 1874

I have just had my dinner—roast beef, lima beans, graham-bread & sweet butter, with a cup of tea, & some stewed cranberries—eat quite a good dinner, & enjoyed it all. I still consider myself getting along very well. O if *this* only holds out, & keeps on favorably, even if ever so moderate & slow—But I seem to have so many of these gleams that delude me into thinking I am on the way to recovery, but soon cloud over again, & let me back as bad as ever—But every time I feel pretty easy, I still keep thinking, *now* I am *certainly* going to get much better *this time*—

Pete, your short letter came to-day, written on the cars—dear son, come whenever you can—As I said on my postal card, if you were here this week, you would find me more like myself, (with the exception of walking) than I have been for fourteen months—whether it will continue or not, God only knows—but we will hope for the best. As I sit here writing to you to-day, it appears to me every way hopeful, & likely that we shall yet have good times. Every thing is quiet—rather lonesome. My little dog is stretched out on the rug at full length, snoozing. He hardly lets me go a step without being close at my heels—follows me in my slow walks, & stops or turns just as I do. We have had a most windy blustering March, but it is pleasanter & milder yesterday & to-day—(I saw the new moon over my right shoulder a week ago—*of course* a *sure* sign of good luck)—Will finish the letter & send it to-morrow.

Friday March 27 noon.

Pleasant & bright weather—have been out on the side walk in front, once or twice, with my shawl around me—walk slow & quite feeble—have some spells of bad head-ache—Went by the West Philadelphia depot yesterday afternoon, in the Market st. horse-cars—saw plenty of RR men & conductors, about the place, lounging & waiting their time—thought if I could only see *you* among them—As I sit here writing I can see the trains of the Camden & Amboy, in full view, some 40 or 50 rods off—makes it quite lively—As I write I am feeling pretty comfortable, & am going out awhile after I finish this—but had a bad night last night. Hope this will find you all right—good bye for this time, dear son.

Walt

MS: Feinberg Collection, Library of Congress

To William Stansberry, a soldier

Camden, May 20, 1874

Dear Wm. Stansberry,[21]

I will just write you a few lines off-hand. Your letter of May 14 has come to hand to-day, reminding me of your being in Armory Square Hospital & of my visits there, & meeting you, in '65. Your writing, or something it has started, strangely, deeply touches me. It takes me back to the scenes of ten years ago, in the war, the hospitals of Washington, the many wounded bro't up after the battles, and the never-to-be told sights of suffering & death. To think that the little gift & word of kindness, should be remembered by you so long—& that the kiss I gave you amid those scenes, should be treasured up, & as it were sent back to me after many years! Dear Comrade—you do me good, by your loving wishes & feelings to me in your letters.

I send you my love, & to your dear children & wife the same. As I write, you seem very dear to me too, like some young brother, who has been lost, but now found. Whether we shall ever meet each other is doubtful—probably we never will—but I feel that we should both be happy, if we could be together—(I find there are some that it is just comfort enough to be together, almost without any thing else)—

I remain about the same in my sickness. I sleep & eat pretty well—go about same, look stout & red, (though looking now *very* old & gray, but that is nothing new)—weigh 185 now—am badly lamed in my left leg, & have bad spells, occasionally days, of feebleness, distress in head, &c. I think I shall get well yet, but may not. Have been laid up here a year doing nothing, except a little writing. As far as room, food, care, &c. are concerned, I am well situated here—but *very lonesome*—have no near friends, (in the deepest sense) here at hand—my mother died here a year ago—a sorrow from which I have never entirely recovered, & likely never shall—she was an unusually noble, cheerful woman—very proud-spirited & generous—am poor, (yet with a little income, & means, just enough to pay my way, with strict economy, to be independent of want)—

DRAFT LETTER: Trent Collection, Duke University

To Ulysses S. Grant

Camden, June 22, 1874

Would it be convenient to the President to personally request of the Attorney General that in any changes in the Solicitor Treasury's office, I be not disturbed in my position as clerk in that office—all my duties to the government being & having been thoroughly & regularly performed there, by a substitute [Walter Godey], during my illness.[22]

I shall probably get well before long.

Very respectfully,

Walt Whitman

MS: National Archives

To Pete Doyle

Camden, July 10, 1874

Dear, dear son,

I am still here—still suffering pretty badly—have great distress in my head, & an almost steady pain in left side—but my worst troubles let up on me part of the time—the evenings are my best times—& somehow I still keep up in spirit, &, (the same old story,) *expect* to get better.

I have been discharged from my clerkship in the Solicitor's office, Treasury, by the new Solicitor, Mr. [Bluford] Wilson.

I think of laying up here in Camden. I have bought a cheap lot—& think of putting up a little two or three room house for myself. My darling son, you must not be unhappy about me—I hope & trust things may work so that we can yet be with each other, at least from time to time—& meanwhile we must adapt ourselves to circumstances. You keep on, & try to do right, & live the same square life you always have, & maintain as cheerful a heart as possible—& as for the way things finally turn out, leave that to the Almighty—

Pete, I shall want you or Mr. Eldridge to see to the sending on here of my boxes at Dr. [George A.] White's. I will write further about it— . . .

Very hot here yesterday & to-day. I don't fret at all about being discharged—it is just as well—I wonder it didnt come before—How are your folks at home—your dear mother & all—write about all, & about Mr. & Mrs. Nash, Wash Milburn, & the RR boys—

Your old Walt

M S: Feinberg Collection, Library of Congress

To Charles W. Eldridge

Camden, December 2, 1874

Dear friend,

. . . I wrote to Nelly about a week ago, stating my condition, & what a plight I have been in—& am partially yet—though slowly coming round to what I was just previous—

The doctor still comes every day—rather a curious fellow—a great bully, vehement, loud words & plenty of them (the very reverse of my valued Dr Drinkard)—& yet I value what *he* says & does for me—He is inclined to think the seat of all my woe has been (what no one ever whispered before,) the *liver*, acted upon largely also, perhaps almost primarily, thro[ugh] the emotional nature—at any rate he is decided that the present botherations are absolutely *liver* troubles, & their radiations—

Charley, I have had a sick, sick three weeks since you were here—havn't been out, except just in front of the house in the sun, & only three times that—but don't be alarmed, my dear friend—the probabilities are, (in my opinion any how), that I shall get partially well yet—

Walt.

M S: Mrs. Doris Neale

To John Burroughs

Camden, April 1, 1875

Dear John,

I have look'd over the Emerson notes[23]—read them all over once—am precluded from any thing more or giving any very deep or elaborate analysis of them, in connection with the Emerson question, (as my brain is in a state not allowing thought, argument or study)—but still I will give you my first impressions of your pages:

In their totality, they produce a not agreeable notion of being written by one who has been largely grown & ripened & gristled by Emerson, but has at last become dissatisfied & finnicky about him, & would pitch into him, but cannot—perhaps dare not—and so keeps running around in a sort of circle of praises & half praises, like a horse tied by a tether.

Your Notes also seem to me (to be plain) a good deal too diffuse, & too Emersony in themselves—I should select *about one third of the MS. as first rate*, (including the opening part)—My opinion is that you had perhaps better work it all over, & leave out at least half—

About the allusions to me, my off-hand thought is that my name might be brought in, in one or two places, as foil or suggestive comparison—but *my name only*, without any praises or comments, (only the silently inferred ones)—to my friends, & circle, who know the relations & history between me & Emerson, the mere mention of the name itself, in that way, will be significant—(& it might give pungency to the sentence)[24]—

I have had a bad time the last two weeks—head & belly—& I almost wonder I stand it so well—for I *do* stand it—I go out most every day, a little—John Swinton,[25] from N. Y., has been to see me—

Love to you & 'Sula—

WW

M S: Barrett Collection, University of Virginia

To Alfred Tennyson

Camden, July 24, 1875

My dear Mr. Tenn[yson],

Since I last wrote you, (your kind response was duly rec'd) I have been laid up here nearly all the time, & still continue so, quite shattered, but somehow with good spirits—not well enough to go out in the world & go to work—but not sick enough to give up either, or lose my interest in affairs, life, literature, &c. I keep up & dressed, & go out a little nearly every day.

I have been reading your Queen Mary,[26] & think you have excelled your-self in it. I did not know till I read it, how much eligibility to passion, charac-ter and art arousings was still left to me in my sickness & old age. Though I am Democrat enough to realize the deep criticism of Jefferson on Walter Scott's writings, (& many of the finest plays, poems & romances) that they fail to give at all the life of the great mass of the people then & there.

But I shall print a new volume before long, & will send you a copy. I send you a paper about same mail with this.

Soon as convenient write me a few lines. (Put in your letter your exact p. o. address.) If you have leisure, tell me about yourself. I shall never see you & talk to you—so I hope you will write to make it up.

DRAFT LETTER: Hanley Collection, University of Texas

To Edwin Einstein

Camden, November 26, 1875

My dear Einstein,[27]

On coming back here, I find your letter of the 20th. It is so kind (bringing up old memories, & making prologue & ceremony unnecessary) that I will at once answer it in its own spirit, & reveal the situation.

My paralysis has left me permanently disabled, unable to do any thing of any consequence, and yet with perhaps (though old, not yet 60) some lease of life yet. I had saved up a little money, & when I came here, nearly three years ago, I bought a nice cheap lot, intending to put on a small house to haul in, & live out the rest of my days.

I had, & yet have, a sort of idea that my books, (I am getting ready, or about have ready, my complete writings, in two volumes—*Leaves of Grass*, and *Two Rivulets*) will yet henceforth furnish me reliably with sufficient for grub, pocket money, &c., if I have my own shanty to live in. But my means, meagre at the best, have gone for my expenses since, & now, while not hitherto actually wanting, (& not worrying much about the future either,) I have come to the end of my rope, & am in fact ridiculously poor. I have my lot yet clear, & it would be a great thing for me to build forthwith a four or five room shanty on it & haul in, snug & quiet, with the sense of security for the rest of my days—for I feel yet about as cheerful & *vimmy* as ever, & may live several years yet—indeed probably will—& may write some—though my days of active participation, & ganging about in the world, are over.

I get out a little nearly every day, & enjoy it, but am very lame—Keep stout & red as ever—grayer than ever—am feeling pretty comfortable as I write—have just returned from a three weeks jaunt to Washington and Baltimore—which has much refreshed me, (the first time I have been away from my anchorage here for nearly three years.) I often recall the old times in New York, or on Broadway, or at Pfaff's—& the faces & voices of *the boys*.

DRAFT LETTER: Feinberg Collection, Library of Congress

To Edward Dowden

Camden, March 4, 1876

Dear friend,

Yours of Feb. 6 with draft[28] reach'd me which I responded to sending new edition "Leaves of Grass" and "Two Rivulets," two or three days since, by mail, same address as this, which you ought to have rec'd now lately—sent postal card briefly notifying you, & asking you to send me word (by postal card will do) immediately on their reception.

To-day comes your affectionate, hearty, valued letter of Feb. 16, all right, with enclosure, draft 12££. 10s.—all deeply appreciated—the *letter* good, cannot be better, but, as always, the *spirit* the main thing—(altogether like some fresh, magnetic, friendly breath of breeze, 'way off there from the Irish Coast)—I wonder if you can know how much good such things do me. I shall send the six sets (six "Leaves" and six "Rivulets") by express, very soon, (probably by next Philadelphia steamer.) The extra copies of "Memoranda of the War" not being ready bound, at present, I will send by mail— six copies, before very long. (I hope the set above mention'd I mailed you by last steamer, will have reach'd you before you get this.) I saw O'Grady's article[29] in the December "Gentleman's" & from my point of view, he dwells on *what I like to have dwelt on*. I was deeply pleased with the article, & if I had O'Grady's address I would like to send him my photograph. I also read the Peter Bayne article.[30] (It was copied in full here at once, & circulated quite largely.) As I write this, I have not read Abraham Stoker's letter,[31] but shall do so, & carefully. (The names shall be written in the Vols. as you mention.) I read with great zest the account of the discussion at the "Fortnightly"[32]—I have learn'd to feel *very thankful* to those who attack & abuse & pervert me—that's perhaps (besides being good fun) the only way to bring out the splendid ardor & friendship of those, my unknown friends, my best reward, art & part with me, in my pages, (for I have come to solace & perhaps flatter myself that it is *they* indeed in them, as much as *I*, every bit.)

My condition physically is pretty much the same—no worse, at least not decidedly. I get out nearly every day, but not far, & cannot walk from lameness—make much of the river here, the broad Delaware, crossing a great deal on the ferry, full of life & fun to me—get down there by our horse cars, which run along near my door—get infinite kindness, care, & assistance from the employés on these boats & cars—My friend, next time you write say more about yourself, family & Mrs. Dowden, to whom with yourself best love and regards—

Walt Whitman

M S: Trent Collection, Duke University

To William M. Rossetti

Camden, March 17, 1876

W. M. Rossetti—Dear friend,

. . . My books are out, the new edition, a set of which, immediately on receiving your letter of 28th, I have sent you (by mail March 15) & I suppose you have before this rec'd them.

My dear friend, your offers of help, & those of my other British friends, I think I fully appreciate, in the right spirit, welcome & acceptive—leaving the matter altogether in your & their hands—& to your & their convenience, discretion, leisure & nicety—Though poor now even to penury *I have not so far been deprived of any physical thing I need or wish whatever— & I feel confident I shall not, in the future*. During my employment of seven years or more in Washington after the war (1865–'72) I regularly saved a great part of my wages—& though the sum has now become about exhausted, by my expenses of the last three years—there are already beginning at present welcome dribbles hitherward from the sales of my new edition which I just job & sell, myself, (as the book agents here for 3 years in New York have successively, deliberately, badly cheated me) & shall continue to dispose of the books myself. And *that* is the way I should prefer to glean my support—In that way I cheerfully accept all the aid my friends find it convenient to proffer—(Prof. Dowden has sent me the money for seven sets—which I have forwarded to him at Dublin. I wish you to loan this letter to him to read.) I wish you to notify me—by postal card will do—soon as you receive your books sent on the 15th—I wish you also to loan this letter to Mrs. Gilchrist, first of all. I shall write to her to-day or to-morrow—but briefly.

To repeat a little, & without undertaking details, understand, dear friend, for yourself & all, that I heartily & most affectionately thank my British friends, & that I accept their sympathetic generosity in the same spirit in which I believe (nay, *know*) it is offered—that though poor *I am not in want*—that I maintain good heart & cheer—& that by far the most satisfaction to me, (& think it can be done, & believe it will be,) will be to live, as long as possible, on *the sales, by myself, of my own works*—& perhaps, if practicable, by further writings for the press.

Walt Whitman

There is a small fury & much eructive spitting & sputtering already among the "literary coteries" here from Robt. Buchanan's lance-slash at them anent of me, in his letter in the London D[aily] News, of March 13,[33] (synopsis cabled here to Associated press, & printed everywhere)—the "coteries" resenting it madly by editorials here & there already in the papers—they fall to berating R. B. first, & then *me*—say, *if I WERE sick, or WERE poor, why then,*—&c. &c. &c.

(If convenient, I should like to have this letter loaned to Mr. Buchanan also. I am prohibited from writing too much, & I must make this candid statement of the situation serve for all my dear friends over there.)

M S: Formerly in Robert H. Taylor Collection

To Anne Gilchrist

Camden, March 17, 1876

Dearest friend,

To your good & comforting letter of Feb. 25th[34] I at once answer, at least with a few lines. . . .

My health I am encouraged to think is perhaps a shade better—certainly as well as any time of late. I even already vaguely contemplate plans, (they may never be fulfilled, but yet again they may,) of changes, journeys—even of coming to London, of seeing you, of visiting my friends, &c.

My dearest friend, I do not approve your American trans-settlement[35]—I see so many things here, you have yet no idea of—the American social & almost every other kind of crudeness, meagreness, (at least in appearance)— Don't do any thing toward such a move, nor resolve on it, nor indeed make any move at all in it, without further advice from me. If I should get well enough to voyage, we will talk about it yet in London—You must not be uneasy about me—dear friend, I get along much better than you suppose. As to my literary situation here, my rejection by the coteries—& my poverty, (which is the least of my troubles)—I am not sure but I enjoy them all. Besides, as to the latter, I am not in want. Best love to you, & to your children.

Walt Whitman

M S: University of Pennsylvania

To William M. Rossetti

Camden, March 30, 1876

Dear friend,

I have already acknowledged yours of 16th—Mine of 17th will have advised you of the situation here, & the general character of my wishes, the way things have shaped themselves in London—Whatever I should do, if I had the planning of it *de novo*, the question is now (like a general making the best of the turn the battle has taken in its own hands, & compell'd to decide quickly & definitely,) what to direct & authorize under the circumstances— While I unhesitatingly accept such kind offerings as Chas W Reynell's (No 1. in your transcript) and J Leicester Warren (No 2)—& authorize you or any of my friends to continue to accept the like, in my name, where offer'd readily & properly, I'd rather you would, after receiving this, either, (to use nautical lingo,) *take in sail*, or at least don't crowd on any more sail at all. The whole business requires to be done with perfect candor to my generous friends—to you & the other mediums of that generosity—& to myself—& must & shall be so done. Of the cheque (No 1) or any other, or any thing of the kind sent by you or through you or any of my friends, the most convenient to me would be to have them remitted to me, to my address here, drawn on some well-known New York or Philadelphia banker, *payable to my order*—(if in Philadelphia, on Drexel & Co. bankers, 34 south 3d street.) Then the p. o. international money order is also a good & safe way to remit—I should like in all cases to have the full & explicit address of the friend & giver, to send him or her at least one special autograph copy, or set, of my books—

As told you in former letter, although I am indeed poor, with means exhausted, I am by no means in a condition of pinching want, nor likely to be. I am boarding here, under the usual, unavoidable expenses. I accept the kind gifts, first for my own help, then perhaps somewhat for the still graver needs of others, forever falling in my way. For the future I really think the income from my books, if it can be utilized, promises amply enough for my support—& *that* decidedly would be most satisfactory to me—

Probably from the tinge of Quaker breed in me the inner convictions & silent dictates of *the spirit* settle these cases, & what I must do in them, more than reason, convention or even delicacy—& those inner dictates I have now obeyed in the decisions of this letter, as *a higher reason & delicacy*, & the final arbiter of the question.

Walt Whitman

If perfectly convenient I should like Buchanan to see this letter—also Dowden—Indeed you can make what use of it, in your discretion, you think best—

A line further about the publication copy, Two Volumes, I sent a couple of days since. I couldn't rest until I had sent that copy to provide for any thing that might happen (my affairs are in such a chaotic state here in America—my health, mentality, from week to week, even *existence*, uncertain)— Now you have it, I feel relieved, & shall consider that the thing is secured, & cannot be lost—*But there is no haste about it*—If you should hear of any proposed London reprint, then try & get my copy published at once, making any decent terms you can—But if there don't appear to be any danger, take your leisure, & hold on. See if you can get any one to pay me something

down ahead—I revoke what I said about the *shilling edition*[36]—let the
books, when printed, be at a price suitable to the trade & market—

W. W.

M S: Formerly in Robert H. Taylor Collection

To Daniel Whittaker(?)[37]

Camden, April 4, 1876(?)

Dear Dan:

I take an interest in the boy in the office, Harry Stafford—I know his
father & mother—There is a large family, very respectable American
people—farmers, but only a hired farm—Mr. Stafford in weak health—

I am anxious Harry should *learn the printer's trade thoroughly—I want
him to learn to set type as fast as possible*—want you to give him a chance
(less of the mere errands &c)—There is a good deal really in the boy, if he
has a chance.

Don't say any thing about this note to him—or in fact to any one—just
tear it up, & *keep the matter to yourself private.*

Walt Whitman

M S: Feinberg Collection, Library of Congress

To Robert Buchanan

Camden, May 16, 1876

Your two letters including the cheque for £25 reached me, for which accept deepest thanks.[38] I have already written you my approval of your three
communications in the L[ondon] D[aily] News & will [say] that in my opinion (& now with fullest deliberation reäffirming it) *all the points assumed as
facts on which your letter of March 13 is grounded, are substantially true, &
most of them are true to the minutest particular*—as far as could be stated in a
one column letter.

Then let me quite definitely explain myself, about one or two things.
I should not have instigated this English move, & if I had been consulted,
should have peremptorily stopt it—but now that it has started, & grown,
and under the circumstances, & by the person, & in the spirit, (& especially
as I can & will give, to each generous donor, my book, portrait, autograph,
myself as it were)—I am determined to respond to it in the same spirit in

which it has risen—to accept most thankfully, cordially & unhesitatingly all that my friends feel to covey to me, which determination I here deliberately express once for all. This you are at liberty to make known to all who feel any interest in the matter.

The situation at present may be briefly & candidly told. I am, & have for three years during my paralysis, been boarding here, with a relative, comfortable & nice enough, but steadily paying just the same as at an inn—and the whole affair in precisely the same business spirit. My means would by this time have entirely given out, but that have been temporarily replenished from sales of my new edition and as now by this most welcome present & purchase—the £25 herein acknowledged.

Though without employment, means or income, you augur truly that I am not in what may be called pinching want—nor do I anticipate it.

My object I may say farther has lately been & still is to build a cheap little three or four room house on a little lot I own in a rural skirt of this town—for a nook, where I can haul in & eke out in a sort of independent economy & comfort & as satisfactorily as may be the rest of my years—for I may live several of them yet. To attain this, would be quite a triumph, & I feel assured I could then live very nicely indeed on the income from my books.

I shall (as I see now) continue to be my own publisher & bookseller. Accept all subscriptions to the New Edition. All will be supplied upon remittance. There are Two Volumes. Leaves of Grass, 384 pages, poems, $5, has two portraits. Then *Two Rivulets*, poems & prose, (including "*Memoranda of the War*") with photos, altogether 359 pages—also $5. Each book has my autograph. The Two Volumes are my complete works, $10 the set.

I wish the particular address of each generous friend given, so as he or she can be reach'd by mail or express—either with the autographic volume *Two Rivulets*, or a complete set of my works in Two Volumes, with autograph & portraits, or some other of my books. It may be some while before the books arrive, but they *will* arrive in time.

DRAFT LETTER: Feinberg Collection, Library of Congress

To John Burroughs

Camden, June 17, 1876

John, I have just been reading your *Galaxy* article,[39] seated by the open window front room in my shirt sleeves, & must write a word about it—Your late pieces show *marked vitality—vivacity* (struggling, almost chafing, under-

neath a continent, respectable form or exterior) & *this is the best of them*—
has those peculiarities, not without one or two foibles, but the *whole* of the
piece is glorious—leaves the impression now upon me (after two readings)
of the noblest piece of criticism on these things yet in America—as much
nobler than the superb Emersonian pages on those subjects as lines & opinions with *the blood of life* & throb of hot conviction in them, are nobler than
the superbest *Marble-statue lines*—

It would be possible that I might be swayed into a warm feeling about the
piece by the magnificent & very 'cute page about me, but as it happens by
accident I had look'd over & read the piece in parts, *accidentally omitting at
first the entire lines in the second column* of the page about me (which finally
please me best)—& had made up my mind very decidedly as aforesaid—
then when I *did* read them, you can imagine *they* didn't hurt me much—nor
my estimation of the piece— [40]

I have much to write—or tell you—about my own concerns—things in
England—here too—&c &c—have been waiting for the chance to write
you fully ever since I got your kind generous note & present [41]—but it dont
seem to occur—Physically I am not much different—get along about as well
as usual these times—am now just going down to an old farm house & big
family,[42] down in Jersey at *White Horse*, to spend a couple of days—and it is
now (4½ p m) while I am waiting for the hack to come & take me to the
depot that I write this—

George and Lou are well—baby only pretty well—hot weather, & teeth-
ing—(but behaves like a little hero)—expect my two nieces here next week
from St Louis—Love to 'Sula—Write soon—

                                                                    Walt

M S: Barrett Collection, University of Virginia

To Ellen M. O'Connor

                                                        Camden, July 13, 1876

Nelly, this is a sad house to-day—little Walt [43] died last evening about ½
past 8. Partially sick but sudden at last—suddenly turned to water on the
brain—is to be buried to-morrow afternoon at 4—

George and Lou are standing it pretty well—I am miserable—he knew
me so well—we had already such good times—& I was counting so much—
My St. Louis nieces are here—they are well—Nelly dear, send me back their

photos & Jeff's—the heat here has been & is dreadful—Love to you—
write—

WW

MS: Feinberg Collection, Library of Congress

To Anne Gilchrist

Camden, December 12, 1876

Thanks, my dear friend, for your hospitable & affectionate letter, & invitations. I too want to come & see you all, & be with you from time to time—hoping it may be good & a comfort to all of us—to *me* surely—[44]

As (though better this winter) decidedly sensitive to the cold—how would it do for me to have a little sheet-iron wood stove, & some wood sawed & cut, & carried up in the south room, immediately adjoining the one I before occupied? Could it be done? Is there a hole in the chimney in that room—or place for stove pipe?

I am getting along quite well—& shall be over very soon—possibly Thursday—

Walt Whitman

(A pretty good fire—& a wood fire—is to me I find the greatest physical comfort I can have this weather—I should want to select & purchase, & have put up myself, the stove, wood, &c.)

MS: University of Pennsylvania

To John H. Johnston [45]

Camden, December 13, 1876

Thanks, my dear friend, for your cheery letter, & for your warm & hospitable invitations—I am, though crippled as ever, perhaps *decidedly better* this winter—certainly in the way of strength & general vim—& it would be very pleasant to me to come on & stay at your house for about a week, if perfectly convenient, & if you have plenty of room—My (adopted) son, a young man of 18, is with me now, sees to me, & occasionally transacts my business affairs, & I feel somewhat at sea without him—Could I bring him with me, to share my room, & your hospitality & be with me?

Glad to hear in your note from Joaquin Miller—first news of him now for three months—Will sit to Mr Waters with great pleasure[46]—& he & you shall have every thing your own way—

I am selling a few copies of my Vols, new Edition, from time to time—most of them go to the British Islands—I see Mr Loag[47] occasionally—Loving regards to you, my friend, & to Mrs Johnston no less—

Walt Whitman

MS: Feinberg Collection, Library of Congress

To John H. Johnston

Camden, December 19, 1876

My dear Johnston,

Yours of yesterday rec'd. Every thing will suit me, just that way—would like to come during or before the close of January—would like to have a room where I could have a fire, table, &c. My nephew & I when traveling always share the same room together & the same bed, & would like best to do so there. I want to bring on a lot of my books, new edition, & sell them, so I can raise a little money—(& that is what my young man is for.)

Fix the time to suit Waters & yourself, that way.

Thanks & affection—

Walt Whitman

MS: Feinberg Collection, Library of Congress

To John H. Johnston

Camden, December 20, 1876

My dear Johnston,

Enclosed find check for $35 for which send me on *immediately* as good a *gold watch*, hunting case, middling showy in appearance & best inside you can give me for that sum. (Let me have it at wholesale price, only paying yourself what you pay for it). I want it for a Christmas present for a young man—*Can't you send it by express to-night or to-morrow morning early?*

Walt Whitman

I might as well leave you some margin. If you think of something a little more [in] price or different any how, better, send it along, as it can be changed, paid for, or made right when I come on in January—

I find I have no revenue stamp to put on check & cannot go out to get one—

M S: Feinberg Collection, Library of Congress

To Mr. and Mrs. Damon Y. Kilgore

Camden, January 24, 1877

My Dear Damon Kilgore & Mrs Kilgore[48]

I will be at the Commemorative meeting. I would like to speak from ten to twenty minutes *before* Mr Phillips's address. What I have to offer might be called *A true Reminiscence of Thomas Paine*. I shall be to-morrow evening & night, and all Friday, & the following night & forenoon, *at 1929 north 22nd street, Phila.* (north of Berks)[49]—& if it would be convenient for you to send a carriage *there* for me at about 1½ p m Sunday it would suit me—Call on or address me there Friday forenoon or evening, or Saturday forenoon before 12.

Walt Whitman

Thanks for the hospitality—hearty thanks—I will accept if I can Sunday—but it is not certain—

M S: Florence A. Hoadley

To John Burroughs

Camden, January 24, 1877

I think *Birds and Poets* not only much the best name for the book, but a first-rate good name, appropriate, original & fresh, without being at all affected or strained.[50] The piece you put 4th should then be *first*—should lead the book, giving it its title, & having the name of the piece changed to "Birds and Poets"—which I think would be an improvement. The whole collection would be sufficiently homogeneous, (and it were a fault to be too much so)—You just want *a hint* for the name of a book—Only it must be in the spirit of the book—& not too much so either. *"Nature and Genius" is too Emersony altogether.*

I will think over the name of the piece devoted to me, & will in a couple of days write you the result. May-be I can think of a better name. I have not rec'd the MS from Church.[51] You send on any thing—any MS—which I will

cheerfully read & will return with any suggestions that may occur to me—I
keep pretty well for me—

W W

M S: Berg Collection, New York Public Library

To Edward Cattell[52]

Camden, January 24, 1877

Dear Ed

I want to write you a few lines particular. Do not call to see me any more
at the Stafford family, & do not call there at all any more—Dont ask me
why—I will explain to you when we meet. When you meet any of the family
I wish you to use them just the same as ever, but do not go over there at all.
I want you to keep this to yourself, & not mention it nor this letter to any
one & you must not speak about it at all to any one.

There is nothing in it that I think I do wrong, nor am ashamed of, but I
wish it kept entirely between you and me—&—I shall feel very much hurt
& displeased if you don't keep the whole thing & the present letter entirely
to yourself. Mr and Mrs Stafford are very near & kind to me, & have been &
are like brother & sister to me—& as to Harry you know how I love him.
Ed, you too have my unalterable love, & always shall have. I want you to
come up here & see me. Write when will you come.

DRAFT LETTER: Feinberg Collection, Library of Congress

To John Burroughs

New York, March 13, 1877

Dear friend[53]

Yours of yesterday rec'd—Shall be very glad to go up with you Friday for
a couple of days or so—Should like to fetch my boy Harry Stafford with me,
as he is my convoy like—We occupy the same room & bed—

We had another reception here last night—very successful—lots of artists, many fine ladies & not a few ministers & journalists—I am feeling
pretty well, but can't stand these things long—Dull half rainy day here—
have been in all day—sitting muchly for my picture[54]—which gets on well—

'Sula, love to you—

W W

M S: New York Public Library

To Harry Stafford

Philadelphia, June 18 and 19, 1877

Dear Harry,

I am still stopping here,[55] & we are having quite nice times, all of us, (Mrs Gilchrist, Mr. Carpenter,[56] Herbert and the two girls and I)—but I miss the creek, a good deal—yesterday, (Sunday) I thought if I could only go down to the creek, & ramble about in the open air by myself & have a leisurely wash & some exercise, it would do me more good than any thing—but I staid in all day. Still it is all very pleasant here, every thing is so gentle & smooth, & yet they are all so jolly & much laughing & talking & fun—we have first rate times, over our meals, we take our time over them, & always something new to talk about. Mr Carpenter has travelled much in England, & met many people & he is one of a large family of brothers & sisters, all in active life in various parts of the world, & he shows us their pictures & tells us about them—

Dear Harry, not a day or night passes but I think of you—I dont suppose it would be so much fun for you here—but it suits an old man like me, (& then it pleases one's vanity to be made so much of)—Harry, I suppose you get the papers I send you—I don't know whether you care about them, but I thought they might amuse you a moment there for a change—I want you always to take them home for your father—At present it is about 11½ o'clock—Herbert is down stairs painting—The girls are sewing—Mrs G is out shopping & at the groceries—Mr Carpenter has gone upstairs to write some letters—& I am sitting here in my front room in the great bay window at a big table writing this—a nice cool breeze blowing in—Why there it goes, the bell for 12 o'clock—right opposite us, the masons &c building a big house, all knock off work, & there are groups sitting down in shady places & opening their dinner kettles—I too will knock off for this time— Dear son, how I wish you could come in now, even if but for an hour & take off your coat, & sit down on my lap—

Tuesday afternoon June 19

Every thing about the same with us—was over to Camden yesterday afternoon—Mrs Gilchrist went over too, & my brother took her out on a good drive about the country—My sister was up & in good spirits—Herbert & Mr Carpenter went out to the park & didn't get back till 9—I came [home?] to Phil. by myself—The girls & I had our supper together, & had a jolly time—the younger daughter came out finely, & she showed that she could make herself very agreeable & interesting when she has a mind to—but the elder one is the noble one[57]—the more I see of her the better I like her—

Harry, how are you getting along there? I suppose you are learning—& I hope you are having good times—Something Mr Carpenter has told me about the effect working at telegraphing has on a person disturbs me a little—but I will talk with you more particularly about it when we are together again—I send you the enclosed from Mr C—I shall be down *Friday* in the 6 o'clock train—I want to see the creek again—& I want to see you, my darling son, & I can't wait any longer—

Your old Walt

M S: Berg Collection, New York Public Library

To Harry Stafford

Camden, August 7, 1877

Dear Comrade & Dear Son

Your letter came this morning, & as I think my loving boy is so touchy ab't it, (he says he has writ *three* letters, but I can't make out but *two*) I will sit right down & send him a letter. I am feeling well—only as I was out with some friends Sunday night, I was foolish enough to take a good strong drink, & eat a couple of slices of rich cake late at night—& *I shan't do any thing of the kind again*. But I am pretty well, dear son, & feel more able & sassy every day—& we will have some good times yet. Harry, I don't know the particulars about the Herbert scrape, but you must let up on him—I suspect you said something pretty tantalizing before he call'd you that—Let it go—Of course I shan't say anything about it to any one[58]—

There is quite a stir here in Camden to-day as the 6th New Jersey Reg't. is coming home this afternoon or evening, & they are going to give the boys a reception & sort of supper. A good many of the young fellows are friends of mine—I am invited, but it will be too boisterous for me, & I shan't go—If you was here you should go, as it would suit you.

I wish I was down by the pond to-day for a couple of hours, to strip & have a good bath—It is very close & hot here—

There is a great rush now to the country—every train most is full—it is quite a sight to go to the ferry, Philadelphia side, & see the stream of people, men, women & children, old & young, some really funny characters—I go once in a while & take a look at the sight—

We are all well—as soon as I finish this I shall go out for a couple of hours before dinner—(it is now between 11 and 12)— . . .

Good bye for a couple of days, my own loving boy. I shall look for you Thursday—

Your old Walt

Harry, I want you to tell (above every one) your mother and father I have written to you & that I send them my love particular, & I will be down again one of these days—

M S: Berg Collection, New York Public Library

To Anne Gilchrist

Kirkwood, New Jersey, February 22, 1878

Dear friend

I am still here—Your kind letter & the papers arrived at noon to-day—Thanks—They are the first visitations of the sort from *the outside world* for a week—

Sunday Mr S[tafford] and I took a long ride (did I tell you before)—Tuesday another, this time to a *farm-auction*, where all the neighbors were gathered, 100 or more—quite a scene, and a real study of character, looks & manners here—I scanned it all well, (& was doubtless scanned in return)—Mr S was to go up last night with a load of straw for market, but it rained furiously, & he did not go—Rain all day till middle of this afternoon, since which we have had a glorious four hours, grand rainbow & gorgeous sunset—but now, as I write, (8½) it looks like rain again—I still keep well—appetite any how quite magnificent—At least two hours forenoon, & two afternoon, down by the *creek*—Passed between *sauntering*—the *hickory saplings*—& "*Honor* is the *subject* of my story"—(for explanation of the last three lines, ask Herby—)[59]

I am glad Bee gets on so well (but I expected it) & my prayers *might* go up, (if it were not for Tyndal)[60] not only toward the success of the *second negative*,[61] but for you & Giddy in *that* ("up to your ears" of) *needle-work*—I shall be up before many days—May be soon—at any rate I think I shall take supper with you by next Tuesday—

W W

M S: University of Pennsylvania

To his niece Mannahatta

Esopus, New York, June 22 and 26, 1878

Dear Hattie (& all the rest) [62]

I came up here last Thursday afternoon in the steamboat from N Y—a fine day, & had a delightful journey—every thing to interest me—the constantly changing but ever beautiful panorama on both sides of the river all the way for nearly 100 miles here—the magnificent north river bay part of the shores of N Y—the high straight walls of the rocky Palisades—the never-ending hills—beautiful Yonkers—the rapid succession of handsome villages & cities—the prevailing green—the great mountain sides of brown & blue rocks—the river itself—the innumerable elegant mansions in spots peeping all along through the woods & shrubbery—with the sloops & yachts, with their white sails, singly or in fleets, some near us always, some far off—&c &c &c—

& here I am, this is now the third day having a good time—Mr Burroughs & his wife are both kind as they can be—we have plenty of strawberries, cream &c & something I specially like, namely plenty of sugared raspberries & currants—(I go out & pick the currants myself, great red things, bushels of them going to waste)—

Albert Johnston, (the Jeweler's son, I am staying with in N Y) is here too on a visit to the Burroughs's—& makes it still more agreeable—

Yesterday we all (Mr B, Al & I) went out on a long drive—I tell you it is very different country here from out west, or down in Jersey—the old stone fences, two feet thick—the scenery—the many splendid locust trees, often long rows of great big ones—the streams down the mountains, with waterfalls—"Black Creek"—the Cattskills, in the distance—all did me good. It is lucky the roads are first rate (as they are here) for it is up or down hill or around something continually—

We pass'd many *tramps* on the roads—one squad interested me—it was a family of five (or six) in a small flat ricketty one-horse open wagon, with some poor household traps huddled together, some new baskets for sale (they were basket makers I suppose) & some three young children—the man driving, the woman by his side, thin & sickly, & a little babe wrapt in a bundle on her lap, its little feet & legs sticking out towards us as we went by—

On our return at sundown a couple of hours afterwards, we met them again—they had hauled aside in a lonesome spot near the woods, evidently to camp for the night—the horse was took out & was grazing peacefully near by—the man was busy at the wagon, with his baskets & traps, & the boy of 11 or so had gather'd a lot of dry wood & was building a fire on the open ground—As we went on a little on the road we encounter'd the woman with the little baby still in her arms, & her pretty-eyed 6 year old barefoot girl trotting behind, clutching her gown—the woman had two or three baskets she had probably been on to neighboring houses to sell—we spoke to her & bought a basket—she didn't look up out of her old sun-bonnet—her voice, & every thing seem'd queer, *terrified*—then as we went on, Al stopp'd the wagon & went back to the group to buy another basket—he caught a look of the woman's eyes & talked with her a little—says she was young, but look'd & talk'd like *a corpse*—the man was middle aged—

I am having a good quiet time here—eat lots of strawberries, raspberries & currants—(O I wish Lou could have a lot of the latter to do up)—I am well—To-day for a change it is raining—but altogether I have enjoyed fine June weather for my trip—Will finish my letter in New York—

1309 Fifth av. near 86th St New York June 26—p m
Came away from Esopus Monday afternoon 4th, by RR, & got here at dark—Still keep pretty well & shall stay here a few days longer—I find it hard to get away—(then I take things quiet, & a change is good for me)—Jeff's telegram came & Mr Johnston tells me he telegraphed back Monday late in the afternoon—I should much have liked to see Jeff—I suppose he has gone back—I suppose you women folks are having great times all to yourselves—

Yesterday I went out on a steamboat sail down the bay to Sandy Hook with a party of Sorosis ladies—very pleasant—a real sea-sail, sea-breeze &c—(I went up with the pilots in the pilot house)—we had dinner aboard—got back before dark—the weather keeps fine—plenty cool enough for me—Love to you, dear Hat, & dear Jess & dear Aunt Lou, & every body—
Uncle Walt.
M S: Whitman House, Camden

To his sister-in-law Louisa

St. Louis, September 12 and 13, 1879
Dear Lou
Came through here all right—seems to be much as I was mentioning to you the other day—at any rate I feel better here now at the end than I did

the two days before I started, & on Wednesday night & morning—Found it comfortable & easy on the sleeping car—suited me perfectly—I see now that *you ought to have come*—you would have enjoyed every thing—it is really nothing difficult to come—To make it more interesting we had a smash about 5½ Thursday p m on our train, just escaped being something very bad indeed—the two locomotives all shivered to splinters—nobody hurt however, (only one man who jumped, the mail agent)—detained us there 2½ hours—I didn't mind it at all—the last 400 miles since we did fly! I never rode so fast before in my life—strangely enough too I slept quite well—only woke up every hour or two—When we got here in St L an hour & a half ago, on alighting from the cars, found Jeff waiting for me—he looks fat & dark, & like work—(which I guess he has plenty of)—We all rode immediately to the Planter's Hotel, where we were expected, & have just had a royal breakfast, perfect beefsteak, broiled chicken, oysters, good cof-fee &c—enjoyed it, for I hadn't eat any thing since yesterday at 3½—This great hotel is crowded with guests—the proprietor puts his private parlor & room at my disposal, & it is in it I am writing this—Jeff is coming in about an hour to take us on a long ride around—I shall stay with him & the girls to-night—To-morrow morning at 8.50 we start for central Kansas, 350 miles further (we are here 1000 miles from Phila:)—

Lou, I will write again, what moves I make—dont exactly know—most likely I shall come back with Col. F[orney] [63] soon, as I find it mighty conve-nient & nice—every thing seen to—

Saturday—8 a m—I have been stopping at Jeffs—they are very nicely fixed—slept like a top—have just had a first rate breakfast—the girls are well, & send love—they much wish you had come—

I now start in an hour for Kansas, (Lawrence)—shall get there about 10 to-night—

Brother Walt

MS: Missouri Historical Society

To Pete Doyle

St. Louis, November 5, 1879

Dear Pete

You will be surprised to get a letter from me away off here—I have been taking quite a journey the last two months—have been out to the Rocky

Mountains and Colorado (2000 miles)—(Seems to me I sent you a paper six weeks ago from Denver)—I got along very well till about three weeks ago when I was taken sick & disabled, & hauled in here in St Louis for repairs, have been here ever since—am fixed comfortable—Still somewhat under the weather, (but have no doubt I shall be well as usual for me before long)—Shall stay here probably two or three weeks longer, & then back east to Camden.

Pete, this is a wonderful country out here, & no one knows how big it is till he launches out in the midst of it—But there are plenty of hard-up fellows in this city, & out in the mines, & all over here—you have no idea how many run ashore, get sick from exposure, poor grub &c—many young men, some old chaps, some boys of 15 or 16—I met them every where, especially at the RR stoppings, out of money & trying to get home—But the general run of all these Western places, city & country, is very prosperous, on the rush, plenty of people, plenty to eat, & apparently plenty of money— Colorado you know is getting to be the great silver land of the world— In Denver I visited a big smelting establishment, purifying the ore, goes through many processes—takes a week—well they showed me silver there by the cart load—Then in middle Colorado, in one place, as we stopt in a mining camp I saw rough bullion bars piled up in stacks outdoors five or six feet high like hay cocks—

So it is—a few make great strikes—like the prices in the lottery—but most are *blanks*—I was at Pike's Peak—I liked Denver City very much— But the most interesting part of my travel has been *the Plains*, (the great American *Desert* the old geographies call it, but it is no desert) largely through Colorado & Western Kansas, all flat, hundreds & even thousands of miles—some real good, nearly all pretty fair soil, all for stock raising, thousands of herds of cattle, some very large—the herdsmen, (the principal common employment) a wild hardy race, always on horseback, they call 'em *cow-boys* altogether—I used to like to get among them & talk with them—I stopt some days at a town right in the middle of those Plains, in Kansas, on the Santa Fe road—found a soldier[64] there who had known me in the war 15 years ago—was married & running the hotel there—I had hard work to get away from him—he wanted me to stay all winter—

The picture at the beginning of this letter is the St Louis bridge over the Mississippi river—I often go down to the river, or across this bridge—it is one of my favorite sights—but the air of this city don't agree with me—I have not had a well day, (even for me,) since I have been here—

Well, Pete, dear boy, I guess I have written enough—How are you getting along? I often think of you & no doubt you often do of me—God bless you, my darling friend, & however it goes, you must try to keep up a good heart—for I do—

So long—from your old

Walt

M S: Feinberg Collection, Library of Congress

To Susan and George Stafford

London, Ontario, June 13, 1880

My dear friends all

I am still laid up here quite sick—last week has been about the same as the previous one with me—I am up & drest, but dont go out—the weather is in my favor here—if it was as hot here as it seems to be most of the time in Philadelphia, it would go hard with me—They are as kind & good as can be, both Dr and Mrs Bucke—then I have a horse & little basket-wagon appropriated to me, to go out by myself, or be driven out just whenever I like—but to be deprest & sick prevents any thing being enjoyed—But enough of this—I have no doubt it will pass over, as it has times before.

The country here is beautiful with hay & wheat—they are just now in the height of harvest for both, & I watch them from my windows—We have rain every third or fourth day (just now a little too much)—Dr Bucke has a big house & a great many visitors—from two or three to five or six here nearly all the time—two fine young ladies staying all the time, with Mrs B & a governess for his younger children—I tell you if I felt well I should have great times—even as it is we have some jovial hours—last evening nothing would do but I had to come in the parlor & sing a couple of verses of "Black Eye'd Susan"—

If I get all right, the plan is three of us, Doctor & another man & myself, to go down the Lakes, and all down the St Lawrence, (the "Thousands Islands" &c) and so on far north to a great river, the Saguenay, I have always wanted to see—& so to Quebec—will take three weeks—but I will have to feel very different from what I do now—

Well I must close—How are you all? Is George well this summer? Is Harry well & in the store? This is about the *eighth* or *ninth* document I have sent to you from Canada—counting papers, letters, postal cards, &c. (one to

Harry from Lake Huron) & *I havn't had a single breath of reply from any of you*—Susan, I enclose you an envelope—Love to all—

Walt Whitman

I shall get well, no doubt, & be coming back like a bad penny toward the end of the summer.

M S: Feinberg Collection, Library of Congress

To Montgomery Stafford

Montreal, Canada, August 4, 1880

Dear Mont

I have come on here (about 500 miles further) & am stopping in this city for a few days, situated very comfortably & feeling pretty well—the journey is doing me good, for I lay quite sick in London about three weeks. I am better, & enjoying everything. I am traveling mostly by water—and spent several days in "the Lakes of the Thousand Islands"—that is what they call a part of the St Lawrence river, some 50 miles long, & 10 to 20 wide, filled with the prettiest islands you ever see, all sizes, some quite big with fine farms on them, & some very moderate—others rocky hills like, of an acre or two covered with cedars—but *the water* every where I travel in this country is the best part—it is more beautiful and bright than you can conceive, very clean & pure, of a sky-blue color & there seems no end of it—I travel for days & days over it, from Lake Huron on through Lakes Erie and Ontario & down the St Lawrence to here (700 miles) & it is just as fascinating to me now as ever—I have been in sight of it or traveling on it ever since I have been in Canada—I never get tired of it—(We have nothing like it our way, so grand & bright & clear.)

This is a large & busy city, the most important in Canada, ships and steamboats, & immense numbers of emigrants—This is in general quite a great farming country—the land not near so rich & good as out west in the United States—dont raise such corn &c—but it is a healthy & beautiful country here, good climate—pretty good for wheat—they raise a good deal of barley here, (perhaps more than any other grain)—but a fair show of wheat—first rate for grass—ditto for apples—then there is so good a chance for a farmer to have his farm run down to the water—As I travel I see hundreds and hundreds of farms, seems to me a majority of them, along the

banks—they set a little up, & sprinkled with trees looks as though the folks
ought to be happy—(but I suppose they are just like all the rest of us)—It is
very different from what I saw out in Kansas last fall—no water there.

I often think of you all, I wish your father could be out here, & travel
through it once, see the country & the water & farming & everything—he
would enjoy seeing it all, & would understand many things about it better
than I do—But *you* ought to take some such trip, Mont boy, it would make
you open your eyes—(Only I must say I like the smell of the *salt and sedge*
along the water, it is what I was born to, like Long Island or Old Jersey—
but it is all *fresh* here)—

I am going on some 400 miles further—north east to the river Saguenay,
(you will see it on the map of Canada toward north east)—Then back again
to stay awhile in the old city of Quebec—give my love to your parents—tell
your mother—I rec'd her letter—love to Debby, I rec'd her letter too—love
to Ed and Harry & Jo and Van, and Ruthey & Georgey[65]—I rec'd a postal
from Harry—Mont, you & your mother write—I send envelope—

                                                              Walt Whitman

Shall be back in London Aug 14—I want Ed and Debby and Jo to read
this—Harry too, if home—

M S: Feinberg Collection, Library of Congress

To Thomas Nicholson

                                                    Camden, October 14, 1880
Dear Tom[66]

I got home all safe—We stopped a day & a night at Niagara & had a first
rate time—Started the next morning early in an easy comfortable palace car
& went on like a streak through New York and Pennsylvania—got into
Philadelphia after 11 at night—(we were an hour late,) but the city looked
bright & all alive, & I felt as fresh as a lark—

I am well, my summer in Canada has done me great good—it is not only
the fine country & climate there, but I found such good friends, good quarters, good grub, & every thing that could make a man happy—

The last five days I have been down on a jaunt to the sea-shore—got back
last night—It is a great change from the beautiful grass and spacious lawns
there around the Asylum—for miles as far as the eye can reach nothing but
flat gray sand & the sea rolling in—& then looking off at sea, always ships

or steamers in sight out in the offing—I sat hours enjoying it, for it suits me—I was born & brought up near the Sea, & I could listen forever to the hoarse music of the surf—Tom, I got your paper & handbill—*Good for you, boy*—believe me I was pleased to know you won—best respects to Tom Bradley, [Edward] Batters—and Dick Flynn & [Henry] O'Connor—Show them this letter—also Canuth[67]—Write to me—I hope you practice & write as I told you—

Walt Whitman

MS: Yale University

To Harry Stafford

Camden, October 31, 1880

Dear Hank

I have just written a postal to your folks to say I wouldn't be down till Saturday afternoon (Ashland Station) & I thought I would write you a line—Every thing goes well with me these times considering—health & feelings better since I come back from Canada than for nine years past—(one of the ferry men told me he heard a lady say to another on the boat yesterday as I went off, "He looks older & savager than ever, dont he? but there is a something—I dont wonder that Aleck is all taken up with him" &c &c—*Aleck*, the ferry man thought, was her husband)—

I am selling quite a good many of my books now[68]—gives me something to do every day—so you see I have enough to put me in quite a good humor. Then upon going to look where I had my bound books boxed & stored away, up in the garret at Mr. Scovel's,[69] (I hadn't been to look after them in three years)—I found them not only in good condition but found I had twice as many as I calculated—yesterday I had the express man to bring two boxes of 'em home, & left three boxes there still. I got a letter from the PM General, Canada—the missing letter not there—I am convinced it came to Haddonfield—

2.40 afternoon

I have just had my dinner & am up here in my third story room finishing this—it is a bright sunny day here, after the three days' storm—I have been alone all day, but busy & contented—my room is just right for all the year except the very hottest months—the sun pours in here so nice, especially afternoons—I wish you was here to-day, Hank (I havn't got any *wine* though)—I see Hoag[70] yesterday, & Seigfried too—every body is flying around—Election excitement now, very hot. Sports, newspaper men, & politicians busy as the devil in a gale of wind—Love to you, dear son—I shall be down Saturday—

Your old Walt

M S: Berg Collection, New York Public Library

To Richard Watson Gilder

Camden, November 26, 1880

My dear Gilder[71]

I wonder if you can help me in the matter of wh' the enclosed two pp are a statement—Havn't you connected with your establishment some one learn'd in copyright law & its infractions, that could take the thing in hand? *injunct* Worthington or something?

I have sent a duplicate of the two pages to John Burroughs—& asked him to call & see you—I am ab't the same as of late years but unable to travel & mainly helpless.

Walt Whitman

Nothing must be done involving heavy fees, as I couldn't pay them—

Nov: 26 1880

R Worthington 770 Broadway New York about a year ago bo't at auction the electrotype plates (456 pages) of the 1860–'61 edition of my book *Leaves of Grass*—Plates originally made by a young firm *Thayer & Eldridge* under my supervision there and then in Boston, (in the spring of 1860, on an agreement running five years.) A small edition was printed and issued at the time, but in six months or thereabout Thayer & Eldridge failed, and these plates were stored away and nothing further done—till about a year ago (latter part of 1879) they were put up in N Y city by Leavitt, auctioneer, & bought in by said Worthington. (Leavitt, before putting them up, wrote to me offering the plates for sale. I wrote back that said plates were worthless, being superseded by a larger & different edition—that I could not use them (the 1860 ones) myself, nor would I allow them to be used by any one else—I being the sole owner of the copyright.)

However it seems Leavitt did auction them & Worthington bo't them (I suppose for a mere song)—W. then wrote to me offering $250 if I would add something to the text & authenticate the plates, to be published in a book by him. I wrote back (I was in St Louis at the time, helpless, sick) thanking him for the offer, regretting he had purchased the plates, refusing the proposal, & forbidding any use of the plates. Then & since I thought the matter had dropt. But I have to add that about September 1880 (I was in London Canada at the time) I wrote to Worthington referring to his previous offer, then declined by me, and asking whether he still had the plates & was disposed to make the same offer: to which I rec'd no answer. I wrote a second time; and again no answer.

I had supposed the whole thing dropt, & nothing done, but within a week past, I learn that Worthington has been slyly printing and selling the Volume of *Leaves of Grass* from these plates (must have commenced early in 1880) and is now printing and selling it. On Nov. 22, 1880, I found the book, (printed from those plates,) at Porter & Coates' store, cor: 9th & Chestnut Sts. Philadelphia. P & C told me they procured it from Worthington, & had been so procuring it off & on, for nearly a year.[72]

First I want Worthington effectually stopt from issuing the books. Second I want my royalty for all he has sold, (though I have no idea of ever getting a cent.) Third I want W. taken hold of, if possible, on criminal proceeding.

I am the sole owner of the copyright—& I think my copyright papers are all complete—I publish & sell the book myself—it is my sole means of living—What Worthington has done has already been a serious detriment to me. Mr Eldridge, (of the Boston firm alluded to) is accessible in Washington D C—will corroborate first parts of the foregoing—(is my friend)—

Walt Whitman

M S: Formerly in Rosamund Gilder Collection

To Harry Stafford

Camden, January 2, 1881

Dear Hank

I hear from you indirectly once in a while by Hoag, (& saw Debbie & Jo some days since)—I suppose you got the postal I sent you about 12 days ago—the weather has been so bad, or I should have come down—I have had quite a good deal to do writing—have finished quite a piece for a big magazine in N. Y.—the *North American Review*—it was ordered—I get $100 for it—I read the proof last night & sent it off[73]—then I have a little poem *the Patrol at Barnegat* probably in next Harper's[74]—(but I think I told you about it)—then to-day I am busy on another order—So you see I have something to do—I will send you the *Review* piece when printed—I am feeling better and *sassier* this winter so far than for some years, am very comfortable here, plain & quiet though—eat my allowance every time—& have a little jug of *good Jamaica rum* from which I take a sip now & then—(but not very often)—came in chill'd & dumpy late yesterday afternoon—made myself a good mug of hot rum, & felt better—

Hank, I hope you are having fair times on the road—I am glad you stick to it—perseverance will conquer. Horner[75] was here again a few evenings ago, an hour—How do you get on with Col: Ingersoll's book?[76] (You mustn't take too much stock in him)—If there is any book particular you want, you tell me, & I will try to get it—Lots of sleighs out, good sleighing—my brother was out day before yesterday, & got overturned—I wanted to go yesterday, but he was afraid for me to venture it—his nag is pretty lively, (but I should have liked that all the better)—

1½—just had dinner, hot soup, cold roast beef, apple pie—all good—the sun is out real warm, & I shall go at my piece for the N Y order—it is for a lady, a friend of mine—she has been for years principal literary editor of the *Herald*, & now she is going to start a paper of her own—pays me[77]—

Is Ed home? I should just like to have a ten mile ride behind his nag with the sleigh bells—Dear boy, I send you my best love & dont you forget it—

Your old Walt

M S: Berg Collection, New York Public Library

To Harry Stafford

Camden, January 27, 1881

Dear Hank—

Dear boy—your letter rec'd & read—Take it easy about the minister & the Ingersoll business—the best answer you can make is to be quiet & good natured & even attentive & *not get mad worth a cent*—True religion (*the most beautiful thing in the whole world*, & the best part of any man's or woman's, or boy's character) consists in *what one does* square and kind & generous & honorable all days, *all the time*—& especially with his own folks & associates & with the poor & illiterate & in devout meditation, & silent thoughts of God, & death—& not at all in what he *says*, nor in Sunday or prayer meeting *gas*—My own opinion is that Ingersoll *talks* too much on his side—a *good life, steady trying to do fair*, & a sweet, tolerant liberal disposition, shines like the sun, tastes like the fresh air of a May morning, blooms like a perfect little flower by the road-side—& all the blowing, talking & powowing *both sides* amounts to little or nothing—Glad, dear boy, you had a good little visit, you & Mont, with me—I enjoyed it too—I am writing this up in the room—the sun shines, but sharp cold & the wind whistling—

Your Walt

M S: Berg Collection, New York Public Library

To Harry Stafford

Camden, February 11, 1881

Dear Hank—

Yours of 9th rec'd—am a little suprised you take to L of G so quickly[78]— I guess it is because the last five years had been *preparing & fixing the ground*, more & more & more—& now that the seed is dropt in it sprouts quickly—my own feeling ab't my book is that it makes (tries to make) every fellow *see himself*, & see that *he has got to work out his salvation himself*— has got to pull the oars & hold the plow, or swing the axe *himself*—& that the real blessings of life are not the fictions generally supposed, but are real, & are mostly within reach of all—you chew on this—

Hank, I am still feeling under the weather—My appetite is fair, (when I can get what I like)—& sleep middling, but I am as weak as a cat, & dull half-dizzy spells every day—I sent off two sets of books to-day, got the money for them—one set to a big lady in England—I enclose you a slip of a piece out to-morrow in the N Y *Critic*, about the old man Carlyle, 85 years old, the grandest writer in England, just dead—they sent for me to write it ($10 worth)—You read it carefully—read it twice—then *show it to your mother*, I want her to read it, without fail—(Hank, *you do not appreciate your mother*—there is not a nobler woman in Jersey)—

Your Walt

M S: Berg Collection, New York Public Library

To Harry Stafford

Camden, February 28, 1881

Dear boy Harry

I sent you a few lines three days ago, but I will write again as I have just rec'd yours of 26—a little wild & nervous & uncertain some parts, (but I am

always glad to get any letters from you, dear boy)—Harry, you certainly
know well enough you have my best honorable loving friendship settled—
Of the past I think only of the comforting soothing things of it all—I go
back to the times at Timber Creek beginning most five years ago, & the banks
& spring, & my hobbling down the old lane—& how I took a good turn
there & commenced to get slowly but surely better, healthier, stronger—
Dear Hank, I realize plainly that *if I had not known you*—if it hadn't been
for you & our friendship & my going down there summers to the creek with
you—and living there with your folks, & the kindness of your mother, &
cheering me up—I believe *I should not be a living man to-day*—I think &
remember deeply these things & they comfort me—*& you, my darling boy,
are the central figure of them all*—

Of the occasional ridiculous little storms & squalls of the past I have quite
discarded them from my memory—& I hope you will too—the other recol-
lections overtop them altogether, & occupy the only permanent place in my
heart—as a manly loving friendship for you does also, & will while life
lasts—Harry, dont be discouraged by any business or other disappointments of the past—It will all turn out right—The main thing, in my opinion,
after finding out as much as possible of life, & entering upon it (it is a
strange mixed business this life) is to live a good square one—This I believe
you are really anxious to do, & God bless you in it, & you shall have all the
help I can give—Your loving ever-faithful old friend & comrade—

Walt Whitman

Hank, I want you to acknowledge this letter—I hope this won't fail to
reach you like some others I have sent—I want to come down before long &
then we will have some good square talks—it is now half past 4 & I see the
sun is going to set clear—

MS: Feinberg Collection, Library of Congress

To Thomas Nicholson

Camden, March 17, 1881

Dear Tom

Your letter has just come aʟ right & I am glad to hear from you again.
Every thing seems to go lovely there with you & the boys & Dr B[ucke]
(which is as it should be)—Tom, I often think of you all, & of the last night

we all got together, & of the friendly parting drink we all had out there on the lawn—seems as if I only got to know you & all best & then time for me to clear out—

I have some good times here in moderation—I cant go around very lively, but I enjoy what's going on wherever I go—This 31st of May coming I shall be 62—but thank the Lord I still feel young at heart & cheery as ever— After I returned last fall from Canada I was first rate all along—put in four good months—had some rare old times—will tell you when we meet, Tom—but some six weeks ago was careless enough to get badly chill'd all through my whole body, & repeated the next day—So I have been since quite under the weather—But I am getting over it & feeling quite myself again—I find I can be well enough if I take very particular care of myself, how I go, &c—

An old doctor here said to me "Whitman you are like an old wagon, built of first rate stuff, & the best sort of frame & wheels & nuts—& as long as you are mighty careful, & go slow, & *Keep to good roads*, you will last as long as any of us—but if you get on bad roads, or cut up any capers, then *look out*"—I go down every week or two (I go tomorrow again) about 20 miles from here right into the country, with a family of farmers, dear friends of mine, named Stafford—Keep a country store also—a big family of boys & girls, & Mrs S one of the kindest & best women in the world—how much happier one can be when there is good women around—Does me good to be with them all. Every thing is very old fashioned, just suits me—good grub & plenty of it. My great loafing place out there is a big old woods, mostly pine & oak, but lots of laurel & holly, old paths & roads every where through the thick woods—I spend hours there every day—have it all to my-self—go out there well-protected, even in a snow storm—rabbits & squir-rels, & lots of birds beginning already—Tom, you would laugh to see me the way I amuse myself, often spouting terrible pieces Shakspere or Homer as loud as I can yell. (But that always was a favorite practice of mine—I used to do it in the din of Broadway New York from the top of an omnibus—at other times along the seashore at Coney Island)—

Tom, my paper is fill'd & I must close—I wanted to write something about the running & matches, but must postpone it—Give my love to all my friends there & you yourself, dear boy—

Walt Whitman

M S: Trent Collection, Duke University

To Susan Stafford

Camden, May 6, 1881

My dear friend

I am sorry to hear of your feeling so unwell, & have thought about it probably more than you think—bad enough any how to feel sick or half sick, & specially so with one that has so much depending upon her, (& a pretty ambitious spirit too)—I thought I would write you a few lines & maybe it might cheer you a little—Things go on quite the same with me—a little more quiet than usual since I got back from Boston[79] (I suppose you got the letter & papers I sent you while I was there)—I had a lively time in Boston—Susan, I wish you could have been there the evening of my lecture—it was such a collection of people as would have suited you, & been a study—different from any I ever saw in my life before—fully one half were women—something different in all of them from the usual crowd—about 300—(I will tell you more when I see you)—

As I write this part of my letter, just come up from dinner—we had a great fat sweet baked shad, just right—what is better once in a while for dinner than good fresh fish, & potatoes?—(I remember you too are fond of fish sometimes)—Shad are unusually good & plenty now—I wish I could send you & George down a couple of big fresh ones, such as I see them bringing in every haul, from the river—

A middling fair rain here to-day & last night—it is raining as I write—well I am glad of it, for it will do a power of good—our street begins to look first rate with the long rows of trees, five squares of them now all out in leaf—Strawberries are already huckstered about the street—I suppose bro't from the south—

Rec'd a long good letter from Mrs. Gilchrist—I think Beatrice must be regularly established as a woman physician in Edinburgh—Mrs. G. is going on there to visit her, & for a change, as she is not yet real well—Herbert is painting away & I guess having a good time, with lots of company & fun &c.—

I was out a few evenings ago to spend an hour or two in north Camden with some friends, a Quaker family, three sisters, quite elderly, one (the oldest) a widow with a grown up son & daughter—they sent for me to come to tea—the five live together—they are neither poor nor rich—Keep no servant—but O such quiet, happy, kind, affectionate ways—cheerful too, & plenty of good things—but *the manners,* "the peace of heaven"—I enjoyed myself first rate just being with them—(besides the good things)—

Susan, what do you hear about old Mrs. [Rachel] Morgan? I suppose she is needy enough, poor old woman, & if you have a chance I should like you to send her things to the amount of *two dollars* a month, as I told you, & I will pay for them—(if you cant go yourself, may-be you can send by Debby or Patience)—

Evening ½ past 8—Well I will finish my letter & put it in the box—maybe you will get it to read Sunday—This afternoon 4 to 6½ I took one of my usual jaunts over in the busiest parts of Philadelphia—Market and Chestnut Streets—crowded with myriads of people & vehicles—all seemed to be going as if the devil was after them—the crowds & rush & excitement seemed to be much greater even than usual—Well I took some three hours of it—then slowly across the river & home—had my supper, & here I am in perfect quiet up in my room, finishing my letter—

Susan, my dear friend, I hope this will find you all right & well again—but if still unwell, try to keep a good heart—Love to all—

Walt Whitman

M S: Feinberg Collection, Library of Congress

1881-1889

As Whitman's health deteriorated toward the close of his life, he was confined to a bedroom cluttered with books, manuscripts, newspapers, and memorabilia, seemingly without any order, although he somehow found what he wanted with little difficulty. The photograph on the table is of John Addington Symonds, who pressed Whitman regarding the meaning of the Calamus poems. About 1889.

AFTER THE FAILURE OF THE FIRM OF THAYER AND EL-
dridge in 1860, Whitman had to wait more than twenty years before an established publisher expressed interest in his writings. The publisher was the
prestigious successor of Ticknor and Fields, James R. Osgood and Company. At once Whitman accepted with "fair warning" that the sexual poems
"must go in the same as ever." In a note obviously written by the poet, *The
Critic* announced on August 13, 1881, that Osgood was to publish *Leaves of
Grass* "without any expurgations, the author having made that a condition
of his contract."[1]

Whitman went to Boston in August and settled in for two months, as in
usual fashion he supervised every step of the publication process. Things
went "swimmingly,"[2] he reported. There was even time for a two-day visit to
Concord, Massachusetts, for his last meetings with Ralph Waldo Emerson,
who was "more eloquent, grand, appropriate & impressive than ever," although he had but one year to live.

On March 1, 1882, Oliver Stevens, the Boston district attorney, informed
Osgood and Company, "We are of the opinion that this book is such a book
as brings it within the provisions of the Public Statutes respecting obscene
literature and suggest the propriety of withdrawing the same from circulation and suppressing the editions thereof."[3] At first Whitman agreed to
make some minor verbal excisions, which were to be concealed by resetting
type, but after he refused to delete "A Woman Waits for Me" and "Ode to a
Common Prostitute," Osgood bowed to the authorities and was "open to
any reasonable arrangement for turning the plates over to you."[4]

The well-publicized scandal lured O'Connor out of his decade-long silence. In a virtuoso performance he lambasted the philistines savagely and
placed the thorny crown of the martyr once again on the forehead of "the
carpenter." At once, in Whitman's words, the two men were "on the same
terms as of yore."[5]

Early in June, Rees Welsh and Company, the Philadelphia booksellers and
publishers, offered to print *Leaves of Grass* and later agreed to publish *Specimen Days*, Whitman's prose miscellany. After the notoriety following the
Boston censorship, Whitman's books for the first (but last) time sold well,
although sales never approximated those of Longfellow and Whittier. In 1882
royalty payments amounted to more than $1400.[6] When interest stimulated
by the incident waned, royalties returned to the usual level of about $200
annually. Once again, then, Whitman had to be his own salesman. He heard
America singing, but America still wasn't listening to his songs. As Whitman
with great honesty and some pain confessed to Traubel in 1888, "I was not

only not popular (and am not popular yet—never will be) but I was *non grata*—I was not welcome in the world. The fellows on top did not want me at any price—not even as a gift: the people, the crowd—I have had no way of reaching them . . . as things are I am a stranger to them."[7] He realized that his relentless self-promotion in the media had failed since it had focused attention not on the poet but on the man. He also knew that "I have always been isolated from my people—in certain senses have been a stranger in their midst . . . they have not known me: they have always missed my intentions."[8] His seemingly unwavering affirmation, then, rested on the painful awareness that at seventy he was still "a stranger" in the crowd and in the family.

George and Louisa Whitman sold their house on Stevens Street and moved to a farm in Burlington, New Jersey, and although Walt was invited to join them, he purchased a "shanty," a most modest house, at 328 Mickle Street. He could not bring himself to leave Camden and Philadelphia, and so on March 26, 1884, he moved into the first house he had ever owned. The transition was not easy. He owned a building, but there was no household. In addition, he was ill, depressed, and lonesome—perhaps somewhat frightened at the prospect of change and attendant uncertainties. "Bad as the weather is," he explained to the Staffords, "I must up & go out & across the river, or I shall have the horrors."[9] His emotional state was not eased when, shortly before he was to move, Tasker Lay, a young friend age fifteen or sixteen, died suddenly of consumption, and he was burdened with still another loss.[10]

In February 1885 he persuaded Mrs. Mary O. Davis, a widow, to become his housekeeper. A motherly soul, evidently with a sense of humor, she managed to get along with the lonely poet. She was no more capable of understanding his poetry than his own mother, but she faithfully attended the poet in the declining years. He provided only $1000 in his will for Mrs. Davis, who claimed that she had spent more than $3000 of her own money on the household and had been promised a more substantial sum.

Whitman was more and more confined to the house, sometimes to the point that he felt "like a rat in a cage day in & day out." Immediately he cautioned himself, "But I must not growl—it might be so much worse." Whitman was more self-disciplined than he superficially seemed, and he venerated, as he advised John Addington Symonds in a famous letter, "restraint." As he said to Bucke, "nature has not only endowed me with immense emotionality but immense bufferism (so to call it) or placid resignation to what happens," which is as perceptive a comment as anyone has ever ventured in dealing with the complexity of this keenly self-aware man.

The man who celebrated "the body electric" and doted on its physical delights was forced to watch his own body slowly atrophy. Friends and acquaintances—including Mark Twain, Oliver Wendell Holmes, and Edwin Booth—raised funds to purchase a horse and buggy, which provided the mobility his body no longer could sustain and granted him the spectatorial pleasures which he sought with the enthusiasm of a child. Boston friends raised funds to acquire a summer cottage so that he could escape the humid heat of Camden summers, but Whitman, who manipulated donors as well as publishers, diverted the funds to suit himself, and in the process lost a few friends. The English again raised money for his assistance, and the poet assured the contributors that "My best help however has come in my old age & paralysis from the British Islands." The statement understandably annoyed American friends, who knew enough about Whitman to recognize the source of the public announcement. Examination of his income in the years 1875 to 1892, including receipts from book orders, royalties, publication, gifts, and lectures, reveals that Whitman received from Americans more than $14,500, from the English slightly more than $5500.[11]

When Whitman required more assistance than Mrs. Davis could provide, there was a procession of male companions or nurses. The first was Billy Duckett,[12] who was also a model for Thomas Eakins, and the list included other young men like Edward Wilkins, who came to Camden from Canada at the suggestion of Dr. Bucke, and Warren Fritzinger, a former sailor and the son of an aged seaman whom Mrs. Davis had attended until his death. Though the roles were reversed, the situation evoked the hospitals of Washington.

Beginning about 1888 Horace Traubel called at 328 Mickle Street once or twice a day and kept almost stenographic records of the conversations and physical state of the poet, which have been published in *With Walt Whitman in Camden*. At eighteen Traubel met Whitman for the first time, in 1876 on the day of the death of Walter Orr Whitman, the son of George and Louisa. Traubel's brother-in-law, Thomas B. Harned, a lawyer, also visited almost daily; he took care of legal matters and, with Traubel and Bucke, became one of the poet's literary executors. Whitman wrote to Bucke several times a week, postcards usually, with details primarily about his health, since he expected and received medical advice. He pretended surprise when he learned that Bucke had carefully preserved his brief letters and postcards: "I'm only sorry that they are not more worthy. They are all so short, so empty—so much the result rather of a desire to write than of any feeling of anything particular to say."[13]

When no mail was delivered he could not conceal his disappointment. His spirits rose and fell, and he chose the exact image to characterize the situation: "I need the fellows—they feed me: lying in here, cribbed here, they are sustenance, life to me." The absence of mail he construed as rejection. "I am sorry for myself," he confessed, "when I think how little John [Burroughs] writes me nowadays." [14]

Despite his illness and constant enervation, he continued to submit pieces to newspapers and magazines. Most were accepted, but gradually, and inevitably, some editors sent rejection slips. Whitman was hurt and deeply wounded, but he also knew that his poems, with few exceptions, in the later years were mediocre, compulsively repetitious, not even deeply felt, and that in his prose he strained for subject matter. Like most authors he continued to write: to stop was to make a frightening admission. "Writing is a disease," he declared. "Look where it has brought me. Do you envy the pass it has brought me to?" [15]

To James R. Osgood, publisher

Camden, May 8, 1881

My dear Mr Osgood

I write in answer to the note on the other side from my dear friend O'Reilly [16]—My plan is to have all my poems, down to date, comprised in one 12 mo: Volume, under the name "Leaves of Grass"—I think it will have to be in brevier (or bourgeois) solid—and I want as fine a (plain) specimen in type, paper, ink, binding, &c. as bookmaking can produce—not for luxury however, but solid wear, use, reading, (to carry in the pocket, valise &c)—a book of about 400 pages to sell at $3—The text will be about the same as hitherto, occasional slight revisions, simplifications in punctuation &c—the main thing a more satisfactory consecutive order—a better *ensemble*, to suit me—some new pieces, perhaps 30 pages—

Fair warning on one point—the old pieces, the *sexuality* ones, about which the original row was started & kept up so long, are all retained, & must go in the same as ever—Should you, upon this outline, wish to see the copy, I will place it in your hands with pleasure—

Walt Whitman

MS: Henry E. Huntington Library

To James R. Osgood

Camden, June 1, 1881

My dear Mr Osgood
    Yours of May 31 just rec'd—Thanking you warmly for willingness, promptness, &c. my terms are:

25 cts on every copy sold if the retail price is put at $2
30 cts on every copy sold if the retail price is put at $2.50 [17]

    If these suit you the bargain is settled—you shall be fully fortified as sole publisher with all legal authority—& you can act accordingly in England— If they do not suit no harm done—the thing is off—but with perfect good feeling left on both sides.

Walt Whitman

M S: Hanley Collection, University of Texas

To James R. Osgood

Camden, June 4, 1881

My dear Mr Osgood
    Yours of yesterday rec'd, which settles the engagement. I shall forward the copy soon. The name will be *Walt Whitman's Poems*—with the sub-title *Leaves of Grass* in its place or places inside. I suggest a 400 page book—in size, thickness, general appearance &c: closely like Houghton & Mifflin's 1880 edition of *Owen Meredith's Poems*, only better paper & print, & at least one size larger type—I think in solid bourgeois (or long primer)—ought to be new type—page the same size as the Owen Meredith (see outline in blue lines on the picture I send) with the same rather narrow margin, which I prefer to wide—in the make up every thing the reverse of free spacing out or free leading—of course not crowding too close either, but with an eye to compacting the matter (for there is quite a good deal to go in the 400 pages)—plain green muslin binding—binding costing say 15 or 16 cts.—no gilt edges—a handsome, stately, *plain book*—
    I shall get a new copyright out—Shall probably write to you in London about the English sale—Can I get a British copyright by going to Canada? If

so I will go—How would the enclosed picture do for a frontispiece? I like it—It is made by Gutekunst 712 Arch St Philadelphia—I think he would furnish them at three to four dollars a thousand.

Walt Whitman

Who of your house shall I specially see & deal with if I should take a notion to come on to Boston in person with the copy—or after the type setting commences?

M S: Yale University

To James R. Osgood and Company

Boston, September 12, 1881

The documents rec'd—but I cannot agree or convey copyright as therein specified. Of course you must be thoroughly fortified in your investment & publication of the book—& I will do any & every thing to secure you to your fullest satisfaction (if not already—which I thought the case—distinctly, amply, legally secured by my letters in the correspondence between us *ante*)—But the copyright of *Leaves of Grass* must remain absolutely & solely in my own hands as hitherto.

The steel engraving—just as good as new I believe—I send herewith. It is required in the book (to face page 29)—in fact is involved as part of the poem. If desired I will sell it to you, as a necessary part of the stock for issuing the book—price $50 cash, & 20 copies of book (without royalty)—I shall want 200 prints from the plate also—(the printer can make that number extra & give me)—

The book will make 390 (to '95) pages. Seems to me every way best for us both that it sh'd be put at *two dollars*—& that it can well be afforded at that price.

Before putting in any thing in adv't'mt or circular advertising L. of G. let me be consulted—Show me first.

Dont forget carefully attending to the English copyright through Trübner—as we concluded about it the other day.

I want to say over again that while I reserve to the fullest degree all my own rights & the means to maintain them, you are to be, & I hereby make & confirm you, the sole issuers and publishers of my completed *Leaves of*

Grass—that I shall coöperate strenuously & loyally in the enterprise—& to add that I do not fix any term or limit of years, because it is my wish that the publication by you, on the conditions & payments of royalty already settled between us, may, while those conditions are fulfilled, continue on and on, quite indefinitely & without limit, as being (I hope) better for you, & better for me too.

Should you wish any thing more in detail let me know. Of course any further points, specifications &c. that may arise as time elapses, or as circumstances or our wishes require, are open to both of us, to be added, modified, revoked or what not, as we may join & agree.

Walt Whitman

M S: Yale University

To John Burroughs

Boston, September 24, 1881

Dear friend

Yours rec'd—I am now back here finishing up—only staid a few days in Concord, but they were mark'd days. Sunday, Emerson & his wife, son Edward & wife &c. gave me a dinner—two hours—every thing just right every way—a dozen people there, (the family & relatives)—for my part I thought the old man in his smiling and alert quietude & withdrawness—he has a good color in the face & ate just as much dinner as any body—more eloquent, grand, appropriate & impressive than ever—more indeed than could be described—Wasn't it comforting that I have had—in the sunset as it were—so many significant affectionate hours with him under such quiet, beautiful, appropriate circumstances?

The book is done & will be in the market in a month or so—all about it has proceeded satisfactorily—& I have had my own way in every thing—the old name "Leaves of Grass" is retained—it will be a $2 book—

I shall probably go on to New York in about a week—shall stay at Johnston's, (address me there Mott avenue & 149th street N Y city) about a week or ten days—

Besides this general death-gloom of the nations [18]—have you heard of the sudden & dreadful death of our young friend Beatrice Gilchrist in performing some chemical experiment with ether?

Joaquin Miller is here—is with me every day—Longfellow has been to see me—I have met O W Holmes & old Mr James.[19]
With love—

Walt Whitman

M S: Mr. and Mrs. Stephen Greene

To Dr. John Fitzgerald Lee[20]

Camden, December 20, 1881

Dear Sir

Your letter asking definite endorsement to a translation of my *Leaves of Grass* into Russian is just received, and I hasten to answer it. Most warmly and willingly I consent to the translation, and waft a prayerful *God speed* to the enterprise.

You Russians and we Americans;—our countries so distant, so unlike at first glance—such a difference in social and political conditions, and our respective methods of moral and practical development the last hundred years;—and yet in certain features, and vastest ones, so resembling each other. The variety of stock-elements and tongues to be resolutely fused in a common Identity and Union at all hazards—the idea, perennial through the ages, that they both have their historic and divine mission—the fervent element of manly friendship throughout the whole people, surpassed by no other races—the grand expanse of territorial limits and boundaries—the unformed and nebulous state of many things, not yet permanently settled, but agreed on all hands to be the preparations of an infinitely greater future—the fact that both peoples have their independent and leading positions to hold, keep, and if necessary fight for, against the rest of the world—the deathless aspirations at the inmost centre of each great community, so vehement, so mysterious, so abysmic—are certainly features you Russians and we Americans possess in common.

And as my dearest dream is for an internationality of poems and poets binding the lands of the earth closer than all treaties or diplomacy—As the purpose beneath the rest in my book is such hearty comradeship for individuals to begin with, and for all the Nations of the earth as a result—how happy indeed I shall be to get the hearing and emotional contact of the great Russian peoples!

To whom, now and here, (addressing you for Russia, and empowering you, should you see fit, to put the present letter in your book, as a preface to it,) I waft affectionate salutation from these shores, in America's name.

Walt Whitman

You see I have addressed you as Russian—let it stand so—go on with your translation—I send you a book by this mail—advise me from time to time—address me here—

W W

M S: Yale University

To Harry Stafford

Camden, January 25, 1882

Dear Harry

Yours rec'd—I am just starting off a few miles out from Phila—probably a day or two only—will look up the book you require (if I can find one) soon as I come back—& send you—I am ab't as usual—nothing very new—

Hank, if I'd known you was coming home last Sunday would have come down Saturday & staid till Monday any way—You say you wrote a *blue letter* but didn't send it to me—dear boy, the only way is to dash ahead and "whistle dull cares away"—after all its mostly in one's self one gets blue & not from outside—life is like the weather—you've got to take what comes, & you can make it all go pretty well if only think so (& provide in reason, for rain & snow)—

I wish it was so you could all your life come in & see me often for an hour or two—You see I think I understand you better than any one—(& like you more too)—(You may not fancy so, but it *is* so)—& I believe, Hank, there are many things, confidences, questions, candid *says* you would like to have with me, you have never yet broached—me the same—

Have you read about Oscar Wilde? He has been to see me & spent an afternoon—He is a fine large handsome youngster—had the *good sense* to take a great fancy to *me*! I was invited to receptions in Phila. am'g the big bugs & a grand dinner to him by Mr & Mrs Childs[21]—but did not go to any—Awful cold here, this is now the third day, but you know all about *that*—(you say you know you are *a great fool*—don't you know every 'cute

fellow secretly knows that about himself—I do)—God bless you, my darling boy—Keep a brave heart—

W W

M S: Feinberg Collection, Library of Congress

To Harry Stafford

Camden, January 31, 1882

Rec'd yours to-day—Sorry you didnt get the letter sent that day I met
you, as I wanted you to have it particular—but perhaps it has come to
hand—that it went to Berlin p. o. I have no doubt, as I mailed it myself,
addressed it to you "care of Sheriff Gibbs" same as this envelope—

I hear Ed has sold the nag, & gone off to seek his fortune, newspaper
canvassing &c. [22]—Whether he will make much money or not, I dont know,
but I feel sure he will learn a good deal & get experience of the world &
people, & *of himself* too—all of which is the *wisdom* described in scripture
as better than riches—rec'd a long letter from Herbert Gilchrist, to-day—he
seems to be well, & working away hard at his painting—he describes to me
some of his new pictures—says his mother was temporarily quite unwell,
when he wrote—Edward Carpenter was visiting them—has a big beard—

Nothing new with me—I keep well as usual—you say when I have a *blue
spell* I must write to you—I don't have any such spells—& seems to me it is
time you grew out of them—my theory is that it is *in onesself* and not from
outside circumstances one suffers such unhappy hours—the more one yields
to them the frequenter & stronger they get until at last they take complete
possession of a fellow—Harry dear, you are a good wrestler—see if you cant
throw them & keep 'em thrown—

But I ought to write you something cheerful—I have been in all day—
quite a deep snow & the wind blowing—I here in my big rocking chair at a
job writing—Oscar Wilde sent me his picture yesterday, a photo a foot & a
half long, nearly full length, very good—

As this letter has little or nothing in it I suppose it will be sure to reach
you & not miss—like the other I wanted you to get—

Your old W W

M S: Berg Collection, New York Public Library

To Dr. Richard Maurice Bucke

Camden, February 7, 1882

I have just sent the MS[23] back by Adams express, same address as this letter.

You will be surprised, probably enraged, at the manner in which I have gone through it—

Upon first looking over it I was divided between two courses—whether to send it back without revision at all—or to go over it *with decision* making all the corrections & changes I felt entirely clear of. After deliberating I decided on the latter—I have acted upon it.

Without explaining each particular point of elision or addition, I will only say that I am convinced if you accept & print this copy as now arranged, you will bless your stars afterward—(printed in the old shape it would have turned out ill, and in very many things would probably have been unendorsed by you, as it certainly would by me.)

The character you give me is not a true one in the main—I am by no means that benevolent, equable, happy creature you pourtray—but let that pass—I have left it as you wrote.

You will see what I have substituted for your argument on the sexual theme. Upon looking it over (pages 166 to 168) after an interval I am satisfied with it, and am willing to let those sections of my poems stand or fall on its support.

I am sure as I can be all of those elaborated and lengthy parts from *Man's Moral Nature*[24] should be ruled out of this book & referred to their own volume, where they are magnificent, (but an intrusion and superfluity here). The whole MS. was far, far far too redundant—some things were often repeated three or four times—several long passages (very likely those you had set your heart on) were very much better out than in. Others would have been nuts to the caricature baboons—There were many errors or half-errors of fact.

But there is enough to make a very creditable, serviceable book—a permanent storehouse of many biographic, personal & other things, and of your glowing & penetrating criticism—

Upon the whole it will justify itself, and (as I have corrected it if you accept) will endure the test of both [readers?] & the best critics of one, ten or fifty years hence—which is the main thing.

Although the MS as it comes back may seem *in a state* to your eyes, I assure you that the printers could take it just as it is, (all numbered with the folios in blue pencil) and get along with ease.

Finally as all the excised pages of the MS are returned (& though it will need considerable writing &c.) it can be restored entirely to the original form, if you should decide to do so.

TEXT: Photostat, University of Pennsylvania

To James R. Osgood and Company

Camden, March 7, 1882

I am not afraid of the District Attorney's threat—it quite certainly could not amount to any thing—but I want you to be satisfied, to continue as publishers of the book (& I had already thought favorably of some such brief cancellation.)

Yes, under the circumstances I am willing to make a revision & cancellation in the pages alluded to—wouldn't be more than half a dozen anyhow— perhaps indeed about ten lines to be left out, & half a dozen words or phrases.[25]

Have just returned from a fortnight down in the Jersey woods, & find your letter—

Walt Whitman

MS: Hanley Collection, University of Texas

To James R. Osgood and Company

Camden, March 21, 1882

Dear Sirs

Yours of 20th rec'd, ab't Dr Bucke's book. I know something about it, & do not object. Dr B. has spent considerable on the illustrations (I have seen them, they are quite creditable) has gathered a variety of biographical information—criticises my poems from an almost passionately friendly point of view (as scientist, student of poetry, medical doctor &c)—& has included what as time goes on may prove a curiously valuable collection of cumulative opinions on L of G. from 1856 to the present day—& I should say it would be a safe publication-enterprise—but you must of course judge & decide for yourselves[26]—

Another thing I must broach—hoping you are not alarmed at the District

Attorney episode, (as I am not at all,) but see your way clear to continue on in earnest—

I have about got into shape a volume (*It* at least will not be liable to any District Att'y episodes—) comprising all my *prose writings* to be called (probably)

Specimen Days
& Thoughts
by Walt Whitman

to be about same size as L of G. This little Dist. Att'y flurry blowing over, & we getting things into good shape—(as of course I suppose *it* surely will, & *we* will)—would you bring it out say late this summer, same terms as L of G? In that case there would be three Volumes gyrating together, the L of G—the S D & T—and Dr Bucke's book—

Upon the whole, & as my friend seems determined to bring out his book, I hope you will take it. I know Dr Bucke well, & have for some years—He is a perfectly honorable, reliable solid man to deal with—a linguist, well conversant with the best German, French & British poetry—of English stock & birth, but grown up in Canada and the California regions of America, & combining in my opinion the best traits of both nationalities. He is now & has been for some years, (in fact he built up & organized it) at the head of the largest & most complete & modernized Asylum for the Insane in America—(one of the largest in the world—1000 persons under his charge)—near London, Ontario, Canada—Though enthusiastic he has a careful eye to practical & business responsibilities—has a fine very large family of children—his social, professional, citizen &c reputation, all first class in Canada.

Walt Whitman

M S: Hanley Collection, University of Texas

To James R. Osgood and Company

Camden, March 23, 1882

Dear Sirs

Yours of 21st rec'd, with the curious list—I suppose of course from the District Attorney's office—of "suggestions" lines and pages and pieces &c. to be "expunged." The list whole & several is rejected by me, & will not be thought of under any circumstances.[27]

To give you a definitive idea of what I meant in my notes of March 8 and

March 19—& of course stick to—I mail you with this a copy of L. of G. with the not numerous but fully effective changes and cancellations I thought of making: see in it pages   84

88

89

& 90

All those lines & passages marked in pencil to come out, & their places to be exactly filled with other matter—so that they will superficially present the same appearance as now. The whole thing would not involve an expense of more than from 5 to $10—

My proposition is that we at once make the revision here indicated, & go on with the regular issue of the book—If then any further move is made by the District Attorney & his backers—as of course there are others behind it all—they will only burn their own fingers, & very badly—

I want the paper copy I send of L of G. returned to me when through.

Walt Whitman

Let this whole matter be kept quiet in the house—no talk or information that may lead to newspaper items—the change to be just silently made—the book, & at casual view all its pages, to look just the same—only those minutely looking detecting the difference—

Inform the official people at once that the cancellation is to be made for future editions.

W W

Write me at once & definitively if all this suits—
M S: Hanley Collection, University of Texas

To James R. Osgood and Company

Telegram
Camden, April 5, 1882

Dated   Camden N J
To   Jas R Osgood & Co
              211 Tremont St Boston

No I cannot consent to leave out the two pieces I am only willing to carry out my letter of March twenty third.

Walt Whitman

M S: Hanley Collection, University of Texas

To James R. Osgood and Company

Camden, April 12, 1882

Dear Sirs

Yours of 10th just rec'd—If you desire to cease to be the publishers of *Leaves of Grass* unless I make the excisions required by the District Attorney—if this is your settled decision—I see indeed no other way than "some reasonable arrangement for turning the plates over" to me—What is the am't of royalty due me, according to contract, from the sales altogether? & what is your valuation of the plates?

Walt Whitman

M S: Hanley Collection, University of Texas

To John Burroughs

Camden, April 28, 1882

Dear friend

Just returned from a fortnight down in the Jersey woods—not feeling well this month, (a bad cold, neuralgia, other head trouble, bowel trouble &c—yet nothing serious—will blow over in a few days)—went down for a change—had bad weather & nothing propitious—but I have just come back & am already better—shall get along—

So Emerson is dead[28]—the leading man in all Israel—If I feel able I shall go to his funeral—improbable though—A new deal in the fortunes of *Leaves of Grass*—the District Attorney at Boston has threatened Osgood with indictment "under the statutes against obscene literature," specifies a long list of pieces, lines, &c.—Osgood is frightened, asks me to change & expurgate—I refuse peremptorily—*he throws up the book & will not publish it any more*—wants me to take the plates, wh: I shall try to do & publish it as before—(in some respects shall like it just as well)—Can you help me? Can you loan me $100?

The next *N A Review* (June number) will have a piece *A Memorandum at a Venture* signed by my name in which I ventilate my theory of sexual matters, treatment & allusion in *Children of Adam*—I shall have some slips & will send you some to England—

Am writing this in great haste, angry with myself for not having responded before to your good letter of April 10—Love to 'Sula & the kid—

Walt Whitman

M S: Henry E. Huntington Library

To William D. O'Connor

Camden, May 28, 1882

Dear William O'Connor

I like the big letter of May 25 the more I have read it—I think it will never die—I am glad the Rev Mr Chadwick[29] appears with his *Tribune* letter to you to-day (as enclosed) for the fine chance it affords to ventilate the real account & true inwardness of that Emerson talk on the Common in 1860— & I at once send you the best synopsis of it I can recall—quite certainly the same in amount as I told you while it was fresh in my memory—the which with hasty scribblings on my relations with Emerson—I hope (working in as from yourself) you will incorporate in your answer to Tribune—

Walt Whitman

for head
?What were Emersons relations to Walt Whitman?
    (for quoting entire in your letter if you think proper)
    "What made, and ever makes the argument of Emerson, in that walk on the Common, so dear and *holy to me, was the personal affectionateness* of it, as of an elderly brother to a younger. It was a vehement, even passionate well-wishing, which I felt then and feel to this hour the gratitude and reverence of my life could never repay. Although perfect from an intellectual and conventional point of view, it did not advance any thing I had not already considered. And my arriere and citadel positions—such as I have indicated in my June *North American Review* memorandum[30]—were not only not attacked, they were not even alluded to.
    While I am on the subject, let me tell you I am sure the same process went on with Emerson, in this particular (it was not needed any where else) that goes on with many other of my readers. Certain am I that he too finally came to clearly feel that the "Children of Adam" pieces were inevitable and consistent—and in that sense, at least, proper—parts of the book. He was not the man to retract any utterance: whatever it had been, it had expressed the truth of the period.
    That he said some transient things, from 1863 to 1873, which are in the critical direction and are acrid, (very likely your discussion will bring them out) there is no doubt. But he permanently loved me, and believed in my poems, of which the "Children of Adam" section, though difficult to unfold, is vertebral."

William, I submit to you whether it wouldnt be well, in your reply to
quote all this, as extracted from a late letter to you from me[31]—
M S: Berg Collection, New York Public Library

To William D. O'Connor

Camden, May 30, 1882

The whole hinge of the Chadwick letter—involving you and yours, with
me, & including the question of veracity—seems to me to be essentially
What are the relations of Emerson to W W? As permanently left by *the sum*
of the transactions and judgments of twenty-five years—(yours of 29th
recd)—(just the same as the Bible means its whole & final spirit, not one or
two picked out verses or texts)—confirmed by a most deliberate and emphatic act of the last year of his E's life—seems to me the mood of your reply
to the Chadwick letter may well be *different* from the other (which the more
I read it, the more it unfolds—it is such a piece of *literary work*)—I see
clearly that the question above is more involved than that of veracity you
speak of—see the other page I send—

Personal information—perhaps nothing but what you knew already—

☞ I suppose you know that the *Life of Emerson*—(& a very good one I
guess)—published nearly a year ago by Osgood—*all with the sanction &
revision of the family & of E. himself*—gives *in full the letter of 1856 you
quote*—thus confirming & sanctioning it—See said *Life.*[32]

Seems to me would be good to bring in quite verbatim—it is certainly
true—

Emerson had much more of a personal friendship for W W than has been
generally known; making a determined visit to Brooklyn soon after the appearance of Leaves of Grass, twenty five years ago, walking out to the little
cottage in the suburbs, several miles from the ferry where Mr W then lived.
From that time regularly for years afterwards whenever he came to New
York he appointed a meeting, and they two generally dined together and
spent some hours. When Mr Whitman was in Boston in 1860 Emerson was
his frequent & cordial visitor. As time elapsed, though officious persons in-
tervened, and there was a lull of some years, I doubt if it could be said that
Ralph Waldo Emerson's affections (and few know how deeply he could
love!) ever went out more warmly to any one, and remained more fixed,
under the circumstances, than toward Walt Whitman.

Mr Chadwick evidently thinks that if the author of Leaves of Grass had any case to state, that walk on the common in 1860 was his time. But it is well known to his intimate friends that Walt Whitman, who has the most simplicity and good nature of any man alive, is also the haughtiest, the most disdainful at those periods when expected to talk loudest and best, and when he probably could do so, is apt to remain perfectly silent. The main reason certainly was, curious as it may seem, that Emerson's objections, on that famous walk, did not at all touch Whitman's principle of treatment which was a moral one, or rather it involved the verteber of all morals. I have heard the author of Leaves of Grass say that what he sought to do in "Children of Adam" seemed all the more necessary after that conversation. Though Emerson's points were of the highest and keenest order, they sprang exclusively from conventional and what may be called the usual technical literary considerations. I know from what he has told me that Whitman himself had long dwelt on these very points in his own mind—that he was anxious to hear the utmost that could be brought forward in their behalf. And now when he heard what the best critic of the age so brought forward, and his inmost soul and brain remained altogether untouched, his final resolution was taken, and he has never changed from that hour.

Then to clench the whole matter of the relations between these two men, I doubt whether there is any thing more affecting or emphatic in Emersons whole career—a sort of last coruscation in the evening twilight of it—than his driving over to Frank Sanborn's[33] in Concord, Sept 1881, to deliberately pay "respects" for which he had obligated himself twenty five years before. Nor was the unusual compliment of the hospitable but formal dinner made the next day for Walt Whitman, by Mr and Mrs Emerson, without marked significance. It was a beautiful autumn Sunday. And if that afternoon, with its occurrences there in his own mansion, surrounded by all his family, wife, son, daughters, son-in-law, nearest relatives, and two or three very near friends—some fourteen or fifteen in all—if that does not mean how Emerson, by this simple yet almost solemn rite, wished, before he departed, to reiterate and finally seal his verdict of 1856, then there is no significance in human life or its emotions or—

MS: Berg Collection, New York Public Library

To Rees Welsh and Company

Camden, June 20, 1882

Let me make my propositions as plain as possible.

Rees Welsh & Co: to publish Leaves of Grass, (in a style as good as the Osgood issue) from W W's electrotype plates to retail at $2—to pay W W a royalty of 35 cts on every copy sold. This agreement to remain in force [*inserted in pencil*: "blank"] and as much longer as both parties mutually agree. R W & Co. to have the privilege of purchasing from W W the plates of L of G., with the steel engraving & the wood cut, for the sum of 400. cash. After so purchasing W W's royalty to be at 25 cts a copy—

Rees Welsh & Co: to electrotype, in the best manner at their sole expense, & publish W W's Prose Writings, Specimen Days (now mostly in MS) as a companion volume to Leaves of Grass, to be of about the same s[ize &] in equally good type, paper & style & to retail at $2—R W & Co: to pay W W a royalty of 22 cents on every copy sold—said R W & Co. to have the sole right to publish *Specimen Days* for five years, and as much longer as mutually agreed—

A special edition of Leaves of Grass for holiday presents in handsome binding, (say half calf, gilt) may be published, price $5. For these W W's royalty to be 87½ cts a copy.

W W is to be the sole owner of the copyright of Specimen Days.

W W to have 25 copies of the first 1000 of *Specimen Days*, without charge.

R W & Co: to publish *Walt Whitman a Study*, by Dr R M Bucke of Canada, in a 12mo volume of about three hundred pages, on condition that Dr. B. secures an American copyright & royalty of [   ] to be paid Dr B.? W W a Study to retail at $2—will call soon—

W W

DRAFT LETTER: University of Pennsylvania

To William D. O'Connor

Camden, October 7, 1882

The *worry* of Ruskin—he has at various times sent to me for six sets of my ($10, two Vol.) centennial Edition—& sent the money for them—with *Leaves of Grass* is that they are *too personal*, too emotional, launched from the fires of *myself*, my spinal passions, joys, yearnings, doubts, appetites &c

&c.—which is really what the book is mainly for, (as a type however for those passions, joys, workings &c *in all the race*, at least as shown under modern & especially American auspices)—Then I think he winces at what seems to him the *Democratic* brag of L. of G.—I have heard from R several times through English visitor friends of his—It is quite certain that he has intended writing to me at length—& has doubtless made draughts of such writing—but defers & *fears*—& has not yet written—R like a true Englishman evidently believes in the high poetic art of (only) making abstract works, poems, of some fine plot or subject, stirring, beautiful, very noble, completed within their own centre & radius, & nothing to do with the poet's special personality, nor exhibiting the least trace of it—like Shakspere's great unsurpassable dramas. But I have dashed at *the greater drama going on within myself & every human being—that is what I have been after—*

P.S. William, (as you seem to be destin'd to defend the banner) I say here once and for all you have my permission to make any extracts, at any time, should you so like from any of my letters—

W W

M S: Berg Collection, New York Public Library

To Sylvester Baxter

Camden, October 8, 1882

Dear Baxter—the book is out & 1st edition quite exhausted—

I send you same mail with this a paper-bound copy of "Specimen Days" for your printing office use [34]—will send you a regularly bound copy in a day or two—the volume is issued in precisely the same style as "Leaves of Grass"—same cloth binding, same butterfly on the back, same size, &c.—It is a great jumble (as a man himself is)—Is an autobiography after its sort—(sort o' synonyms & yet altogether different—"Montaigne," Rousseau's "Confessions" &c)—is the gathering up, & formulation, & putting in identity of the wayward itemizings, memoranda, and personal notes of fifty years, under modern & American conditions, a good deal helter-skelter but I am sure a certain sort of orbic compaction and oneness the final result—dwells long in its own peculiar way on the Secession War—gives glimpses of that event's strange interiors, especially the Army Hospitals—in fact makes the resuscitating and putting on record the *emotional aspect* of the war of 1861–'65 one of its principal features.

The years from 1876 to the present date Whitman has been a partial para-
lytic. Very much of his days—(and nights also as it appears)—he has spent
in the open air down in the country in the woods and fields, and by a se-
cluded little New Jersey river—His memoranda on the spot of these days
and nights fill a goodly portion of the Volume—Then comes the "Collect,"
embodying "Democratic Vistas," the Preface to L of G. of 1855, and much
other prose.

It is understood that Whitman himself considers "Specimen Days" the ex-
ponent and finish of his poetic work "Leaves of Grass," that each of the two
volumes is indispensable in his view to the other, and that both to-gether
finally begin and illustrate his literary schemes in the New World. Talking
lately in a half jocular vein to a friend he termed them his Adam and Eve,
sent out in "this garden the world."

(don't fail to copy this—can't it conclude your notice?)

Four Phila: editions of "Leaves of Grass" have been issued & sold within
the last three months—they are now on the fifth—The first edition of
"Specimen Days" has been exhausted in less than a week. They are now on
the *second*—

Dear B, if you notice,—send me a paper—don't fail— . . .

Dear B I have dash'd off all this to help you—to use (incorporate) or not
as you think fit—you will understand—

Of course use whatever of this you want—incorporate it I mean in your
article.

M S: Berg Collection, New York Public Library

To Susan Stafford

Germantown, Pennsylvania, August 6, 1883

Dear friend,

Sitting here in the library, alone in a great big house, I thought I would
write you a few lines to pass for a letter—though the Lord only knows what
I shall write about, for I have no news to tell, & nothing special to say—

I came out here on a visit to an old friend[35] a few days ago, & shall stay
here perhaps the ensuing week—The family, (& a fine one they are) are at
Newport for the summer—my friend, the father, goes to his business in
Philadelphia, absent all day, & I am left here master of a large house, garden,
library &c. with servants, horses—a good dinner at 1 o'clock every day—
have to eat it all by myself, but I enjoy it—It is a Quaker family I am very

much attached to—(I believe I have mentioned them to you before)—all kind & good—but the ones that seem most to me are the eldest daughter Mary (ab't 21) the brightest happiest sunniest cutest young woman you ever saw, & probably you would say upon knowing her, a new & different combination of character from any you ever saw—& one I am sure you would like—And then the father himself, my friend—he is in business in Phila:— he has been a great traveler in Europe, & something of a preacher—he is a good talker—& very kind—we always have a good long ride, from 5 to 7½ afternoons—which I enjoy very much—& then return to supper—& a couple of hours talking, reading &c.

Then there is (all now at Newport as I said) another daughter & a son, a young man—all dear friends of mine—I have been here quite a good deal the last year & a half, when they were all home—but now no one but the father & myself here—I wish you could have two or three good drives with me about here—we have a fast, strong, gentle young sorrel mare—first rate—the roads & views are the finest you ever saw—& now they show at their best—Yesterday (Sunday) afternoon & evening seem'd to me one of the most perfect for weather &c I ever knew—we drove out to a hill, about an hour from here, & had a view over twenty miles towards Bethlehem— fields & farms & rolling country—some woods—the richest tract in Pennsylvania. It was an hour before sundown. It was like Paradise. (It will have a good effect upon me the rest of the summer.)

Mont was in to see me ab't a week ago—By his acc't you must have a house full. I hope you keep up health & spirits—Love to Ruth—Ed also— (I havn't forgot those rides evenings off among the *pea-pickers*)—Respects to Messrs. Wyld and Edwards[36]—Nothing specially new with me—I am only middling well—seem to be getting clumsier than ever, more *loguey*— rheumatic & other ailments—My loss (money, dues, &c) I alluded to, from the letter rec'd when I was down there, is worse than I expected[37]—(I knew all the spring & early summer there would be *something*, for I was feeling too well & prosperous & *sassy*)—

If I could only feel well & sleep well, though (which I do not), I should not care a straw for pecuniary botherations & losses. What a beautiful ten days we have had past! I hope Ed's things are all turning out well. So good bye for this time, dear friend—

W W

Ruth, fatten up some o' them chickens & have 'em ready for early fall—
MS: Feinberg Collection, Library of Congress

To Susan and George Stafford

Camden, February 14, 1884

Dear friends

I send the within letter just rec'd from Harry—I am about as usual, & nothing new in my affairs. Susan, this will be a mean short letter this time— better luck next time—It is heavy and bad outside, the wind blowing a gale—(I should like to put on my overshoes & old overcoat & *go off in the woods* for an hour or two)—

I havn't heard from Deb—I hope she is all right—Well, bad as the weather is, I must up & go out & across the river, or I shall have the horrors. The Lord A'mighty bress[38] you all—good bye.

W W

M S: Feinberg Collection, Library of Congress

To Susan and George Stafford

Camden, March 13, 1884

Thank you for the nice chicken—had some for my dinner—was glad to see Van & hear from you all—

I am getting over my bad spell of health—but very slowly—& have been depressed a great deal by the sudden taking down & death by hasty consumption of a dear friend, a young man in his 19th year[39]—I was there all Saturday and Sunday—till he died ab't noon—I hadn't been out of the house for three weeks, before—& was only able to get there with assistance—he sent for me to be with him—The funeral was yesterday afternoon—I did not intend to go to the cemetery & burial, but his father wished me to so earnestly, I went—So all these things hang like a cloud for a while— but I shall without doubt soon be nearly as usual—(though I think likely a little weaker & clumsier [consequently?]).

I have got to get out of this house too, & very soon—for the new tenants take possession April 1. Don't know yet what move I shall make—but shall have to do something in a few days—If it hadn't been for my sick spell should have been out before this—I will let you know—(most likely shall come down & tell you myself)—

I am sorry I missed Harry—I want to see him & have him with me—was in hopes he would come up in the Friday (or Saturday) morning train—& still have some hopes—but I have just rec'd his postal card from Haddonfield that he would try to come up early next week—I send him my best love, & always welcome—

Susan, I rec'd your good letter—If we only lived near, so I could come in & spend a couple of hours every day or two I know it would do me good— Harry, come up soon—

W W

M S: Feinberg Collection, Library of Congress

To Herbert Gilchrist

Camden, December 15, 1885

Dear Herbert

I have rec'd your letter. Nothing now remains but a sweet & rich memory—none more beautiful, all time, all life, all the earth—

I cannot write any thing of a letter to-day. I must sit alone & think.[40]

Walt Whitman

M S: University of Pennsylvania

To John Burroughs

Camden, December 21, 1885

My dear friend

Real glad to hear from you once more, as by yours of 18th—The death of Mrs: Gilchrist is indeed a gloomy fact—she had cancer, & suffered much the last three months of her life with asthma—for a long time "every breath was a struggle," Herbert expresses it—the actual cause of death was dilatation of the heart. Seems to me mortality never enclosed a more beautiful spirit—

The trouble ab't my eyesight passed over, & I use both eyes now same as before—I am living here, rather monotonously, but get along—as I write, feel ab't the same as of late years—only the walking power seems quite gone from me, I can hardly get from one room to another—sometimes quite force myself to get out a few yards, but difficult & risky—

O'Connor seems to be holding on at Washington—I think he is middling well, except the leg power—his "gelatine legs" he calls them—will pass over I rather think—

I drove down yesterday (Sunday) to my friends the Staffords, 10 miles

from here, & staid three hours, had dinner &c—I go *there* every Sunday—
So I get stirr'd up some, but not half enough—three reasons, my natural
sluggishness & the paralysis of late years, the weather, & my old, stiff, slow
horse, with a lurking propensity to stumble down—

The "free will offering" of the English, through Rossetti, has amounted in
the past year to over $400—I am living on it—I get a miserable return of
royalties from McKay, my Philad. publisher—*not $50 for both books L of G.
and S D for the past year* [41]—

John, I like *both the names* in your note—I cannot choose—if I lean at all
it is in favor of "Spring Relish" [42]—either would be first rate—Did you get
W S Kennedy's pamphlet "the Poet as a Craftsman"—I hear from Dr Bucke
quite often—he was the past season somewhat broken in physical stamina
& health—but is better—he gives up for the present his European tour,
but is coming here soon for a week—As I close, my bird is singing like a
house afire, & the sun is shining out—I wish you were here to spend the day
with me—

                                                                        W W

Merry Christmas to you and 'Sula and the boy—
M S: Berg Collection, New York Public Library

To Susan Stafford

                                            Camden, January 9 and 10, 1886
As I shall not get down to Glendale to-morrow I will write a few lines &
send Edward Carpenter's letter, rec'd this morning, which may interest
you—As I look out, the ground is all cover'd with snow, a foot deep, & the
wind blowing quite a gale—& freezing cold—But I have a good fire—Mrs.
Davis has gone out to market, & shopping—So I am alone in the house—
One of my Quaker girls Alys Smith from Germantown has been over to see
me to-day—I told her I considered it indeed a compliment to pay a visit to a
fellow such weather—she said she liked the snow & breeze—liked to whack
around in it—

                                                    Sunday Jan 10—noon—
Cold, cold, & snow everywhere outside—bad luck all around—the fire
goes out, the clock stops, & the water-pipe bursts in the bath room—but the
sun shines, the bird sings away, & Mrs. Davis is in jovial humor—Susan, I

wish I had something interesting to write you—but I havn't—the Lord be
with you all—

W. W.

M s: Feinberg Collection, Library of Congress

To John Burroughs

Camden, March 18, 1886

Dear friend

I send to-day by mail the three Vols. of your Emerson so long detained—
deepest apologies for not returning them before[43]—I don't know that I have
any thing to tell you of any account. I am not writing any thing. Have a small
screed of three or four pages to appear in A T Rice's forthcoming *Reminiscences of Lincoln*, but I consider it unworthy the theme. James Redpath, who
manages things for A T R, has been very good to me—persistently so—& it
is to his urgency I have responded—

Have not yet finished the *Army Hospital* article for the *Century*, but intend to do so forthwith. Had a violent spell of illness ab't a week ago—
remained in bed all last Friday—am up since, & go out a little, but dont feel
even as half-well as usual. Beautiful here to-day & I am enjoying the sunshine, sitting here by the window, looking out—

Have read my *Death of Abraham Lincoln* paper *twice* this spring, on applications ($25 and $30)[44]—got along with it rather slowly, but didnt break
down, & seems to have given a sort of satisfaction—

Want to scoop up what I have (poems and prose) of the last MSS since
1881 and '2, & put in probably 200 page book (or somewhat less) to be
called perhaps *November Boughs*—

I am getting along comfortably enough here—spirits generally good—my
old horse has quite given out—we have a canary bird, dog, & parrot—all
great friends of mine (& teachers)—

Best love to you & 'Sula—not forgetting the little boy—

Walt Whitman

M s: Estelle Doheny Collection, St. John's Seminary

To William M. Rossetti

Camden, May 30, 1886

My dear friend

Yours of May 17, enclosing the fifth instalment £29.18.3 is just now safely received, making altogether—

September	1885	£ 22.	2.6
October 20	''	37.12.	
November 28	''	31.19.	
January 25,	1886	33.16.	
May 17	''	29.18.3	
		£ 155. 9.9	

for which I indeed, indeed thank you, and all—We have beautiful sunshiny weather here, & I am sitting by my open window writing this—If Herbert Gilchrist prints the circular you spoke of, send it me—send me three or four copies. I send best respects & love to my British contributor-friends—they have done me more good than they think for.[45]

Walt Whitman

M S: Hanley Collection, University of Texas

To Mary Smith Costelloe

Camden, January 3, 1887

Henry Norman, of the *Pall Mall Gazette*, has sent me £81 over, in a very kind & good letter—enclosing some printed slips from paper—one written by you ab't my Camden *entourage*—very satisfactory & right to me—In the Reminiscences stick as much as possible to personal descriptions, anecdotes, & sayings—& *don't make me too good*—I am no angel by a long shot[46]—

Walt Whitman

M S: Feinberg Collection, Library of Congress

To William Sloane Kennedy

Camden, February 25, 1887

Dear W. S. K.

It is of no importance whether I had read Emerson before starting L. of G. or not. The fact happens to be positively that I had *not*. The basis and body and genesis of the L[eaves] differing I suppose from Emerson and many grandest poets and artists was and is that I found and find everything in the *common concrete*, the broadcast materials, the flesh, the common passions, the tangible and visible, etc., and in *the average*, and that I radiate, work from, these outward—or rather hardly wish to leave here but to remain and celebrate it all. Whatever the amount of this may be or not be, it is certainly *not Emersonian*, not Shakspere, not Tennyson—indeed, the antipodes of E. and the others in essential respects. But I have not suggested or exprest myself well in my book unless I have in a sort included them and their sides and expressions too—as this orb the world means and includes all climes, all sorts, L. of G.'s word is *the body, including all*, including the intellect and soul; E.'s word is mind (or intellect or soul).

If I were to unbosom to you in the matter I should say that I never cared so very much for E.'s writings, prose or poems, but from his first personal visit and two hours with me (in Brooklyn in 18[55] or [56]) I had a strange attachment and love for *him* and his contact, talk, company, magnetism. I welcomed *him* deepest and always—yet it began and continued *on his part*, quite entirely; HE always sought ME. We probably had a dozen (possibly twenty) of these meetings, talks, walks, etc.—some five or six times (sometimes New York, sometimes Boston) had good long dinners together. I was very happy—I don't think I was at my best with him—he always did most of the talking—I am sure he was happy too. That visit to me at Sanborn's, by E. and family, and the splendid formal-informal family dinner *to me*, next day, Sunday, Sept. 18, '81, by E., Mrs. E. and all, I consider not only a victor-event in my life, but it is an after-explanation of so much and offered as an apology, peace-offering, justification, of much that the world knows not of. My dear friend, I think I know R. W. E. better than anybody else knows him—and loved him in proportion, but quietly. Much was revealed to me.

Walt Whitman

TEXT: W. S. Kennedy, *Reminiscences of Walt Whitman* (1896), 76–77

To Harry Stafford

Camden, April 26, 1887

Harry boy, we have missed you two or three days, & both I & Mrs D[avis] wondered & wanted you—but Ed has been here this forenoon & says you are not coming up any more to have the cut dress'd—So I hope it is healing all right & will be no more trouble—Nothing new or special with me—Sold one of my books to-day, which helps along—Am not feeling quite as well as usual—(but nothing particularly bad)—Pretty dull—If I did not have naturally good spirits I don't know what would become of me, run in here like a rat in a cage day in & day out—But I must not growl—it might be so much worse—If the weather is good I shall be down to Glendale Sunday next— Love to E[va] and little D[ora]—

Walt Whitman

M S: Feinberg Collection, Library of Congress

To Susan Stafford

Camden, May 3, 1887

Dear friend

I got home all right Sunday afternoon—had a nice enjoyable ride— enjoyed my visit anyhow—Yesterday I felt pretty dry, up in my room, & made a glass of drink, water, sugar & vinegar—from that bottle you gave me—such as I remember my dear mother[47] making sixty years ago, for my father, of a hot day, when I was a little boy—& my drink went well too—

Nothing new of any importance with me—Send you enclosed a letter just rec'd from Edward Carpenter—the dear good young man—I have just written him a few lines—told him ab't Harry—

Warm & sunny to-day & I am sitting here with my window open—Mrs. D[avis] is off to Phil. & I shall be here alone all the forenoon. The bird is singing—the cars are puffing & rattling, & the children of the neighborhood are all outdoors playing—So I have music enough—Best love to you all—

Walt Whitman

M S: Feinberg Collection, Library of Congress

To William Sloane Kennedy

Camden, June 13, 1887

Yours of 11th just rec'd—it is a fine bright morning, just the right temperature—I am feeling better to-day—freer (almost free) of the heavy congested condition (especially the head department) that has been upon me for nearly a week—Took a long drive yesterday & have been living much on strawberries of late—Don't write much—just sold & got the money for—& it comes in good, I tell you—a poem to *Lippincotts*—(Mr Walsh editor—friendly to me)—poem called "November Boughs," a cluster of sonnet-like bits, making one piece, in shape like "Fancies at Navesink"—that ("November Boughs") is the name, by the by, I think of giving my little book, I want to have out before '87 closes—shall probably print it here in Phila: myself—it will merely give the pieces I have uttered the last five years, in correct form, more permanent in book shape—probably nothing new—I see a piece in Saturday's June 11 N Y *Times* that Boyle O'Reilly is treasurer of my *summer cottage fund*—(dear Boyle, if you see him say I sent my best love & thanks)—I wish you fellows Baxter, Mrs F[airchild], yourself &c, to leave the selection, arrangement, disposal &c of the cottage, (where, how, &c) *to me*—the whole thing is something I am making much reckoning of—more probably than you all are aware—the am't shall be put of course to that definite single purpose, & *there* I shall probably mainly live the rest of my days—O how I want to get amid good air—the air is so tainted here, five or six months in the year, at best—As I write Herbert Gilchrist is here sketching in my portrait for an oil painting—I hear from Dr Bucke often—nothing now of late from O'Connor, who is still in So: Cal— . . .

Walt Whitman

M S: Trent Collection, Duke University

To William T. Stead[48]

Camden, August 17, 1887

First thank you again for the handsome money present of some months ago, wh' did me more good than you perhaps think for—it has helped me in meals, clothing, debts, &c., ever since. My best help however has come in my old age & paralysis from the Br: Islands. The piece in yr paper (was it early in May last?) from "a distinguished American man of letters" abt me was a very large inflation into fiction of a very little amt of fact—in spirit it is altogether, & in letter mainly untrue (abt my affairs &c.). My income from my books, (royalties &c.) does not reach $100 a year. I am now in my 69th year—living plainly but very comfortably in a little wooden cottage of my own, good spirits invariably, but physically a sad wreck, failing more and more each successive season, unable even to get abt the house without help—most of the time though without serious pain or suffering, except extreme weakness wh' I have a good deal—the paralysis that prostrated me after the Secession war (several shocks) never lifting entirely since—but leaving mentality unimpaired absolutely (thank God!) I have a few, very few, staunch & loving friends & upholders here in America. I am gathering a lot of pieces—uttered within the last six years & shall send them out under the name of *November Boughs* before long—a little book (200 pages or less) some new pieces—a sort of continuation or supplement. Then I think of printing a revised ed'n of complete writings (*Leaves of Grass, Specimen Days & Collect* & *November Boughs* all in one volume) soon. Please accept *personal thanks* from me (never mind the literary) & I know you will accept the impromptu Note in the same spirit in wh' it is written. Best thanks and love to all my British helpers, readers & defenders.

TEXT: *Pall Mall Gazette*, August 30, 1887

To Dr. Richard Maurice Bucke

Camden, February 25, 1888

Nothing special with me. Rainy & dark to day—not cold. Yours rec'd with *Critic* letter—A letter from Mrs: Costelloe this mn'g—all well & busy, baby growing & well—I am not surprised at the refusal to publish in C [49]— the opposition & *resentment* at L of G. is probably as concentrated & vital & determined in New York (my own city) as anywhere, if not more vital—& I do not count the Gilders as essentially *on our side*—they are smart & polite but worldly & conventional—as to the literary classes anyhow I will get a few exceptional dips out of them—but mainly I will have to wait for another generation—But this I have long known—

I am sitting here all alone to-day—I do not eat dinner these short days— only breakfast & supper—my appetite fair—had some buckwheat cakes & raw oysters for my breakfast. Shall most probably not write you at F[lorida] again—

Walt Whitman

MS: Feinberg Collection, Library of Congress

To Sidney H. Morse[50]

Camden, February 28, 1888

Eakins' "pict." is ab't finished—It is a portrait of power and realism, ("a poor, old, blind, despised and dying king"). Things with me ab't the same. Mrs. D[avis] is well—is in the back room working. My canary is singin' away as I write.

TEXT: *In Re Walt Whitman* (1893), 389

To William D. O'Connor

Camden, April 18, 1888

Dear W. O'C.

Your kind good copious letter came to-day & has been read & reread. Nothing new in the monotony of my life—I have rec'd a good plaster bust of Elias Hicks, (size inclined to colossal)[51] wh' I have put open in the corner of my room—& I think it does me good—perhaps *needful* almost to me— Elias at the latent base was *sentimental-religious* like an old Hebrew mystic— & though I may have some thing of that kind 'way in the rear it is pretty far in the rear & I guess I am mainly sensitive to the wonderfulness & perhaps spirituality of things *in their physical & concrete expressions*—& have celebrated all that—

My writing for the *Herald* continues on—they have lately written to me to continue—they have paid me so far $165, wh' I call first rate—25 for the Whittier bit, also enclosed—The little slip enclosed (Lilt of Songs) I sent first (a week or ten days ago) to the *Cosmopolitan* N Y—asking $12—it came back at once *rejected*—So I sent it to *Herald*—The *Cosm.* man stopt here last fall & urged me to send him something—but I think they now have new men—Yes I think Stedman inclined to be friendly & receptive—(L of G. though has to fight ag't a most infernal environment there in New York)— Best love to you—Best love to Nelly—

Walt Whitman

MS: Berg Collection, New York Public Library

To William D. O'Connor

Camden, June 14, 1888

Dear friend W. O'C

Here I am sitting up in the big chair—I got up ab't noon, (& shall keep up an hour or two, & send you my actual *sign manual* to show proof)—Have been pretty ill, indeed might say pretty serious, two days likely a close call[52]— but Dr Bucke was here, & took hold of me without gloves—in short, *Monday last* (four days since) I turned the tide pronouncedly & kept the favorable turn Tuesday forenoon—havnt since kept the good favoring turn the last two days—but the indications are still favorable (good pulse the Dr says last two days) for my getting sort abt as usual—Dr B went back to Canada last Tuesday night, R.R. train—I am half thro' on my little "November Boughs"—& am stuck of it & proofs &c—

Walt Whitman

Best love to you & to Nelly—get your good letter to-day—

M S: Berg Collection, New York Public Library

To Dr. Richard Maurice Bucke

Camden, June 30 and July 1, 1888

The sun is out again after three days—good temperature, neither hot nor cold to-day—I neither *improve* nor really go back—Keep my room rigidly yet—have had today a bowel movement—& sit up most of the time—eat my meals sufficiently—*take no brain grip* (real writing, reading, examining proofs) definitely yet, (nor anything like it plainly as of old)—

I will very soon send proof pages onward following from "Sands at Seventy" for proof pieces of ab't 50 pages further—(you have now ab't 40 proof pages)—Of course I have for all June *stopp'd writing the Herald bits*—& the H. paper ceases by mail wh' is just as satisfactory—I have written, formally completed &c. the *will document* (witnessed by ocular witnesses as this state statute requires) and the designation of my copyrights to be supervised by you, Harned and Horace Traubel—& now when "Nov. Boughs" are completed all will be attended to, the same—

Sunday afternoon early July 1

Feeling miserably to-day so far—am sitting up—not rain, but cloudy and cool and raw—bad feeling in belly and head regions, all day so far—had the

preluded coca-wine, & then my breakfast, moderate—pretty good spirits—
Mrs Davis has been up ten minutes—good company, good gossip—a pretty
rose bouquet from Agnes Traubel—Tom Harned ret'd last evn'g from N Y
three days (likes N Y much)—I am wretchedly weak in knees & anything
like *body strength*—tho' pretty good arm muscular hold as I hold on—
    Love to you & to Mrs B & the childer—

                                                                    Walt Whitman
M S: Feinberg Collection, Library of Congress

To John Burroughs

                                                    Camden, July 12 and 13, 1888
    It gets very tedious here—(I have now been in my room and bed five
weeks)—I am sitting up in a rocker and get along better than you would
think—I think upon the whole I am getting mending—slowly and faintly
enough yet sort o' perceptibly—the trouble is sore and broken brain—the
old nag gives out and it hurts to even go or draw at all—but there are some
signs the last two days that slight ambles will justify themselves—even for
old habit, if nothing else—
    It was probably the sixth or seventh whack of my war paralysis, and a
pretty severe one—the doctors looked glum—Bucke I think saved my life as
he happened to be here—Shimmering, fluctuating since, probably gathering, recruiting, but as I now write I shall rally or partially rally—only every
time lets me down a peg—I hear from you by Horace Traubel—I have an
idea that O'Connor is a little better.
    A rainy evening here, not at all hot, quiet—
    Friday July 13—Just after noon—Ab't the same. I am sitting up, had a
fair night—rose late, have eaten my breakfast—have rec'd a good letter
from O'C—nothing very special or new—fine, clear, cool. Today my head
thicks somewhat today. Love to you, dear friend. Love and remembrance to
'Sula, to July, too. I am on to 90th page Nov. Boughs—it will only make 20
more.

                                                                    Walt Whitman
M S: Barrus, 280–81

To Dr. Richard Maurice Bucke

Camden, July 24, 1888

Better quite perceptibly—fluctuating considerable, with bad days or hours—but a general and prevailing improvement—

I have put together the *Elias Hicks* fragments last night & sent off the "paper" to the printer—not knowing how it will look in print—but with some fear & trembling—then three or so pages (all done now) on *George Fox*—evolutionary on the E[lias] H[icks] piece—& the *Nov. Boughs* will be *done*—will make from 120 to 130 (or possibly 135) pages—(those solid long primer pages eat up the copy at a terrible rate!)—I have not worried at it—& do not—indeed it has probably been more benefit to me than hurt—I have been unspeakably helped by Horace Traubel—& by the best printers I have ever yet had—The *Century* people have just sent me again my *Army Hospitals & Cases* proof—I judge it is intended for the October number—bowel movements continue every day or other day—I take no drugs at all—have not moved from my room yet—Keep good spirits—young Dr Mitchell[53] has just come—weather pleasant continued—warmish but I am satisfied—Tom Harned comes every day, often bringing his nice always welcome children—

2 p m—y'rs of 22d has come—I have enjoy'd a partial wash—

Walt Whitman

M S: Feinberg Collection, Library of Congress

To Susan Stafford

Camden, September 10, 1888

Your letter came in the noon mail & I will write a few lines—Glad to hear little Susie[54] is well & send her my love & hope she will grow on & up first rate—Yes, dear friend, come up & stay a little with us, & of course bring the chicken for me—it will be acceptable—Herbert [Gilchrist] was here this forenoon but did not come up to my room—though I was sure I would have been glad to see him & talk a bit—I think he has some scheme (painting most likely) on the carpet—At any rate I tho't he looks hearty & well—I am still kept in my sick room—don't get worse but don't gain any thing it

seems—& I almost doubt if I ever will—weakness extreme—I have sold the
mare & phæton—I sold her for a song—my brother Eddy is boarding at
Blackwoodtown Asylum now—my sister got quite dissatisfied with the
Moorestown place—My books are being printed nicely—I have two on the
stocks—one little one "November Boughs"—and one big 900 Vol. to contain all my works—you shall have them, when ready—Harry too—I send
my love to Harry & to Eva & little Dora—it is a rainy, cloudy, coolish day, &
I am sitting here alone in the big chair in better spirits & comfort than I
deserve—

Walt Whitman

MS: Feinberg Collection, Library of Congress

To Dr. Richard Maurice Bucke

Camden, September 22, 1888

Still here in my big chair in the sick room yet—a coolish wave to-day, but
pleasant enough—John Burroughs has been to see me, the good hearty affectionate nature-scented fellow, very welcome[55]—he left yesterday en route
to visit Johnson (Century staff) at Sea Girt, on the N J sea coast—J B lodged
at Tom Harned's, & T H and Horace liked him muchly—J B is not so hardy
& brown & stout as formerly—that bad fiend insomnia haunts him as of
old—he thinks himself it affects his literary power, (style, even matter)—
Horace told him my half-suspicion that his association with the supercili-
ousness & sort o' vitriolic veneering of the New York literati had eat into
him, but he denied & pooh-pooh'd it—attributed it to his bad health, insomnia &c—said he knew himself he could not (or did not) write with the
vim of his better days—(probably makes more acc't of that by far, than
really *is*)—

I expect to get a specimen copy of *November Boughs* from the binder this
evening—Shall not feel out of the woods & all safe, until I see the October
Century, with my Army Hospital piece printed—accepted & paid for by
them two years ago—as I consider myself obligated not to print from it until
it has been *first* published by them—(But I have heard they give it—intend
to—in the Oct. number)—

Afternoon—Horace comes with spec[imen] of *Nov. B* bound for sample—
it is satisfactory—looks plain, larger than expected—I give an order or two
changing the lettering on cover, &c.—the picture printing gives satisfac-

tion—In fact *all will do*—("Only think" said the Irish girl "what ye'd said if it was ever so worser")—I have been expecting Alma Johnston[56] of N Y to-day (or yesterday)—but no sign—a dear & prized friend—"good roots" for the meter[57] (slang from N Y vagabonds, for favorable prophecy)—It gets cooler & I have donn'd my big blue wool overgown—as I end with love & thanks to you—

Walt Whitman

M S: Feinberg Collection, Library of Congress

To Dr. Richard Maurice Bucke

Camden, September 25 and 26, 1888

Of late I have two or three times occupied spells of hours or two hours by running over with best & alertest sense & mellowed & ripened by five years your 1883 book (biographical & critical) about me & L of G—& my very deliberate & serious mind to you is that you *let it stand just as it is*—& if you have any thing farther to write or print book shape, you do so in an *additional* or further annex (of say 100 pages to its present 236 ones)—leaving the present 1883 vol. intact as it is, any verbal errors excepted—& the further pages as (mainly) reference to and furthermore &c. of *the original vol.*—the text, O'C[onnor]'s letters, the appendix—every page of the 236 left as now—This is my spinal and deliberate request—the *conviction* the main thing—the details & reasons not put down.[58]

Sept: 26 noon

Dr Osler[59] has call'd—evidently all right—I have a good deal of pain (often sort of spasmodic, not markedly violent) in the chest & "pit of the stomach" for the last three days. O says it is nothing serious or important—& prescribes a mustard plaster—lately we have a sort of cold wave & I shouldn't wonder if that was behind it—(I have the mustard plaster on now)—It is bright & sunny—rather cool—I have rec'd a long letter from Sidney Morse from Chicago—no special news—Mr Summers, M P from England, has just call'd & we've had a talk[60]—a nice fellow (how much more & more the *resemblance* between the cultivated Englisher and Americaner)—I have been reading Miss [Julia] Pardoe's "Louis XIIII"—I wonder if as a sort of foil to the Carlyle reminiscences (T[homas]'s and J[ane]'s)—the same sort of business in another sphere & land—Your letters come &

are always welcome—As I close I am sitting in my big chair in my room 1½ p m quiet & measurably comfortable—

Walt Whitman

MS: Feinberg Collection, Library of Congress

To Dr. Richard Maurice Bucke

Camden, December 16 and 17, 1888

Am sitting here a while to contrast the fearful tedium of lying in bed so long—eking a half hour more, to sit up here—though slowly & moderately, seems to me *I am decidedly better*, wh' sums all at present—seem to fall from one pit to a lower pit—what is to come remains to be seen—Dr Walsh (who is not very definitive) says it is an extreme case (this very last) of prostration & gastric trouble from indigestion—Monday, Tuesday & Wednesday last were worst—Tuesday was deathly—yesterday & to-day I begin at milk & broth & sit up more—feel pretty fair as I sit here this moment—have drink'd some sherry mix'd with milk—(wine, whey)—Hope you have rec'd the copies of the big book, sent by Canadian Express (sent last Thursday)—Hope you are not disappointed (or vex'd) at its looks—as it is, for all nine-tenths of L of G. are from normal al fresco genesis (beef, meat, wine, sunny, lusty) and three fourths of the rest of the trilogy ditto—it is fished out of one of Dante's hells, considering my physical condition the last three months—

Well, I will get to bed, with Ed [Wilkins]'s help—

Monday afternoon Dec. 17—Fairly passable last night & some chicken broth for breakfast—anticipated a pretty good day & a good bath in the wash room, but not accomplish'd yet—Yours of 15th rec'd—Am sitting up—a dismal dark sticky rainy day—Suppose the big books must be to hand now—sweat easily, the least encouragement—quite great thirst—drink milk a good deal—have just eaten some vanilla ice cream—just rec'd an Italian (Palermo) paper[61]—& the Paris *Revue Independent* for Nov: with notice of L of G,[62] wh' I mail you—send me the synopsis when you have an opportunity—my head is in a sore poor condition—

Walt Whitman

MS: Feinberg Collection, Library of Congress

To Dr. Richard Maurice Bucke

Camden, December 21 and 22, 1888

I scribble away as perhaps you care to hear even minor affairs—sent off Mrs: O'C[onnor]'s letter to me describing the situation wh' you must have rec'd—My poor dear friend Wm O'C—my brother in affliction—I have been out & had a thorough bath in the tub, (with Ed's assistance,) & complete clothe change, specially under—

Saturday 22d—9 a m—Feeling pretty well—& shall tackle my breakfast presently, had a fair night—sent big books off, (by express) to Boston yesterday afternoon to Kennedy, Baxter, Mrs. Fairchild, Harland[63] & Frank Sanborn, (for Christmas presents)—yours of 20th rec'd this morning—

Noon—cold & bright—bowel movement, decided—(first in four days)—my brother George comes every day—bro't from Lou a good quilted lap robe to go over my knees & feet as I sit, very useful & acceptable—

Evn'g—Well I believe this has been, upon the whole, the nearest approximation for a tolerable day for six months and more—I am fearfully weak yet but *the feeling* & the comparative ease are like something toward sanity—I may fall back—but O that I can keep up the standard of to-day, moderate as it is—had my mutton-broth & couple of good raw oysters for my supper, 4¾, (no dinner)—as it is I am sitting by the wood fire—comfortable—Ed is snoozing on the couch—every thing is quiet—Christmas is near at hand & seems to be made extra much of here—Hope it will be a merry one with you all—

Walt Whitman

M S: Feinberg Collection, Library of Congress

To William Sloane Kennedy

Camden, February 1, 1889

Y'rs of 29th Jan: rec'd & welcom'd as always—I continue on much the same—the last two days I fancy a little plus, something like strength—have got so when negative favors (to be free from special botherations) quite set me up.

Had my breakfast & relish'd it—three or four hot stew'd oysters, a stout slice of toasted Graham bread, & a mug of coffee—My housekeeper Mrs: Davis is compell'd to be temporarily absent these two days & Ed my nurse gets my breakfast & gets it very well.

I get along here without any luxury or any special *order*, but I am satisfied & comfortable & often bless the Lord & congratulate myself that things are as well with me as they are—that I retain my mentality intact—that I have put my literary stuff in final form—that I have a few (but sufficient) real & competent & determined advocates & understanders & *bequeathers* (important as much as any thing)— . . .

Enclosed find a proof of y'r condensed translation of Sarrazin[64] (I don't mind its hasty, somewhat broken form) wh' read & correct if anything & return to me at once—& I will send you some impressions—I like it well— Best love to you—

Walt Whitman

TEXT: Photostat, Feinberg Collection, Library of Congress

To Susan Stafford

Camden, February 6, 1889

Quite sharp & cold this forenoon, & I am sitting by a good oak fire—Am still imprison'd in the sick room—Keep up spirits pretty fair, but weak as ever in my movements, & being kept indoor for most nine months begins to tell on me—I almost wonder I keep as well as I do—but I have been pretty low—the doctors—even Dr Bucke—gave me quite up more than once— They just kept life like a little light prevented from being all put out (& this was the reason why I often had to deny friends from seeing me)—& for a month or so I was in a horrible plight—a nuisance to myself & all—but my nurse (Ed Wilkins, the Canadian young man Dr. B. sent) stuck to me & it has sort o' pas'd over—or at any rate the worst of it—At present I sit here in the room—Mrs Davis has just been in & wishes to send her love to you, & says come up & see us—my mentality ab't the same as ever (tho' I get very soon sore & tired reading, or being talked to)—& not much show of being any better—thankful that things are as well as they are with me—for they might be much worse—

Susan, your good letter came this forenoon & I was glad enough to hear from you all—I thank you so much for it—I write all this rigmarole at once— . . .

My books are all completed, these last editions, wh' is a great relief. Eddy my crippled brother is still at Blackwood—(I yesterday paid the three months board bill $45:50 there) he is well, & seems to be well off & satisfied—young Harry Bonsall died there three or four weeks ago—my sisters

at Greenport L I and Burlington, Vermont are ab't as usual—my brother &
sister Lou are well at Burlington this state—I think quite often of Harry, &
wish you would send this letter over to him without fail the first chance you
get—it is written largely to him—I have what I call *sinking spells* in my sickness, & I had one the day he last visited me—Love to you & George, Ed,
Van, Deb & Jo and all—

W W

M S: Feinberg Collection, Library of Congress

To Dr. Richard Maurice Bucke

Camden, March 21, 1889

Noon—Feeling pretty well—dark & rainy (the third day)—News not
favorable from O'C[onnor] as you will see by enc'd card—I write a few lines
every day to him & send Mrs. O'C the Boston paper. . . . Horace was in this
forenoon—faithful & invaluable as ever—Mrs: Davis has come in for a few
moments to see if I am "all right"—Ed has been making up the bed.

Toward sunset

Had a good thorough bath this afternoon, hot water—my "cold" has not
altogether withdrawn—I feel it in the head perceptibly enough an hour or
two now and then—heavy sloppy muddy day—I almost envy your having
such lots to do, responsibilities & strong & well & energetic to do 'em—My
lassitude is one of the worst points in my condition—but whether Sidney
Morse's man's answer (when reproach'd for drunkenness) "Suppose 'twas so
intended to be," was right or no—Mrs: Davis's woman's remark is "So it
really *is* any how"—& answers all philosophy & argument (up to a certain
line you probably say)—Well I will adjust myself for dinner, & hope you &
Mrs B & all are having good times—& send my love to all—

Walt Whitman

M S: Feinberg Collection, Library of Congress

To Dr. Richard Maurice Bucke

Camden, May 2, 1889

Feeling ab't fairly—weather not unpleasant, cloudy, & a little cool—am
sitting here by the oak fire—a middling fair bowel action an hour ago, I go
out to the closet myself & return—Horace has been in—the L of G. pocket-

book ed'n is getting along—(probably the press-work to-day—also some of the plates at the plate press)—Well the big N Y show seems to have all pass'd over successfully—to me *the idea* of it is good, even grand, but I have not enthused ab't it at all—(may be a whim, but the most insignificant item in the whole affair has been Harrison himself, President for all he is)—So the circus here was a success last night—Ed enjoy'd it hugely—& I suppose Dr Baker[65] has gone off (to Minneapolis) immediately after his graduation— Mrs. Davis was there—Osler spoke well & was treated to great applause— all this in the Phila: Academy wh' must have look'd gayly—

I have been looking over the May *Century*, the *Book News* and the *Critic* (so I may be supposed to be posted with current literature)—read Whittier's long N Y centennial ode[66] . . . Ed gives me a good *currying* every evening— Sleep fairly—Sun bursting forth as I write—the great long *burr-r-r* of the Phila. whistles from factories or shores often & plainly here sounding, & I rather like it—(blunt & bass)—some future American Wagner might make something significant of it—Guess you must have all good times there— occupied & healthy & sufficiently out door—I refresh myself sometimes thinking (fancying) ab't you all there—I enclose Mrs. O'C[onnor]'s yester- day's card—I send card or something every evn'g—Love to you, Mrs B & the childer—

W W

M S: Feinberg Collection, Library of Congress

To Dr. Richard Maurice Bucke

Camden, May 4 and 5, 1889

Sarrazin's book (from him from Paris) has come, & looks wonderfully in- viting all through but is of course sealed to me—I enclose a slip of title de- tailedly, as you may want to get one from New York—(but of course you can have my copy as much as you want)— . . .

Fine & sunny here—am rather heavy-headed—& *hefty* anyhow to-day— nothing specially to particularize—ate my breakfast, (mutton broth & Graham bread with some stew'd apple,) with ab't usual zest—(nothing at all sharp, but will do, & even thankful it's as well as it is)— . . .

Sunday May 5

Fine & sunny to-day—feeling fairly—all going smoothly—In general ab't the world, I guess we are now floating on *dead water* in literature, politics, theology, even science—resting on our oars &c. &c.—criticising, resuming—at any rate *chattering* a good deal (of course the simmering, gestation, &c. &c. are going on just the same)—but a sort of *lull*—a good coming summer to you & Mrs. B & all of you—

Walt Whitman

M S: Feinberg Collection, Library of Congress

To Ellen M. O'Connor

Camden, May 12, 1889

After a great trouble, or death, a sort of *silence* & *not* trying words or to depict y'r feelings come to me strongest—But I will send a word any how to you, dear friend, of sympathy & how the death of William, for all I have for some time anticipated, comes very bitterly[67]—

I am somewhat better, & late yesterday afternoon I was taken out & jaunted around for an hour—my first experience of out door for most a year, & it was very refreshing—then when I came back & up to my room I spent the sunset & twilight hour thinking in silence of W and you & old times in Wash'n—

Best love to you, & send me word when you can—

Walt Whitman

M S: Berg Collection, New York Public Library

To Dr. Richard Maurice Bucke

Camden, May 25 and 26, 1889

Well, Maurice, every thing here goes on much the same, & fairly enough—As I write, it is abt 1 P M, Saturday, clear but not sunny & neither cool nor warm—I have just had a midday currying—partial bowel action two hours ago—feel middling (but cold in the head, or catarrh or gathering or whatever it is yet)—get out a little in the wheel chair—they are all going out, Mrs. D[avis] and all, to an East Indian ship for two or three hours this afternoon—I told Ed to go too as he was invited, (& he will go)—the ship is here from Bombay, & our sailor boys know some of their sailors—

We broke a big bottle of good wine yesterday & all of us (seven—me at the head) drank health & respects to Queen Victoria—(it was her birthday you know—) . . .

Night—9½—Have been out twice to day in the wheel-chair—short excursions—T B H[arned] has been here this evn'g—150 dinner tickets taken now—y'r letter rec'd by H[orace]—(I have not seen it yet)—coolish temperature three days & now stopping sweat exudation & somewhat bad for me but well enough as I sit here alone, every thing quiet, but some sailors from the ship downstairs—

Sunday toward noon May 26

A clouded rather rawish day—Am going up to my friends Mr & Mrs: Harned's in an hour, in my wheel chair—to stay a few minutes, & probably get a drink of champagne—(of which H always has the best & treats me to galore)—Havn't now had such a tipple for a year.

Nothing particular to write—My head is a little heavy & thick—no pocket-book copies yet, but I count on them in a couple of days—All goes fairly as c'd be expected—

Walt Whitman

M S: Feinberg Collection, Library of Congress

To Dr. Richard Maurice Bucke

Camden, June 1, 1889

Well here I am, feeling fairly, commencing my 71st year. The dinner last evening came off & went off, all right, & was a great success—they say they had a mighty good *dinner* (nothing to drink but Appollinaris water)—I was not at the eating part, but went an hour later—Ed wheel'd me in the chair, & two policemen & two other good fellows just carried me from the sidewalk, chair & all as I sat, up the stairs & turning (which were fortunately wide & easy) to the big banquet hall & big crowd, where I was roll'd to my seat, & after being rec'd with tremendous cheering they bro't me a bottle of first rate champagne & a big glass with ice, (Tom Harned sent to his house for the wine)—The whole thing was tip top & luckily I felt better & more something like myself, and nearer chipper, than for a year—I made a short talk, wh' you will see in the paper I enclose—also Herbert's speech—It was largely a home & neighbors' affair (wh' I liked) although there were (& speeches from) outsiders—The compliments & eulogies to me were *excessive* & without break—But I fill'd my ice-glass with the good wine, & pick'd out two fragrant roses f'm a big basket near me, & kept cool & jolly & enjoy'd all—

I suppose you have the pocket-book copy L of G wh' I mailed yesterday—have just sold one & got the 5 for it—Hamlin Garland has been to see me to-day—also Tom Harned—The Phila: papers have long reports—a little rainy & broken to-day, but pleasant—

Walt Whitman

M S: Feinberg Collection, Library of Congress

To Horace Traubel

Camden, June 2, 1889

Horace, I was just thinking the *pamphlet* notion might be improved & expanded on by having a nicely 60 or 70 page (thick good paper, with portrait for front piece) *book*, trimmed & gilt edged—good job—bound in crepe—thick paper (like my Passage to India, robin-blue-egg color with white inside)—to be publish'd by Dave [McKay], & sold at 50cts retail—to be call'd

Camden's Compliment

to Walt Whitman on his finishing his 70th year.

putting in enough appropriate stuff to the occasion & latest developements—(if needed) to make out 60 or 70 pp—

Mention this to Tom, Harry Bonsall & Buckwalter[68]—then see if Dave w'd undertake & publish it at his expense—I don't think it needed be stereotyped—print it f'm the types—1000 copies—Us here, Dr B[uckle], Tom, other Camdenites, Johnston in N Y, &c, to subscribe for 100 & pay the cash down when ready—

The more I think of it *this way*, the more I believe it worth doing, & that it will pay for itself, at least—& I think Dave will go in—(no great risk or money investment any how.) The whole thing of the dinner was such a success & really a *wonder* it ought to be commemorated—

W W

M S: Feinberg Collection, Library of Congress

To Thomas B. Harned

Camden, June 9, 1889

Have had such a good time with the Champagne you sent me, must at least thank [you] for it. I drank the whole bottle (except a little swig I insisted on Ed taking for going for it) had it in a big white mug half fill'd with

broken ice, it has done me good already (for I was sort of "under the weather"
the last 30 hours.)

Walt Whitman

TEXT: *Whitman at Auction* (1978), 46

To Dr. Richard Maurice Bucke

Camden, July 10, 1889

Fearful heat here now a week & at present looks like continued—thro'
wh' tho' I get along better than you m't suppose. Am taking the tonic—it
(or something) relieves me the last two days of the worst of the weakness,
caving-in & head inertia—but I feel it, the dose, for an hour after taking in
my head & stomach very perceptibly & very uncomfortably—bowel action
yesterday & also this forenoon, quite good—Ed stands it first rate— . . .

Have been dipping in the new French book Amiel's *Journal Intime* translated by Mrs: Humphrey Ward. He is evidently an orthodox conservative
determined to stand by his (moth-eaten) colors, tho' modern science & democracy draw the earth from under his very feet—He is constantly examining, discussing *himself*, like a health-seeker dwelling forever on his own
stomach—I heard it was a great book & going to be *established*—but I say
no to both—he is one of those college pessimistic *dudes* Europe (& America
too) sends out—

I am sitting here in my big chair—every thing still—just drank a great
drink of iced lemonade (pleasant but non-healthy)—After a New York boy's
slang, I conclude by sending you *good roots*—

Walt Whitman

MS: Feinberg Collection, Library of Congress

To Dr. Richard Maurice Bucke

Camden, October 5, 1889

Sunny & coolish & fine—have a good oak fire—I think the press work of
Horace's dinner book must have been done yesterday or day before, & the
binding will follow soon & you shall have it.

. . . Are you interested in this All-Americas' Delegates' visit here & convention at Washington?[69]—their trip R R, 50 of them, between five & six thousand miles in U S without change of car interests me much—it is the biggest best thing yet in recorded history—(the modern *is* something after all)—They say this racket is in the interest of *protection*—but I sh'd like to know how it can be prevented f'm helping free trade & national brother-hood—You fellows are not in this swim I believe—but you tell the Canadi-ans we U S are "yours faithfully" certain, & dont they forget it—

Walt Whitman

M S: Feinberg Collection, Library of Congress

To William Sloane Kennedy

Camden, October 10, 1889

Y'rs of 9th just come—Whittier's poetry stands for *morality* (not its *en-semble* or in any true philosophic or Hegelian sense but)—as filter'd through the positive Puritanical & Quaker filters—is very valuable as a genuine ut-terance & very fine one—with many capital local & yankee & *genre* bits—all unmistakably hued with zealous partizan anti-slavery coloring. Then all the *genre* contributions are precious—all help. Whittier is rather a grand figure—pretty lean & ascetic—no Greek—also not composite & universal enough, (don't wish to be, don't try to be) for ideal Americanism—Ideal Americanism would probably take the Greek spirit & law for all the globe, all history, all rank, the $^{19}\!/_{20}$ths called evil just as well as the $\frac{1}{20}$th called good (or moral)—

The sense of *Mannahatta* means *the place around which the hurried (or feverish) waters are continually coming or whence they are going*—

Walt Whitman

M S: Berg Collection, New York Public Library

To Dr. Richard Maurice Bucke

Camden, October 15, 1889

Well, Maurice, you must have rec'd Horace's "Camden's Compliment" sheets, as he sent them to you last evn'g, as soon as he could get a copy f'm the printing office—I have just been looking over them—a curious & in-teresting collection—a concentering of praise & eulogy rather too single

& unanimous & honeyed for my esthetic sense—(for tho' it has not got around, *that same esthetic* is one of my main governments, I may candidly say to you)—

I am sitting here alone & pretty dull & heavy—fairly, though, I guess—bowel movement—rainy, raw, dark weather—oak wood fire— . . . few visitors lately—a steady shower of autograph applications by mail—carpenter & mason here propping up this old shanty—it was giving out & down—I have been reading (4th time probably) Walter Scott's "Legend of Montrose" and other of his Scotch stories—Dave McKay sent them over—Mary Davis is good to me, as always—had a pretty fair night, (Ed generally gives me a good currying before)—had an egg, cocoa & bread & honey for breakfast—

Walt Whitman

M S: Feinberg Collection, Library of Congress

To Dr. Richard Maurice Bucke

Camden, October 21, 1889

Ed has left[70]—goes in the 4.15 train—I send you by him a parcel of portraits—tell me if they reach you in good order—Am feeling in one of my easier spells just now—the man who was to come to-day has *not* put in an appearance—I am sitting here as usual—Mrs: D[avis] is just making up the bed—cloudy raw to-day—don't be uneasy ab't me in any respect—nature has not only endowed me with immense emotionality but immense bufferism (so to call it) or placid resignation to what happens—

W W

M S: Feinberg Collection, Library of Congress

To Dr. Richard Maurice Bucke

Camden, October 31, 1889

"The same subject continued"—good bowel passage last evn'g—my sailor boy nurse (Warren Fritzinger, he is just making up the bed) had a letter from Ed this morning—so he got there all right any how—buckwheat cakes & honey for my breakfast—Did you not see (he got £250 for it) Tennyson's "Throstle" & a burlesque of it in one of the papers I sent you? Gosse

I sh'd call one of the amiable conventional wall-flowers of literature (see Thackeray—"Yellowplush" I think)—We too have numbers of good harmless well-fed sleek well-tamed fellows, like well-order'd parlors, crowded all over with wealth of books (generally gilt & morocco) & statuary & pictures & bric-a-brac—lots of 'em & showing first rate—but no more real *pulse and appreciation* than the wood floors or lime & sand walls—(one almost wonders whether literary, even Emersonian, culture dont lead to all that)—

Toward noon weather here turns to rain—bet'n 12 and 1 had a good massage, pummeling &c.—bath also—have had a visit f'm some of the Unitarian conference—y'rs of 29th rec'd—my head, hearing, eyes, bad to-day, yet I am feeling pretty fairly—a present f'm R P Smith of a cheque for $25 to-day—sent him the pk't-b'k morocco ed'n L of G—Mrs: Davis off to-day to Doylestown, Penn: (20 miles f'm here) to visit & comfort a very old couple—returns to-night—my sailor boy has just written to Ed & has gone to the p o to take it—it is towards 3 P M & dark & glum out & I am alone—have a good oak fire—am sitting here *vacant* enough, as you may fancy (but it might be worse)—have myself for company, such as it is, any how—God bless you all—

Walt Whitman

M S: Feinberg Collection, Library of Congress

To Dr. Richard Maurice Bucke

Camden, December 25 and 26, 1889

Dec. 25 6 p m—have been out to-day in the wheel chair—& down to the kitchen at the table for my supper—now sitting as usual up in my den—J A Symonds from Switzerland has sent the warmest & (I think sh'd be call'd) the most *passionate* testimony letter to L of G. & me yet[71]—I will send it to you after a little while—

Yesterday went out (two hours drive) to the Harleigh Cemetery & selected my burial lot—a little way back, wooded, on a side hill—lot 20 x 30 feet—think of a vault & capping all a plain massive stone temple, (for want of better descriptive word)—Harleigh Cemetery is a new burial ground & they desire to give me a lot—I suppose you rec'd the *Critic*—

Dec 26 noon Perfect sunny day—Tom Donaldson[72] here last evn'g—sold a little pocket-book L of G. to-day, & got the money—am feeling fairly (inclined to heavy) to-day—plain indications of rheumatism in my right arm—

both my parents had r but not yet in me—Shall have a currying & then get out in the wheel chair—

Walt Whitman

Sudden death of a special friend & neighbor I have known from her 13th—a fine young handsome woman—typhoid—buried to-day—

MS: Feinberg Collection, Library of Congress

1890-1892

Walt Whitman
Feb: 3 '90

Jacques Reich (1852–1923), an artist employed by the United States Mint, asked for permission, though unknown to Whitman, to sketch "my phiz" on February 3, 1890. Apparently the last drawing or portrait made in the poet's lifetime, it resembles some of the well-known photographs of Thomas Eakins. Reich later made an etching based on an Eakins photograph, which is the frontispiece of the first collected edition of Whitman's writings.

Collection of the editor

"GOOD-BYE MY FANCY" (1891), WHITMAN SAID, IS "mostly to untune (let down) clinch what I have said before, pass the fingers again carelessly over the strings . . . & *to close the book* avoiding any thing like trumpet blasts." He acknowledged "its spurty (old Lear's irascibility)— its off-handedness, even evidence of decrepitude & old fisherman's seine character as part of *the artism*," and declared it part of "the determin'd cartoon of Personality" unveiled in *Leaves of Grass.*

More than a year earlier the observant Traubel had been reminded of Shakespeare's tragic hero: "How much like Lear—the waking Lear— Whitman seemed: shaken, on the boundary of reason, to-night: his gray hair long and confused."[1] There was a kind of grandeur in Whitman's ability to bear the limitations his deteriorating body placed upon his movements and freedom as well as the constant awareness of his failing imaginative powers. Like Lear, Whitman was deeply pained by the contraction of his family: Anne Gilchrist in 1885, Mannahatta, Jeff's daughter and his favorite niece, in 1886 (at twenty-six), O'Connor in 1889, Jeff in 1890, and George Stafford in February 1892. He was supported and comforted not by his own family, although George came to 328 Mickle Street occasionally, but by Harned, Bucke, and, above all, Traubel, who had a fidelity rare among true sons.

There were, however, new admirers, new families, to the last. From Australia came the lengthy letters of a future poet, Bernard O'Dowd, who discovered Whitman in a period of personal crisis and in his poetry found solace and stability. O'Dowd and his friends established the first Walt Whitman Society in that far-off land. "Take our love," O'Dowd wrote, "we have little more to give you, we can only try to spread to others the same great boon you have given to us."[2] With great delight Whitman welcomed the Australians into the family: "I write to you as an elder brother might to the young bro[ther]s & sisters, & doubtless repeat parrot-like," which is a delicate touch of domestic understanding. The image of the elder brother evokes perhaps the greatest passage in his poetry, the account of his epiphany in Section 5 of "Song of Myself."

In Bolton, England, James Wallace and Dr. John Johnston also organized a Whitman society. Both men, like O'Dowd, were experiencing personal crises: Wallace was recovering from the trauma of his mother's death, and Johnston was probably suffering from the effects of a vanishing godhead in the twilight of a troubled century. Both journeyed to America and to Camden to see the poet and to be emotionally and physically healed. Neither was disenchanted by exposure to a man whom they had already apotheosized; such was the aura or electricity of an enfeebled man to those almost desperate for certainty amid life's uncertainties. To Johnston, Whitman was a father figure; to Wallace, a mother. When it came time for Wallace to return to England, Whitman "was as tender as a mother, and as our lips met he showed unmistakable emotion." In a letter in 1891 Wallace wrote, "You remind me so much of my dear mother. . . . You seem to me now as near & intimate as well as dear as my own Kith & Kin—Nay, dearer."[3]

As the body weakened and the end approached, from his bedroom which was littered with the effects accumulated during a lifetime, Whitman slowly and meticulously provided for his future reputation and for his family. With the faithful assistance of Horace Traubel, he saw through the press the so-called death-bed edition, which was to supersede the earlier editions of *Leaves of Grass* and to establish the definitive text. In this gathering of his poetry he presented his masterpiece to posterity with the excisions and revisions he alone had decided upon.

Whitman carefully designed and supervised the erection of a lavish mausoleum in Harleigh Cemetery in Camden which seemed a tribute to the ornateness and vanity of the Gilded Age rather than to the achievements of a democratic poet of humble origins. The tomb was an extravagance, the cost certainly excessive for a man of Whitman's means. Although the contractor finally settled for less, the original price was $4000, which was more than twice the cost of his "shanty." If some of the disciples were surprised, perhaps shocked, there was nothing inconsistent in Whitman's desire to have an enduring monument in granite.

The mausoleum was no more grandiose and vain than that wonderfully witty and self-inflating line in the first edition of *Leaves of Grass*, "Walt Whitman, an American, one of the roughs, a kosmos." In planning the tomb Whitman was again about his father's business. It was to be the last and the finest of the Whitman homes.

In a last will and testament in 1888 he provided bequests for his survivors. To his two sisters mired in poverty he left $1000 each, and he did not forget the attention and affection of Mrs. Stafford and Mrs. Davis in the twilight years. He directed that the residue of his estate be used for the care of the most helpless member of the family, Eddy, who was now institutionalized in New Jersey.

In the last painful months of his life Whitman wrote only to his favorite sister, Hannah, who could hardly contain her gratitude and her sorrow: "But your writing to me now—there is no words to say & I wont try. you are the only one in the whole world, would be, so good to me.—What does me good or what is a comfort to me is nothing, you, are the one I care for my darling."⁴ It is only fitting that Hannah received the last letter he wrote, in which, elder brother to the end, he remembered to enclose $4.

Whitman directed that the remains of his parents be buried at his side. He accomplished at death what life for complex reasons had denied: the reunion of mother, father, and child, that eternal trio finally at peace in an eternal home. Walt's instructions provided that they be surrounded by other members of the family. Louisa, George's wife, and Eddy were buried there a few months after his death in 1892, George in 1901, and Horace Traubel in 1918.

In death he was no longer a stranger.

To Dr. Richard Maurice Bucke

Camden, January 7, 1890

Close to my den the last two or three days—pretty dull every thing—alone nearly all the time—very moderate temperature (but cold probably by the time you get this)—I guess matters physiological are as well with me as could be expected *considering*—when exhilarated with visitors or friends here I probably feel & throw out sort o' extra (wh' probably acc'ts for Horace's glowing picture probably having a very flimsy background or none at all)—the main things are a pretty good (born) heart & stalwart genesis—constitution—*these the main factors*—Keeping hearty—Y'r letters always welcomed—

Walt Whitman

M S: Feinberg Collection, Library of Congress

To Dr. Richard Maurice Bucke

Camden, January 22, 1890

Sunny & cold & dry to-day—(*most* yet this winter)—I keep on much the same—probably slowly certainly *ebbing*—fairly buoyant spirits—rare egg & tea & bread for breakfast—good bowel action—Shall probably have a poemet (8 or 9 lines) in Feb. *Century*⁵—Shall send it you in slip, soon as out—Stead has sent me his "Review of Reviews" f'm London—shall I send it to you? Horace has it now—

I have written to Mrs. Costelloe—Alys comes quite regularly—R[obert] P[earsall] S[mith] is well—Logan writes—am sitting here dully enough—

stupid—no exhilaration—no massage or wheel-chair to day—my nurse has disappear'd for the day—now 3½ oclock—If I had a good hospital, well conducted—some good nurse—to retreat to for good I sometimes think it w'd be best for me—I shall probably get worse, & may linger along yet some time—of course I know that death has struck me & it is only a matter of time, but may be quite a time yet—But I must get off this line—don't know why I got on it—but having written I will let it remain—enclosed (I have just come across it & I tho't I w'd send it to you) is Sylvanus Baxter's Pension Proposition two years ago—Peremptorily declined by me—but for all that & against my own decision put before the U S H[ouse of] R[epresentatives] *pension committee* at Washington & passed, (did I send you the U S H R Committee report?)—but not definitively pass'd by Congress—Perhaps I had better tell you, dear Maurice, that the money or income question is the one that *least* bothers me—I have enough to last. This is a sort of crazy letter but I will let it go—

Walt Whitman

finish'd toward 4 P M—all right—
M S: Feinberg Collection, Library of Congress

To Mary Smith Costelloe

Camden, January 22, 1890

Dear Mary Costelloe

Sunny, cold, dry, very seasonable day, I continue on much the same—get out a little in wheel chair (but doubtful to-day—pretty sharp cold)—have quite rousing oak fire, & great wolf skin fur on my big-limb'd ratan chair—Alys was here Sunday, & I rec'd yesterday a nice letter f'm Logan—a day or two before the "Spectator" f'm thy father—(so I am not neglected or forgotten)—Give my best thanks & love to all— . . .

Probably every thing in our great United States (now 42 of them) goes on well all in a monotonous & matter of fact way—"blessed is that country that has *no* history"—we have an unprecedently humdrum President & big men, but down in the myriad inner popular currents the moral & literary & pecuniary & even political flow & *good flow* are grand—we can console our hearts with that—on a great democratic scale the present & here are probably ahead & better than all time past, or any other land—*& thats what America is for*—& that satisfies me—that general unmistakable certain

trend does—I dont mind little bothers & exceptions & some hoggishness—
Love to you all—

                                                                    Walt Whitman

M S: Feinberg Collection, Library of Congress

To Ernest Rhys[6]

                                                        Camden, January 22, 1890
My dear E R
    Y'rs regularly rec'd & welcom'd (I often send them afterward to Dr Bucke,
Canada)—
    I am still here, no very mark'd or significant change or happening—fairly
buoyant spirits &c—but surely slowly *ebbing*—at this moment sitting here
in my den Mickle Street by the oak wood fire, in the big strong old chair
with wolf-skin spread over back—bright sun, cold, dry winter day—America continues generally busy enough all over her vast demesnes (*intestinal
agitation* I call it)—talking, plodding, *making money*, every one trying to get
on—perhaps to get toward the top—but no special individual signalism—
(just as well I guess)—I write without any particular purpose, but I tho't I
w'd show you I appreciate y'r kindness & remembrance—The two slips enclosed you are at liberty to do what you like with—affectionate remembrance to the dear sister—

                                                                    Walt Whitman

T E X T: *Pall Mall Gazette*, February 8, 1890

To Richard Maurice Bucke

                                                          Camden, April 13, 1890
    Had a much better night, & got up late & better—Horace came & I told
him I w'd try to go thro' the Lincoln Death Piece Tuesday night (I can't bear
to be *bluff'd off* & toward the last, even in minor ways)—But I by no means
know how it will go off—or but I sh'l break down—no strength no en-
ergy—a little stimulus (the personal exhiliration of calling friends & talk)
keeps me up ten minutes but then down flops everything.
    It is a beautiful sunny warm April day & I want to get out a little yet—
fortunately keep up pretty good spunk but the body & physical brain are
miserable yet—the enclosed note is f'm Dr Brinton[7] to whom I had sent the

big book in response to his many kindnesses & liberalities &c. As I sit here
every thing is beautiful & quiet—Warren has gone over to T Donaldson's—
I expect him (W) back presently—have a headache (not severe)—of course
we shall post you of all happenings &c. Of course all will be well. "What are
yours and Destiny's O Universe," said Marcus Aurelius, "are mine too."
Have sent word to Kennedy and John Burroughs.

　　God bless you & all—

　　　　　　　　　　　　　　　　　　　　　　　　　Walt Whitman

M S: Feinberg Collection, Library of Congress

To William Sloane Kennedy

　　　　　　　　　　　　　　　　　　　　　　Camden, June 18, 1890

　　Fairly with me these days—Did I tell you my last piece (poem) was rejected by the *Century* (R W Gilder)[8]—I have now been shut off by *all* the
magazines here & the *Nineteenth Century* in England[9]—& feel like closing
house as poem writer—(you know a fellow doesn't make brooms or shoes if
nobody will have 'em)—I shall put in order a last little 6 or 8 page annex
(the second) of my *Leaves of Grass*—& that will probably be the finish—

　　I get out almost daily in wheel chair—was out yesterday down to river
shore & staid there an hour—cloudy weather now fourth day, but entirely
pleasant—appetite fair—had oatmeal porridge, honey & tea for breakfast—
shall probably have stew'd mutton & rice for early supper (do not eat dinner
at all, find it best)—have massage every day—bath also—have a good nurse
Warren Fritzinger—sell a book occasionally—get along better than you
might think anyhow—have some pretty bad spells—some talkers bores
questioners (hateful)—two splendid letters lately f'm R G Ingersoll—I
enclose Dr B[ucke]'s, rec'd this morning—Love to Mrs: K—God bless
you both—

　　　　　　　　　　　　　　　　　　　　　　　　　Walt Whitman

M S: Trent Collection, Duke University

To Dr. Richard Maurice Bucke

　　　　　　　　　　　　　　　　　　Camden, July 18 and 19, 1890

　　Pleasant and sufficiently cool & breezy to-day, (after some exhaustingly
hot weather lately, but I am here ab't the same after it all)—Dr John

Johnston f'm Bolton, England, has been here three or four days, & I have seen quite a good deal of him & like him well—I believe he intends to go to Ontario & call upon you—I am sure you will be interested in him—he is a great reader &c of L of G—he yesterday went to Brooklyn, to visit Andrew and Tom Rome[10] & intends going down to Huntington L I to visit Herbert Gilchrist—Sh'd suppose he might come y'r way ab't a week or thereab't fr'm now—

J A Symonds has sent me his (formidable) finely printed "*Essays Speculative & Suggestive*," *two Vols. duodecimo, Chapman & Hall, London*—one essay being devoted to me, "*Democratic Art, with special reference to Walt Whitman*"—Have run it over & a few other pages—I guess there is meat in the vols. but I doubt whether he has gripp'd "democratic art" by the nuts, or L of G. either—then the pretty magazine here "*Poet Lore*" for July 15, (Lippincott, Phila:) has an article "*Walt Whitman's View of Shakspere*," signed *Jonathan Trumbull*, very friendly respectful & complimentary to me—but dont get to marrows hardly at all[11]—

Saturday P M—Fine day—sunny—cool enough—Am feeling fairly—this enclosed slip is cut f'm Horace's little paper—y'r letters rec'd—am sitting here the same in cane chair in my Mickle Street den—the big whistle has sounded 1 o'clock—my good nurse Warry has just bro't me some nice ice cream, wh' I have duly eaten—A NY man has offered me $100 for a novel (shortish story, 5000 words)—shall probably not try[12]—

Love to Mrs: B and the childer—

Walt Whitman

M S: Feinberg Collection, Library of Congress

To William Sloane Kennedy

Camden, August 8, 1890

Y'rs of 6th just comes—(are you not a little *blue*?—it's no use—one has to obey orders, & do duty, & face the music till he gets formal dismissal—& may as well *come up to the scratch* smiling)—

I am still getting along thro' the hot season—have things pretty favorable here in my shanty, with ventilation, (night & day) frequent bathing, light meals & *lassaiz faire*—all wh' makes it better for me in my utterly helpless condition to tug it out here in Mickle street, than transfer myself some where to sea-shore or mountain—It is not for a long time any how—then Elias

Hicks's saying to my father "Walter, it is not so much *where* thee lives, but how thee lives."

Symonds's new vols: are deep, heavy, bookish, infer not things or thoughts at first hand but at third or fourth hand, & after the college point of view— the essays are valuable, but appear to me to be elderly chestnuts mainly— Horace is preparing an article ab't me for N[ew] E[ngland] Magazine[13]—I make dabs with the little 2d Annex & licking it in shape—I made my break- fast on bread, honey & a cup of coffee—a cloudy drizzling day, pleasant— Love to you & the frau—

                                                           Walt Whitman

M S: University of Pennsylvania

To John Addington Symonds[14]

                                              Camden, August 19, 1890

Y'rs of Aug: 3d just rec'd & glad to hear f'm you as always—Abt the little portraits, I cheerfully endorse the Munich reproduction of any of them you propose or any thing of the sort you choose—(I may soon send you some other preferable portraits of self)—Suppose you have rec'd papers & slips sent of late—Ab't the questions on Calamus pieces &c: they quite daze me. L of G. is only to be rightly construed by and within its own atmosphere and essential character—all of its pages & pieces so coming strictly under *that*— that the calamus part has even allow'd the possibility of such construction as mention'd is terrible—I am fain to hope the pages themselves are not to be even mention'd for such gratuitous and quite at the time entirely undream'd & unreck'd possibility of morbid inferences—wh' are disavow'd by me & seem damnable. Then one great difference between you and me, tempera- ment & theory, is *restraint*—I know that while I have a horror of ranting & bawling I at certain moments let the spirit impulse, (?demon) rage its utmost, its wildest, damnedest—(I feel to do so in my L of G. & I do so). I end the matter by saying I wholly stand by L of G. as it is, long as all parts & pages are construed as I said by their own ensemble, spirit & atmosphere.

I live here 72 y'rs old & completely paralyzed—brain & right arm ab't same as ever—digestion, sleep, appetite, &c: fair—sight & hearing half- and-half—spirits fair—locomotive power (legs) almost utterly gone—am propell'd outdoors nearly every day—get down to the river side here, the Delaware, an hour at sunset—The writing and rounding of L of G. has been to me the reason-for-being, & life comfort. My life, young manhood, mid-age, times South, &c: have all been jolly, bodily, and probably open to criticism—

Tho' always unmarried I have had six children—two are dead—One living southern grandchild, fine boy, who writes to me occasionally. Circumstances connected with their benefit and fortune have separated me from intimate relations.

I see I have written with haste & too great effusion—but let it stand.

DRAFT LETTER: Feinberg Collection, Library of Congress

To Dr. Richard Maurice Bucke

Camden, September 13, 1890

Medley sort of weather half rain half sunshine some breeze—will probably send you Kennedy's Dutch piece soon [15] (see enclosed letter f'm him)—Am looking over the Kreutzer Sonata & have Ingersoll's criticism in N[orth] A[merican] Review—the political *intestinal agitation* here in U S is essentially ab't unrestricted trade (general reciprocity) and the damnable diseased policy the Harrison gov't typifies call'd protectionism—thats the bottom of it, below every thing else—probably the world never saw such a mean dog-in-the-manger principle so thoroughly attempted & made the base of a great party (the remains, dead cadaverous trunk of the once glorious live Lincoln party of '60 to '64 and '5) as to-day & in the U S—But *agitation, experiment* &c: *must* be a gain one way or another here in U S [16]—

I told you Mrs. Davis has gone on a visit to Kansas—It is a long jaunt—she gets there 14th—

Walt Whitman

MS: Feinberg Collection, Library of Congress

To Mary D. Davis

Camden, September 15 and 16, 1890

Dear Mary Davis,

Every thing is going on right here, & ab't as usual—I keep ab't the same, & well enough considering—went out yesterday afternoon, (Warry wheel'd me up of course in the chair) to Mr & Mrs: Harned's where we had a first-rate dinner (my 5 o'clock supper) of champagne & oysters—the best & plenty—come back just after 8. Both Mr and Mrs H so hospitable & gener-

ous & good to me—Mrs Doughty and Maggy are well & Mrs D does very
well—gives me plenty for my meals & all right—we've killed one of the
roosters, (he behaved very badly & put on airs) and had a chicken pot pie &
I had some of the c[hicken] for my breakfast this morning—& some new
coffee better than the old, (wh' was not good)—My appetite is good as
ever—Warry is well & jolly & keeps first rate & good to me—we go out
towards evn'g as ever—last night it rained & keeps it half-up to day, &
is cloudy & dark & half warm—Warry has just been in to make up the
bed, &c:—

The most important event is Harry's marrying,[17] which is to come off this
evn'g, to be by Squire Tarr at his house—

Harry was up with me yesterday noon to talk ab't it—I felt quite solemn
ab't it (I think more of the boy, & I believe he does of me, than we knew)—
He kissed me & hung on to my neck—O if he only gets a good wife & it all
turns out lasting & good (Mary, I think more of Harry than you suppose)—
at any rate one first-rate point, it may anchor him in a way that nothing else
might, & give him a definite object & aim to work up to—(& perhaps he
needs that)—I am sitting up in my big den, in the old chair as I write, every
thing comfortable—

5 P M—Chicken pot pie & rice pudding to-day—& oysters & champagne
yesterday—so you see, Mary, we are not starving—

Tuesday forenoon Sept: 16—Harry and Becky were married last evn'g, &
they came around here afterward a little while, at my special invitation—I
have had my breakfast (Warry broiled a bit of meat for me, very nice)—the
sun has been under a cloud, but I see it is plainly coming out—Love to you
f'm me & all of us—I enclose $5, 2 for Mrs: M[apes], 2 for the dear mother
& 1 for dear boy Glen & my best respects & well wishes to all—

                                                        Walt Whitman

M S: Barrett Collection, University of Virginia

To Bernard O'Dowd

                                                Camden, October 3, 1890

Dear Bernard O'Dowd[18] (& all the friends)

Y'r good letter of Sept: 1 has just come, & is welcomed—I like to hear
every thing & anything ab't you all—& ab't the Australian bush & birds and
life & toil & idiosyncrasies there—& how it looks—& all the sheep work

&c: &c:—you please me more than you know by giving such things fully—
write often as you feel to & can—The Dr Bucke book (that I had dispatch'd
by mail hence early in July) came back to me after a long interval for more
post stamps wh' I put on & re-sent hence July 25 last, same address as this—
& I sort o' hope & trust it has reached you safely by this time—if not I will
send another—Ingersoll is to come to Philadelphia & make a public address
(the bills call it a "testimonial" to me) the latter week of this month & to
raise moneys for me I suppose—(thank him, the true Christian of them
all)—They refused to rent him the hall he wanted—but I believe he has
found one yet—If reported I will send you the acc't & speech—Cloudy &
wet here lately but today is sunny & perfect & I shall get out this afternoon
in wheel chair—I remain much the same—spirits good—sleep, appetite, digestion &c: not bad—but the grip (a catarrhal, cold-in-the-head affection)
and bladder trouble seem tenaciously on me—good right arm volition—
mentally not seriously impair'd &c: &c: (I write to you as an elder brother
might to the young bro's & sisters, & doubtless repeat parrot-like)—what
books of mine have you?—I sh'd like to send you a little pocket-book b'd L
of G. as a present to be used by any of you & may be handy, & indeed am
only restrain'd by the uncertainty of the mails f'm sending many more
things. But I already get enough to know I have your good will & love & that
my missives have struck deep even passionately into dear human hearts—

Walt Whitman

M S: Melbourne Public Library, Australia

To Bernard O'Dowd

Camden, November 3, 1890

Dear friend Bernard O'Dowd (& dear friends all)

Y'r good letter 29/9 & the newspaper came this mn'g & was welcome, as
always—am cheer'd to hear f'm you all, & y'r affectionate treatment of me,
thro' L of G. See you must have rec'd all my letters, papers, slips & scraps, &
Dr Bucke's book (remember that Dr B gives his coloring f'm the eye of a
zealous friend—I know well enough that W W is not a quarter as good as B
makes him out, but is full of defects & vagaries & faults)—I have since sent
you report of R G Ingersoll's big lecture in Philadelphia here Oct. 21—I
have rec'd from it (& him) $869.45 wh' keeps me in bread & [milk] &
shanty-keeping a good time yet—I also send to you printed slip, "Old

Poets" my latest piece—am not sure but this internationality of P O & mails
(I got a letter this mn'g. all safe f'm Nagasaki, written very fair English, f'm a
young Japanese reader & absorber of L of G) is the grandest proof of modern civilization, practical brotherhood & Christianity—we feel it here in the
U S f'm Canada to Texas, & f'm Atlantic side to Pacific shore—& you must
too in Australia—

Am mainly ab't same in health but slowly dimming & the pegs coming
gradually out as I call it—this *grip* has hold of me thoroughly, & bladder
trouble badly—but I keep fair spirits & I suppose mentality & (as before
written) fair appetite & sleep—have a good nurse, Warren Fritzinger, a
strong hearty good natured young American man, has been f'm boyhood a
sailor & all round the world—go out in propell'd wheel chair—was out last
evn'g to a friend's & wife's to supper, (drank a bottle of first rate champagne)—when you write don't be afraid to send me ab't Australian idiosyncrasies, the woods, special trees & birds & books, life, people, peculiarities, occupations &c. (Under the thin glaze-surface of conventionalities, as
here, a vast plummetless-depth of democratic humanity is existing, thinking,
acting, ebbing & flowing—there no doubt—that I would like O so like to
flatter myself I am giving or trying to give voice to)— . . .

Barney, you don't know how much you & all there have done me—words
by pen & ink are poor perhaps but O how I wish to give you all & each a
God bless you & my love to you & the dear wife & baby & to Fred [Woods]
& Jim [Hartigan] & Kate, & Ada, Eve, & Mr & Mrs Fryer & Mr Bury[19] &
other friends I fear I have not specified—

Walt Whitman

MS: Melbourne Public Library, Australia

To his brother Ed

Camden, November 28, 1890

Dear Ed:

It is pretty sad days just now for me here—our dear brother Jeff died last
Tuesday at St Louis, Missouri, of typhoid pneumonia. Jessie[20] went on first
train soon as she heard he was sick, but poor Jeff was dead when she arrived—George has gone on—(must have got there this morning)—Hannah
is poorly at Burlington Vermont, but gets about the house. Very cold here. I
am still about (not much about for I can only move by help) but have the

grip badly, & bladder trouble. I often think of you & hope you have comfortable times—I have heard you have a good kind attendant who has been there some time in the asylum—I wish he would stop here at 328 Mickle & see me a few minutes when he is in Camden. My best respects to Mr and Mrs. Currie[21]—My love to you—

Walt Whitman

M S: Feinberg Collection, Library of Congress

To Wallace Wood

Camden, March 3, 1891

Y'rs, & the third kind solicitation, rec'd; to wh' I hurriedly respond.[22] The answer to such questions ought to be the thoughts and results of a life time & w'd need a big volume. Seems to me, indeed, the whole varied machinery, intellect, & even emotion, of the civilized universe, these years, are working toward the answer. (My own books, poems & prose, have been a direct & indirect attempt at contribution.) No doubt what will be sent you will be salutary & valuable, & all fit in. Though the constituents of "perfect manhood" are much the same all lands & times, they will always be sifted & graduated a good deal by conditions, and especially by the United States. Then I sh'd say, with emphasis, we c'd not have (all things consider'd) any better chances than mainly exist in these States to-day—common education, general inquiry, freedom, the press, Christianity, travel, &c. &c. But perhaps I may vary and help by growling a little as follows: For one thing out of many, the tendency in this Commonwealth seems to favor & call for & breed specially *smart men*. To describe it (for reasons) extra sharply I sh'd say we New Worlders are in danger of turning out the trickiest, slyest, 'cutest, most cheating people that ever lived. Those qualities are getting radically in our business, politics, literature, manners, and filtering in our essential character. All the great cities exhibit them—probably New York most of all. They taint the splendid & healthy American qualities, & had better be well understood like a threatening danger, & well confronted & provided against.

Walt Whitman

M S: Feinberg Collection, Library of Congress

To Dr. John Johnston

Camden, March 30 and 31, 1891

Pleasant sunny day out & I am getting on fairly considering—the long fearful obstinate *bowel-block* seems to be edged upon, even started, (or suspicion of it)—have pretty good nights—must have five or six hours sleep— no vehement pain night or day that I make acc't of—bladder trouble not pronounced at present—use the catheter most every day—eat my two meals daily or something of them, farina, roast apple, rare fried egg, mutton & rice, &c. &c.—Dr Longaker, (652 north 8th st: Philadelphia) comes every 2d day, & I like him & his doings— . . . the proofs of "Good-Bye My Fancy" are slowly getting along—have sent back 31 pp: to be corrected—(there may be ab't 45)—don't you look out for anything stirring—it is small any how, & mostly to untune (let down) clinch what I have said before, pass the fingers again carelessly over the strings & probably some parrot-like repetitions & *to close the book* avoiding any thing like trumpet blasts or attempts at them—intend it to be bound in with "November Boughs" & make it supplementary part.

Tuesday 31st 1 pm—Dr L has just been—thinks matters are going along satisfactorily—Dark glum day—& I am too, but it is blessed to be no worse, & even indication of turning better—am sitting here same way in big chair alone &c:—drizzling out—God bless you & all[23]

Walt Whitman

M S: Library of Congress

To Dr. Richard Maurice Bucke

Camden, May 5, 1891

Bad days—bad condition. Was taken out to Harleigh yesterday, had to be led, assisted every movement, to see the tomb—it is well advanced—is a hefty very unornamental affair not easily described—is satisfactory to me & will be to you—some pieces stone weigh 6 or 8 tons—splendid weather— Mrs. D[avis] & Warry good to me—Dr L[ongaker][24] sick & home—

W W

M S: Feinberg Collection, Library of Congress

To Dr. Richard Maurice Bucke

Camden, May 23, 1891

Nothing very new or different—bad bad enough—*the fiendish indigestion block* continued—heavy torpor increasing—the burial house in Harleigh well toward finished—I paid the constructor $500 last week—(as far as I can see I am favor'd in having Ralph Moore[25] as my *alter ego* in making it)—I wish to collect the remains of my parents & two or three other near relations, & shall doubtless do so—I have two deceased children (young man & woman—illegitimate of course) that I much desired to bury here with me—but have ab't abandon'd the plan on acc't of angry litigation & fuss generally & disinterment f'm down south—

Kennedy has printed a short criticism of "Good-Bye"—finds it without the sign-marks of early L of G—praises it highly tho'—As I get toward estimate—but that is more in the forming than settled state—f'm my own point of view I accept without demur its spurty (old Lear's irascibility)—its offhandedness, even evidence of decrepitude & old fisherman's seine character as part of *the artism* (f'm my point of view) & as adherence to the determin'd cartoon of Personality that dominates or rather stands behind all of L of G. like the unseen master & director of the show—

W W

MS: Feinberg Collection, Library of Congress

To J. W. Wallace

Camden, May 28, 1891

Still badly prostrated—horrible torpidity—Y'rs & Dr [Johnston]'s letters rec'd, & cheer me much—am sitting here in big chair at this moment.

I guess I have a good deal of the feeling of Epictetus & stoicism or tried to have—they are specially needed in a rich & luxurious & even scientific age—But I am clear that I include & allow & probably teach some things stoicism would frown upon & discard—One's pulses & marrow are not *democratic* & *natural* for nothing—Let Plato's steeds prance & curvet & drive at their utmost, but the master's gripe & eyes & brain must retain the ultimate power for all, or things are lost—Give my loving compliments to all the boys, & give this scrawl to Wentworth Dixon to keep if he cares for it—

Walt Whitman

MS: Feinberg Collection, Library of Congress

To Dr. John Johnston

Camden, June 1, 1891

Well here I am launch'd on my 73d year—We had our birth anniversary spree last evn'g—ab't 40 people, choice friends mostly—12 or so women— Tennyson sent a short and sweet letter over his own sign manual—y'r cable was rec'd & read, lots of bits of speeches, with gems in them—we had a capital good supper (or dinner) chicken soup, salmon, roast lamb &c: &c: &c: I had been under a horrible spell f'm 5 to 6, but Warry me got[26] dress'd & down (like carrying down a great log)—& Traubel had all ready for me a big goblet of first-rate iced champagne—I suppose I swigg'd it off at once— I certainly welcom'd them all forthwith, & at once felt if I was to go down I would not fail without a desperate struggle—must have taken near two bottles champagne the even'g—so I added ("I felt to") a few words of honor & reverence for our Emerson, Bryant, Longfellow dead—and then for Whittier and Tennyson "the boss of us all" living (specifying all)—not four minutes altogether—then held out with them *for three hours*—talking lots, lots impromptu—Dr B[ucke] is here—Horace T is married[27]—fine sunny noon—

Walt Whitman

Doctor, if easy & cheap photo (fac-simile) this June 1 note, *not* the mask, & give one to each of the friends that desires—send Tennyson one—send Symonds one—send Whittier one (Amesbury, Mass:) & half a dozen to me— W W

just send them without explanation— M S : Library of Congress

To Dr. Richard Maurice Bucke

Camden, June 4, 1891

I ought to have written before, but there has been & is nothing partic- ular—Both y'r letters have duly come f'm Niagara—am pulling al'g so-so, stomachic and bladder bother & fearful lassitude—Warry went out to Harleigh yesterday—the *date* is chipp'd off (W says an improvement)— the ponderous door is *not* yet hung, baffles even the machinist & stone-

cutters—when done &c: will probably be the rudest most undress'd structure (with an idea)—since Egypt, perhaps the cave dwellers—am sitting
here in the big chair—my supper has appear'd & is waiting before me—
Seems to me at any rate a suspicion of easier & let up as I conclude. How
delightful the country you are in & must have pass'd thro' surely looks—
   God bless you, & love to all—

                                                      Walt Whitman

M S: Feinberg Collection, Library of Congress

To his sister Hannah

                                          Camden, October 26, 1891
Dear sister
   Am sitting here so-so—Nothing very different—get along fairly, considering—have buckwheat cakes for b'kfast—relish my meals fairly—visitors,
some f'm a distance—some f'm Calcutta not long ago—fine sunny weather—
children in to see me, bro't a big bunch of fall wild flowers—the big stout
Dutch woman is out in front playing f'm "Sonnambula" on a capital organ
& a little boy going all around collecting the pennies—How hearty (& dirty)
they look—
   God bless you, Han dear—$2 enc'd—

                                                              W W

M S: Feinberg Collection, Library of Congress

To Dr. Richard Maurice Bucke

                            Camden, October 31 and November 1, 1891
   Wallace[28] is down stairs taking a lunch, & photoing Warry, (at my request)—nothing very new or distinctive—the N Y papers are (I believe
every evn'g) telegraphing questions here wh' are answer'd "Walt Whitman
is *not dead yet*"—my disease is now call'd *progressive paralysis* with a more
or less rapid tendency (or eligibility) to the heart—formidable isn't it?—the
worst is there may be something in it—fine bright sunny day—am sitting
here ab't as usual—head bad—water w'ks trouble bad—frequent visitors—
Harrison Morris and Miss A Repplier[29] yest'dy—

Nov: 1—noon—Still the same—J W W[allace] is going off in City of
Berlin f'm N Y Wednesday mn'g—good slip enc'd ab't Schleimann's (almost) funny discoveries[30]—cloudy half-raw day—

Walt Whitman

M S: Feinberg Collection, Library of Congress

To Dr. Richard Maurice Bucke

Camden, November 12–14, 1891

Sunny fine Nov. day—have pann'd oysters for my meals—continued
bowel stoppage—rise late—feelings ab't "same subject continued"—probably a little more heavy headed & inertia—lots of pieces ab't me in newspapers (especially N Y) frequently horribly erroneous & silly—Horace and
Tom H[arned] are quite excited ab't a (supposed) plot or black mail or ex-
tortion to get a big sum of money out of me (or friends) for *the tomb*—Tom
H has it in hand—& I have too—don't anticipate much f'm it—but we will
see—have paid them $1500, & am willing to pay same am't more wh' is cer-
tainly ⅓d more (altogether) than square—But I wanted much to collect my
parents' & two or three relatives (dead relics) with my own—& this is the
result—& I am & think I shall be satisfied[31]—

Nov: 14—Fine sunny Nov: weather cont'd—feeling ab't same—buckwh't
cakes & coffee for brkf't—no specific news of J W W[allace]'s arrival yet—
no word yet f'm [H. Buxton] Forman ab't the Eng: publishing nibble—fearful rush lately of autograph fiends upon me—20 or 30 this week—sitting
here same in big chair—have rec'd copy of O'C[onnor]'s "Three Tales"[32]—
books & papers galore—head uneasy or congested or aching all the time—

Walt Whitman

M S: Feinberg Collection, Library of Congress

To Dr. Richard Maurice Bucke

Camden, December 6, 1891

Send same time with this first copy, (rude, flimsy cover, but good paper,
print & stitching) of L of G. *at last complete*—after 33 y'rs of hackling at it,
all times & moods of my life, fair weather & foul, all parts of the land, and

peace & war, young & old—the wonder to me that I have carried it on to accomplish as essentially as it is, tho' I see well enough its numerous deficiencies & faults—(At any rate

"From waiting long & long delay
Johnny comes marching home")

The cumulus character of the book is a great factor—perhaps even the jaggedness, or what might be call'd so f'm the conventional & tidy principles of "art"—probably *is* so anyhow³³—

Bad days & nights with me, no hour without its suffering—

Walt Whitman

M S: Feinberg Collection, Library of Congress

To Dr. Richard Maurice Bucke

Camden, January 23, 1892

Am deadly weak yet—otherwise inclined to favorable—bowel drain sufficient—appetite fair—the plaster cast come safe to Dr J[ohnston] Bolton³⁴—Ralph Moore is dead—Tom Harned well—my doctors & attendants cont[inue] first rate—Horace ever faithful—am propp'd up in bed—

God bless you all—

Walt Whitman

M S: Feinberg Collection, Library of Congress

To his sister Hannah

Camden, January 24, 1892

Just a line, sister dear—Have been very sick & suffered—& they say am better, but still at death's door—

Have the best attention & watching—send *best love* & God bless you, always—5 enc'd—bodily functions better than you might suppose—

It is all right whichever way—Lou & Geo & Jess often come—

W W

M S: Feinberg Collection, Library of Congress

To his sister Hannah

Camden, January 27, 1892

Much the same—weak & restless—otherwise fairly—y'r letter came—$2 enc'd—Geo was here—my new fuller best ed'n is out—have written to Mary[35]—very cold to day—am propp'd up in bed—read the papers &c—appetite fair—body sore & feeble—Best love & God bless you—

W W

M S: Feinberg Collection, Library of Congress

To Dr. Richard Maurice Bucke

Camden, January 27, 1892

Feeble & weak & restless but not without favorable points—appetite holds out—eat two meals every day—bowel movement every day (rather strange after such a long interregnum)—McK[ay] was here—paid me $283—I enc' two adv't slips—to me the 1892 ed'n supersedes them all by far—adv. intended for N Y Trib[une]—God bless you—

W W

M S: Trent Collection, Duke University

To Dr. John Johnston

Camden, February 6 and 7, 1892

Well I must send you all dear fellows a word from my own hand—propp'd up in bed, deadly weak yet but the spark seems to glimmer yet—the doctors & nurses & N Y friends as faithful as ever—Here is the adv. of the '92 edn. Dr Bucke is well & hard at work—Col. Ingersoll has been here, sent a basket of champagne. All are good—physical conditions &c. are not so bad as you might suppose, only my sufferings much of the time are fearful—Again I repeat my thanks to you & cheery British friends may be last—my right arm giving out—

Walt Whitman

Feb 7 Same cond'n cont'd—More & more it comes to the fore that the only theory worthy our modern times for g't literature, politics & sociology

must combine all the bulk people of all lands, the women not forgetting—
But the mustard plaster on my side is stinging & I must stop—Good bye
to all—

W W

M S: Library of Congress

To his sister Hannah

Camden, February 8, 1892

Much the same cond'n cont'd. Am probably growing weaker. Will not
write much—$2 enc'd—Best love & God bless you—

W W

Geo here yesterday—
M S: Feinberg Collection, Library of Congress

To Dr. Richard Maurice Bucke

Camden, February 8, 1892

Geo Stafford the father is dead—buried to morrow—I keep on much
the same—probably growing weaker—bowel movement an hour ago—
bad steady pain in left side what I call under belly—Dr McA[lister] here
daily[36]—God bless you all—

Walt Whitman

M S: Feinberg Collection, Library of Congress

To his sister Hannah

Camden, February 24, 1892

Still very poorly—wearing—Much same—Lou here—Jess back in St
L[ouis]—Geo sick rheumatism—$5 enc'd—Best love as always—

W W

M S: Feinberg Collection, Library of Congress

To his sister Hannah

Camden, March 4, 1892

Still lingering along pretty low—Lou here yesterday—Jess well St L[ouis]—[$5?] enc'd—Best love to you & God bless you—

W W

MS: Feinberg Collection, Library of Congress

To his sister Hannah

Camden, March[37] 17, 1892

Unable to write much—$4 enc'd—y'r good letter rec'd—God bless you—

W W

MS: Feinberg Collection, Library of Congress

NOTES

INTRODUCTION

1. Traubel, 1:137.
2. Traubel, 2:195.
3. *Corr.*, 1:134.
4. Traubel, 2:51.
5. *Corr.*, 1:134.
6. Traubel, 1:71.
7. Traubel, 1:316.
8. Traubel, 2:96.
9. Barrus, 157.
10. Traubel, 3:525.
11. Traubel, 3:110.
12. Traubel, 1:69.
13. See *Temple Bar Magazine*, 113 (1898): 200–12.
14. Traubel, 3:525.
15. *In Re Walt Whitman: Edited by His Literary Executors, Horace L. Traubel, Richard Maurice Bucke, Thomas B. Harned* (Philadelphia: McKay, 1893), 34.

1840–1841

1. These letters to Leech, now in the Library of Congress, were published by Professor Arthur Golden in *American Literature* 58 (1986): 342–60. I am greatly indebted to his article and annotations as well as to his generosity in supplying me with additional materials.
2. Switchel or switchell: a drink made of molasses, honey, or maple syrup, to which was added water and rum, usually flavored with ginger and vinegar.
3. People who live in or frequent bogs.
4. Probably, as Golden suggests, a private joke, with reference to the suspension of payments by banks following the panic of 1837.
5. A follower of Sylvester Graham (1794–1851), who advocated temperance and the consumption of whole wheat (hence graham flour).
6. A reference to the marriage ceremony in the Book of Common Prayer.

Golden suggests that it is not "an early expression of the 'Calamus' sentiment on Whitman's part" (353n).

7. Whitman probably intended to write "ipecacuanha." "Antimonial wine" is an irreverent allusion to antimonial powder, an emetic, sometimes called James's powder.

8. Martin Van Buren, the Democratic opponent of William Henry Harrison, the Whig, for the presidency in 1840.

9. The language of the Choctaw people; in jargon the gibberish of a strange language.

10. A radical group among New York Democrats. After Charles King, a Whig, in the *Long Island Farmer* on October 6, 1840, branded Whitman a "loco-foco," he replied to "this slanderous and contemptible scoundrel" on the same day in an unidentified newspaper. Whitman was particularly incensed that King had accused Van Buren and the Democratic party of upholding the doctrine of a "community of goods, wives, and children." In uttering this "*lie*," King "acted as *no gentleman* would act."

11. Fort Totten Battery was completed in 1846; see Golden, 356n.

12. See "Song of Myself," 1855 edition, lines 552–63.

13. An adhesive disk of dried paste used as a seal on letters.

1842–1860

1. See Gay Wilson Allen, *The Solitary Singer* (New York: Macmillan, 1955), 101.

2. Bennet Dowler, M.D., in *Tableaux of New Orleans* (1852?), 22, writes: "Probably no city of equal size in christendom receives into its bosom every year a greater proportion of vicious people than New Orleans."

3. Found: room and board.

4. Moses S. (1822–1892) and Alfred E. (1826–1896) Beach were the owners of the *New York Sun*, and Carlos D. Stuart the editor.

5. Fredrika Bremer (1801–1865), a Danish novelist, was in the United States from 1849 to 1850. Whitman commented on her novels in the *Brooklyn Eagle* on August 18, 1846.

6. Bernhard Severin Ingemann (1789–1862), the Danish Sir Walter Scott, wrote *The Childhood of King Erik Menved* in 1828. It is not known whether Whitman's adaptation appeared in the *Sun* or elsewhere.

7. Hale (1806–1873) was a senator from New Hampshire when he accepted the nomination of the Free-Soilers in 1852.

8. Members of the conservative faction of the Democratic party in New York in the 1840s and 1850s.

9. Mrs. Tyndale, an abolitionist from Philadelphia, met Whitman in the company of Bronson Alcott and Henry David Thoreau. Alcott describes her as "a solid

walrus of a woman spread full many a rood abroad, kindly taking the slaves' and Magdalens' parts and advocate for general justice and equality in all relations"; *Journals*, ed. Odell Shepard (Boston: Little, Brown, 1938), 289. Her son Hector was a Philadelphia importer of china.

10. Mrs. Tyndale commented on this passage: "If [Emerson] or any one else expected common etiquette from you, after having read Leaves of Grass, they were sadly mistaken in your character" (*Corr.*, 1:42n).

11. The Prices were friends of Whitman's mother. Edmund Price operated a pickle factory in Brooklyn. Whitman was particularly fond of his wife and the three children, Helen, Emma, and Arthur. John Arnold, a Swedenborgian, lived in the same house with the Prices. Henry Ward Beecher (1813–1887), brother of Harriet Beecher Stowe, was the somewhat notorious pastor of the Plymouth Church in Brooklyn. His father was Lyman Beecher (1775–1863).

12. Cora L. V. Hatch, a well-known medium, wrote *Discourses on Religion, Morals, Philosophy, and Metaphysics* (1858). Davis (1826–1910), a celebrated spiritualist of the age, proudly claimed that he had read only one book (presumably Swedenborg or the Bible) and proceeded to write about thirty books.

13. Elbert Stothoff Porter was pastor of the Williamsburgh Church in Brooklyn for almost forty years and editor of the *Christian Intelligencer* from 1852 to 1868.

14. Orson S. and Lorenzo Fowler, the phrenologists, formed the publishing firm of Fowler and Wells with S. R. Wells in 1844.

15. This fragment is known only from an auction record and may have been part of a letter or a notation for inclusion in one of Whitman's notebooks. At this time Whitman was considering a career as a lecturer.

16. *Harper's* rejected the poem, which became Number 4 of "Chants Democratic" when it was printed for the first time in the 1860 edition of *Leaves of Grass*; later it was titled "Our Old Feuillage."

17. Lowell (1819–1891), the editor of *The Atlantic Monthly*, was not one of Whitman's admirers. He apparently printed the poem at the suggestion of Emerson or Edward Howard House (1836–1901), music and drama critic of the *Boston Courier* and later of the *New York Tribune*. The poem eventually became "As I Ebb'd with the Ocean of Life."

18. On this occasion Emerson attempted to persuade Whitman not to publish the sexual poems later included in the section of *Leaves of Grass* entitled "Enfans d'Adam." Whitman's firm but no doubt respectful refusal did not undermine the relationship of the two men.

19. Charles Heyde, the husband of Whitman's favorite sister, Hannah, was an itinerant painter who settled in Burlington, Vermont, and an alcoholic who frequently threatened to leave his neurotic wife. Whitman had arranged the marriage but over time had nothing but contempt for the whining painter and deep sympathy for Hannah, whom he supported with frequent monetary gifts.

20. Until the end of his life Whitman was a devoted practitioner of currying, the use of a coarse brush supposedly to stimulate circulation and well being.

21. Stephen Alonzo Schoff (1818–1904), famous for his engraved portraits.

22. "Ned Buntline" was the pseudonym of Edward Z. C. Judson (1823–1886), the first of the dime novelists and the originator of the Buffalo Bill series. The *New York Ledger* was a popular weekly with a circulation of 400,000 in 1860.

23. A bill in the Albany legislature affecting the operation of the Brooklyn Water Works, where Jeff was employed.

1861–1865

1. *Corr.*, 1:58–59n; and see *Civil War Letters of George Washington Whitman*, ed. Jerome M. Loving (Durham: Duke University Press, 1975).

2. Traubel, 1:115.

3. Traubel, 2:371.

4. *Corr.*, 1:188n.

5. Traubel, 2:380.

6. Martha, Jeff's wife, whom Whitman often called "sister."

7. Mannahatta, the daughter of Martha and Jeff.

8. Moses Fowler Odell (1818–1866), member of the House of Representatives from New York.

9. Edward Ferrero (1831–1899), colonel in the Fifty-first New York Volunteers, later a brigadier general.

10. William Henry Seward (1801–1872), Secretary of State from 1861 to 1869; Salmon Portland Chase (1808–1873), Secretary of the Treasury from 1861 to 1864; Charles Sumner (1811–1874), chairman of the Committee on Foreign Affairs in the United States Senate from 1861 to 1871.

11. "Our Brooklyn Boys in the War" appeared in the *Brooklyn Daily Eagle* on January 5.

12. The *Monitor* foundered at sea on December 30, 1862. The report of the disaster was received on January 3, 1863.

13. A contribution to Whitman's hospital work from two employees of the Brooklyn Water Works, Louis Probasco and Moses Lane, chief engineer.

14. William Starke Rosecrans (1819–1898), a Union general.

15. Here Whitman replied to Jeff's almost hysterical letters asking him to persuade George to quit the army in order to spare the life of their mother.

16. Stone (1808–1875) served as a surgeon in the Patent Office Hospital from 1862 to 1865.

17. Whitman published these notes for the first time in 1874 in the *New York Weekly Graphic* as "Memoranda During the War."

18. United States Senator from New York from 1857 to 1863.

19. George arrived in Brooklyn on March 7 on a ten-day furlough.

20. His sister Mary Van Nostrand.

21. "The Great Washington Hospital," which appeared in the *Brooklyn Eagle* on March 19, later became "Life Among Fifty Thousand Soldiers."

22. Professor Joseph-Charles d'Almeida (1822–1880), author of *Problèmes de physique* (1862), came to the United States in 1862.

23. Bloom and Gray were part of what Whitman facetiously called the Fred Gray Association, along with Charles Russell, Charles Chauncey, Edward F. Mullen (or Mullin), an artist, Benjamin Knower, a clerk, and others.

24. The O'Connors. Matilda Agnes Heron (1830–1877) was a famous interpreter of Legouvé's *Medea*.

25. Construction began in 1848, was abandoned from 1855 to 1877, and finally completed in 1884.

26. This is the first extant letter Whitman wrote to a soldier in the Washington hospitals.

27. D. Willard Bliss (1825–1889) was a surgeon and practiced in Washington after the war. In 1887 he recommended that Whitman receive a pension for his services in the military hospitals.

28. Admiral Samuel F. du Pont suffered the worst naval loss of the war at Charleston on April 7, 1863.

29. General Joseph Hooker (1814–1879) replaced General Ambrose E. Burnside as the commanding general of the Army of the Potomac on January 26.

30. At this point Whitman deleted the following: "What I have written is pretty strong talk, I suppose, but I mean exactly what I say."

31. Like the preceding one, this is a draft letter and is dated in an unknown hand.

32. Jeff informed Whitman that Andrew was going to New Bern, North Carolina, "to take charge of the building of some fortifications," which was to be described later as military service.

33. Jessie Louisa Whitman was born on June 17, 1863.

34. Elias Hicks (1748–1830), the famous American Quaker preacher.

35. Among the numerous agencies involved with the soldiers, Whitman had praise only for the United States Christian Commission.

36. Vicksburg formally surrendered on July 4.

37. At this time Lee was at or near Chambersburg, Pennsylvania.

38. General George Meade (1815–1872) replaced Hooker on June 28, two days before the engagement at Gettysburg.

39. A grim account of the squalor in this camp appeared in the *New York Herald* on February 27, 1863.

40. Whitman characterized Hugo Fritsch as "one of my New York boys (Fifth Avenue)"; he was the son of the Austrian Consul General.

41. Lewis K. Brown (1843–1926). His leg was amputated in 1864, and he was mustered out of the army in the same year. He spent the rest of his life until his retirement in the United States Treasury Department but apparently had no contact with Whitman after the war.

42. James Redpath (1833–1891) was the author of *The Life of John Brown*, a correspondent for the *New York Tribune* during the Civil War, and later editor of *The North American Review*.

43. Years later Whitman did not think that this paragraph in the draft letter had been recopied in the letter sent to Fritsch: "It was too damned nonsensical for a letter otherwise so dead serious" (Traubel, 3:368). It is lined through in the extant manuscript.

44. Whitman was not quite accurate: he composed a rough copy which he recopied and then mailed to the soldier's parents.

45. John Mahay was wounded in the bladder at second Bull Run in August 1862. "A painful and long-lingering case," he died late in 1864. Whitman visited him in the hospital for fifteen months. "Poor Mahay," Whitman writes in *Specimen Days*, "a mere boy in age, but old in misfortune. He never knew the love of parents, was placed in infancy in one of the New York charitable institutions, and subsequently bound out to a tyrannical master in Sullivan county, (the scars of whose cowhide and club remain'd yet on his back.) . . . He found friends in his hospital life, and, indeed, was a universal favorite. He had quite a funeral ceremony" (*Prose Works 1892*, 84).

46. See Lawrence Lader, "New York's Bloodiest Week," *American Heritage* 10 (June 1959):44–46, 95–98.

47. Davis, a lawyer in Worcester, Massachusetts, sent the contribution to Whitman on behalf of his brother, who was one of Jeff's friends.

48. "Letter from Washington," dated October 1, was printed in the *New York Times* on October 4, 1863.

49. Donizetti's *Roberto Devereux*.

50. At this time Arthur Price was a naval officer.

51. On November 5 the *New York Herald* announced: "The agony is over. . . . The copperheads . . . have been routed, horse, foot and artillery" (*Corr.*, 1:176n).

52. When Whitman wrote to Wintersteen in 1875, the former soldier replied: "I can not place you as I did not learn your name but havent forgot the kindness I recived while in the Armory Square Hospital" (*Corr.*, 1:177n).

53. Giuseppini Medori appeared in Donizetti's *Lucrezia Borgia* on November 4.

54. The letter is evidently not extant.

55. In the letter Fox wrote: "Dear Father: You will allow me to call you Father wont you. I do not know that I told you that both of my parents were dead but it is true and now, Walt, you will be a second Father to me won't you. For my love for you is hardly less than my love for my natural parent. I have never before met with a man that I could love as I do you. Still there is nothing strange about it for 'to know you is

to love you,' and how any person could know you and not love you is a wonder to me" (*Corr.*, 1:186–87n).

56. Trowbridge (1827–1916), novelist, poet, author of juvenile stories, and biographer, met Whitman in Boston in 1860.

57. Turner Ashby (1828–1862), a Confederate cavalry officer.

58. Edward Brush Fowler (1827–1896) became the commanding officer of George's regiment in 1862 and, after being badly wounded, was mustered out in 1864.

59. According to an article in the *Brooklyn Daily Eagle* on February 12, George received the honor "in recognition of his services in the field."

60. Franz Sigel (1824–1902), a German-born Union general, was relieved of his command after a serious defeat in the Shenandoah Valley on May 15, 1864.

61. William M. Baldwin was mustered out of the army on June 6, 1864.

62. Brown, usually inarticulate, was deeply moved in his reply on July 18: "I was also very sory to hear of your illness & to think that it was brought on by your unselfish kindness to the Soldiers. There is many a soldier now that never thinks of you but with emotions of the greatest gratitude & I know that the soldiers that you have bin so kind to have a great big warm place in their heart for you. I never think of you but it makes my heart glad to think that I have bin permitted to know one so good" (*Corr.*, 1:237).

63. George Brinton McClellan (1826–1885), the deposed Union general, was the Democratic presidential candidate in 1864.

64. William Tod Otto was assistant Secretary of the Interior, and J. Hubley Ashton assistant Attorney General.

65. George was taken prisoner on September 30, 1864, and, according to his first report to the family, was "well and unhurt" (*Corr.*, 1:243n). The family tried to arrange for a prisoner exchange.

66. Edward Ruggles (1817?–1867), a Brooklyn physician and friend of the Whitman family and later the inventor of cabinet pictures called Ruggles Gems.

1866–1873

1. See *Corr.*, 2:61.

2. Traubel, 4:514.

3. John Burroughs (1837–1921), the famous American naturalist, was magnetically drawn to Whitman, to "his great summery, motherly soul": "I loved him as I never loved any man. We were companionable without talking. I owe more to him than any other man in the world" (*Corr.*, 1:14).

4. The printing of the fourth edition of *Leaves of Grass* was proceeding slowly. Once again the poet was his own publisher and had to assume all costs.

5. Henry Stanbery (1803–1881) was appointed to the post on July 23, 1866, and

served until March 12, 1868, when he resigned to serve as President Johnson's chief counsel during the impeachment proceedings.

6. Jeff was again collecting funds from fellow employees at the Brooklyn Water Works to support his brother's endeavors.

7. Pseudonym of Elizabeth Chase Allen (1832–1911), who heartily disliked Whitman. Her *Poems* (1866) includes the work upon which her fame rests, "Rock Me to Sleep."

8. Henry Jarvis Raymond (1820–1869) established the *New York Times* in 1851. He termed O'Connor's *The Good Gray Poet* "the most brilliant monograph in our literature" (Barrus, 35) and invited O'Connor to review *Leaves of Grass* on December 2, 1866.

9. Pasquale Brignoli (1824–1884), an Italian tenor, and Euphrosyne Parepa-Rosa (1836–1876), an English soprano, gave a recital at Metzerott Hall.

10. William Michael Rossetti (1829–1919).

11. Conway (1832–1907), an American liberal clergyman who spent most of his life in England, lauded Whitman in *The Fortnightly Review* in 1866. Later Conway cooled, as did Whitman. This letter was written by Whitman for William O'Connor to recopy and send to Conway. Whitman still had trouble spelling "Rossetti."

12. Rossetti on December 8 informed Whitman that the "form of title-page which you propose would of course be adopted by me with thanks & without a moment's debate, were it not that my own title-page was previously in print" (*Corr.*, 1:351).

13. Burroughs's *Notes on Walt Whitman, As Poet and Person* was published earlier in the year at Burroughs's expense; it was written under the supervision of the poet.

14. In his letter Rossetti stated his principles of selection: "1. to omit *entirely* every poem which contains passages or words which modern squeamishness can raise an objection to—and 2, to include, from among the remaining poems, those which I most entirely & intensely admire" (Traubel, 3:303–4).

15. Whitman was preparing "Personalism" for *The Galaxy*, where it appeared in May 1868.

16. Celebration of the opening of trade and diplomatic relations with China.

17. Schuyler Colfax (1823–1885), Speaker of the House of Representatives, was Grant's running mate. At this time Chase was chief justice of the United States Supreme Court.

18. This is the third but the first extant letter of Whitman's correspondence with Pete Doyle. Both William and Henry James admired these letters in which, according to Henry, "there is not even by accident a line with a hint of style."

19. "Whispers of Heavenly Death."

20. The Washington Nationals defeated the Olympics 21 to 15 on September 21.

21. The item was printed under "Minor Topics" in the *New York Times* on October 1 much as Whitman outlined it here.

22. Ferdinand Freiligrath (1810–1876), a German poet and translator, reviewed the English edition of Whitman's poems in the *Augsburg Allgemeinem Zeitung* on April 24, 1868. It was among the first notices of Whitman in Europe.

23. Another one of the workers at the Railroad Company.

24. The October 3 issue of the *Clipper* contained Paul Preston's article "On the 'Five Points,'" one of the city's most notorious and squalid sections of whorehouses and bars.

25. William F. Channing (1820–1901), the brother-in-law of Ellen O'Connor and son of William Ellery Channing, was a doctor as well as the inventor of the first fire-alarm system.

26. William James quotes this paragraph in *Talks to Teachers on Psychology* (1899), 252, with this question: "Truly a futile way of passing the time, some of you may say, and not altogether creditable to a grown-up man. And yet, from the deepest point of view, who knows the more of truth, and who knows the less,—Whitman on his omnibus-top, full of the inner joy with which the spectacle inspires him, or you, full of the disdain which the futility of his occupation excites?"

27. The next edition of *Leaves of Grass* appeared in 1871–72.

28. Pennsylvania went Republican on October 13, and Grant's election was assured.

29. In Providence Whitman stayed alternately with the Channings and Davises. Pauline Wright Davis was a well-known abolitionist and suffragette, and Thomas Davis a manufacturer of jewelry.

30. Signed "Pete XX."

31. "Proud Music of the Sea-Storm" (later "Proud Music of the Storm") was accepted by James Fields and published in *The Atlantic Monthly* in February 1869.

32. According to Dr. Richard M. Bucke, Doyle was suffering from a skin eruption popularly known as barber's itch. Whitman would appear to have chosen his words carelessly in mentioning syphilis, and Doyle's apparent threat of suicide was an extreme overreaction, although the young man was seemingly given to periods of depression.

33. This letter is apparently lost.

34. This letter is evidently not extant.

35. John A. Rawlins, Grant's aide-de-camp during the Civil War and in 1869 Secretary of War.

36. Anne Gilchrist.

37. Stoddard (1843–1909), poet, author of tales of the South Pacific, and briefly Mark Twain's secretary, was strongly attracted to Whitman's Calamus poems. His letter of April 2 begins: "In the name of CALAMUS listen to me!" (*Corr.*, 2:97n). "A South-Sea Idyl" records Stoddard's only thinly veiled homosexual relationship with a sixteen-year-old native boy, Kána-ána.

38. Probably Charles H. Russell, who lived at 417 Fifth Avenue.

39. Napoleon III was deposed and the French army surrendered on September 2, 1870.

40. Although Whitman kept a thousand or more letters addressed to him, he destroyed at one time or another most of Doyle's letters. Hence it is not possible to explain this paragraph.

41. The *New York World* reported a street fight "over the merits of an Irish battle fought and won in 1690," in which 45 were killed and 105 wounded.

42. Because of his mother's continued illness, Whitman had his leave extended and returned to Washington on July 31, 1871.

43. When Whitman delayed in replying to her letter of September 3, 1871, Mrs. Gilchrist, impatient, her ardor undiminished, wrote on October 23: "I am yet young enough to bear thee children, my darling, if God should so bless me. And would yield my life for this cause with serene joy if it were so appointed, if that were the price for thy having a 'perfect child'" (*Corr.*, 2:141n).

44. Burroughs called on Dowden in Dublin in 1871.

45. Emerson's lecture on January 16, 1872, was reprinted at length the following day in the *Washington Daily Morning Chronicle*.

46. A draft letter to Symonds (1840–1893), author of *Renaissance in Italy, Sexual Inversion*, and a collection of poems entitled *Love and Death*, which was dedicated to Whitman. In his letter of October 7 Symonds noted the similarity of "Love and Death" to "Scented Herbage of My Breast," one of the Calamus poems. After Whitman replied, Symonds asked for clarification of "athletic friendship" in a vain attempt to have Whitman admit the homosexual undertones of his poetry.

47. "The Mystic Trumpeter."

48. Whitman was slightly inaccurate. The third edition was published by Thayer and Eldridge.

49. Probably Katharine Hillard; see *Corr.*, 2:224–25n.

50. *Democratic Vistas*.

51. Noel (1834–1894), a minor English poet and essayist, was, like Symonds, strongly attracted to Whitman's treatment of male friendship: "The proclamation of comradeship seems to me the grandest & most tremendous fact in your work & I heartily thank you for it" (*Corr.*, 2:162n).

52. This volume, on its appearance in 1872 titled *American Poets*, was dedicated to Whitman, "the greatest of American poets."

53. Whitman's mother was to live with George and Louisa in Camden. After Jeff and his family moved to St. Louis, no member of the family except Eddy lived with her.

54. This was one of Whitman's fibs to explain his delay in replying to what he must have construed as assault.

55. Mrs. Gilchrist refused to heed his warnings. "O, I could not live," she wrote, "if I did not believe that sooner or later you will not be able to help stretching out your arms towards me & saying, 'Come, my Darling'" (*Corr.*, 2:170n).

56. *The History of Civilization in England* (1857, 1861).

57. Martha had come East two months earlier for consultations with doctors in New York and Camden.

58. A veiled reference to the connubial relations of the tormented Heydes.

59. Miller (1839–1913), a colorful poet of mediocre ability, concluded his letter of September 30, 1871: "Grand old man! The greatest, and truest American I know, with the love of your son. Joaquin Miller" (*Corr.*, 2:154–55n).

60. The wife of J. Hubley Ashton, who obtained a position for Whitman in his office after Secretary Harlan fired him.

61. Whitman contributed to the support of his mother and his brother Eddy.

62. George Whitman's wife.

63. Mrs. Whitman had adjusted neither to her secondary role in the household of George and his wife nor to the absence of her Brooklyn friends. To her old friend Helen Price she complained: "i wouldent mind living here if i had a place of my own but this living with and not being boss of your own shanty aint the cheese" (*Corr.*, 2:201n).

64. Mrs. O'Connor's sister.

65. Whitman was mistaken: it was Colonel E. C. Mason, not his friend Julius. The war between the Modocs, an Indian tribe in Oregon, and the United States government, lasted from November 1872 to October 1873.

1873–1881

1. Traubel, 2:39.

2. Traubel, 2:354

3. Traubel, 2:265.

4. See *Corr.*, 6:xiii–xiv.

5. Clifton Joseph Furness, *Walt Whitman's Workshop* (Cambridge: Harvard, 1928), 245–46.

6. *Corr.*, 3:20, and see 6:xi–xii.

7. Barrus, 164.

8. *Corr.*, 3:4.

9. See *Corr.*, 3:108 and n.

10. *Corr.*, 3:5–7.

11. Son or brother of Dr. J. P. Milburn, a Washington druggist and manufacturer of "Milburn's UNRIVALED POLAR SODA WATER."

12. Louis Fitzgerald Tasistro (1808–1886) edited a newspaper in New York, had a brief career on the stage, and later served as translator for the State Department in Washington.

13. The river steamer *Wawassett* caught on fire on August 8 on the Potomac River with a frightful loss of lives.

14. "The Birds of the Poet," in which Burroughs quotes at length from "Out of the Cradle Endlessly Rocking."

15. Towner was a clerk in the Treasury Department, and George B. McCartee was the general superintendent of the building.

16. Written by the Irish novelist Regina Marie Roche (1764?–1845) and published in 1798 in four volumes.

17. "'Tis But Ten Years Since" appeared in the *New York Weekly Graphic* from January 24 to March 1. The articles were later published as "Memoranda During the War."

18. Schmidt (1836–1899), a poet as well as the editor of the Danish journal *For Idé og Verkelighed*, informed Whitman on October 19 that he was preparing an article for "all the Scandinavian countries" (*Corr.*, 2:142n).

19. Carl Rosenberg, according to Schmidt, was "a silly little fellow, who understands nothing between heaven and earth, and least of all, you" (*Corr.*, 2:286n).

20. A Danish friend of Schmidt's, at this time a draftsman and patent agent in Washington.

21. On December 9, 1873, this former soldier wrote to Whitman, who did not reply until April 27, 1874 (lost). This is Whitman's answer to Stansberry's letter of May 12. Whitman sent "22 News Pappers," which were acknowledged on June 28. Mrs. Stansberry in July informed Whitman of her husband's failing health and poverty as well as his need for a pension. Stansberry himself wrote on July 21, 1875, asking for "the Lone of 65¢," so that he could go to West Virginia to look for witnesses to support his application for a pension.

22. A bill approved by Congress on June 20, 1874, directed a reduction in the Department of Justice. Wanting to bring his case to the attention of the President, Whitman enclosed with his letter a clipping from a Camden newspaper which included one of his poems, "Song of the Universal," as well as comments on his illness, no doubt written by Whitman himself.

23. Burroughs published "A Word or Two on Emerson" and "A Final Word on Emerson" in *The Galaxy* in February and April 1876; they were later included in *Birds and Poets* (1877).

24. As requested, Burroughs deleted the paragraph.

25. John Swinton (1829–1901), a journalist and editor associated with the *New York Times* and *New York Sun*, discovered *Leaves of Grass* on the day of its publication in 1855. "Since then," he wrote to Whitman in 1884, "you have grown before me, grown around me, and grown into me." Whitman characterized Swinton's protestation "almost like a love letter—it has sugar in it" (Traubel, 1:24, 23).

26. The work was published in 1875.

27. Edwin Einstein, a tobacconist and a friend of Whitman's Pfaffian days, wrote from the Union League Club on Madison Avenue to inquire about the accuracy of a newspaper report that Whitman was "needy" and to offer assistance.

28. Dowden enclosed a draft for $10.

29. Standish James O'Grady (1846–1928), pioneer of the Celtic renaissance, published "Walt Whitman: The Poet of Joy" in *The Gentleman's Magazine* in December 1875.

30. Bayne (1830–1896), a Scottish journalist, blasted the poet and his English admirers in *The Contemporary Review* in December 1875; the article was reprinted in *The Living Age* on January 8, 1876.

31. Stoker (1847–1912), the author of *Dracula*, wrote a letter to Whitman on February 18, 1872, but did not send it until February 14, 1876: "How sweet a thing it is for a strong healthy man with a woman's eyes and a child's wishes to feel that he can speak so to a man [Whitman] who can be if he wishes, father, and brother and wife to his soul" (Traubel, 4:185).

32. There was a discussion of "The Genius of Walt Whitman" at the Fortnightly Club on February 14, 1876; see Traubel, 1:302–3.

33. Buchanan's article was based on excerpts from the account in the *West Jersey Press* which Rossetti had inserted in *The Athenaeum*.

34. Her letter upset the poet, who preferred to have her and her passion three thousand miles away. "Soon, very soon I come, my darling," she wrote, "this is the last spring we shall be assunder. . . . Hold out but a little longer for me, my Walt" (*Corr.*, 3:30n).

35. In March she rejected his advice, "for it has been my settled steady purpose . . . ever since 1869." On April 21, she offered herself: "Surely I was made as the soil in which the precious seed of your thoughts & emotions should be planted— they to fulfil themselves in me, that I might by & bye blossom into beauty & bring forth rich fruits—immortal fruits" (*Corr.*, 3:31n). How we deceive ourselves about our Victorian ancestors!

36. Apparently in an unlocated letter.

37. Whittaker worked as a printer for the *Camden New Republic*, where Harry Stafford was an errand boy. This is the first reference to the youth who was to be Pete Doyle's successor.

38. In an April 18 letter marked "Private," Buchanan asked for clarification of Whitman's economic circumstances. Conway, he said, "has denied authoritatively that you wanted money." The problem was that although Whitman's income was limited, he was not in need, but at the same time he welcomed gifts from English admirers, who sometimes sent as much as $25 and in return received the two-volume 1876 edition of his writings.

39. See the letter to Burroughs on April 1, 1875.

40. In 1907 Burroughs commented on this passage: "I think he must have had a glass of whisky, or some champagne, when he wrote that" (Barrus, 135).

41. A gift of $50.

42. The Staffords.

43. Walter Orr Whitman, the only child of George and Louisa, was born on November 4, 1875, and died on July 12, 1876. Whitman's account of the child's death appeared in the *New York Tribune* on July 19.

44. The Gilchrists arrived in Philadelphia on September 10, 1876, and almost at once Whitman began to visit them and frequently to stay there. Visits with the Gilchrists alternated with trips to see the Staffords, both of which activities indicate improvement in his health.

45. A wealthy New York jeweler with a store at 150 Bowery, near Broome Street. Whitman stayed occasionally at the Johnston residence on Fifth Avenue near 86th Street.

46. George Waters (1832–1912), a portrait and landscape painter.

47. Samuel Loag, a Philadelphia printer.

48. Damon Kilgore (1827–1888) was a well-known Philadelphia lawyer and a member of the Liberal League. In 1875 he prepared a petition to exclude the Bible from the public schools. Whitman delivered "In Memory of Tom Paine" at Lincoln Hall, Philadelphia, on January 28, 1877. It was another major step back into the world for the paralyzed poet.

49. The residence of the Gilchrists.

50. Burroughs was gathering essays which he had published over a period of years (see August 14 and 15, 1873). For a month Whitman offered suggestions for revisions of the manuscript and proposed many alterations in the chapter devoted to him, "The Flight of the Eagle."

51. Probably a reference to "Our Rural Divinity," an essay Burroughs published in January 1877 in *The Galaxy*, which was edited by F. P. Church.

52. Cattell was a young semiliterate farmhand and a friend of the Staffords. Whitman met him, it appears, in May 1876. After the first meeting Whitman made enigmatic entries in diaries such as "the hour (night, June 19, '76, Ed & I.) at the front gate by the road." Apparently this was another of the ephemeral Calamus relationships. See *Corr.*, 3:76n.

53. On March 4, 1877, Whitman, accompanied by Harry Stafford, went to New York to stay at the home of J. H. Johnston, and later visited Burroughs at Esopus, New York, from March 16 to 20.

54. Burroughs was not fond of Waters's oil painting because it made Whitman "look rather soft, like a sort of Benjamin Franklin" (Barrus, 164).

55. At the home of Mrs. Gilchrist.

56. Edward Carpenter (1844–1929), Anglican minister, socialist, anthologist of friendship (*Iolāus*), and author of *Days with Walt Whitman*. He wrote to Whitman for the first time on July 12, 1874: "Because you have . . . given me ground for the love of men I thank you continually in my heart" (*Corr.*, 3:41n).

57. Grace and Beatrice Gilchrist.

58. Herbert Gilchrist, according to Harry, called him a "dam fool. . . . If I had

been near enough to smacked him in the 'Jaw' I would of done it." Harry wanted Whitman to discuss the matter with Herbert, who "is fooling with the wrong one. . . . I will be up to see you on Thursday to stay all night with you" (*Corr.*, 3:92n).

59. A cryptic reference to Harry Stafford ("*hickory saplings . . . Honor . . . subject*"). Perhaps the *c* in "*creek*" referred to Ed Cattell, another one of Whitman's young Kirkwood friends. Herbert Gilchrist noted that Whitman was fond of quoting Cassius' speech to Brutus, "Well, honour is the subject of my story." Whitman placed a large bracket about this passage in the margin.

60. An allusion to the investigations of John Tyndall (1820–1893), the British physicist.

61. Perhaps a reference to an experiment conducted by Beatrice Gilchrist at the medical school she was attending in Philadelphia.

62. Much of the material in this letter appears with minor alterations in "A Poet's Recreation" printed in the *New York Tribune* on July 4, 1878, and later in *Specimen Days*; see *Prose Works 1892*, 165–72.

63. On September 10 Whitman left for St. Louis, accompanied by Colonel John W. Forney (1817–1881), owner and editor of various Washington and Philadelphia newspapers in which Whitman had published articles over the years. Whitman had accepted an invitation to address the Old Settlers of Kansas Committee at Lawrence.

64. Ed Lindsey, with whom Whitman stayed at Sterling, Kansas, on September 24 and 25.

65. This is the only known letter Whitman wrote to Montgomery, one of the sons of George and Susan Stafford. Whitman referred to the other Stafford children: Edwin, Debby, who was married to Joseph (Jo) Browning, Van Doran, Ruth, and George (the son).

66. Nicholson, a twenty-one-year-old attendant in Bucke's asylum from April 12, 1880, to September 14, 1882.

67. Young employees like Nicholson at the asylum. Canuth is probably Gomley Canniff.

68. Whitman filled at least fifty-eight orders for his books from here and abroad during 1880; see *Corr.*, 6:xxvii.

69. James Matlack Scovel, a Camden lawyer, member of the New Jersey legislature, and later special agent for the United States Treasury. In the late 1870s Whitman frequently had Sunday breakfast with the Scovels.

70. F. A. Hoag, a young reporter who died at thirty-five. Seigfried may also have been a reporter.

71. Gilder (1844–1902) was assistant editor of *Scribner's Monthly* from 1870 to 1881 and editor of its successor, *The Century*, from 1881 until his death. Whitman considered him one of the few sane men "in that New York art delirium" (Traubel, 2:93).

72. Although Whitman here outlines the details of the sale of the plates of the

1876 edition of *Leaves of Grass*, he is not always consistent and perhaps candid: on at least four occasions he accepted royalties amounting to $143.50 from Worthington and by so doing sanctioned the "pirate" printing. See *Corr.*, 3:196–97.

73. "The Poetry of the Future," later called "Poetry To-day in America," appeared in the February issue.

74. "Patroling Barnegat" was printed in April.

75. Jacob H. Stafford (1850–1890), Harry's cousin, whose middle name was "Horner," the maiden name of his mother Mary.

76. Robert G. Ingersoll (1833–1899), noted lawyer and agnostic, was an enthusiastic admirer of Whitman: "You have nobly defended the human body and the sacred passions of man from the infamous placebos of the theologian. For this I thank you" (*Corr.*, 3:175n).

77. Jeannette L. Gilder (1849–1916), sister of Richard Watson and Joseph Gilder. With the latter she founded *The Critic* in 1881.

78. When Harry visited Whitman on February 7, 1881, the poet apparently gave him a copy of *Leaves of Grass* for the first time.

79. Whitman delivered his speech commemorating the death of Abraham Lincoln in Boston in April.

1881–1889

1. *Corr.*, 3:237n.
2. *Corr.*, 3:238.
3. *Corr.*, 3:267n.
4. *Corr.*, 3:273n.
5. *Corr.*, 3:301.
6. *Corr.*, 6:xvi.
7. Traubel, 3:467.
8. Traubel, 3:525.
9. *Corr.*, 3:265.
10. See *Corr.*, 3:366–67.
11. See *Corr.*, 6:xvii–xviii.
12. See Gordon Hendricks, *The Photographs of Thomas Eakins* (New York: Grossman, 1972), 136–37, 141.
13. Traubel, 5:130.
14. Traubel, 3:9.
15. Traubel, 3:358.
16. John Boyle O'Reilly (1844–1900), a colorful and fierce Irish patriot, became co-editor of the *Boston Pilot* in 1876 and evidently approached Osgood on Whitman's behalf.

17. This was Whitman's counterproposal to the publisher's offer of a ten per cent royalty. Osgood accepted the offer, as the next letter confirms.

18. The assassination of President Garfield on September 19.

19. Henry James, Sr., the father of the novelist.

20. Lee was a student at Trinity College, Dublin, and no doubt learned of Whitman through Edward Dowden and T. W. H. Rolleston. On November 28 Lee requested permission to translate *Leaves of Grass* into Russian. Nothing came of the proposal.

21. Whitman excused himself when the Childses invited him to dine with Wilde on the grounds that he was "an invalid." Wilde came to Camden on January 18, and the men hit it off. The meeting was satirized in Helen Gray Cone's piece entitled "Narcissus in Camden," in *The Century Magazine* for November. George W. Childs (1824–1894) was the co-owner of the *Philadelphia Public Ledger*.

22. Harry's brother Edwin was now in Indiana, Pennsylvania.

23. In the 1870s Bucke began to assemble material for a critical biography of the poet. He sent the manuscript to Whitman, who revised it at will, corrected errors, made some of his own, and in effect became Bucke's collaborator. In addition to arranging for the publication of the study, Whitman later vetoed Bucke's plans for a revised edition, and decreed that it was to be the official biography.

24. The dedication of *Man's Moral Nature* (1879) reads: "I dedicate this book to the man who inspired it—to the man who of all men past and present that I have known has the most exalted moral nature—WALT WHITMAN" (*Corr.*, 3:142n).

25. On March 4 Osgood asked Whitman's "consent to the withdrawal of the present edition and the substitution of an edition lacking the obnoxious features" (*Corr.*, 3:267n).

26. Whitman was replying to a letter from Osgood asking whether the book met with his approval. The firm did not know that Whitman was an unacknowledged co-author.

27. The publisher submitted to Whitman a list of passages to be expurgated from "Song of Myself," "From Pent-Up Aching Rivers," "I Sing the Body Electric," "Spontaneous Me," "Native Moments," "The Dalliance of the Eagles," "By Blue Ontario's Shore," "Unfolded Out of the Folds," "The Sleepers," and "Faces." See *Corr.*, 3:270n.

28. Emerson died on April 26, 1882. On April 29 Whitman sent an essay to the *The Critic* entitled "By Emerson's Grave," which appeared in the May issue along with Burroughs's "Emerson's Burial Day."

29. John White Chadwick, pastor of the Second Unitarian Church in Brooklyn, replied to O'Connor's attack on the Boston censorship in the *New York Tribune* on May 28. O'Connor promised Whitman to answer "this clerical blackguard, who has the audacity to accuse me of wilfully and consciously lying" (*Corr.*, 2:285n).

30. "A Memorandum at a Venture"; see the preceding letter.

31. As directed, O'Connor quoted Whitman's remarks in his reply to Chadwick.

32. George W. Cooke's *Ralph Waldo Emerson: His Life, Writings, and Philosophy* (1881) was not an official biography, and Cooke's account of the relationship of the two men was therefore speculative.

33. Franklin B. Sanborn (1831–1917), an abolitionist and friend of John Brown. Whitman was in the courtroom in 1860 when Sanborn refused to testify before a committee of the United States Senate. Sanborn was later editor of the *Springfield Republican* and the founder of a school in Concord, Massachusetts.

34. Baxter (1850–1927), a Boston journalist, evidently met Whitman for the first time when he delivered his Lincoln lecture in Boston earlier in the year. The letter supplied material for the review of *Specimen Days* that Baxter was to publish in the *Boston Herald*. It appeared with many acknowledged and unacknowledged quotations from Whitman's letter.

35. The family of Robert Pearsall Smith and his wife Hannah (1832–1911), the latter a famous Quaker leader. They had three children, Mary, Alys, and Logan. Mary, while a student at Smith College, persuaded her somewhat reluctant family to visit the poet in Camden. Mary married B. F. W. Costelloe, an English Catholic, separated, and at his death was at last able to marry Bernard Berenson. Alys was for a time the wife of Bertrand Russell, and Logan (1865–1946) developed some reputation as an essayist and biographer.

36. Two of Mrs. Stafford's boarders.

37. The dividend on his investment in the Sierra Grande Mines of New Mexico due July 6 had not been received.

38. A black expression.

39. Tasker Lay.

40. A month after his mother's death, Herbert Gilchrist informed Whitman that he intended to reprint some of her essays and asked Whitman to return his mother's letters: "Never did son have such a sweet companionable dear mother as mine" (*Corr.*, 3:413n). *Anne Gilchrist* appeared in 1887.

41. Whitman understated his income for the year: book orders, $118; royalties, $119; publications in journals, $350; gifts, $746. Total: $1333. See *Corr.*, 6:xvi. In a few instances receipts had to be estimated, drawing upon inadequate and unsystematic records. The total is no doubt on the low side.

42. "A Spring Relish" became the title of a chapter in *Signs and Seasons* (1886).

43. Whitman borrowed the volumes during the Washington years (Traubel, 2:86–87).

44. He read the Lincoln essay in Elkton, Maryland, in February and at Morgan Hall, Camden, in March.

45. Rossetti distributed a facsimile of Whitman's letter, on the verso of which appeared the names of more than eighty donors.

46. In her reply on January 17, Mrs. Costelloe asked: "Has thee never thought of

expanding *Specimen Days* into autobiographical sketches? Then thee could tell the world thy wickedness to the full, which thy friends are so uncomprehending as not to see!" (*Corr.*, 4:62n).

47. On May 23, 1887, Whitman noted in his Daybook the "anniversary of dear mother's death—1873"; *Walt Whitman—Daybooks and Notebooks*, ed. William White (New York: New York University Press, 1978), 2:424.

48. As editor of the *Pall Mall Gazette* and later *The Review of Reviews*, Stead (1849–1912) was most sympathetic to Whitman and his poetry. On May 6, 1887, he printed passages from a "private letter," perhaps written by Moncure D. Conway, which alleged that Whitman was being well taken care of by American friends.

49. The editors of *The Critic* rejected Bucke's "One Word More on Walt Whitman": "We have printed a great many 'words' on Whitman, & can only print 'more' . . . when he issues a new book, or does something to attract general attention to his work" (*Corr.*, 4:153n).

50. Morse, at one time the editor of *The Radical*, eventually became a self-taught sculptor. In 1876 he began one of numerous busts of the poet, all of which were wretched. He was again at work when Thomas Eakins completed the most celebrated literary portrait of the century.

51. One of Morse's works.

52. This attack, which Whitman attributed to his "war paralysis," marked the beginning of a deterioration from which there was little relief until his death.

53. Dr. J. K. Mitchell was the son of S. Weir Mitchell, a celebrated neurologist and novelist.

54. Mrs. Stafford's granddaughter, Susan Browning.

55. In his journal Burroughs wrote: "He presses my hand long and tenderly; we kiss and part, probably for the last time. I think he has in his own mind given up the fight, and awaits the end" (Barrus, 283).

56. The wife of J. H. Johnston, the New York jeweler.

57. Bucke and a friend expected to get rich from their invention, a water meter. Whitman scoffed.

58. As expected, Bucke agreed, although he had planned "considerable changes"; "Your wishes will be religiously respected" (*Corr.*, 4:215n).

59. Sir William Osler (1849–1919), at that time a professor at the University of Pennsylvania. His *Principles and Practice of Medicine* (1891) is a medical classic.

60. William Summers came to Camden with a letter of introduction from Mrs. Costelloe. His version of the meeting appeared in the *Pall Mall Gazette* on October 18, 1888.

61. Perhaps a review of the translation *Canti Scelti* (1887) by Luigi Gamberale.

62. Translations by Francis Vielé-Griffin.

63. Mrs. Elizabeth Fairchild, wife of Colonel Charles Fairchild, and Hamlin Garland (1860–1940), the novelist.

64. Gabriel Sarrazin's "Poètes modernes de l'Amérique, Walt Whitman" appeared in *La Nouvelle Revue* on May 1, 1888; reprinted in the following year in *La renaissance de la poesie anglaise, 1798–1889.*

65. Nathan M. Baker, after serving briefly as one of Whitman's nurses, left to complete a medical degree.

66. Whittier's "The Vow of Washington" appeared in the *New York World* and elsewhere on May 1.

67. The poet who sang of death so tenderly retreated into silence when death came to friends like O'Connor and Mrs. Gilchrist.

68. Henry (Harry) L. Bonsall, Sr., the editor, and Geoffrey Buckwalter were among the local people who served on the committee to celebrate Whitman's seventieth birthday.

69. The International Congress of American States assembled in Washington on October 2, and two days later the delegates began a grand tour of the United States.

70. Wilkins returned to Canada to pursue the career of a veterinarian.

71. Symonds, who like Whitman was a dying man, stricken with tuberculosis, asked for Whitman's blessing, and then said: "I cannot find words better fitted to express the penetrative fate with which you have entered into me, my reliance on you, & my hope that you will not disapprove of my conduct in the last resort" (*Corr.*, 4:408n). Symonds wanted confirmation of what he intuited in the Calamus poems and the acceptance of his own homosexuality. Whitman would neither confess nor bless.

72. Thomas Donaldson, a Philadelphia lawyer and the author of *Walt Whitman the Man* (1896), and a group of friends had purchased a horse and buggy for Whitman in October 1885.

1890–1892

1. Traubel, 3:287.

2. *Corr.*, 5:3.

3. *Corr.*, 5:3–4.

4. *Corr.*, 5:8.

5. "Old Age's Ship & Crafty Death's."

6. English writer and editor (1859–1946), Rhys arranged for the English publication of a one-shilling edition of Whitman's poetry that sold 10,000 copies.

7. Daniel G. Brinton (1837–1899), a pioneer in the study of anthropology and author of *Giordano Bruno: Philosopher and Martyr* (1890), with a prefatory note by Whitman.

8. "On, on the Same, Ye Jocund Twain!"

9. Whitman sent "Old Age Echoes," a cluster of poems, to *Nineteenth Century*

in November 1889 and asked £20. The editor returned the manuscript on February 21, 1890.

10. The printers of the first edition of *Leaves of Grass.*

11. Whitman's reply, "Shakspere for America," appeared in the magazine in September.

12. Franklin File, of a newspaper syndicate, made the proposal on July 16, 1890.

13. "Walt Whitman at Date."

14. This important letter exists only in the draft version, which was in Whitman's possession at his death. The assertion in the last sentence that he wrote "with haste & too great effusion" is refuted by the many corrections he made. Symonds's reply revealed his disappointment, but in *Studies in Sexual Inversion*, published posthumously in 1897, Symonds accepted Whitman's statements: "No one who knows anything about Walt Whitman will for a moment doubt his candour and sincerity. Therefore the man who wrote 'Calamus,' and preached the gospel of comradeship, entertains feelings at least as hostile to sexual inversion as any law-abiding humdrum Anglo-Saxon could desire. It is obvious that he has not even taken the phenomena of abnormal instinct into account. Else he must have foreseen that, human nature being what it is, we cannot expect to eliminate all sexual alloy from emotions raised to a high pitch of passionate intensity, and that permanent elements within the midst of our society will emperil the absolute purity of the ideal he attempts to establish" (1964 ed., 186).

15. Kennedy had trouble finding a publisher for "Walt Whitman's Dutch Traits," which finally appeared in February 1891 in *The Conservator*, which was edited by Traubel.

16. "*Must*" is heavily underscored.

17. Harry Fritzinger, Warren's brother. In another letter Whitman wrote, "One of my two boys 26 yrs old was married last evn'g—he came yesterday to talk ab't it & hung on my neck & kiss'd me twenty times" (*Corr.*, 5:87).

18. Dowd (1866–1953), a self-styled "poor clerk in an obscure library" in Melbourne, Australia, wrote to Whitman for the first time on March 12, 1890. The son of an Irish policeman, he had a lonely and loveless childhood, gave up Catholicism to become a freethinker, became a teacher at an early age (like Whitman), and then drifted from job to job. Now married, he was in his own eyes "a failure" and "an enigma to myself," evidently in search of a father figure. "Had Carlyle," he wrote, "added another chapter to his 'Hero Worship' the 'Hero as Nurse' with Walt Whitman as subject would have worthily capped his dome" (*Corr.*, 5:62n).

19. Friends and members of the O'Dowd circle. The baby was the O'Dowds' first child, Montaigne Eric Whitman O'Dowd.

20. Jessie, Jeff's daughter, was in Camden when her father died on November 25, 1890.

21. The superintendent of the asylum where Ed was staying.

22. Wood, of the *New York Herald*, wrote several times asking Whitman to partici-
pate in a symposium "on the anthropological and ethical subject of the 'Coming
Man.'" Whitman's reply appeared in Wood's *Ideas of Life. Human Perfection. How
to Attain It. A Symposium on the Coming Man* (1892).

23. Dr. Johnston was especially grateful for this letter which recalled "the sound
of your 'valved voice,' . . . those two red letter—nay rather epoch-making—days of
my life which I spent with *you*, my dear, old Camerado & Elder Brother."

24. Daniel Longaker was Whitman's attending physician until his death. A fund
contributed by friends and managed by Traubel and Bucke paid Longaker $30 or
$40 a month for his almost daily visits.

25. Superintendent of the Harleigh Cemetery.

26. Whitman reversed the words.

27. Traubel married Anne Montgomerie on May 28, 1891.

28. Dr. Johnston came to Camden in 1890 and Wallace in 1891.

29. Harrison S. Morris (1856–1948), a translator and later author of *Walt Whitman* (1929), met the poet in 1887. Agnes Repplier (1858–1950) was a Philadelphia
essayist and biographer.

30. A strange characterization of Heinrich Schliemann's widely praised explorations of Homeric sites.

31. Confusion as to the amount Whitman owed to the firm that constructed the
mausoleum led to legal proceedings in which Harned represented the poet and, in
Whitman's words, "got me out of a hole" (*Corr.*, 5 : 265 n, 267).

32. *The Brazen Android and Other Tales* (1891), with a preface by Whitman.

33. On December 3 Bucke wrote to Whitman: "What scholars will ponder it in
the ages to come! What commentators darken it! What annotators load it with heavy
& weary notes! but also what thousands and thousands of young men and young
women and middleaged men & women will rejoice in it and find their lives deepened
& widened by it! . . . When it becomes known for long & long it will be THE
BOOK—all others will stand on a lower plane. I am satisfied that I know something
of it and of you—that is greatness enough for me—yes and greatness enough to
carry my name down thro' all the ages" (*Corr.*, 5 : 270–71 n).

34. The bust by Morse.

35. This letter is apparently not extant. Whitman wrote infrequently to his sister Mary.

36. Dr. Alexander McAlister, a Canadian physician, assisted Longaker in attending Whitman in his final illness. Whitman's letter to his sister was written on the
verso of one from Hallam Tennyson on January 26: "My Father thanks you cordially
for yr new Edition of 'Leaves of Grass'—He is not allowed by his doctors to write
more than is absolutely necessary—We are very sorry. I hear that you have been unwell, but hope that—as the spring advances—your health will improve" (*Corr.*,
5 : 276 n). Tennyson died on October 6, 1892.

37. Whitman wrote "June" and then corrected himself.

INDEX OF WHITMAN'S

CORRESPONDENTS